THE S. MARK TAPER FOUNDATION

IMPRINT IN JEWISH STUDIES

BY THIS ENDOWMENT

THE S. MARK TAPER FOUNDATION SUPPORTS

THE APPRECIATION AND UNDERSTANDING

OF THE RICHNESS AND DIVERSITY OF

JEWISH LIFE AND CULTURE

The publisher and the University of California Press Foundation gratefully acknowledge the generous support of the S. Mark Taper Foundation Imprint in Jewish Studies.

Trans Talmud

Trans Talmud

Androgynes and Eunuchs in Rabbinic Literature

Max K. Strassfeld

UNIVERSITY OF CALIFORNIA PRESS

University of California Press
Oakland, California

© 2022 by Max Strassfeld

First Paperback Printing 2023

Library of Congress Cataloging-in-Publication Data

Names: Strassfeld, Max K., author.
Title: Trans Talmud : androgynes and eunuchs in rabbinic literature / Max K. Strassfeld.
Description: Oakland, California : University of California Press, [2022] | Includes bibliographical references and index. |
Identifiers: LCCN 2021037411 (print) | LCCN 2021037412 (ebook) | ISBN 9780520382053 (hardcover) | 9780520397392 (paperback) | 9780520382060 (ebook)
Subjects: LCSH: Gender nonconformity—Religious aspects—Judaism. | Sex in rabbinical literature. | Androgyny (Psychology—Religious aspects. | Eunuchs—Religious aspects. | Masculinity—Religious aspects—Judaism.
Classification: LCC BM729.T65 S77 2022 (print) | LCC BM729.T65 (ebook) | DDC 296.3086/7—dc23
LC record available at https://lccn.loc.gov/2021037411
LC ebook record available at https://lccn.loc.gov/2021037412

CONTENTS

Acknowledgments   *vii*

    Introduction   *1*

1. Transing Late Antiquity: The Politics of the Study of Eunuchs and Androgynes   *33*
2. The Gendering of Law: The Androgyne and the Hybrid Animal in Bikkurim   *55*
3. Sex with Androgynes   *89*
4. Transing the Eunuch: Kosher and Damaged Masculinity   *115*
5. Eunuch Temporality: The Saris and the Aylonit   *151*

    Conclusion: Rereading the Rabbis Again   *183*

Bibliography   *203*
Glossary   *237*
Index   *243*

ACKNOWLEDGMENTS

In this political moment, many activists are invoking ancestors. In the context of these activist calls, I understand ancestors to include the collective wisdom of all those who make our current work possible. I wish to mark my gratitude for all my transcestors, and in particular, for the radical trans and intersex Jewish thinkers whose names I may never know. I am also grateful for the trans and intersex Jews radically reimagining Judaism today, and my fellow conspirators at Transtorah and WAITRRS, who ensure that trans and intersex Jewish youth inherit a different landscape than we did. Finally, I am grateful to all the scholars who have worked to carve space in academia, including Susan Stryker, who advocated for the trans studies cluster hire at the University of Arizona. All these people make my work possible.

This book is especially indebted to the generous efforts of Charlotte Fonrobert, Susan Stryker, Rafe Neis, Julia Watts Belser, and Joseph Marchal, all of whom read early drafts and contributed feedback that enriched this work immeasurably. Any mistakes in the book are my own and do not reflect any errors in their painstaking efforts.

There are many people whose efforts in training me are reflected in this volume. I am particularly grateful to my teachers, primarily Charlotte Fonrobert, who took me on as a "nontraditional" student. Charlotte was and is enormously supportive; she is the main reason I survived graduate school and am a professor today. Barb Voss served as a mentor to me, read my dissertation, and has helped me navigate academia with excellent and down-to-earth advice. My dissertation committee member, Steve Weitzman, was generous with his responsiveness and incisive critique. I feel very lucky to have had such a stellar committee. At the defense, both Sarra Lev and Steve Zipperstein created a generative conversation that was invaluable in planning to turn the dissertation into a book.

I am grateful to Daniel Boyarin and his students—in particular Zvi Septimus. I also deeply appreciate my fellow Stanford graduate students, John Mandsager Mira Balberg, James Redfield, Timothy DeBold, and David Levinsky, all of whom taught me much. My unofficial writing bootcamp buddies, Maura Finkelstein, Zoe Weiman-Kelman, Ana Minian, and Clare Bayard, made the process of writing the dissertation almost pleasurable.

I appreciate the supported time I had to complete this book. I am especially grateful for the Frankel fellowship at the University of Michigan from 2013 to 2014, and to all the fellows whose feedback strengthened the second chapter. I am thankful for the support of Auburn Seminary and the Coolidge Fellows for their feedback on my revisions. And I am enormously indebted to my department chair, Karen Seat, and to the Wellspring Foundation for their grant to the Trans Studies Initiative, which enabled my junior sabbatical year and allowed me to work on this book.

The anonymous reviewers at the University of California Press provided lengthy and detailed responses that pushed me to think more broadly about the audience for the book and to rewrite boldly. I am grateful for mentorship and professional encouragement from Susan Stryker, Judith Plaskow, Martha Acklesberg, Karen Seat, Marla Brettschneider, Fabian Alfie, Joe Marchal, Rafe Neis, Julia Watts Belser, Ed Wright, and Melissa Wilcox, all of whom helped me navigate the tenure-track and book-writing process. I am deeply appreciative of all the other members of Bnot Esh and their support throughout this process. I am grateful to the fantastic group of assistant professors in the Department of Religious Studies and Classics at the University of Arizona, and to all my colleagues in Judaic Studies, Classics, and in the Trans Studies Initiative.

Several people helped me to prepare the manuscript. Michael Strassfeld, Scottie Elton Bradford-LaMay, and Sari Fein helped me to prepare the initial manuscript for review and provided excellent and sharp readings. Nina Judith Katz (www.askthewordnerd.com) gave expert assistance with the glossary in particular and in preparing and rewriting the entire manuscript; her help was invaluable. My editor, Eric Schmidt at the University of California Press, offered practical advice on how to write a book, and very patiently worked with me during the pandemic. The editorial assistants at the University of California Press walked me through the stages of preparing the manuscript. The members of the Writing Every Day group on Facebook cheered me on and instilled in me my regular writing habit.

I am also deeply grateful to my family. Graduate school and the beginning years of the tenure track process were personally tumultuous. Becoming a single parent under challenging circumstances required lots of familial support. My parents—Sharon Strassfeld, Michael Ramella, Michael Strassfeld, and Joy Levitt—helped me pick up the pieces. My brothers, Noam Strassfeld and Ben Strassfeld, helped me care for my son in difficult moments. To my queer and trans family, my birth team (Elliot Kukla, Maura Finkelstein, Zohar Weiman-Kelman, Ben Doyle), the house of queer magic, Reuben Zellman and Erika Katske who took us in, and all the trans and queer uncles and aunties enriched those years for my son and me: I would not be where I am today without all my family.

Finally, I am grateful to my son and my partner. My son always inspires me to put one foot in front of the other. I love them beyond measure. And I am so lucky to have Carlyn Arteaga, my shipmate, who feels everything in the world so intently and has taught me so much.

. . .

On the day I am finishing writing these acknowledgements, Daunte Wright was murdered by the police. A reckoning of white supremacist violence is long overdue. There are debts that cannot be fully figured, even though reparations, land back movements, and mutual aid are important attempts to acknowledge those debts.

As I sit typing these acknowledgements on the ancestral lands of the Tohono O'odham and Pascua Yaqui peoples, I want to offer gratitude to all the BIPOC, decolonial, immigrant, labor, prison abolitionist, trans liberation, feminist, queer, and crip activists whose collective wisdom guides our struggles in this moment. Their vision of a world of rest, liberation, and healing justice sustains us all.

Without all those whom I have acknowledged this work would not have been possible.

Introduction

You and I have bodies that make people pray.
THEA HILLMAN, INTERSEX (FOR LACK OF A BETTER WORD)[1]

I first encountered androgynes and eunuchs in the Talmud through a scholar-in-residence weekend with Rabbi Benay Lappe at the queer and trans synagogue in San Francisco. The study session was part of Svara, a queer yeshiva (traditional Jewish school) founded by Rabbi Lappe and Rabbi Elinor Knepler. Lappe, an engaging teacher, introduced me to sources that I had not realized the Jewish corpus contained. I had studied Talmud, had run queer Jewish groups as an undergraduate, and had helped to start Shabbat rituals at the Friday night trans march in San Francisco, but I had never met the androgyne before. I was hooked.

I had recently completed my bachelors in Hebrew literature and taken a job selling sex toys at a woman-owned and worker-owned cooperative. During my breaks, I searched for more sources about androgynes and eunuchs to explore with my study partner. I was sitting at my desk during lunch hour when I encountered this story on b. Yevamot 84a:[2]

> Rabbi [Yehudah HaNasi] relayed [the following story]: "When I went to learn rabbinic teachings with Rabbi Elazar ben Shamua, his students banded together against me like the [famously aggressive] roosters of Beit Bukiya.[3] They allowed me to learn only one teaching [and it was this]: "Rabbi Eliezer says that [in the case of the] androgyne: [the

---

1. Hillman, *Intersex (for lack of a better word)*, 19.
2. I will use the standard abbreviations for citing rabbinic sources: a lowercase *b.* indicates a source found in the Babylonian Talmud, with the name of the tractate and page number found after. A lowercase *m.* refers to the Mishnah; a lowercase *t.* refers to the Tosefta; and a lowercase *p.* refers to the Palestinian Talmud.
3. Beit Bukiya is a place name. I explore this text further (and have a longer note on it) in chapter 3 of the book.

man who penetrates the androgyne anally] is liable for [the penalty of] stoning [for transgressing the prohibition against sex with a man, just] as [he would be if he had anal sex with a non-androgyne] male."[4]

This first-person narrative tells the story of Rabbi Yehudah HaNasi, who goes to study with a teacher named Rabbi Elazar ben Shamua. The students of Rabbi Elazar ben Shamua are portrayed as aggressively territorial; they deny Rabbi Yehudah HaNasi access to their teacher. These students are likened to the fighting cocks of a place named Beit Bukiya—apparently the aggression of these roosters was widely known. Rabbi Yehudah HaNasi only manages to glean one piece of information through the impenetrable barrier posed by the students. That teaching concerns the androgyne and tells us that a man who has sex with an androgyne transgresses the biblical prohibition against "lying with a man."

I could feel the gendered complications of that short narrative pulsing just below the surface of the text. The penetrated body of the androgyne seemed to function as a type of currency, used to negotiate the borders between two groups of rabbis. There is a poetic aspect to the contrast between the hypermasculine barrier presented by the rooster/students, who nevertheless allow this one teaching to slip through. There is a palpable disjunction between the doubly penetrable body of the androgyne and the—almost—impenetrable border presented by the students. The text leaves us with the haunting question: how is sex with an androgyne like sex with a man?

I ardently desired the tools (intellectual, philological, and theoretical) to pursue the implications of this short narrative. This story sparked my interest in graduate school; I wrote about Rabbi Yehudah HaNasi's tale in my applications. Ever since then, I have been trying to write about these same four lines of text, and their tantalizing mixture of sex, gender, sexuality, the boundaries of rabbinic society, and the violent regulation of bodies.

This book represents the culmination of my obsessive interest in that single four-line story. It is my attempt to untangle some of the questions that continue to haunt me about that narrative: How does nonbinary gender figure in rabbinic laws?[5] How do messy, unruly, and multiply penetrable bodies fit within the ordered taxonomies of ritual and legal obligation? What can we understand about the categories of sex and gender from the link between the body of the androgyne and the body of a man, a link built on the sexual "violation" of that masculinity?

In the course of unraveling these questions about sex, gender, and sexuality, this book will make two interventions simultaneously. First, I will argue that centering

---

4. All translations of rabbinic sources are mine, unless otherwise noted. The brackets indicate phrases not in the original, that I have added to facilitate the reader's understanding. The language of the original is terse and often assumes prior knowledge, so translators often interpolate to provide the context and complete the sentences.

5. On using the term "nonbinary" historically, see DeVun, *The Shape of Sex*.

eunuchs and androgynes shifts our understandings of how gender functions in rabbinic literature. The study of gender has been, for the most part, structured by a focus on the relationship between men and women in Jewish sources. This focus established a much-needed criticism of rabbinic androcentrism. It is not my intention to blunt that essential feminist critique. At the same time, when we focus on eunuchs and androgynes, we gain a fuller picture of the way gender works in rabbinic literature.

To the extent to which eunuchs and androgynes fail to perform a stable sex and gender, they can represent a challenge to systemic binary gender. In some of the sources I analyze in this book, we see the ways that eunuchs and androgynes do not fit easily into the conventions of rabbinic gendered obligation. There are ways, therefore, that eunuchs and androgynes carve nonbinary space into the tradition. Simultaneously, however, eunuchs and androgynes are sometimes forcefully incorporated into gendered law by the rabbis, which raises questions about the viability of nonbinary space. The mutability of sex, therefore, has some paradoxical effects in the sources.[6]

In calling the book *Trans Talmud*, it is not my intent to trumpet the Talmud as essentially subversive or trans; this would have the effect of obscuring the darker aspects of these sources. The distance between contemporary radical trans critique and the Talmud is vast. I am, at times, quite critical of the gendered projects of the rabbis in this book. And yet, I will argue that there are ways in which the Talmud is more trans than is sometimes imagined in contemporary Jewish communities.

My second intervention in this book is to contribute to the burgeoning fields of trans and intersex history. Recent scholarship has engaged theoretically with the questions of what it means to study sex and gender variance before contemporary trans and intersex frameworks existed.[7] Any study of rabbinic sources must account for the radical differences between the ways sex, gender, and sexuality were organized in the past, and contemporary formulations. As such, to even translate and organize eunuchs and androgynes through the lens of the categories of "sex" and "gender" is itself anachronistic.

---

6. For foundational work on the way sex changes in the sources, that influences my thinking in this book, see Kessler, "Bodies in Motion," 389–430. I am also influenced in my thinking here by Mira Balberg, who argues that the boundaries of the body are in flux in tannaitic literature. See Balberg, *Purity, Body, and Self.*

7. Scholarship within the fields of trans premodern history in particular is now so broad, that this note cannot be comprehensive. For antiquity, see the recent anthologies by Campanile, Carlà-Uhink, and Facella, eds., *TransAntiquity*, and Surtees and Dyer, eds., *Exploring Gender Diversity in the Ancient World*. Mary Wiesmantel has proposed a practice of "ungendering" history: see Weismantel, "Towards a Transgender Archaeology," 319–34. On trans history more generally, see the special issue of *Transgender Studies Quarterly*, edited by DeVun and Tortorici, "Trans*historicities." In chapter 1 I will look specifically at the scholarship about castration in antiquity and late antiquity, and I will continue to discuss trans historiography throughout the book. The book *Arresting Dress* by Clare Sears was particularly helpful in conceptualizing how law can produce normative gender.

Greta LaFleur's recent monograph about sex in eighteenth-century US history argues that approaches to studying sex in the past can broadly be divided into two groups.[8] In one group are those historians who wish to create a "usable past," and who often see themselves as working within and responding to a particular political moment in time.[9] These scholars tend to make connections between the present and the past.[10] In the other (Foucaultian-influenced) camp are those who have traditionally assumed a strict historicism.[11] From this perspective, transhistorical connections between the present and the past flatten the true variety of ways that people have made meaning of bodies and sex acts. Refusing anachronism allows for the possibility of the true alterity of the past.[12]

For either of these two camps, the project of history is political. As LaFleur argues, for example, discussions of racialized difference are often played out over and against sex, so that sodomy laws are enlisted to maintain racial order. The project of history can undermine the naturalization of these efforts; if the world was not always organized to manage and produce racialized ideas of binary gender, then the possibility of a different future emerges. We live in a time and place, as Lourdes Ashley Hunter has put it, where "every breath a Black trans woman takes is an act of revolution."[13] In that context, historical projects that explore the racialization of gendered mutability and that describe a trans past are urgent.[14]

---

8. LaFleur, *The Natural History of Sexuality*, 1–32. See also Marchal, who schematizes the division as between the altericist and continuist camps: *Appalling Bodies*, 16–29.

9. Faderman, "A Usable Past," 171–78. LaFleur also cites Faderman in the introduction of *The Natural History of Sexuality*, 1–32.

10. Take, for example, Plato's *Symposium*, a text I address in the next chapter. The *Symposium* became the center of a debate about nondiscrimination laws in Colorado. Martha Nussbaum famously offered a "neutral" translation of Plato that presented pederasty in a more positive light in order to argue that a range of attitudes toward same-sex sexuality existed in antiquity. While Nussbaum is not precisely making a strong claim for "gay" identity in antiquity, she implicitly connects same-sex acts across time. See Nussbaum, "Platonic Love and Colorado Law," 1515–1651.

11. Marchal suggests that these altericists are in fact misinterpreting Foucault, drawing on Sedgwick's critique, among others. See Marchal, *Appalling Bodies*, 16–29.

12. This schematization into two camps are overgeneralizations. For example, David Halperin softens his earlier strict historicist approach in response to Eve Sedgwick's critique that he had overemphasized historical discontinuities between the present and the past. See Halperin, *How to do the History*, 1–24. For an excellent response to this debate, see Marchal, *Appalling Bodies*, 16–30. For an elegant summation of the ways that historicism allows us to contextualize contemporary schemes of sex and gender, see DeVun, *The Shape of Sex*, 1–16.

13. See Hunter, "Every Breath a Black Trans Woman Takes."

14. C. Riley Snorton's work is particularly significant in this regard. At the same time, there is an important critique of using Black and trans people of color to capacitate scholarly (and other) projects. See Snorton and Haritaworn, "Trans Necropolitics," 66–76. I am aware that these critiques could be applied to this book; my intention is not to efface the category of race but rather to center important developments in trans of color critique.

Any study of eunuchs and androgynes in the past has to grapple with the relationship between sex and gender and how these categories are mobilized across time. Recent research has argued that the framework of "gender" emerges from conservative medical contexts. As scholars like C. Riley Snorton and Jules Gill-Peterson show, "gender" is imbricated with anti-Blackness, racialized ideas about the plasticity of sex, and conservative medical approaches to the treatment of intersex bodies.[15]

Sex and gender are embroiled social categories. Gill-Peterson shows that this entanglement of sex/gender, alongside the conceptual attempts to distinguish between them, becomes a part of the technology of managing and disciplining contemporary trans and intersex embodiment.[16] Thus a sex/gender system is particularly problematic from a trans studies or intersex studies perspective, and we must consider the implications of importing that framework into the past.

I do not believe that contemporary trans and intersex identities translate easily to the *aylonit, saris, androginos,* or *tumtum*. This discontinuity is, in part, because rabbinic sources are not formed within the same contemporary milieu that produces the conceptual imbrication of sex/gender. In some sources, the rabbis assume a connection between body parts and social and legal obligations. So, for example, I will treat a source in chapter 4 where damage to the penis creates certain restrictions within a priestly marriage. In that source, body parts become connected to kinship structures. Other sources seem to draw distinctions between bodies and social roles, such as in chapter 2 when I discuss a text that debates how an androgyne with dual genitalia fits within gendered legal obligations. Still other sources associate transgressive sexual acts with particular sex/gender configurations, or link what we would understand as sex or gender to other attributes like membership in the priesthood, sacrifices, and the practice of levirate marriage. To explore what eunuchs and androgynes mean to the rabbis, therefore, requires us to connect to an entirely different conceptual framework. If the person who is born with variant sexed anatomy (whom we might call intersex) and the person who changes their genitalia (whom we might call trans) are both understood as different facets of the same phenomenon—a eunuch—then our conceptual distinctions do not mesh with the local taxonomies of the rabbis.

Moreover, sex/gender systems, situated as they are within particular colonial, racialized, and ableist modes of knowledge production, can obscure the fact that rabbinic taxonomies of eunuchs and androgynes are formed within their own context of power and knowledge. It is not an accident, for example, that the word the rabbis use for the androgyne is a Greek loan word. Early rabbinic sources

---

15. Snorton, *Black on Both Sides*, 139–76, and Gill-Peterson, *History of the Transgender Child*, 97–128.
16. For a foundational work on the history of the entanglement of sex, gender, and sexuality, see Meyerowitz, *How Sex Changed*.

explore androgynes and eunuchs within the context of Roman imperialism. As Joseph Marchal points out, contemporary identification with the eunuch is fraught precisely because of the important distinctions in the way sex/gender was understood in the past. For example, castration was sometimes practiced as a punishment in antiquity and at times was linked to enslavement.[17] The use of the terms "sex" and "gender," therefore, can function to obscure the particular relations of power and knowledge that operate within the rabbinic context.

Despite all these misgivings, I will use the terms "sex" and "gender" in this book. In part, I use these terms because when the rabbis link different kinds of eunuchs and androgynes together they are demonstrating some type of larger conceptual category that connects the two. There are chapters in the Mishnah that group eunuchs and androgynes, and there are also sources that make analogies between androgynes and eunuchs. This suggests to me that even early layers of rabbinic literature conceptually link these various types of embodiment. Sex and gender therefore describe the rabbinic attempt to think with eunuch and androgyne bodies as a meaningful category of embodiment. As I use sex/gender, however, to pay attention to the ways these concepts can become so embroiled, I will also pay attention to the specific meanings assigned to the mutability of the body in discrete rabbinic disputes. And I will examine the whole host of characteristics that are intimately intertwined with sex/gender and the bodies of eunuchs and androgynes: the focus on pubic hair as a pivotal bodily marker; frameworks of bodily "damage"; and the way anal sex can shift gender, to name a few.

Throughout this book, I will also deliberately put eunuchs and androgynes to many nonrabbinic usages; for example, I engage intersex activist opposition to medical interventions, the anti-trans so-called "bathroom bills," and the regulation of trans embodiment in US law. In my conclusion, I examine the way that trans and intersex Jews use these categories to critique contemporary transphobia within Jewish communities. I am in part addressing the continuing currency of these texts; in many Jewish communities today, both Rabbi Yehudah HaNasi and anti-trans regulations are remarkably present. While I argue in this book that the rabbis use the bodies of eunuchs and androgynes to sketch the contours of the normative, I also want to pay attention to the potential these categories have to exceed their parameters.

Following Joseph Marchal, who argues in favor of juxtaposing the present and the past as part of his strategy for reading Paul's letters, I am giving these sources an anachronistic reading in order to demonstrate the context and politics of the

---

17. Marchal, *Appalling Bodies*, 16–29. The punishment for castration within the Roman Empire varied, but at some points included the castration of the offender. There is debate over how often that might have been enforced, but given the rates of survival for castration, this may have entailed a death sentence for some. See Horstmanshoff, "Who is the True Eunuch," 101–18.

questions I ask throughout the book. Even as I am cautious about importing contemporary taxonomies, situating my questions within their current political milieu is a part of what it means to me to trans the Talmud. In that sense, I am foregrounding the problem of anachronism within my argument. As I attend to the dynamics of reading sex and gender variance in a premodern context, my strategy will be to play up the contradictions rather than to try to minimize them. I will embrace anachronism as part of embracing a "bad/trans" reading strategy designed to acknowledge the particular ontologies that govern contemporary trans and intersex politics, as I will explore shortly.

. . .

Because I wrote this book to engage multiple kinds of academic audiences, I have created a glossary, which is found at the end of the book. The glossary includes common terms in rabbinics. I encourage readers unfamiliar with this body of literature to refer to it as they move through the book.

Both sets of readers should find the next section defining eunuchs and androgynes a helpful starting place. After that, I will signpost sections that are intended primarily for certain audiences.

INTRODUCING ANDROGYNES AND EUNUCHS

I want to begin by introducing the cast of characters, since rabbinic categories do not translate easily into our idiom. This section will familiarize the reader with the various types of androgynes and eunuchs in rabbinic literature. There are ways to complicate these definitions, but this section is intended as a basic primer.

Rabbinic sources from the first six centuries of the common era discuss eunuchs and androgynes over a hundred times. In this book, I write primarily about five rabbinic categories of eunuchs and androgynes: the born (male and female) eunuch, the man who becomes a eunuch, the dually sexed person, and the person without a clear sex.[18] While the sources sometimes link these five different kinds of eunuchs and androgynes, these categories are also used to consider distinct legal issues.

The word *saris* is often translated as eunuch.[19] Within the rabbinic context, "eunuch" is an umbrella term that can describe a number of different kinds of bodies. *Saris* may refer to someone who becomes a eunuch later in life; in this context

---

18. In addition to the categories named here, there are also three biblical categories of genitally "damaged" men that the rabbis import: the *p'ẓua daka'*, *krut shafkhah*, and *m'roah 'ashekh*. Not all scholars would characterize these biblical figures as eunuchs. I will discuss genitally "damaged" men in the book, but I focus on the five that I list in the body of the text.

19. Based on the advice of the publisher, I will use simple English spelling to facilitate easier reading by nonspecialists. See my note on transcription at the end of the introduction.

the word is sometimes translated as "a castrate," a term that I will avoid.[20] I will refer to this type of eunuch as an *acquired saris* since they acquire their status as a eunuch at some point after birth.[21] The *acquired saris* is most analogous to our contemporary English term *eunuch*, which usually refers to a man who has been castrated.

Saris, however, can also refer to someone who was born a eunuch; by this the rabbis mean a person born with bodily differences that preclude reproduction. I will call the latter type of eunuch the *born saris*. The rabbinic category of someone who is a born eunuch might be more analogous to our contemporary concept of intersexuality than to how we define eunuch today. The rabbinic *saris*, therefore, does not neatly correspond to our contemporary definition of the term "eunuch."

In addition, for the rabbis, eunuchs are not only male. There is also the *aylonit*, a female eunuch. The *aylonit* is a parallel figure to the born *saris*; she is born with a body that will not develop reproductive capabilities. As there is no real English equivalent for the *aylonit*, I have chosen to retain the untranslated term in the book. The *aylonit* is often paired with the born *saris*. In that sense, even though the *aylonit* has her own word, both men and women can be born as "eunuchs."

To sum up, for the rabbis the concept of the eunuch is capacious enough to include several different kinds of bodies. When I use the word *eunuch* without distinctions, I mean to refer to all three kinds of rabbinic eunuchs: the born *saris* and *aylonit*, and the acquired *saris*.

In addition to eunuchs, the rabbis have two other categories, which, for simplicity's sake, I am grouping together under the heading *androgyne*. The rabbis describe the *androginos* as a person with dual genitalia.[22] In early sources, the rabbinic *androginos* is portrayed as being capable of both menstruation and seminal emissions, for example.

---

20. Referring to a person as "a castrate" is problematic and sounds about as awkward as "a transgender." I will do my best to avoid the term throughout.

21. I am not happy with my translation choices of "acquired *saris*," which is awkward and pathologizing. I tried "become *saris*," which was less medicalized, but it scanned awkwardly when worked through the book. *Eunuch* is difficult precisely because of the ways that our contemporary term does not line up with the full spectrum of meanings in the rabbinic word *saris*. After ten years of writing about these categories, I have experimented with language in multiple ways to try and address some of the difficulties in translation. I have yet to find a satisfactory solution to any of these translation issues. Thanks are due to Rafe Neis who generously agreed to discuss the translation issues with me.

22. The assumption that the androgyne has dual genitalia comes from various texts that refer to the circumcision of the androgyne, as well as other sources that refer to menstruation. These descriptions appear in early (tannaitic) layers of rabbinic literature.

There is also the category of the *du parẓuf*—the two-faced human. I address the *du parẓuf* in the second chapter of this book, but since this category is mostly found in the midrashic context, and would require its own in-depth analysis, I do not discuss it here. There is not a substantial overlap between the androgyne and the *du parẓuf* in the legal sources.

The second category that I have grouped under the heading of androgynes is the *tumtum*. The *tumtum* is distinct from the *androginos* but is often paired with them. Some rabbinic sources describe the *tumtum* as a person with a flap of skin covering their genitals. If the flap of skin were to be removed, the *tumtum*'s sex would be revealed. The *tumtum* is conceptually linked to the *androginos*; while the *androginos* has a surplus of visible genitalia, the *tumtum* has a dearth. Because no English term is roughly equivalent to the *tumtum*, I have chosen to leave this word untranslated in the book. When I refer to androgynes without further qualification, I mean to include both the *androginos* and the *tumtum*.

There are ways to contextualize this rabbinic taxonomy within discussions of eunuchs and androgynes circulating in broader cultural contexts. We might turn to Greco-Roman legal, literary, and medical sources, or to Sasanian ideas about sex, gender, and sexuality, for example. I will undertake contextualization of this sort throughout my book; context is important, and the rabbis are not cloistered from their surroundings. Nonrabbinic primary and secondary sources from late antiquity often seek to explain the presence of eunuchs and androgynes in the world. These attempts to explicate eunuchs and androgynes are often polemical. For example, in Greco-Roman sources, eunuchs and androgynes are sometimes invoked to characterize "foreign" sexed and gendered practices, and eunuchs can become rhetorical shorthand to describe the exoticized East. The discussion of androgynes and eunuchs is, and always has been, both political and polemical.

INTRODUCING THE RABBIS

In this section I will introduce the rabbis and the rabbinic period to orient nonspecialists in the field. Like most such generalized introductions, mine will paper over many of the unresolved dilemmas of the field, but it will provide an essential framework for readers unfamiliar with either the general history of the rabbinic movement in late antiquity or the genres of rabbinic literature.

When scholars write about *the* rabbis, they are not talking about contemporary Jewish religious leaders. They are instead referring to a movement whose roots extended from a period before the common era into the sixth century.[23] This rabbinic movement stretched between Roman Palestine and Babylonia, and we can see the traces of this geography reflected in the rituals, ideas, and languages of rabbinic literature. Judaism was already well-established by this time. Some of the contours of the Hebrew Bible existed, as did some central aspects of Jewish practice, including the practice of proffering offerings at a central temple in Jerusalem.

---

23. Scholars in Judaic studies tend to prefer the terms "BCE" and "CE" (before the common era and common era) instead of "BC" and "AD." While the transition point to the common era still measures time through a Christian lens, this is a nod to acknowledging that discomfiting fact.

In the first half of the rabbinic period, the movement was centered in the Galilee. In 63 BCE Judea became a client state of the Roman Empire—when the Roman general Pompey conquered Jerusalem and the central Temple after a local power struggle. Generally speaking, both political and religious power had traditionally been held by the Temple priests. Under Roman rule, the power and governance structures in Judea slowly shifted.

By the beginning of the first century, Judea was governed directly by Roman procurators, some of whom were tolerant of the Jewish refusal to participate in Roman religion and its attendant worship of the Roman emperor. Others, like the infamous Pontius Pilate, seem to have been less lenient. The increasing tension finally erupted in a war (66–70 CE), when Jews rebelled against Roman rule.

While historical sources (both within rabbinic literature and without) attest to the revolt, it is from Josephus that we have the most information about "the Jewish War," and his account must be taken with a grain of salt. What is clear, however, is that the rebellion also quickly became a civil war; there were tensions between groups of Jews who had a more conciliatory orientation toward Rome and those that radically rejected Roman rule. Jerusalem was besieged by the Roman general Titus, and in 70 CE it fell, resulting in the destruction of the central sanctuary, the Temple. The Arch of Titus, which was erected in Rome to commemorate this victory, famously depicts the looting of the Temple treasures in the wake of this destruction. As a consequence of this war, the Romans imposed the *fiscus Judaicus* (or Jewish tax), which routed the money that had previously supported the Temple in Jerusalem to a temple dedicated to Jupiter in Rome.

When the Romans destroyed the Temple in Jerusalem, a central pillar of Jewish practice disappeared. The Jewish festival year and many Jewish rituals had been attached to animal and produce offerings that were regularly sacrificed at the central Temple. The Hebrew Bible sets forth the outlines of the practice, and the attendant institutional structure of the priesthood had also been historically linked to political power. The destruction of the Temple, therefore, had much broader implications than the obvious exercise of Roman colonial power.

Older scholarly historical narratives credit the rabbis with reinventing Judaism in the wake of the destruction of the Temple. In these narratives, the rabbis tend to play the part of the heroes who ensured Judaism's survival by reimagining Judaism in the face of chaos and disaster. Historical evidence demonstrates that, in truth, Jewish sectarianism predated the destruction of the Temple and flourished well into the subsequent "rabbinic" period. Recent historiography has also tended to downplay the influence of the rabbinic movement on the larger Jewish populace even during the first couple of centuries of the common era and to emphasize instead that the rabbis were likely only one voice in a hotly contested field of Jewish continuity. The growth of synagogues and eventually of study halls provided an alternate structure for Jewish life, but this shift was probably a slower process than has been previously believed.

During the same time period, the Roman Empire very slowly Christianized.[24] Recent scholarship has argued that the rabbinic movement spread as Christianity was becoming the official state religion. While rabbinic literature is not a historical chronicle in the contemporary sense, we can see various elements of this historical context within the texts themselves.

Early layers of rabbinic traditions arose within this historical and cultural milieu. The first layer of rabbinic literature is called tannaitic literature, so named because it was produced by the tannaim, the generations of sages who flourished in the period that extended until the middle of the third century CE. This tannaitic (early) rabbinic strata of the literature emerged within the context of Roman imperialism, and in the immediate aftereffects of several crushing Jewish military defeats.

Later layers of rabbinic literature, however, are more complicated to situate. The border between the Roman Empire and the Persian Empire was hotly contested, and border skirmishes between the two polities lasted for centuries. During the rabbinic period, there were two main Persian dynasties: the Parthian and the Sasanian. The Parthian Empire (247 BCE–224 CE) stretched from the Mediterranean to India and China in the East. The Parthians even briefly took over Judea in 40 BCE. Conflicts between Rome and the Persian Empire continued into the Sasanian period (224–651 CE), where we see, for example, Shapur I (roughly 240–270 CE) fighting with the Romans in Syria. The disputed and shifting borders sometimes resulted in forced migrations.

Over the course of the Sasanian period, Zoroastrianism was consolidated and eventually became the national religion of the Persian Empire. Even so, significant Jewish and Christian minorities remained in their lands, as did pagans, Manichees, and Buddhist communities in the eastern parts of the Empire. Well-established communities of Jews had been living in the region for centuries, particularly in Mesopotamia, where Jewish communities had remained since the fall of the kingdom of Judah in 586 BCE had brought with it the capture and deportation of Jews. Some Jews also migrated in the wake of political, military, and social upheaval.

Relations between Jewish communities and the Persian Empire were not always antagonistic—there is evidence, for example, that at some points Jews collaborated with the Parthians to oppose Seleucid and Roman rule. Similarly, some historians think that Jews had relatively peaceful relations with their neighbors for several centuries following the rise of the Sasanian dynasty in the early third century CE. These good relations laid the groundwork for established communities to flourish.

---

24. The slow processes of Christianization (and the effects on rabbinic Judaism), are laid out in Schwartz, *Imperialism*, 179–203.

In the second half of the rabbinic period, the major centers of the rabbinic movement slowly began to shift eastward.

The Sasanian Empire was not continuously tolerant of its religious minorities, however. For example, as the Roman Empire slowly Christianized in the wake of Constantine's conversion in the fourth century, the Sasanian government sometimes singled out Christians suspected of collaborating with the Romans. Jewish communities may have been persecuted in the fifth century. Nor were minority interrelationships always pacific. The introduction of Islam at the end of the Sasanian period brought both more conflict and further religious richness into the region. Late antiquity, therefore, across both the Roman and Persian Empires, was a period of enormous religious contestation and innovation. This is the broader historical context within which we should regard the rabbinic project.

These rabbinic movements, spread across the Roman and Persian Empires, produced what would become one of the most influential bodies of Jewish literature. This body of works continues to inform and shape Jewish practice today. In the interest of space, I will introduce only the two works that I discuss most frequently: the Mishnah and the Babylonian Talmud, although I do address some other compilations in the glossary. The Mishnah and the Talmud are primarily composed in Hebrew and Aramaic, with significant numbers of loan words reflecting the various geographies of rabbinic Judaism.

The Mishnah is usually dated to the early third century of the common era, and it is situated within the context of Roman Palestine. Since the Mishnah is a compilation of traditions that may have circulated for hundreds of years, some of the teachings contained in it originate from before the destruction of the Temple in 70 CE. The compiling of the Mishnah is traditionally associated with Rabbi Yehudah HaNasi (the rabbi whose story begins my introduction). It is organized topically in six "orders" (broad subject headings); individual tractates come under those headings. Scholars continue to debate the precise process of how the Mishnah came to be compiled; there is no reliable historical account of how (or why) these oral traditions were arranged, nor of exactly when they changed from oral compilations to written text. The Mishnah is primarily (but not exclusively) made up of legal discussions on a broad range of topics.

The Babylonian Talmud is often described as the apex of rabbinic achievement. Scholars surmise that the editors may have put together some version of it in the sixth century. The Babylonian Talmud takes its structure from the topical organization of the Mishnah and is therefore also organized into orders and tractates. However, unlike the Mishnah, it is also organized around the *sugya*, a coherent unit of discussion that was edited together. These individual *sugyot* make up the basic structure of discussion in the Talmud. The Talmud comments on the Mishnah, cites other traditions that never made it into the Mishnah, and debates the significance, reach, and applicability of the legal obligations that are laid out in the Mishnah. Famously, the Babylonian Talmud rarely tells us which side wins any particular debate; it is difficult to extract a coherent legal code from it. In addition to discussions conventionally described as "legal," the Talmud shares stories about the sages, creative interpretations of the Hebrew Bible, and parables.

The Sasanian cultural and religious milieu influenced the Babylonian Talmud in ways that scholars are still only beginning to appreciate. Recent scholarship has demonstrated points of convergence between Jewish and Zoroastrian practices, examined loan words, and considered the Sasanian context for the rabbinic culture that developed.

While the contents of the Mishnah and the Babylonian Talmud are related but not the same, scholarship tends to emphasize the legal aspects of both more heavily than the narrative aspects. Calling these rabbinic sources "legal" should not be construed to mean that they correspond to the genre of contemporary law codes with which many of us may be more familiar. The word *halakhah* itself, while conventionally translated as law, can contain all kinds of materials that we do not associate with law. There is excellent scholarship questioning whether "law" is even an appropriate label for these traditions; in rabbinic discussions the rabbis may be practicing medicine, outlining ethical obligations, or describing rituals, and all of this would come under the heading of *halakhah*. In short, neither the Mishnah nor the Babylonian Talmud conforms to any contemporary literary genre that readers will be familiar with. I will use the term "law" in this book advisedly, as a heuristic device, while recognizing that this division between "legal" and narrative or exegetical materials is neither obvious nor uncontested.

TRANSING THE TALMUD

One of the central methodological interventions of this book is what I am calling "transing" rabbinic literature. Before I explain what I mean by using the term "trans" as a verb, I want to introduce some basic terminology used within trans communities. This language has rapidly developed, and terms that were in use when I first came out have been discarded. Therefore, this overview should be understood as reflecting a snapshot in time.

Both the term "transgender" and the more colloquial term "trans" may describe a range of different kinds of gendered identifications. As a broad category, trans can include those who were assigned a sex at birth that does not match the gender they currently identify with. For example, I was assigned female at birth, but I do not currently identify as a woman. *Trans* may also include those who do not identify within the gender binary altogether, sometimes also called nonbinary. Trans people may or may not seek medical assistance to transition. The term "transsexual" has sometimes been used as a synonym for transgender, but it has also been used to differentiate between those trans people who desire medical intervention and those who do not. The common denominator, in all these contexts, is that any use of "trans" often functions as an adjective (or, on occasion, particularly in languages that are not English, as a noun).

And yet, the grammar of trans is decidedly more complicated; scholars have interrogated the nature of the prefix "trans-." Eva Hayward, in the article "More Lessons from a Starfish," explores the ways that "trans" indexes a type of movement: "The transsexual . . . energetically ripples the body, marks the meat, with *re*-form, *re*-grow, *re*-shape so that subjective transformation may occur: transition, transsex, *trans*-be; this is prefixial rippling."[25] Hayward is exploring the prefix "trans-" from a nonteleological perspective as it transforms the words around it. Thus, Hayward recontextualizes the prefix "trans-" as a movement rather than using "trans" as a stable referent. Instead, "trans" indexes a mode of becoming.

It is in the context of this (nonteleological) understanding of trans that I wish to explore the term "transing." In their introduction to a special issue of *Women's Studies Quarterly* on trans studies, editors Paisley Currah, Lisa Jean Moore, and Susan Stryker offered this definition of the term "transing":

> "Transing" . . . is a practice that assembles gender into contingent structures of association with other attributes of bodily being, and that allows for reassembly. Transing can function as a disciplinary tool when the stigma associated with lack or loss of gender status threatens social unintelligibility, coercive normalization, or even bodily extermination. It can also function as an escape vector, line of flight, or pathway towards liberation.[26]

In other words, transing has a few meanings. The first, and most important for this book, is that it unpacks the mechanisms by which genders are formed (and reformed) through their association with other bodily characteristics. In this definition gender is both contingent and inextricably bound up with other aspects of the body that we attribute meaning to. This meaning of transing allows us to think about the bodily characteristics that the rabbis give meaning to in order to historically contextualize the processes by which the rabbis assemble sex/gender.

The second definition of transing describes the way gender functions as a set of practices that both discipline and manage populations. The disciplinary effects that transing has can be violent—up to and including death. In this definition of transing we can feel the weight of the homicidal aggression directed at trans women, and in particular trans women of color. Finally, transing also means uncovering paths of fugitivity, and the potential of movement toward liberation. In a general sense, then, the framers of "transing" organize the term around a ten-

---

25. Hayward, "More Lessons from a Starfish," 81.

26. Stryker, Currah, and Moore, "Introduction," 13. The first usage of the term "transing" should be credited to a talk by Joanne Meyerowitz: "A New History of Gender."

sion: transing describes the mechanism of assigning gendered meaning to bodily attributes, and transing recognizes both disciplinary and liberatory possibilities.

This tension between the disciplinary and liberatory potential of transing will be found throughout this book. On the one hand, encountering rabbinic culture, which does not naturalize binary sex, can feel liberating to those of us who suffer under the current regimes of sex and gender. The alterity of the past is fodder that we can use to imagine our current world differently. The past demonstrates the ephemeral nature of our contemporary definitions of sex, gender, and sexuality.

And yet, at the same time, these sources are not intuitively liberating. Nowhere in the story by Rabbi Yehudah HaNasi does the androgyne express their desires, for example. Trans (and queer) liberation is not obviously present in a debate over what kinds of sex with an androgyne are punishable by death. When I am transing the Talmud, then, I will be playing with all three pieces of transing: transing as a mechanism by which genders are assembled into relationship with bodies, and transing as a tension between liberation and discipline. At some points I literally rewrite the text, such as when I reimagine the story told by Rabbi Yehudah HaNasi from the perspective of the androgyne and the rooster. At other points I examine sources in which the disciplinary functions of law and the potential of fugitivity coincide.

The editors of the special issue of *Women's Studies Quarterly* who coined the term "transing" play with the way that the prefix "trans-" crosses gendered space in their introduction. This makes sense in a context where so much attention is paid to regulating gender through space—as in contemporary legal battles over trans people's right to access public facilities. In order to trans late antique sources, we must consider the crossing of temporal boundaries, as well as spatial ones, as I have already begun to discuss. On the question of the transgression of historical boundaries there is a growing body of scholarship attending to these issues within trans studies and intersex studies; there is also a well-established field of scholarship discussing these questions in the field of the history of sexuality.[27]

In the field of the history of sexuality, Thomas Laqueur has written one of the most famous accounts of sex. In his introduction, Laqueur gives an example of a sex-change narrative in order to outline the difficulties in interpreting the story:

> Girls could turn into boys, and men who associated too extensively with women could lose the hardness and definition of their more perfect bodies and regress into effeminacy ... One might, of course deny that such things happened ... the girl chasing her swine who suddenly sprung an external penis and scrotum ... was really suffering from androgen-dihydrotestosterone deficiency ... This, however, is an

---

27. I discuss some of this scholarship directly in this chapter, chapter 1, and the conclusion. But see also the roundtable in *Transgender Studies Quarterly*, Bychowski et al.: "Trans*historicities: A Roundtable Discussion," 658–85.

unconscionably external, ahistorical, and impoverished approach to a vast and complex literature about the body and culture.[28]

In this passage, Laqueur gives us the narrative of a girl who suddenly manifests an external penis and scrotum. One possible way to understand that story is to diagnose the girl retroactively as having a hormone imbalance that explains her sudden bodily transformation. For Laqueur, the problem with reading hormonal imbalances into a sixteenth-century narrative is that this explanation is both ahistorical and external to the text. The rich sources that Laqueur invokes describe a world where different understandings of (and possibilities for) sexed embodiment exist. To impose the contemporary framework of hormones onto the sources, therefore, impoverishes our ability to read the varied depictions of sexed embodiment. If liberation from contemporary norms of sex and gender can come in part through noticing the ways in which the past organized sex and gender differently, then diagnosing the past removes the possibility of the alterity of the past. Diagnosing the past is not only essentialist and ahistorical, then, it also works against the project of denaturalizing contemporary regimes of sex and gender.

Laqueur is making us aware of the problems of ordering the past through contemporary categories in this passage. At issue in the (rejected) reading of the girl who grew a penis, however, is also a specific attempt to diagnose her as intersex. This understanding of sex as disordered and therefore as diagnosable engages a medical framework for interpreting sex. It is therefore both the diagnostic frame and sex itself that can be historically contextualized. The attempt to read intersex bodies into the past becomes a bad reading.

While I have called this book *Trans Talmud*, I (alongside Laqueur) do not believe that eunuchs and androgynes in antiquity are trans and intersex or that there is any easy correspondence among the categories. I am also concerned, alongside Lacquer, with flattening the tantalizing differences between the way the rabbis ordered sex and gender and contemporary schemata by imposing our categories onto the past.

At the same time, however, I am curious about this "bad" reading of the materiality of sex. In other words, in Laqueur's critique, glossing the girl's sex change as intersex is too literal; it constitutes a bad reading. I find the idea of the bad (material) readings of sex particularly evocative for two reasons: on the one hand transgender bodies have been construed as a "bad reading" of sex and gender in some queer and feminist theory, on the other hand, Jews are often portrayed in late

---

28. Laqueur, *Making Sex*, 7. Laqueur's one-sex theory has been influential, and, in recent times, it has also been subject to criticism. For an overview of the debate in *Isis* and response to Laqueur, see King, *The One-Sex Body on Trial*, 1–31. King also examines the way Laqueur's theories work less well for the Hippocratic corpus than Galen.

antiquity as "bad and literal readers."²⁹ To unpack these convergences further will require me to explore some of the politics of language, and the border clashes between queer theory and trans theory.

While the popular adoption of the term "transgender" is a complex phenomenon, certain strains of feminist and queer theory deliberately mark sex change as outmoded.³⁰ We can trace positive depictions of nonbinary frameworks as subversive and disruptive to gender binaries in this literature. In contrast, these same scholars often construe certain kinds of trans embodiment as shortsightedly attached to the gender binary. I want to give one example—to demonstrate how trans bodily practices have sometimes been sacrificed on the altar of gendered subversion. The example that follows has already been analyzed by Susan Stryker; I want to build on her insights by contextualizing within a broader picture of "bad/literal" reading strategies.

In the groundbreaking special issue of *GLQ* on trans studies, Jack Halberstam invokes the variety of different relationships between "queer" and "trans." He argues as follows:

> Sometimes, transgender and queer are synonyms whose disruptive refigurations of desires and bodies are set in opposition to (nonhomosexual) transsexuality's surgical and hormonal recapitulation of heteronormative embodiment—its tendency to straighten the alignment between body and identity.³¹

When we examine the language here, we can see that transgender is aligned with queer positively, as a disruptive and nonnormative force. Transsexuality, on the other hand, is heteronormative. Halberstam's use of the word *straighten* here is not accidental. This dichotomy, of course, completely erases the possibility and existence of transsexual queers. As part of creating oppositions between queer/straight and transgender/transsexual, transsexuality itself is straightened.

It should be noted clearly that Halberstam is not trying to advance this particular view of trans embodiment. Rather, he is analyzing different conceptions of

---

29. I will expand on the politics of "bad trans readings" in short order, but I am also thinking of the early Christian polemical accusations that Jews are bad/literal interpreters of bodily practices like circumcision. The literature on this polemic is vast; but see, for example, Fredriksen, "Secundum Carnem," 26–41. Fredriksen summarizes the reception of the Jews as carnal, and Augustine's response to these earlier arguments against the Jews. Simultaneously, Jewishness is often associated with embodying problematic genders. On the association between androgyne sex and the uncleanness of Jews in the medieval period, see DeVun, *The Shape of Sex*, 70–102.

30. On the genealogy of the term "transgender," see Valentine, *Imagining Transgender*, 29–67.

31. Susan Stryker quotes this passage in her introduction to the issue, where she explicates the difficulties with it, so this entire critique is indebted to her insights. See "The Transgender Issue," 145–58. Halberstam is, in fact, trying to correct misreadings of their work as anti-trans. See Halberstam, "Transgender Butch," 287–310. Still, it is a compelling summary of a common correlation drawn between some trans bodies and normativity.

"trans" that circulate in the theorist Jay Prosser's work. Still, this passage summarizes admirably the characterization of trans found in some strains of both feminist and queer theory. In this formulation, "nonhomosexual" trans recapitulates heterosexual normativity. Trans people become straight by being attached to the materialities of sex in their desire for medical interventions. In other words, trans people perform "bad and literal" readings of sex.

It is not only that trans people have been portrayed as "bad" readers of sex, however. Given the widespread and continued characterization of trans women as particularly bad/literal readers of sex/gender, the effects of the "bad reader" theory are not distributed equally.[32] The logic by which transgender replaces transsexual (women), specifically with "queerer" forms of contemporary transgender identification, simultaneously renders trans women *themselves* anachronistic. In the many trenchant critiques of transmisogyny, we can see the ways in which trans masculinity is not subject to the same forces.[33] It is this concern that should give us pause about the transmisogyny embedded in the rejection of the bad reading. While I am not trying to recuperate the figure of the transsexual over and against the framework of transgender,[34] or to assume that the two are mutually exclusive, I am interested in the linguistic politics of effacing certain forms of trans embodiment.

To return to our sixteenth-century swine-chasing maiden who suddenly sprouts a penis and testicles: Laqueur has argued that reading hormonal sex change into narrative is an "external, ahistorical, and impoverished" way to read history. Laqueur is critiquing the impulse to "explain away" the sixteenth-century narrative with a diagnostic reference to hormone imbalance. And yet, both the reader who interpolates hormones into the sixteenth century and the bad/literal trans figure are asserting the importance of the materiality of sexed bodies. It is this stubborn insistence on the materiality of sex and sex change that has been labeled a too-literal reading of sex. In other words, in both cases, sex changes constitute a "bad" reading of sex.

---

32. In previous decades trans men tried to disrupt the association of transsexuality with trans women because of the ways in which it renders trans men invisible. See, for example, Jamison Green, *Becoming a Visible Man*, 53–89. Today there is a sharper critique of the effects of transmisogyny and the ways this renders trans women hypervisible. On questions of trans visibility, see Gossett, Stanley, and Burton, *Trap Door*. For the association between visibility and surveillance, also see Beauchamp, *Going Stealth*, 1–23.

33. For the origins of the term "transmisogyny," see Serano, *Whipping Girl*, 11–23. For a critique of the whiteness and class position of Serano's work (and the more general critique of white saviorism implicated in the desire to "save" trans women of color), see Krell, "Is Transmisogyny Killing Trans Women of Color?" 226–42.

34. My purpose is not to revalorize the term "transsexual" over and against "transgender"; both frames have their limitations. As someone who identifies as both transsexual and transgender, I am not interested in relitigating these debates. For one of the foundational works on this question, see Stone, "The *Empire* Strikes Back," 150–76.

Perhaps I have encountered too many early Christian polemics against Jewish hermeneutics. It seems as if late antique Jews are always being accused of reading the sources stubbornly, literally, and materially: Jews insist on literal circumcision instead of metaphorical circumcision, and so on. In other words, Jews are often accused of being bad (literal) readers of the body. But I have begun to wonder what it might mean to embrace the label of being a "bad" trans/Jewish reader.[35] I am not insisting on literal hormonal imbalances in the sixteenth century or in rabbinic literature. And yet, embracing the deliberately "bad" reading might be a productive mechanism to rethink these questions.

In using the term "transing," then, I mean to explore these bad/literal reading strategies. Transing must pay particular attention to the politics of rendering certain (bodies, conceptual frames, lines of argumentation) outmoded or illegible just as the queer "transsexual" becomes illegible in Halberstam's anatomizing of Prosser's work.[36] Transing means paying attention to the forces of transmisogyny—the way that trans women specifically are subject to heightened scrutiny, gender policing, and misogyny. Transing address the attendant forces of racialization, the ways that anti-Blackness and settler colonialism fundamentally shape conceptualizations of both gender and "progress." Transing should track the material costs to those bodies that are "left behind."

C. Riley Snorton, in his monograph *Black on Both Sides: A Racial History of Trans Identity*, asks the reader to consider how some pasts have been discarded in order to create distinct categories of Blackness and transness. Or, as Snorton puts it: "What does it mean to have a body that has been made into a grammar for whole worlds of meaning?"[37] In examining the ways in which the necropolitical management of racialized gender capacitates certain historical projects, Snorton is also focusing our attention on what stories are simultaneously suppressed. I do not, in this project, search out and recuperate alternative voices that have been suppressed by rabbinic literature per se. And yet I will, in Snorton's words, pay attention to whose bodies are enabling meaning in rabbinic discourse.

---

35. Trans studies scholar Cáel Keegan has recently suggested that we might embrace the "bad transgender object"—films that are not governed by contemporary trans respectability politics. See Keegan, "In Praise of Bad Transgender Objects." I am also inspired by Joseph Marchal's rejection of the divine spiritual androgyne in his reading of First Corinthians. See Marchal, *Appalling Bodies*, 30–67.

36. For a transmasculine take on questions of anachronism, see the dialogue between J. Halberstam and C. Jacob Hale, "Butch/FTM Border Wars," 283–85. For a historical approach, see Kunzel, *Criminal Intimacy*.

37. Snorton, *Black on Both Sides*, 11. The reference to grammar is an allusion to the classic article by Hortense Spillers, "Mama's Baby, Papa's Maybe," 65–81. There is an established reception history of Spillers in Black trans studies: see, for example, Bey, "The Trans*ness of Blackness, the Blackness of Trans*ness," 275–95.

By transing I also mean noticing the ways bodies change. Bodies experience changes through time: some bodies transform in puberty, some bodies become ill, some bodies change in ways that make it difficult to access restrooms, workplaces, or school classrooms. Only some of those changes are understood as either natural or desirable. Often, bodily change (as in the changes that accompany aging) can be couched as a loss. By the same token, many different kinds of bodies undergo hormonal shifts; menopause, for example, can be a time of hormonal change that can have a variety of bodily effects. Yet only some hormonal shifts are labeled "sex changes."

Transing, therefore, means paying attention to the materialities of bodies and bodily change. I want to attend to the way certain bodies carry the weight of sex change, thereby naturalizing other types of bodily transformation. More broadly, however, transing recognizes the particular scrutiny that singles out certain types of bodies and the way that all bodies, in their propensity to change and shift through time, thwart expectation and orderliness. When I trans rabbinic sources, I will note where eunuchs and androgynes bear the weight of the changeability of bodies, marking other kinds of bodies as static and unchanging. I will argue, for example, that eunuchs are stigmatized for reproductive failure, obscuring the fact that all bodies may "fail" to reproduce at certain times and that many bodies do not reproduce altogether.

I also mean transing to center a conversation about sex and gender in rabbinic literature. In embarking on this agenda, I am responding to the privileging of an analytical frame of sexuality in historical projects. This dynamic is most obvious in the field of the history of sexuality, which has focused particularly on "homosexuality" in antiquity.[38] Unfortunately, this attention to sexuality (and in particular masculine sexuality) has meant that categories like androgynes and eunuchs are often relegated to the footnotes of a debate about same-sex eroticism, as I shall explore in my next chapter.[39] Centering rabbinic discussions of eunuchs and androgynes allows us to resituate gender in the literature.[40] Sexuality will certainly play a role in my analysis; it is a part of Rabbi Yehudah HaNasi's story about the

---

38. I will not cite the entire body of literature, instead confining myself to a classic work: Kenneth Dover, *Greek Homosexuality*.

39. For a critique of the way so much of the classic literature focuses on male-male sex, see Bernadette Brooten's masterful work: *Love Between Women*. On these questions of sexuality and gender, David Valentine argues that the historical separation between gender and sexuality was crucial to the establishment of the category of transgender. In the end, however, Valentine argues this distinction is used to marginalize discussions of gender variation in the past. See Valentine, *Imagining Transgender*.

40. Many terms that have been used to discuss gender historically, such as "sex/gender deviance," "sex/gender variance," nonbinary, and so on have been critiqued in recent years. I will use these terms provisionally.

androgyne, for example. But I avoid treating eunuchs and androgynes as a subset within a conversation primarily focused on sexuality.

By the same token, while I use queer theory throughout the book, I am framing this as a trans and intersex book. When I have presented this work at conferences, I have often been asked by colleagues why I do not frame eunuchs and androgynes in terms of their queerly subversive potential. I hope that my discussion in this section of the politics of queer subversion and the way it has been used to efface certain types of trans embodiments, for example, will form a partial answer to this question. I also think a part of my answer lies in my argument about the very different ontological stakes for queer and trans historical projects, as I will explore in chapter 2 and the conclusion to this book. More generally, however, I do not wish to purchase queer subversion on the backs of eunuchs and androgynes.

Finally, transing the Talmud means commitment to unpacking the contemporary politics that surround trans and intersex bodies, as well as the ways in which these politics are often litigated through an appeal to history. Attention to the political is not born of a desire to collapse the distinctions between the present and the past; it is, rather, to acknowledge that our contemporary scholarly questions are formed in a particular time and space. My questions in this book are shaped in the particularly vindictive and punishing political moment of the Trump presidency. They are also typed within my private office in my tenure-track job by my white, Ashkenazi, transmasculine hands. This office is simultaneously located in a public university experiencing drastic cutbacks to education within the neoliberal higher educational system that is founded on the exploitation of contingent labor, frontline workers, and graduate students. My questions about eunuchs and androgynes in rabbinic literature are shaped by the landscape in which I write.

STUDYING GENDER IN RABBINICS

I want to begin this section on methodology and the history of the study of gender in rabbinics by relating a story. This story takes place in a trans/religion symposium, where I was invited to present my work. Together with my colleague, Sarra Lev, I wove close readings of rabbinic sources with contemporary trans and intersex political questions in our respective papers. Following our talks, a senior scholar in a different field within Jewish studies delivered the keynote address. Much of his keynote responded to our papers by critiquing the imposition of what he called modern "goggles" on late antique texts. He took issue with feminist, intersex, trans, and queer frameworks. The next day he granted an interview to the Jewish press identifying us as particularly misguided.

There are numerous ways to critique this interaction, which is a stark example of the larger dynamics in the field. In particular, it is important to name the gatekeeping that structures Jewish studies broadly and rabbinics in particular. Sexism, homophobia, and transphobia all played a part in that exchange and are some of the forces that can make the field so unlivable for scholars who find themselves at its margins.

For the moment, however, I wish to take the senior scholar's methodological provocation literally and examine what it means to study gender in rabbinics. This section of the introduction is mainly written for specialists in the field, as I will move rather quickly through some scholarship that will be familiar to my colleagues. But it may also interest anyone who has considered the gendered politics of studying rabbinic sources.

While I do not agree with this scholar's critique, I do have some misgivings of my own about the "application" of feminist, queer, and trans theory to rabbinic sources. Tal Ilan traces the study of women in rabbinic literature to the nineteenth century, when scholars in the *Wissenschaft des Judentums* (Jewish studies) movement began to investigate the status of women within the context of larger debates over the changes of modernity.[41] Contemporary feminist work in rabbinics, however, interacts more with feminist scholarship from the 1970s and 1980s. Beginning in the 1970s, Christian feminists argued that the misogyny of rabbinic culture set the stage for the success of a "protofeminist" Jesus movement. Thus Jesus' purported rejection of Jewishness was (at least in part) a rejection of Judaism's treatment of women.[42] Bernadette Brooten, among others in the field of early Christianity, intervened in this Christian feminist (and anti-Jewish) critique of rabbinic Judaism.[43]

The study of gender in rabbinics, therefore, has historically been tied to supercessionist (or downright anti-Jewish) logics. Jewish activists and scholars who consider the question of the status of women in law have done so within this freighted context of Christian polemics.[44] Feminist rabbinics as a field has histori-

---

41. See Ilan, *Jewish Women in Greco-Roman Palestine*, 1–22. Her introduction is one of the most thorough accounts of early scholarly approaches to the question of gender in rabbinic literature.

42. Leonard Swidler's article "Jesus Was a Feminist" is perhaps the most famous articulation of these ideas, as is Judith Plaskow's equally iconic response in *Lilith* magazine, where she calls out Christian feminist scholarship for its anti-Judaism. See Swidler, "Jesus Was a Feminist," 177–83; Plaskow, "Blaming the Jews," 11–12.

43. See Brooten, "Jewish Women's History in the Roman Period," 22–30. See also Brooten's earlier monograph, which argues from the inscriptional evidence that there were Jewish women leaders in synagogues. Brooten uses this data as a rejoinder to those feminists who had argued that Jewish women were completely excluded from public life. See Brooten, *Women Leaders in the Ancient Synagogue*.

44. For classic feminist works on women in Jewish law, see Biale, *Women and Jewish Law*; Adler, *Engendering Judaism*; Plaskow, *Standing Again at Sinai*. On the feminist preference for aggadah over law, see Fonrobert, "The Handmaid, The Trickster, and the Birth of the Messiah," 245–77. I do not mean to assume that we can easily define and separate between midrash and halakhah—a complicated and fraught project to say the least. There are also good reasons to question the translation of halakhah as law. See Neis, "The Seduction of Law," 119–38.

cally faced the unappetizing choice between an apologetic approach bent on justifying the rabbis in the face of these attacks, and a condemnatory approach primarily concerned with indicting the androcentrism (and at times downright misogyny) of the rabbis. Many foundational scholars in early feminist rabbinics carefully navigated between these two poles, and this polemical debate shaped the contours of those early efforts.[45]

It is worth paying attention to the legacy of those scholarly encounters. We need to consider whether anti-Judaism and the investigation of gender in rabbinics are still imbricated. In recent years, there have been attempts to read eunuchs and androgynes for Christian liberatory purposes, in order to help contemporary trans and intersex Christians find a place within the Church. Some of these efforts rely on demonizing the rabbis in order to elevate early Christian attitudes. In that sense, while gender theory is certainly not to be blamed for supercessionism, these bodies of scholarship are created without rabbinic sources in mind.

At the same time, however, the senior scholar's critique of our talks positioned my colleague and me as standing "outside the texts," and as analyzing them through the "goggles" of modernity.[46] The language of his critique is unsubtle: he stands within the sources. I, on the contrary, employ a modern frame external to the text and therefore, in his view, stand outside of it. I am separated from my sources by both time and space, and perhaps, also, by my (trans)gender. The gatekeeping elements of his critique are almost too obvious to require comment: who is presumed to be "internal" to the tradition?

But the scholar's rejection of "modern goggles" is not just a rejection of women and trans people in the field; the critique was meant as a rejection of gendered analysis itself. In this perspective, modernity becomes the provenance of gender. Given Tal Ilan's exploration of the gendered politics of modernity that shaped the research originating in nineteenth-century *Wissenschaft* scholarship, there is, therefore, a well-established tradition within Judaic studies of deploying gender to negotiate the boundaries of modernity.[47] And yet, if the rabbis enter into intimate, theoretical, and sustained consideration of questions of sex, gender, ethnicity, embodiment, and sexuality, in what ways is gender modern?

Clearly, this scholar and I disagree. I want to call our attention, however, to a more fundamental aspect of his argumentation. When this scholar renders gender as external to the text, he is simultaneously proposing a hermeneutic for reading rabbinics. This scholar's methodology conceptualizes the boundaries of the sources.

---

45. See, for example, Wegner, *Chattel or Person?*; Hauptman, *Reading the Rabbis*; Boyarin, *Carnal Isarel*; and Peskowitz, *Spinning Fantasies*.

46. The visual metaphor of goggles or glasses that he used throughout the talk is also quite interesting. More could be said about the ableist logics of assistive devices (glasses) being deployed as "blinding," but that is not the main thrust of my discussion here.

47. Ilan, *Jewish Women in Greco-Roman Palestine*, 1–22.

What is the implication of hypothesizing a text that has insides and outsides? Obviously, this was meant as a metaphor, but it is a metaphor with profound implications. To overstate the case in order to drive the point home: If he argues that I, as a scholar, stand on the exterior of my texts, and penetrate them with my "foreign" theoretical frames, then my analysis is figured as a violent (sexualized/ethnic) boundary-crossing imposition. Is he not, then, characterizing feminist inquiry, in an ironic shift, as a type of sexualized violence operating on the defenseless rabbinic text? In other words, the rabbinic sources themselves are feminized in this gendered and sexualized hermeneutic and violated by my imposition of feminist theory.[48] Therefore, it is only the (cis/male?) scholar that stands already within the sources, who may properly interpret them. For a rejection of feminist theory, this is an incredibly gendered and sexualized account of the practice of reading rabbinic literature.

This story of my interaction is certainly not unique. Most critiques of this sort target women, like my copanelist, rather than trans masculine people like myself. At the Association for Jewish Studies Annual Conference in 2018, on panels addressing topics as broad as the future of philology, the question of the gendered dynamics of the field was repeatedly raised. Beth Berkowitz called some of the narrowly practiced versions of philology forms of toxic masculinity.[49] Sara Ronis collected the reflections of fellow scholars anonymously, and many discussed their encounters with misogyny in the field.[50] From 1982 (the year that Judith Hauptman became the first woman to earn a PhD in Talmud) to the present, we continue to struggle collectively with painful levels of sexism and misogyny. Nor are these questions confined to the academy; there are growing (but still limited) resources for women who want to learn rabbinic literature, which has traditionally only been taught to men. This has a direct correlation to the number of women who pursue doctoral degrees.

I am deliberately weaving together the methodological questions of studying gender in rabbinics, with the complicated gendered politics of the field itself. It is my general contention that these two seemingly separate questions are intertwined. The gendered politics of the field has led to a systematic undervaluation of the ways in which feminist and queer scholarship has revolutionized methodology

---

48. I am not trying to sidestep the issue of my shared masculinity with the speaker, which implicates me as transmasculine within the logics of sexual violence. However, I am quite positive that he was not trying to render a feminist critique of transmisogyny.

49. I am paraphrasing Beth Berkowitz's remarks as moderator and respondent at the 2018 Association of Jewish Studies Annual Conference: "What is the Place of Philology and Source Criticism in Talmudic Studies?" The exact quotation is: "Philology also has a habit of creating a class of knowers and a class of ignoramuses. Elitism is baked into the enterprise. I'll go even further than Moulie on this point: philology exudes an atmosphere of toxic masculinity." The exclusionary character of the elitism does not just impact women but anyone who does not fit the image of a white, cis, straight, Jewish student of the Talmud.

50. Ronis, "Different Approaches to Rabbinics Research: Between the United States and Israel."

in rabbinics. This undervaluation is, at least in part, owing to sexism and misogyny in the field.

While there were certainly earlier attempts to interpret rabbinic literature alongside contemporary theory in the humanities (for example, Susan Handelman's early work with literary theory), it is feminist scholarship that chafes most under the strictures of a narrowly defined philological method.[51] Building on the feminist scholarship of the 1980s, in the 1990s such scholars as Miriam Peskowitz, Judith Romney Wegner, and (later) Charlotte Fonrobert began to draw on different theoretical tools in order to be able to formulate new questions about the sources. In doing so, these scholars prompted a sea change in the practice of rabbinics. It is feminist and queer scholarship that is largely responsible for the dramatic shift.

Charlotte Fonrobert has referred to *Carnal Israel* as the midwife of a new approach to gender studies. At the same time, it might be argued that feminist and queer scholarship served as midwives to a new methodology in rabbinics more broadly.[52] Put another way, not only is gender as a category integral to rabbinic thinking as these scholars have demonstrated but, regardless of whether current scholarship acknowledges its debts or not, it is an integral part of the turn to cultural studies that makes large swaths of contemporary work in rabbinics possible. The study of sex, gender, and sexuality transformed the field.

Moreover, feminist scholarship has broadened the types of conversations rabbinics has entered into: postcolonial theory, critical race theory, disability theory, animal studies, and queer theory are just some areas of recent inquiry.[53] In several different respects, then, my project of transing the Talmud is only possible because of the interventions of feminist scholars in the field. The contemporary practice of rabbinics generally has been profoundly and irrevocably shaped by feminist theory. Feminist theory is not a violent interpolation into the sources; feminist theory enables contemporary critical reading practices in much of the field.

OUTLINE OF THE BOOK

In this book I weave together various bodies of theory—in particular trans and intersex studies. In doing so, I am not trying to imply that the contemporary

---

51. Handelman, *The Slayers of Moses*.
52. Fonrobert, "On Carnal Israel and its Consequences," 462–69.
53. On queer theory, see Rafe Neis, *The Sense of Sight in Rabbinic Culture*, and Gwynn Kessler, "Bodies in Motion," 389–430. On disability theory, see Julia Watts Belser, *Rabbinic Tales of Destruction*. On gender and material culture, see Cynthia Baker, *Rebuilding the House of Israel*. On animal studies, see Beth Berkowitz, *Animals and Animality in the Babylonian Talmud*. On the category of the human see Mira Wasserman, *Jews, Gentiles, and Other Animals*. Many of these scholars engage with more than one body of theory. This is just a sampling of representative work; this footnote cannot be comprehensive.

distinctions among intersex, trans, and queer are either uncontested or unimportant. The disciplinary divides index real material and political differences. The struggles with health care in both trans and intersex communities, for example, can manifest very different desires.[54] My intention in transing the Talmud is not to colonize other bodies of theory (including intersex theory), or historical configurations of sex/gender.[55] Rather, while trans studies is my theoretical home, I hope, in this book, to facilitate further conversations between trans and intersex theory.

Transing, as I have argued, centers eunuchs and androgynes. My first chapter, "Texts and Contexts," examines the phenomenon of eunuchs and androgynes within the broader history of the ancient Near East, Greco-Roman late antiquity, and the Sasanian context. There are long-established and varied traditions circulating throughout the region that phobic scholarship has misread. In this chapter I argue that when we center eunuchs and androgynes, we fundamentally shift the way we narrate the history of this time period.

Having established the importance of these categories in contemporaneous cultures and literatures, my second chapter, "The Gendering of Law: The Androgyne and the Hybrid Animal in Bikkurim," explores the most central tannaitic (early) rabbinic source that discusses the androgyne. In this tradition the rabbis ask a series of questions: How is the androgyne like a man? How is the androgyne like a woman? How is the androgyne like both? How is the androgyne like neither? The rabbis, in other words, pose questions about sex/gender and the capacity of rabbinic law to incorporate the androgyne. In this chapter I produce a bad (trans) reading of these sources by weaving through an anachronistic discussion of contemporary anti-trans "bathroom bills" in order to think through the material costs of unintelligibility in the law.

Building on this discussion of gendered unintelligibility, my third chapter, "Sex With Androgynes," explores a *sugya* (edited unit of text) in tractate Yevamot of the Babylonian Talmud. This discussion treats the oft-cited biblical prohibition against "lying with a man." The rabbis pose the question: does sex with an androgyne constitute "lying with a man"? Just as transing can draw attention to the way transsexual bodies carry the weight of sex changes, in this chapter I will pay attention to the multiple orifices of the androgyne. I argue that the penetrability of all masculine bodies is displaced onto the body of the androgyne, who becomes the prototypical subject of the biblical prohibition against "lying with a man."

---

54. See, for example, the battles trans people fight to gain access to health care, and likewise the battles intersex people fight to avoid surgical intervention for infants.

55. There is substantial research into the way both queer and trans people configure relations transnationally. In queer studies, see, for example, Boelstorff, *The Gay Archipelago*. In trans studies, see Aizura, *Mobile Subjects*.

My fourth chapter builds on my arguments about transgressive masculinity by examining debates that center on "genitally damaged" men. The chapter, "Transing the Eunuch: Kosher and Damaged Masculinity," thinks with disability theory about what it means when the rabbis label certain kinds of masculine bodies "kosher." I demonstrate that disability, ethnicity, sex, gender, and sexuality are all intertwined in Mishnah Yevamot through a focus on bodies and genitalia. Transing, in this chapter, attends to the way the rabbis socially impair certain types of eunuchs because of genital differences.

My fifth chapter engages a discussion (*sugya*) in the Babylonian Talmud through the lens of theories of trans and intersex temporality. In this discussion in Yevamot, eunuchs disrupt the rabbinic normative expectations of the way bodies develop through infancy, puberty, and old age. This chapter, "Eunuch Temporality: The Saris and the Aylonit" argues that the anxieties over reproductive failures center on eunuchs, obscuring the way reproduction and bodily development is a fraught enterprise for all.

In my conclusion, I argue that the mutability of sex in rabbinic sources, which I have demonstrated in a variety of different texts, is used to establish rabbinic authority as an interpreter of sex. I also analyze the reading strategies of contemporary activists, theologians, and rabbis who have translated androgynes and eunuchs into contemporary idioms. In the face of the way trans and intersex people are often not allowed to name (or claim) history, these creative reimaginings perform a type of historical and religious work.

. . .

I want to address one final peculiarity about the format of the book, and this section is intended primarily for scholars of rabbinics. Most monographs that treat a specific topic in rabbinic literature tend to organize the materials diachronically, and to follow the development of rabbinic thinking through the layers of sources. This mode of analysis implicitly suggests that the sources evolve.

In the special roundtable of the *AJS Review* devoted to the Mishnah scholars describe a number of recent trends that interpret tannaitic literature as a distinctive project.[56] Steven Fraade, in his introduction, points to the ways that recent research positions the Mishnah as a rabbinic enterprise in its own right. This pushes back on the notion that tannaitic literature represents a less developed version of the Babylonian Talmud. These insights are particularly important in light

---

56. See Fraade, "Introduction to the Symposium," 221–23, for an outlining of the different approaches represented. It is worth noting that Fraade is not arguing that the textual layers are completely independent of one another but rather that they should be read intertextually. This is contra Jacob Neusner, who, in his documentary hypothesis, understands each of the "documents" of rabbinic literature to be independent of one another. See Neusner, *Three Questions of Formative Judaism*, 94–148 (among other places).

of the fact that there is not a strong consensus on the genre or function of either compilation; this, in turn, leaves open the possibility that any evolutionary approach is simply comparing two radically different types of objects.[57]

My book takes up the challenge issued by these scholars of tannaitic literature to resist portraying earlier strata as underdeveloped. This kind of evolutionary model has been critiqued in queer theory, critical race theory, and disability theory as well, albeit to different ends.[58] Within the context of rabbinics, this idea of the increasing sophistication of the sources tends to rest on a theory of the development of the Talmud that understands the later layers as building on earlier ones.

Moulie Vidas's recent monograph *Tradition and the Formation of the Talmud* explicitly takes up again the question of the redaction of the Talmud and its relationship to the earlier sources it cites.[59] Vidas summarizes the main schools of thought in the field that characterize the relationship between the creators of the anonymous materials and the attributed traditions.[60] In contrast to other scholars, Vidas points out that citation, or the practice of marking something as tradition, has the paradoxical effect of drawing a boundary around it to denote it as past. In contrast, the voice of the creators of the Talmud is unmarked, and through their anonymity the creators situate themselves as the (present) authoritative representative of the Talmud.

If Vidas is correct, the anonymous layer is what transforms apodictic statements into tradition. The creators of the Talmud, through their citational practices, produce a temporal boundary that marks off the past. In contrast to understanding rabbinic literature as a progressive enterprise culminating in the Babylonian Talmud, the aesthetic of the *sugya*, which often creates improbable conversations between rabbis living generations apart from each other, is not

---

57. On the question of the purpose of the Mishnah, see Elman, "Order, Sequence, and Selection," 53–81. Elman summarizes the prolific scholarship on this question.

58. Progress narratives work (or fail) differently in these various fields. For a critique of progress narratives from the perspective of queer history, see Love, *Feeling Backward*, 1–31. For a recent exploration of Black time and the debate about afropessimism in Black studies, see Sexton, "The Social Life of Social Death," 61–75. For a critique of the triumphalist progress narratives in disability studies, see McRuer, "Crip Eye for the Normate Guy," 586–92.

59. Vidas, *Tradition and the Formation of the Talmud*.

60. Vidas contrasts Weiss-Halivni with Shamma Friedman. See Weiss-Halivni, *Midrash, Mishnah and Gemara*. Weiss-Halivni's thinking on the *stammaim* has also changed over time. See, for example, the collection of his introductions to the various individual volumes of his commentary: Weiss-Halivni, *Mevo'ot l'm'korot u'mesorot*. On the other hand, Shamma Friedman would seem to be diametrically opposed to Weiss-Halivni: see Friedman, "Pereq Ha'Ishah Rabah b'Bavli," 274–441. Vidas argues that there is more overlap between Weiss-Halivni and Friedman than is commonly assumed.

meant to be linear. Rather, one of the functions of the *sugya* is to make disparate temporalities, genres, and geographies touch.[61]

I am not claiming the *sugya* as some kind of essentially queer literary production that transgresses temporal boundaries. Rather, I am building on the work of scholars who note the peculiar characteristic of rabbinic time. Yosef Hayim Yerushalmi has, perhaps most famously, characterized the whimsical nature of rabbinic time: "the rabbis seem to play with time as though with an accordion, expanding and collapsing it at will ... that acute biblical sense of time and place often gives way to rampant and seemingly unselfconscious anachronism."[62] The image of time as an accordion is one in which disparate elements can be both expanded and collapsed into one another, or, put another way, made to "touch."

Models that suggest linear development in analyzing the Babylonian Talmud, therefore, are subject to criticism not only from the perspective of those who want to take tannaitic literature as an object worthy of independent analysis; linear models also work against the aesthetic of the Babylonian Talmud itself. This point has been made in the work of Sergey Dolgopolski. Dolgopolski claims that the *stammaitic* (late anonymous rabbinic) argumentation does not reproduce the logic of linear progressive time.[63] While Dolgopolski is specifically discussing the distinction between oral and written tradition, he is linking the rhetorical function of the *sugya* to its predilection for alternative temporalities. For Dolgopolski, the *sugya* promiscuously undermines temporal boundaries, even as, if Vidas is right, it establishes them.

While my title is *Trans Talmud*, I am, in fact, addressing both tannaitic and later layers of literature in the Talmud. I have paired chapters on the tannaitic sources with chapters on *sugyot*. This paired structure is meant to address the ways in which the layers of sources may simultaneously stand in conversation with one another and have distinct projects.

---

61. On the dialogical structure of rabbinic literature, see Boyarin, *Socrates and the Fat Rabbis*; Dohrmann, "Reading as Rhetoric," 90–115; and Hidary, *Rabbis and Classical Rhetoric*. On the way narrative is a woven within the *sugya*, see Wimpfheimer, *Narrating the Law*, 147–64; and Simon-Shoshan, "Halakhic Mimesis," 101–23. In talking about "touch" across time I am referencing work in queer temporality. See Dinshaw, *Getting Medieval*, 1–55. Dinshaw explores the erotics of cross-temporal touches.

62. Yerushalmi, *Zakhor*, 17. See also Neusner, *The Idea of History in Rabbinic Judaism*. A more recent summary that is particularly strong in its discussion concerning the issue of the rabbinization of biblical history is Gafni's "Rabbinic Historiography," 295–313. Gafni discusses Yerushalmi's *Zakhor*.

63. I am using the term "stammaitic" because Dogolpolski does, but I am not adjudicating between *saboraim*, *stammaim*, and Vidas's term "creators of the Talmud." See Dolgopolski, *The Open Past*.

There are some clear drawbacks to the structure of my book;[64] I am not recommending this format for others. Rather, this is an experiment in shifting the conventions, in order to continue a conversation on how we might write rabbinics differently. I am responding to the challenges of scholars of tannaitic literature that goad us to new forms of organizing our research.

TECHNICAL ISSUES
Terminology

I will use the term "hermaphrodite" sparingly (mostly when it is the word that the sources themselves are using), but I want to begin by acknowledging the ways intersex activists have problematized the term. *Hermaphrodite* is still used in certain medical contexts. The word comes from antiquity; it was most likely a combination of the names of Hermes and Aphrodite. Intersex communities have protested against these mythological associations. Contemporary medical practices, including "disambiguating" surgeries that purport to solve the problem of intersex bodies, are still practiced today in the United States. Activists have argued that the medical management of intersex "conditions" has been tantamount to a concerted effort to make intersex bodies disappear. In this context, the term "hermaphrodite" is particularly problematic; its connotations extend the ways intersex people living today are rendered invisible or mythical. Just as surgery can be understood in some cases to efface intersex bodies, so too naming intersexuality in mythical terms seems designed to erase contemporary intersex existence.

The term "intersex" is itself fiercely contested, but I will use it instead of "DSD" (Differences/Disorders of Sexed Development). Many of the major organizations in the United States now use the term "DSD" in their advocacy work.[65] Some of these activists have found that speaking the language of medical professionals yields better results when advocating for improved medical treatment, and "DSD" is more intelligible to the medical community. At the same time, some activists decry the pathologizing flavor of "DSD" or dislike the way it assumes a sexed norm

---

64. One obvious drawback is that the Palestinian Talmud is mostly found in the footnotes or body of the chapters on the Babylonian Talmud and does not receive its own chapter discussions. This replicates the same teleological logic that I was trying to avoid; it positions the Palestinian Talmud as a precursor to the Babylonian Talmud rather than as a project in its own right.

65. For the Intersex Society of North America's (ISNA) position on why it switched to DSD, see http://www.isna.org/node/1066. This is before the group closed its doors in 2007 and reformed under the name Accord Alliance. See Emi Koyama's endorsement of the switch and her comments on the controversy over Alice Dreger: http://www.intersexinitiative.org/articles/intersextodsd.html. From the opposing camp, the Organisation Intersex International rejected the term "DSD" and maintains the use of the term "intersex." See http://www.intersexualite.org/Response_to_Intersex_Initiative.html.

that all bodies should conform to. I have chosen to use "intersex" throughout, but I do not intend that as a condemnation of the strategic use of "DSD" in the context of medical advocacy. Both terms are equally anachronistic, but I prefer to mark the diagnostic frame associated with "DSD" as the contemporary enterprise that it is.

Pronouns represented another challenge in writing this book. I use the singular "they" throughout the book when I discuss androgynes, particularly when the rabbis are debating their sex. Over the years, I have used numerous pronouns for the androgyne—sometimes the nonbinary pronouns "ze" or "hir," sometimes "s/he." Occasionally I have also used "he," which is a more literal translation of the Hebrew, but only because in Hebrew the default "neutral" grammatical gender is masculine.[66] All of these pronouns are less than ideal; I am faced with the unappetizing choice of papering over the androcentrism of the sources or erasing the kinds of sexed indeterminacy that the rabbis are explicitly attempting to describe. I continue to struggle with the constraints and limitations of both English and Hebrew in translating these sources.

Transliteration, Manuscripts, and Sources of the Hebrew Texts

Common words (for example "kosher") have been transliterated into English in ways that will be easily recognizable to most readers. At the request of the press, I have also used a simple transcription style for the ease of nonspecialist readers.[67]

Unless otherwise noted, citations of the Mishnah follow the Kaufmann manuscript; citations of the Tosefta follow Saul Lieberman's critical edition; citations of the Palestinian Talmud follow the Leiden edition; and citations of the Babylonian Talmud follow the Munich manuscript.[68] I have mostly confined textual criticism to the endnotes and have only cited variants when they were especially pertinent to the topic of discussion. All the manuscripts I consulted were available online,[69] except for Lieberman's critical edition of the Tosefta, some fragments of

---

66. For an early rendering of nonbinary pronouns, see Minnie Bruce Pratt, *S/he*.

67. I originally transcribed most terms using a fully reversible SBL style. In SBL style, for example, the Deuteronomic terms for genital damage would have been rendered *pṣû ʿa dakkā ʾ* and *kərût šāpkā*. In the much simpler AJS transcription system, those same words would appear is *p'zua daka'* and *krut shafkhah*. While I prefer the accuracy of a technical transcription, I understand the concerns of the press about readability and have changed the transcriptions accordingly.

68. MS Kaufmann. Hungarian Academy of Sciences, Budapest, MS A 50. I also consulted MS Parma (de Rossi 138); MS Munich, Bayerische Staatsbibliothek Cod. Heb. 95.

For the Tosefta I also rely on Lieberman's commentary in the *Tosefta Kifshuta*. I have also consulted Zuckermandel, *Tosefta*.

69. Most of the manuscripts were available through the Saul and Evelyn Henkind Talmud Text Databank, Bar Ilan, and the National Library of Israel (in partnership with Hebrew University) .

Yevamot found in the Vatican Library,[70] and the Sussman edition of the Palestinian Talmud.[71]

Finally, all translations of rabbinic texts are mine, while translations of the biblical texts follow the Jewish Publication Society Bible, unless otherwise noted.[72] I have inserted some glosses into my translations; these insertions are indicated by square brackets. Translations of Greek and Latin texts follow the Loeb editions, unless otherwise noted.

---

70. See Sherry, *Manuscripts of the Babylonian Talmud from the Collection of the Vatican Library*. This three-volume set contains two relevant manuscripts of Yevamot, Vat. Ebr. 114 and Vat. Ebr. 111, the latter of which is available through the National Library of Israel website, but the former of which is only available in this facsimile edition.

71. Sussman, *Talmud Yerushalmi*.

72. Jewish Publication Society, *The Jewish Publication Society Hebrew-English Tanakh* (New York: Jewish Publication Society, 1999).

1

Transing Late Antiquity

The Politics of the Study of Eunuchs and Androgynes

One chapter cannot comprehensively cover all the different materials on eunuchs and androgynes circulating in late antiquity or in the broader Mediterranean world. Instead, I will explore a series of case studies that provide a snapshot of different traditions and that serve as an introduction to the study of eunuchs and androgynes. More information is available on each of the rabbinic categories (and their precursors) in the chapters that follow. In this chapter, I demonstrate the ways in which contemporary attitudes toward transgender and intersex people have profoundly influenced the study of eunuchs and androgynes. I argue that centering eunuchs and androgynes reshapes our historical narratives.

MONSTROUS EUNUCHS, LATE ANTIQUITY, AND THE DECLINE AND FALL OF THE ROMAN EMPIRE

Recent scholarship has contextualized the rabbinic movement within the period of late antiquity. In this section, I will trans late antiquity by demonstrating how eunuchs are central to the stories that scholars have told of this era. In so doing, I want to imagine the rabbinic engagement with eunuchs within this moment of the slow decline of the Roman Empire. Transing can offer us a different perspective from which to challenge received narratives about late antiquity.

Late antiquity is a period comprising approximately the second to the eighth centuries of the Common Era.[1] Situating the rabbis in late antiquity positions

---

1. This periodization for late antiquity follows that offered by Peter Brown in *The World of Late Antiquity*. On questions about periodization and late antiquity, see Marcone, "A Long Late Antiquity," 4–19. Each of these suggested periodizations of late antiquity includes only part of the rabbinic period.

them in a time of cultural and religious innovation: in late antiquity, Jewish sectarianism waxes and wanes; Christianities are invented and discarded; Zoroastrianism transforms Iranian political culture; Islam spreads beyond the Arabian Peninsula; and Roman (pagan) religions continue to thrive. Scholars have argued that this rich environment of religious and political transformation profoundly shaped rabbinic culture as the rabbis navigated between Greco-Roman and the Sasanian Persian milieus.[2] The later layers of rabbinic oral traditions, according to this argument, are formulated within the tensions between empires and religions.[3]

That the rabbis function within these broader (and competing) cultural contexts does not mean that these cultures "influenced" them in any straightforward way. There are several problems with the model of influence, including the following: that it supposes two distinct and separate entities; and that it ignores the power dynamics of Roman imperialism.[4] Moreover, staging the interaction between rabbinic sources and the Greco-Roman and Sasanian worlds as "influence" plays into the dynamics of interreligious polemics of late antiquity. In the context of a world in which the authenticity of religious traditions is often measured by how old they are, the question of whose tradition has influenced whom led to intense (and polemical) debates. For example, early Christians accused devotees of the Magna Mater goddess tradition of copying the rite of baptism.[5] At the same time, in order to avoid hermetically sealing off the rabbis from their environment, it is important to position the rabbinic movement within its historical and cultural context.

This scholarly desire to contextualize the rabbis within late antiquity coincides with a general increase of interest in this period and its contributions.[6] The por-

---

Even as I contextualize the rabbis within late antiquity, therefore, it is useful to consider the ways in which these narratives of history are not designed around rabbinic Judaism.

2. See, for example, Saul Lieberman, *Greek in Jewish Palestine* and *Hellenism in Jewish Palestine*. In general, linguistic models work better for the Greco-Roman materials than for the Sasanian; Greek and Latin loanwords in rabbinic literature vastly outnumber Iranian loan words. See Secunda, *The Iranian Talmud*, and Mokhtarian, *Rabbis, Sorcerers, Kings, and Priests*. Robert Brody points to this linguistic disparity in order to argue against the recent push to explore Iranian parallels. See Brody, "Irano-Talmudica: The New Parallelomania?" 209–32. Galit Hasan-Rokem has explored the way narratives can cross cultural divides. See Hasan-Rokem, *Tales of the Neighborhood*, 28–54.

3. The model of cultural "influence" has been roundly and deservedly critiqued in rabbinics. Michael Satlow helpfully lays out the ways in which different scholars have approached this question: see Satlow, "Beyond Influence," 37–53.

4. The concept of borrowing is also not benign; it can mean cultural appropriation in the context of colonialism. For a contemporary exploration of these dynamics within Indigenous studies, see Joanne Barker, "Introduction," 1–44.

5. Fear, "Cybele and Christ," 37–51. On the sexual politics of these questions of "copies" and "originals," see Seidman, *Faithful Renderings*, 37–73.

6. Some examples of the innovations attributed to this time period: On the development of the self in this time period, see Miller, "Shifting Selves in Late Antiquity"; on the invention of the category of religion, see Daniel Boyarin, *Borderlines*, 1–36.

trayal of late antiquity as an era of innovation and transformation (as I sketched briefly above) is a relatively recent revision; the previous, long-standing narrative of late antiquity depicted an age of cultural decline in which the innovations of the classical world were frittered away as the Roman Empire slid slowly toward the "Dark Ages."[7] Edward Gibbon's *History of the Decline and Fall of the Roman Empire* popularized this traditional (perhaps even lachrymose) narrative. Gibbon's work is an elegy to the classical period sketched against a backdrop of the crumbling edifice of Roman imperial power. For Gibbon, the growth of Christianity contributed greatly to the demise of the cultural and political accomplishments of Greece and Rome.

Gibbon's narrative about the decline of the Roman Empire is not only a narrative about religion (and Christianity specifically); it is also decidedly gendered. For Gibbon, the Christianization of the Roman Empire transforms and weakens Roman masculinity, and this weakening results in Rome's waning political and military power. Christianity "emasculates" Rome, and it is therefore at least partly to blame for Rome's fall. Recent scholarship engages Gibbon's intertwining of gender, religion, and the decline of empire in a variety of ways.[8]

Although scholarship has explored Gibbon's gendered rhetoric, few scholars have noted his specific focus on eunuchs, or the way he connects the figure of the eunuch to the emasculation of Rome.[9] For example, in his section on Constantine (who is often described as the first Roman emperor to convert to Christianity), Gibbon relays the story of Constantine's famous victory and unification of the empire. Directly following this investigation of Constantine's conversion, Gibbon argues that this unification of the Roman Empire served only to "establish the reign of the eunuchs over the Roman world."[10] When Gibbon connects Constantine, who is so often tied to the Christianization of the Roman Empire, with eunuchs, he simultaneously attaches the softening of Roman masculinity to Christian deviance.[11] At the same time, Gibbon marks this transformation as Eastern, calling the spread of eunuchs "the contagion of Asiatic luxury." The rhetorical effect of this characterization positions eunuchs as a contagious disease that

---

7. Medievalists would take issue with the depiction of the Middle Ages as synonymous with decline. See, for example, Caroline Dinshaw's exploration of the term "medieval" in *Getting Medieval*, 183–207.

8. See, for example, Cooper, "Gender and the Fall of Rome," 187–200; and Halsall, "Gender and the End of Empire," 17–39.

9. In his review of the anthology *Eunuchs in Antiquity and Beyond*, Donald Lateiner connects Gibbon and the study of eunuchs, although he does so mostly in order to note that the volume fails to discuss Gibbon. Some historians have engaged Gibbon's negative portrayals of individual historical eunuchs. See, for example, Hopkins, "Eunuchs in Politics in the Later Roman Empire," 62–80. There has also been critique of Gibbon's treatment of Jews. See Langmuir, *Toward a Definition*, 26–31.

10. Gibbon, *The History of the Decline and Fall of the Roman Empire*, vol. 1, ch. 19, 337.

11. Kuefler, *The Manly Eunuch*, 1–15.

spreads throughout the empire, penetrating Roman households. This orientalizing and racialized narrative about the deviant spread of eunuchs forms the basis of a fantasy of an inviolate, masculine, Western Greco-Roman past.[12] In a footnote, Gibbon asserts that while individual eunuchs may, on occasion, distinguish themselves, the rise of eunuchs inevitably spells doom for empires—specifically the Persian, Indian, and Chinese empires. In the process of characterizing the importance of eunuchs, therefore, Gibbon also describes them as monstrous.[13]

One could, of course, simply excuse Gibbon's theories as outdated and therefore irrelevant, despite the way the field continues to argue implicitly against this narrative of late antiquity. Rather than arguing against Gibbon, I want to entertain his thesis for the moment: if we assume that he is right, might we then imagine, alongside him, that eunuchs, in all their exoticized emasculation, have the power to spell doom for the collective imperial might of Rome, Persia, India, and China? If, as Gibbon claims, eunuchs are monstrous, then perhaps with that monstrousness comes great power.[14]

HOW (NOT) TO DO THE HISTORY OF CASTRATION: EUNUCHS IN THE SCHOLARLY LITERATURE[15]

Having explored some of the potential benefits of transing late antiquity, I will now discuss the impact of transphobia in general, and of eunuchphobia in particular, on the existing scholarship. Disgust, especially toward castration, has conditioned the interpretation of ancient and late antique sources. My goal in this section is not to call out the "failings" of any individual scholar; to identify scholarship from a hundred years ago that does not conform to contemporary queer and trans politics would not, after all, signify much. Rather, my intention is to describe a systemic problem that exceeds any one particular field.[16]

---

12. In this, Gibbon is reflecting the prejudices of Greco-Roman sources. See Tougher, "Eunuchs in the East, Men in the West?" 147–63. Horstmanshoff argues that the association between eunuchs and "oriental despots" dates back to Herodotus. See Horstmanshoff, "Who is the True Eunuch?" 101–18. Leah DeVun explores the ways hermaphrodites are similarly displaced onto foreign lands. She cites Pliny, who maps hermaphrodites onto Africa, but she follows this trend up to the medieval period. See DeVun, *The Shape of Sex*, 40–70.

13. Gibbon, *Decline and Fall*, vol. 1, chapter 19, 338n7 on Xenophon and Cyrus.

14. On monstrosity in trans studies, see the classic article by Susan Stryker, "My Words to Victor Frankenstein," 237–54.

15. The title of this section is a reference to the work of David Halperin: *How to Do the History of Homosexuality*.

16. I am not the first to call out an academic field for its limitations in addressing historical sex and gender variance. See, for example, McCaffrey, "Reconsidering Gender Ambiguity in Mesopotamia," 379–91; and Weismantel, "Towards a Transgender Archaeology," 319–35.

In his introduction to the volume *Eunuchs in Antiquity and Beyond*, Shaun Tougher optimistically states: "It can be reported that the growth of eunuch studies shows no sign of abating."[17] Currently, there is research that addresses eunuchs in early Christianity, the Hebrew Bible, Greek literature, medical literatures, Pagan rituals and religious traditions, and the broader ancient Near East. Scholars have emphasized the numerous material remains that challenge conventions on sex and gender. For example, there is much interest in the seated figure of Ur-Nanshe, whose gender presentation is ambiguous in the context of Mesopotamian cultures. There is also a significant body of literature on the Sumerian figure of the *gala* (Akkadian *kalû*), which has been variously interpreted as a eunuch, an impotent man, a homosexual, or a man wearing women's clothing.[18] Almost universally, this scholarship is either reacting to or built on a foundation of research that evinces clear disdain for eunuchs and androgynes.

And yet, scholarly disdain cannot entirely obscure the evidence that eunuchs and androgynes excited broad interest in the ancient world. Castration was widely practiced, for example. The Hebrew Bible refers to castration, but the practice certainly predates the Hebrew Bible. Some scholars argue that castration is already so widespread by the second millennium BCE that the ancient Near East becomes singularly associated with it.[19]

Still, the study of castration has been mired in controversy. Take, for example, the field of research on castration in Egypt, a field of research that has focused on both the historical phenomenon and the literary representations of it.[20] Since the evidence that attests to the presence of eunuchs in Egypt relies primarily on Greek and Latin historiography, modern historians struggle to ascertain the genuine scope of the historical phenomenon.[21] Given the polemical ways in which eunuchs are often invoked, the historiography cannot straightforwardly mobilize Greek

---

17. Tougher, ed., *Eunuchs in Antiquity and Beyond*, 1.

18. On Ur-Nanshe and the problems of interpretation, see McCaffrey, "Reconsidering Gender Ambiguity in Mesopotamia," 379–91. McCaffrey refers to these remains as "proto-trans." On the *gala*, see Gabbay, "The Akkadian Word for 'Third Gender,'" 49–56.

19. This idea is contested, but see N'Shea, "Royal Eunuchs and Elite Masculinity," 214–21. Cf. Peled, *Masculinities and Third Gender*. See also the evidence of Kassite-period Babylonian seals that attest to the presence of eunuchs as described in Yalçin, "Men, Women, Eunuchs," 121–50.

20. Many scholars address the famous scene in Egyptian mythology where Horus castrates Seth as punishment. See Te Velde, *Seth God of Confusion*, 53–59. We find this theme of castration as punishment as well in the New Kingdom story, "Tale of Two Brothers." For a discussion of the "Tale of Two Brothers" that links it to the Joseph narrative in the Hebrew Bible, see Kadish, "Eunuchs in Ancient Egypt," 55–62.

21. Matić, "Gender in Ancient Egypt," 174–83. Some Egyptologists have argued that castration in Egypt does not occur until the Persian period. See Assante, "Men Looking at Men," 42–83. Assante cites MAL A15. This is not the only instance of castration as punishment in the ancient Near East. See, for example, the prophecy of Isaiah in II Kings 20:18. Similarly, Herodotus describes the Persians as castrating prisoners in war. For more on this subject, see Vikman, "Ancient Origins," 21–31.

and Latin sources as history. But these prosaic challenges to assessing the historicity of sources cannot fully explain the scholarly aversion to discussing castration in the ancient Near East.[22]

Scholars of rabbinics have not avoided the topic of castration, but they have often treated it with disdain. For example, Julius Preuss's work on biblical and Talmudic medicine remains a classic resource for anyone working on the body and medicine in rabbinic literature. Preuss begins his section on castration: "The abnormalities of the genitalia enumerated here are individual cases of the commonly practiced abomination called *serus*, meaning castration."[23] While there is little pretense of neutrality, the use of the word *abomination* relies on the premise that both the reader and the texts themselves share the disdain for castration that Preuss evinces so unquestioningly. A type of historical connection, animated by disgust, links the scholar to his subject.

Traces of this apparent disgust can be found, albeit much more subtly, within the literature on castration in studies of the Hebrew Bible. The term "saris" appears forty-five times in the Masoretic text of the Hebrew Bible, but biblicists disagree on the question of how frequently the term refers to someone who has been castrated. Often, there are no contextual clues—take, for example, 1 Chronicles 28:1: "David assembled all the officers of Israel . . . with the *sarisim* and the warriors, all the men of substance to Jerusalem."[24] In this verse (and many others), the term "saris" is used without any explanation, and it is unclear from the context whether it refers to someone who has been castrated or not.[25]

---

22. On the case of Egypt, for a discussion of the way scholarship has avoided the self-castration theme of the "Tale of Two Brothers," see Dundes, "Projective Inversion in the Ancient Egyptian," 378–94.

23. Here I am using Rosner's translation of the German, although Preuss's German term "Verstümmelungen," which Rosner translates as "abnormalities" can also be rendered as the somewhat stronger "mutilations." See Preuss, *Biblical and Talmudic Medicine*, 222. The term "abomination" is not simply a citation of the biblical attitude toward castration. Leviticus 22:24 does not use the word *abomination*. This verse is interpreted as a blanket ban on castration only in the later literature; see b. Ḥagigah 14b. See also Josephus *Antiquities* 4.41 and his gloss on the Bible.

24. This is one of the verses that the Septuagint does not translate as "eunuch" per se but rather as δυνάστας. The Septuagint most often translates saris as εὐνοῦχος, less often as σπάδων (a term that literally means "tear out" but that refers to eunuchs). On the terminology, see Cornelius, "'Eunuchs?'" 321–33.

25. In order to determine the meaning, scholars turn to the Akkadian loan word from which the word *saris* derives, but there are numerous translations of the Akkadian as well. The most common of these is "(he) of the head." Given other Akkadian usages, J. D. Hawkins argues that this means "attendant," whether castrated or noncastrated. See Hawkins, "Eunuchs Among the Hittites," 217–33. Stephanie Dalley disagrees and thinks Mesopotamian two-sexed creation myths are the ground for the semantic shift to the meaning of "eunuch." See Dalley, "Evolution of Gender in Mesopotamian Mythology and Iconography," 117–22. Karlheinz Deller believes that the plural "two heads" in the Akkadian might be a euphemism for the testicles: see Deller, "The Assyrian Eunuchs and their Predecessors," 303–11. Janet Everhart argues that *ša rēši* is best understood as a nonprocreative male. See Everhart, "The Hidden Eunuchs of the Hebrew Bible, 71–77.

Several scholars have pointed out that there seems to be a contradiction in the status of the saris in the biblical text. On the one hand, there are verses that refer to the saris as a high official, such as 1 Chronicles quoted above, which lists the saris among "all the men of substance." On the other hand, there are also verses that seem to disparage the saris. Some scholars have argued, therefore, that any reference to a saris with a high social status could not possibly refer to a castrated man but should instead be translated as "attendant."[26] There is an underlying assumption that anyone who has been castrated must have a low social status in biblical cultures. At the heart of this philological debate over translation is eunuchphobia in the scholarship.

At times, this eunuchphobia becomes explicit, as when scholars refuse to justify their translation choices, instead assuming that the saris must mean attendant as the default. Hayim Tadmor has repeatedly critiqued the tendency of the Akkadian dictionaries to translate the term as eunuch only in cases where it would be impossible to translate it otherwise. As Tadmor puts it:

> I should venture to suggest that the rather emotional scholarly reaction of claiming that *šūt rēši* is never a eunuch, should be viewed as ensuing from a *Weltanschaung* that wished to see Assyria as the prototype of the Indo-European military society which never accepted castration and even emphatically rejected it, as Romans did.[27]

Tadmor here suggestively calls out a fantasy of a racialized Indo-European lineage that traces a masculine genealogy through an imagined Assyrian rejection of castration. At the same time, Assyrian masculinity is analogized to Rome's imperial masculine culture. The effect of this hypermasculine, racialized translation practice is to literally write eunuchs out of the historical record.

A second type of scholarship does not evince the same overt aversion to castration, but instead situates eunuchs solely as literary tropes, or metaphors.[28] In his otherwise excellent book *Roman Homosexuality*, for example, Craig Williams writes: "Castration is an extreme instance of a conceptual all-or-nothing tendency that pervades Roman texts: softening a male constitutes a direct infringement on his masculine identity."[29] In this passage, Williams uses castration to advance his

---

26. T. M. Lemos, who believes that the Akkadian term always referred to a eunuch, pushes back against the idea that eunuchs were only abject. Lemos argues that both statuses existed simultaneously: the eunuch was both degraded and, at the same time, was also able to hold positions of authority in the ancient Near East. See Lemos, "'Like the Eunuch Who Does Not Beget,'" 47–67.

27. Hayim Tadmor, "The Role of the Chief Eunuch," 604.

28. There is also a tendency in contemporary scholarship to use intersex and transgender bodies as a conceptual backdrop to sexual orientation. This has been roundly critiqued in transgender studies. See Prosser, *Second Skins*, 135–70; and Nameste, *Invisible Lives*, 9–23; *and* Stryker, "(De)Subjugated Knowledges," 1–17.

29. Craig Williams, *Roman Homosexuality*, 129. Williams's treatment of the eunuch must be understood within the context of his distinction between gender deviance, on the one hand, and sexual object choice, on the other. The reference to softening masculinity is to the Roman use of the word *mollitia* ("softness"), a quality said to characterize both women and effeminate men.

larger argument—that Roman sexual cosmology stigmatized specific sex acts rather than the gender of those performing them.

I want to linger for a moment over his wording. Although in this context Williams is pointing out the *Roman* tendency to think of castration as extreme, his own use of the term "extreme" as a label for castration has a profound rhetorical effect.[30] By framing castration as a "conceptual tendency," Williams's reading implicitly invokes a ghostly castration that haunts Roman literary masculinity.[31] Like Roman masculinity, castration lacks subtlety, is an all-or-nothing proposition, and literalizes the fear of effeminacy. In that sense, castration functions as a fundamentalist reading strategy—a too-literal reading of sex and gender.

As I have argued in the introduction, transing means attending to what happens when we center categories of sex and gender variance rather than treating them as a subset of the scholarly interest in sexuality. Scholarship has had a tendency to either actively ignore eunuchs or to treat them as the conceptual backdrop for same-sex sexuality. In that sense, marking eunuchs as beyond the pale facilitated the project of bringing sexuality into the bounds of accepted scholarly discourse. In order to cement that focus on sexuality, scholars have, at times, insisted on castration as a metaphor, or, at most, a literalization of masculine fears. Yet there is evidence that castration happened. If transing the sources means that we embrace bad and literal readings of sex, what other possibilities may emerge if we interpret the literal embodied nature of castration? Fear and violence certainly characterize many of the sources, and castration sometimes served as a punishment, or otherwise occurred nonconsensually, throughout these periods. But if we did not weight these traditions down with quite so much disgust, might we also occasionally find space in them for longing or even suppressed desire? If we suspend, at least temporarily, the idea that castration must be understood within the context of fear and disgust, we open up the possibility of exploring the multiple meanings of eunuchs more fully.

EUNUCHS IN BIBLICAL, SECOND TEMPLE, AND GRECO-ROMAN SOURCES

Given the widespread problems with the way eunuchs have been interpreted, what have scholars determined about eunuchs in antiquity? We know, for example, that there are certain terms that are unambiguous, which are impossible to interpret as

---

30. On the category of the *kinaidos/cinaedus* and the argument about whether this is equivalent to queerness in antiquity, see Richlin, "Not before Homosexuality," 523–73. On the question of the queerness of slaves, eunuchs, barbarians, and androgynes in early Christianity, see Marchal, *Appalling Bodies*.

31. For a classic discussion of Roman invective and eunuchs, see Richlin, *The Garden of Priapus*, 105–63.

meaning anything other than a person whose genitalia have changed. While scholars debate whether the saris in the Hebrew Bible refers to someone who has been castrated, other categories in the Hebrew Bible are unambiguously defined by a change to the genitalia. There are three categories of genital "damage" found in the Hebrew Bible. Leviticus contains a discussion of genital damage among priests. After a priest's genitals become damaged, his priestly activities are restricted. The second discussion of genital damage is found in Deuteronomy, where men with genital damage are prohibited from "being admitted into the congregation of the LORD." While the Hebrew Bible itself sometimes discusses the saris in more positive terms, these "damaged" men are the subject of legal restrictions (a topic I shall discuss at length in chapter 4.)

Each set of verses uses distinct terms; the words for "genital damage" in Leviticus are different from the terms used in Deuteronomy, and neither set of verses use the word *saris*. We might, therefore, reasonably conclude that categories of genital damage (in Leviticus and Deuteronomy) have nothing to do with the saris/eunuch. And yet, if we examine some strains of the interpretation of the Hebrew Bible in the Second Temple period, we find traditions that connect eunuchs with the genitally damaged men of the Hebrew Bible. At least some Jewish sources from the Second Temple and Rabbinic periods, then, suggest that castration should be understood as a type of genital damage, and therefore, perhaps, as linked to restrictions.[32]

The first-century Hellenistic Jewish author, Philo, glosses the presence of the saris in Genesis 40:7. This chapter of Genesis describes a scene in which the eunuch courtiers of Pharoah are distraught over their bad dreams. They express their upset to Joseph, whom they ask to interpret their dreams. Philo extends this brief scene from the Bible and writes in the voice of the eunuch:

---

32. While the sources from Qumran do not equate the saris with genitally damaged men, it is worth noting that the scrolls are, in general, invested in extending the restrictions on people with bodily "blemishes" and therefore have some bearing on the discussion. In Qumran sources, the scope of both the bodies listed as "blemished" and the restriction is expanded to encompass not just priests but all "blemished" Israelites. See Shemesh, "'The Holy Angels are in their Council,'" 179–206. The scroll omits people with genital damage from the list. Some scholars suggest that terms like "blindness" functioned as an umbrella term meant to stand in for an expanded list.

Scholars also debate whether the text understands the whole of Jerusalem as a holy community where God dwells. This draws on stringent interpretations of the verses in Prophets (Isaiah 52:1; 2 Samuel 5:8) that seem to imply exclusion from the city. Saul Olyan believes that spatial restrictions refer to the entire city. See Olyan, *Disability in the Hebrew Bible*, 101–18. Lawrence Schiffman, on the other hand, thinks that "holy city" must refer more narrowly to the Temple. See Schiffman, "Exclusion from the Sanctuary and the City of the Sanctuary," 301–20. See also Schiffman, "The Eschatological Community of the *Serekh Ha-'Edah*," 105–29.

Thus I, the servant of that Pharoah . . . am a eunuch (Gen. 40:7), gelded of the soul's generating organs, a vagrant from the men's quarters, an exile from the women's, a thing neither male nor female, unable to either shed or receive seed, twofold yet neuter, base counterfeit of the human coin, cut off from the immortality which, through the succession of children and children's children, is kept alight forever, roped off from the holy assembly and congregation: "For he that hath lost the organs of generation is absolutely forbidden to enter therein."[33]

In this passage, Philo imagines the eunuch excoriating themself and lamenting the way that they do not belong in either men's or women's spaces. The image of the counterfeit eunuch is an image of deceit.[34] Elsewhere Philo explains that the eunuch appears to be a man, but in fact they do not function as one. Thus, at least some of the transgressive nature of the eunuch derives from their appearance of masculinity, which "conceals" their reproductive disability. At the same time, Philo's eunuch describes themself as cut off from the holy community; this is a clear reference to Deuteronomy, which prohibits genitally damaged men from entering into the community. For Philo then, the saris/eunuch from Genesis is connected to the genitally damaged man of Deuteronomy.[35]

33. Philo, *On Dreams* 27.184. This is not Philo's only citation of the verses in Deuteronomy. See also *The Unchangeableness of God* 24; *The Migration of Abraham* 12; and *On Drunkenness* 51. Philo clearly understands the saris here to refer to a literal eunuch. For a discussion of Philo's interpretation of the Joseph story, see Ra'anan Abusch, "Eunuchs and Gender Transformation," 103–22. Abusch argues that Philo's interpretation of eunuchs should be understood within the context of cultural tension over circumcision and Philo's desire to make a strong distinction between castration and circumcision. Philo is not alone in his characterization of the practice of castration. See, for example, the fourth-century author Claudius Mammertinus: "Eunuchs, who are, so to speak, exiles from the society of the human race, belonging neither to one sex nor the other as the result of some congenital abnormality or physical injury" (*The Emperor Julian*, 19.4). Both Philo and Mammertinus employ a rhetoric of eunuchs as nonhuman. This translation of Mammertinus is from Samuel N. C. Lieu, ed., *The Emperor Julian*, 26.

34. In *On Joseph* Philo describes the eunuch: "A eunuch, possessing to all appearances the organs of generation but deprived of the power of using them, just as those who suffer from cataract have eyes but lack the active use of them and cannot see." See Philo, *On Joseph* 12.58. While this passage may simply be addressing reproduction and not sex more generally, in the phrase "lack the active use of them," it seems possible that Philo understands the eunuch as asexual. See, for example, the passage where he describes castration as a possible cure for sexual temptation: Philo, *Allegorical Interpretation* 3.84. For an earlier (but similar) sentiment of the eunuch's asexuality, see *Sirach* 30:20, which seems to assume a frustrated desire in the eunuch. For a discussion of Ben Sira, see Bolle and Llewelyn, "Intersectionality, Gender Liminality," 546–69.

35. In Deuteronomy, it is not entirely clear what the verse means when it says that genitally damaged men "shall not enter into the congregation of the LORD." For the rabbis, being "admitted into the congregation" is interpreted as marriage to an Israelite woman. For the community at Qumran, this verse seems to have been interpreted as a spatial ban. Aharon Shemesh argues that, in fact, both the rabbis and the community at Qumran understand the prohibition in Deuteronomy to refer to both marriage and space. The difference in opinion between the rabbis and the Qumran sect comes from their different understanding of what area of space was considered "sacred." The rabbis interpret the

Josephus, the first century Roman Jewish author and historian, similarly describes eunuchs in subhuman terms:

> Shun eunuchs [γάλλους] and flee all dealings with those who have deprived themselves of their virility and of those fruits of generation, which God has given to men for the increase of our race; expel them even as infanticides who withal have destroyed the means of procreation. For plainly it is by reason of the effeminacy of their soul that they have changed the sex of their body also. And so with all that would be deemed a monstrosity by the beholders: Ye shall castrate neither man nor beast.[36]

Here Josephus interprets Leviticus 22:24 ("You shall not offer to the LORD anything with its testes bruised or crushed . . .") as a blanket prohibition on castration, including the castration of humans. In an oblique reference to Genesis and the command to "be fruitful and multiply," Josephus's equation of castration with infanticide blames eunuchs in advance for the loss of their potential to procreate. Josephus refers to an "effeminacy of soul" that causes a change in bodily sex; interestingly, the effeminacy in the soul seems to predate the castration rather than be caused by castration. In both authors, the lack of reproduction has gendered implications.

The tone of this passage is uniformly negative, as the association of eunuchs with monstrousness makes clear. Josephus's negative view of castration suggests that his use of a word for eunuch that alludes to the castrated priests of Cybele is no accident; in choosing that word, he links eunuchs to pagan worship and foreign cults. Josephus thus suggests that eunuchs are incompatible with the biblical tradition; the ubiquitous presence of eunuchs in the Hebrew Bible seems to make his fervor only more intense.

This type of rhetoric is not uncommon in Greco-Roman literature more broadly; by far the most dominant treatment of the eunuch is one involving invective. Greek and Roman authors characterize eunuchs as sexually voracious, as lacking in self-control (considered an important aspect of male virtue), as effeminate, and as deceitful. Maud Gleason's monograph *Making Men* follows Favorinus, a rhetorician and born eunuch in the Second Sophistic movement. His frequent rhetorical opponent, Polemo, makes statements of this sort: "Hence no one is

---

space as narrower (between the sanctuary and the altar), so that in rabbinic law, the ban has no relevance outside of pilgrimage times. See Shemesh, "The Holy Angels are in their Council," 179–206. If Shemesh is right, the legislation may differ but the underlying conceptualization is shared. Still, in Mishnah Yevamot 8, the rabbis rather explicitly interpret this phrase as a marriage prohibition in relation to genital damage. There is a fragment in the Dead Sea Scrolls (fragment 8 of 4QMMT) that seems to refer to marriage as well.

36. Josephus, *Jewish Antiquities* 4.40. Ironically, Josephus is held up as evidence for the ubiquity of eunuchs: see, for example, Guyot, *Eunuchen als Sklaven und Freigelassene*.

more perfectly evil than he who is born without testicles."[37] While Polemo's statement must be understood within the context of a war of words with Favorinus, such extreme rhetoric is neither uncommon nor limited to rhetoricians in the Second Sophistic movement. Authors from Juvenal to Claudian famously characterize eunuchs in extremely negative terms.[38]

Another widely dispersed and polemical characterization is of the eunuch as foreigner, or as a figure used to sketch the boundaries of ethnic identity. The passage from Josephus above may allude to this trope of the foreign eunuch in his reference to Cybelianism, but other sources characterize eunuchs as foreign much more explicitly.[39] Lloyd Llewellyn-Jones, for example, discusses the problems of studying Persian eunuchs when most of the sources are Greek. Greek sources employ the eunuch as a symbol of the effeminate Persian court, and thus they may be of limited historical value.[40] As Llewelyn-Jones complains, the well-known rhetorical use of the eunuch as "foreign" has colored even scholarship on the topic. Ruth Bardel analyzes classical Greek literary sources that represent castration as the subversion of Hellenic values. In her analysis of Sophocles's play *Troilus*, Bardel notes that Hecabe (the queen) herself castrates an enslaved eunuch. This action associates her barbarian royal body with the feminine and effeminizing.[41] J. L. Lightfoot examines the *galli*, eunuch priests who were associated with Magna Mater, the mother goddess (to whom Josephus alludes). Lightfoot discusses the

---

37. Gleason, *Making Men*, 47.

38. I am summarizing and generalizing a vast body of literature ("Greco-Roman") and vast bodies of scholarship. For famous examples of eunuchs and invective, see Juvenal's sixth satire; and Claudian, *In Eutropoium* 1.277–81. For a more complete survey of the literature, see Asikainen, "'Eunuchs for the Kingdom of Heaven,'" 156–88. There is a whole subfield of scholarship on Roman masculinity, some of which directly (or indirectly) addresses eunuchs and androgynes. See, for example, Foxhall and Salmon, eds., *When Men were Men*. There is also literature on the construction of Roman women that relates to the rhetoric of "softened" men. See Richlin, ed., *Arguments with Silence*; and Kraemer, *Unreliable Witnesses*. On sexuality specifically, see Hallett and Skinner, eds., *Roman Sexualities*. Keith Hopkins's work on the eunuch in antiquity is considered a classic in the field. Hopkins examines structural reasons for the importance of eunuchs in court and political settings. He has written several pieces on the topic, including "Eunuchs in Politics in the Later Roman Empire," 62–80.

39. Biblical literature may also suggest a connection between castration and "foreignness." In Deuteronomy 23, the verses that address men with damaged genitalia are grouped with a parallel interdiction against others, such as the Ammonites and Moabites. The rabbinic interpretation of the verse understands it to refer to a ban on marriage with an Israelite woman. This reinforces the connection between the boundaries of the community and eunuchs, as I shall explore in chapter 4. Isaiah 56 also creates a proximal link between foreigners and eunuchs.

40. Llewelyn-Jones, "Eunuchs and the Royal Harem in Achaemenid Persia," 19–51. Most of the sources that Llewelyn-Jones cites would be earlier than our period, but he includes some later Hellenistic and Roman authors. David Hester discusses the ways in which the eunuch is used to feminize the "other" in Greco-Roman discourse. See Hester, "Queers on Account of the Kingdom of Heaven," 809–23.

41. Bardel, "Eunuchizing Agamemnon," 51–71.

methodological difficulties of reconstructing the practices of the cult when all the Greco-Roman literary sources portray the galli as "the exotics *par excellence* in an exotic cult."[42] Similarly, Shelley Hales treats the galli as a case study in the processes by which Rome absorbs "foreign" bodies.[43] In contrast to previous scholarship, Hales argues that the surviving images of the priests reject the standard visual markers of Roman acculturation, and this absence is a deliberate choice by the artists to negotiate the "foreignness" of the galli.[44]

In addition to literary and material representations of the eunuch, legal discourse similarly depicts eunuchs as a foreign phenomenon. Roman legal sources explicitly ban the castration of slaves. The emperor Nerva (96–98 CE) broadens the ban to include castration of any kind. Justinian's *Digest* records a rescript on this subject clarifying that the ban on castration pertained to both voluntary and involuntary castration, as did the penalties prescribed for a violation of the ban.[45] The *Digest*, however, preserves what was essentially a legal loophole: castration was outlawed within the boundaries of the Roman Empire, but trade in "barbarian" eunuchs was allowed.[46] Given the ubiquity of eunuchs in private upper-class households in some periods, historians generally surmise that there was a thriving trade in eunuchs.[47] The frequent reiteration and updating of the laws banning castration, however, has led some scholars to posit that not all eunuchs were imported, and that the laws may have been flouted frequently.[48] Whether eunuchs were actually castrated domestically or brought into the empire already castrated,

---

42. Lightfoot, "Sacred Eunuchism in the Cult of the Syrian Goddess," 74. See, however, Jacob Latham's excellent survey, which argues that perceptions of the *galli* change through time. Latham contends that the image of the *galli* as foreign is much more characteristic of the late Republic period than late antiquity. See Latham, "'Fabulous Clap-Trap,'" 84–122.

43. Hales, "Looking for Eunuchs," 87–103.

44. For an alternative reading of depictions of Attis and the "foreign" nature of the cult of Cybele, see Butler, "Notes on a Membrum Disiectum," 236–55.

45. Ra'anan Boustan argues that the limits on castration need to be understood in the context of larger legal changes addressing the status of slaves. His general argument is that Hadrian's prohibition treated castration, not circumcision. See Boustan, "Negotiating Difference," 71–92. For a classic article on the question of the sources for Hadrian's ban on circumcision, see Geiger, "Hag'zeirah al hamilah u'mered Bar Kochba," 139–47. In some cases, the punishment for those caught practicing castration was that they would be castrated themselves. Horstmanshoff argues that, given the rates of survival for castration, the practice itself may have amounted to a death sentence in some cases. He also cites Pliny, who says that eunuch slaves were three times as expensive, creating economic incentives for castration. See Horstmanshoff, "Who is the True Eunuch?" 101–18.

46. Piotr O. Scholz, *Eunuchs and Castrati*, 112. There is some evidence for the importation of eunuchs into the Roman Empire. See the discussion of the inscription of Euphrates the Eunuch in Horstmanshoff, "Who is the True Eunuch?" 101–18.

47. Hopkins, "The Political Power of Eunuchs," 172–97. Cf. Tougher, *The Roman Castrati*.

48. Hopkins, "The Political Power of Eunuchs," 172–97. See Shaun Tougher's response: "In or Out?" 143–61.

significant cultural energy was expended in literature, visual arts, and legal discourse to highlight their foreignness. Eunuchs may have frequently functioned as a metaphor in these depictions, but castration was not only a literary trope.

While Greco-Roman sources displace eunuchs to Persia as a mechanism to situate eunuchs as a foreign phenomenon, independent sources seem to confirm the presence of eunuchs within the Persian Empire from the Achaemenid to the Sasanian period. For example, some evidence suggests that castration was practiced along the borders of the Roman Empire in order to supply the Roman demand for eunuchs.[49] There are also accounts of eunuchs in the Achaemenid court.[50] In later sources, the Sasanian king, Yazdegerd II, is described as castrating eight thousand subjects to act as servants. Although these narratives may be exaggerated, they nonetheless testify to the fact that both Persians and Romans considered eunuchs to be particularly loyal servants.[51] We have evidence of a "chief of the royal eunuchs"[52] and of a seal that scholars believe belonged to a eunuch who served in the Sasanian Court. These pieces of evidence, along with other indications, show that eunuchs held prominent offices and functioned as priests, administrators, and military officers.[53]

If numerous sources attest to the presence of eunuchs in the Persian court, it is not clear how the eunuchs came to be there. While eunuchs generally have Persian names in the sources, it is possible that eunuchs originally came to the court as tributes or through the slave trade and that their enslavers gave them new names. Given some Zoroastrian attitudes about the value of bodily integrity and procreation, some scholars have suggested that eunuchs were primarily imported.[54] If this

---

49. Thomas Sizgorich examines the narratives about Abasgian castration. See Sizgorich, "Reasoned Violence and Shifty Frontiers," 167–79.

50. The Old Persian term for eunuchs does not survive. In the Sasanian period there are citations of the Middle Persian *shābestān*, which Omar Coloru believes indicates the title of the eunuch as a master of the "women's sleeping quarter." Coloru notes that the Shapur I inscription translates shābestān into Greek as *eunuchos*. See Coloru, "Ancient Persia and Silent Disability," 61–74.

51. See McDonough, "A Question of Faith?" 69–85. On Antiochus, the eunuch in the Persian court, see Greatrex and Bardill, "Antiochus the 'Praepositus,'" 171–97. From the same time period, see also the figure of Chrysaphius: Chew, "Virgins and Eunuchs" 207–27. See also the figure of Mār Abā, who served as chief eunuch, as described in Macuch, "The Case Against Mār Abā," 47–58. Finally, for changes in the position of eunuchs in the court over the Sasanian period, see Kolesnikov, "Eunuchs," 64–69.

52. Tafazzoli, "An Unrecognized Sasanian Title," 301–5.

53. Lerner and Skjaervø, "A Seal of a Eunuch in the Sasanian Court," 113–19. Lerner dates the seal to the third century. See also Skjaervø, "A Postscript on the Seal of a Eunuch in the Sasanian Court," 39. Analyzing a passage from the *Dēnkard*, Skjaervø argues that the term "shābestān" definitely refers to a castrated eunuch and is not just a job title.

54. Except Mithridates, who is attested to by Diodorus of Sicily. See Coloru, "Ancient Persia," 69–70.

is so, it would be particularly ironic in view of the ways Greco-Roman literature works so hard to portray the eunuch as a racialized symbol of Persian decadence.

. . .

Writers like Josephus and Philo are working specifically with biblical texts and it is noteworthy that they link the biblical categories of "genital damage" to the saris/eunuch. They are not alone in their expansive understanding of what kinds of bodies the general category of "eunuch" might include. Second Temple authors who understand a variety of different bodies as "eunuchs" are tapping into the flexibility of the Greek term itself.[55] Nowhere is the semantic range of the Greek word *eunuch* clearer than in Matthew 19:12, which lays out three kinds of eunuchs:

> For there are eunuchs who have been so from birth, and there are eunuchs who have been made eunuchs by others, and there are eunuchs who have made themselves eunuchs for the sake of the kingdom of heaven.[56]

Matthew sketches out three separate categories: the born eunuch, the eunuch who is created by others, and eunuchs for the sake of the kingdom of heaven. This division of eunuchs mirrors that in other Greco-Roman texts—for example, the Roman jurist Ulpian distinguishes between "eunuchs by nature" and "those who are made eunuchs."[57] Although the specific framing of these different kinds of eunuchs may be significant ("by nature" or "from birth"), still, a basic understanding that both bodies that are born as eunuchs and bodies that become eunuchs fall under the same umbrella category is well established.

The precise meaning of this verse in Matthew has been hotly debated by both early Christians and contemporary biblical scholars. Historically, scholars and

---

55. The Greek word for eunuch is εὐνοῦχος. Most scholars believe the term derives from the amalgam of the Greek terms for "bed" and "to keep." In other words, eunuchs were the "keepers of the bed" in courts; they became associated with castration. In the Augustan period, the practice of employing eunuchs in the Roman household spread. See Walter Stevenson: "To complicate the issue further, there clearly are a variety of 'eunuchs' living at the time of our early Christian authors. I would break these down into those who are born in a variety of conditions without strong masculine characteristics, those who had 'moderate' destruction of the gonads (θλαδίας, and θλιβίας) and those who had radical surgery (ἀποκεκομμένος and *castratus*)" (Stevens, "Eunuchs and early Christianity," 124). Paulus Aeginata discusses the extant techniques for castration. See Horstmanshoff, "Who is the True Eunuch?" 101–18.

56. The English translation of the verse is from Michael Coogan, ed., *The New Oxford Annotated Bible*. In the Greek, the same word εὐνοῦχος is used to describe all three types of eunuchs.

57. Matthew Kuefler cites Ulpian's statement: "'The name of eunuch is a general one,' he wrote; 'under it come those who are eunuchs by nature, those who are made eunuchs [*thlibiae thlaisae*], and any other kind of eunuchs [*aliud genus spadonum*].'" See Kuefler, *The Manly Eunuch*, 33. See also Candida Moss's commentary: "Mark and Matthew," 275–301. This category of "those that are made eunuchs" probably comes closest to a translation of *s'ris adam*, the term I am translating as "acquired saris," which could be more literally rendered as "human-made" eunuch.

theologians have mostly understood the invocation of the eunuch in Matthew as allegorical, and they have variously interpreted the verse as addressing sexual temptation, celibacy, or second marriages.[58] A minority of commentators and scholars believe that the verse addresses eunuchs per se.[59] We know from the surrounding pagan religious movements (e.g., Cybelianism) that the idea of religious castration was in circulation, so there is certainly a counterpart for the concept of "eunuchs for the sake of the kingdom of heaven."

Regardless of how scholars interpret this verse, Matthew 19:12 demonstrates the way that the Greek term "eunuch" could refer to different kinds of bodies. Castration is only one way to become a eunuch; some eunuchs are born without the ability to procreate. Some people, whom we would probably label as intersex in contemporary times, would have been understood as having a congenitally infertile body in antiquity and would have been labeled a eunuch. As we will see, the rabbis also understand the word *saris* to refer to both those people who were born as eunuchs and those people who become eunuchs. While the term "eunuch" in antiquity could reference a wide range of bodies, scholarship does not always highlight that range successfully; it sometimes relies implicitly on our contemporary understanding of the term "eunuch" as denoting a castrated man. In doing so, scholars tend to sideline the category of the born eunuch in particular.[60]

---

58. See, for example, these four different allegorical readings: R. Jarrett Van Tine interprets the verse as addressing the dangers of adultery. See Van Tine, "Castration for the Kingdom," 399–418. Carmen Bernabé argues that these verses are a commentary on forms of marriage: see Bernabé, "Of Eunuchs and Predators," 128–34. Retief, Cilliers, and Riekert argue that Matthew is addressing the practice of celibacy: see "Eunuchs in the Bible," 247–58. Rick Talbott claims that this verse speaks to the status of women: see Talbott, "Imagining the Matthean Eunuch Community," 21–43. J. David Hester, on the other hand, argues that allegorical readings of the verse were attempts to sanitize a tradition about eunuchs: see Hester, "Eunuchs and the Postgender Jesus," 13–40.

59. At least some early Christians probably understood this verse literally. See Caner, "The Practice and Prohibition of Self-Castration," 396–415. See also Brower, "Ambivalent Bodies." The question of castration in early Christianity often emerges in the debate over whether Origen castrated himself. See Hanson, "A Note on Origen's Self-Mutilation," 81–82. For a theoretically sophisticated take on the question of identifying these eunuchs as intersex or trans, see Marchal, "Who Are You Calling a Eunuch?!," 29–54.

60. One illustrative example of the tendency to sideline the born eunuch can be found in the essay by Vern Bullough, "Eunuchs in History and Society," 1–17. Bullough connects the study of historical eunuchs to the modern category of intersex through his opposition to unnecessary genital corrective surgery on intersexed infants. His argument that surgery on intersex infants creates a type of eunuch links these contemporary "eunuchs" to the eunuchs of antiquity. While I admire Bullough's foregrounding of political issues that urgently require our attention, this argument also highlights his failure to recognize that some births that we now term "intersex" would *already* have fallen under the category of "eunuch" in antiquity by virtue of their sexed ambiguity, even without "corrective" surgery.

The verse in Matthew is only one example of a rich tradition of discussing eunuchs in early Christianity. Scholars have written about eunuchs and androgynes in the Christian Bible,[61] as well as in early Christian literature.[62] Regardless of whether Matthew (or any other early Christian source) addresses the question of castration figuratively, early Christian literature betrays a fascination with the figure of the eunuch.[63]

It is within this rich and varied discussion of the different kinds of eunuchs that we must contextualize the extensive rabbinic interest in the saris. We will see the rabbis conceptualize the distinction between different kinds of eunuchs very similarly to some of these late antique sources. When they discuss eunuchs, the rabbis are participating in a much broader contemporaneous conversation.

ANDROGYNES AND EUNUCHS IN ROMAN LEGAL DISCOURSE

Just as there is a broad fascination with the figure of the eunuch, androgynes of various types are widely discussed throughout the ancient Near East. Androgynes, while absent from the Hebrew Bible, are found with regularity in both ancient and late antique sources. I discuss the popularity of the Hermaphroditus narrative in the next chapter.[64] Given the association of Hermaphroditus with protection, we might assume that people born with sexed variation would have been held in societal esteem. Instead, in Rome, there is a long history of various types of violence (both rhetorical and material) against nonbinary sex. In this section I will survey

---

61. On the figure of the Ethiopian eunuch in Acts 8:26–40, see Burke, "Queering Early Christian Discourse," 175–91; Villalobos, "Bodies Del Otro Lado," 191–223; and Brittany Wilson, "'Neither Male nor Female,'" 403–22. For a fuller discussion of the implications of the discussion in Galatians, see Marchal, "Bodies Bound for Circumcision and Baptism," 163–82. On Corinthians, see Marchal, "The Corinthian Women Prophets and Trans Activism," 223–47. For a general reading of the biblical sources as they relate to intersex categories, see DeFranza, *Sex Difference in Christian Theology*.

62. See the discussion of Clement of Alexandria in Horstmanshoff, "Who is the True Eunuch" 101–18. For a survey of early Christian sources, see Davis, "Crossed Texts, Crossed Sex," 1–36. Patricia Cox Miller reads the cross-dressing of Pelagia, an important saint in the Syriac tradition, as an intensification of her masculinity. See Cox-Miller, "Is There a Harlot in This Text?" 419–35.

63. Other early Christian texts certainly deploy eunuchs rhetorically and critically. See, for example, Chrysostom's association of Jewishness and effeminacy. Joshua Levinson discusses these sources in his article "Cultural Androgyny in Rabbinic Literature," 119–40.

64. The degree to which the figure of Hermaphroditus and the androgyne are coextensive is debatable. There are scholars who try and make a clear distinction between the two. See DeVun, *The Shape of Sex*, 16–40. Other scholars note the ways in which late antique sources are fuzzy about the differences between the two. See Marchal, *Appalling Bodies*, 30–68.

some of the more troubling history of eunuchs and androgynes in the Roman Empire, as best as we can reconstruct it.

In Rome, before the time of the empire, the birth of an androgyne would have been considered a "monstrous birth."[65] While the full text of the Twelve Tables is no longer extant, a citation from Cicero on the topic of the fate of all "monstrous births" has been preserved: "Quickly killed, as the *Twelve Tables* ordain that a dreadfully deformed child shall be killed."[66] This quotation from Cicero comes from the section that enumerates the rights of a father, rights that granted him the ability to expose his child.

The custom of exposing a child or leaving them to die was practiced for a variety of social reasons. Exposure by the state, on the other hand, was "ordained" (in the words of Cicero) in order to dispel the ill omen of a monstrous birth.[67] Exposure resulted in the deaths of those infants that had birth "defects" that were considered monstrous, including those infants born with mixed sex signs.[68] The practice of exposure is predicated on the idea that the monstrous birth itself is unnatural; the state resets the natural order by ordaining the infant's death. Scholars have argued that exposure was not actively practiced in great numbers. Regardless, the formulation of mixed sex signs as a monstrous birth demonstrates a particular construction of sexed variation as counter to the natural order.[69]

---

65. For an etiology of the androgyne's birth, see, for example, Hippocrates: "But if the male be secreted from the woman but female from the man, and the male get the mastery, it grows just as in the former case, while the female diminishes. These turn out hermaphrodites [in the Greek "androgyne"] ("men-women") and are correctly so called." See Hippocrates, *Regimen* I, 38.30.

66. E. H. Warmington, trans., *Remains of Old Latin: The Twelve Tables* 4.1. This is from Table 4, where the *paterfamilias* is granted the rights of life and death. The treatment of "monstrous births" in Greece is less clear; Diodorus Siculus seems to refer to a woman in the first century BCE being burned alive for having mixed sex characteristics. There are earlier references to mixed sex infants in the Mesopotamian omen series that prognosticated based on the type of "birth defect." See Scurlock and Anderson, *Diagnoses in Assyrian and Babylonian Medicine,*" 391.

67. Leaving the infant exposed to the elements would result in its death but allow the father to avoid actively killing the child (which might potentially create angry spirits). For an overview of the practice, see Dasen, "Multiple Births in Graeco-Roman Antiquity," 49–63. On the question of hermaphrodites specifically, see Graumann, "Monstrous Births and Retrospective Diagnosis," 181–211. On the connection between monstrous races (as popularized by Pliny the Elder), the discussion of the way that the androgyne straddles the ontological border between human and nonhuman, see DeVun, *The Shape of Sex*, 40–70.

68. For an overview of lists of "prodigies" (records from the Republican period that list abnormal births in humans and animals), see Luc Brisson, *Sexual Ambivalence*, 8–30.

69. Martha Rose has argued that exposure happened much less frequently than is often supposed. See Rose, *The Staff of Oedipus*, 29–49. Nicole Kelley discusses Soranus, Cicero, and other sources that attest to the practice of exposure in "Deformity and Disability in Greece and Rome," 31–47. On the concept of monstrousness as related to intersex historical projects, see Malatino, *Queer Embodiment*, 39–66.

By late antiquity, a major shift had taken place. Instead of the framework of monstrous births, Roman legal sources now tended to advocate assigning the androgyne a stable sex/gender category. Pliny the Elder comments on the concomitant shift in social attitude to the hermaphrodite: "Persons are also born of both sexes combined—what we call 'Hermaphrodites,' formerly called '*androgyni*' and considered as portents, but now as entertainments."[70] This shift from portent to a figure of entertainment traces a transformation in disposition toward the androgyne, whom Roman society no longer perceives as a threat to the natural order. By default, then, this suggests a recognition that the body of the androgyne is a natural variation, if perhaps still "freakish" enough to provide entertainment. While some scholars argue that the birth of an androgyne was still associated with monstrousness even into late antiquity, the accompanying practice of exposing androgynes seems to have ended, at least for the most part.[71]

Jane Gardner, a historian of Roman legal systems, argues that the primary method for determining sex was visual and the criterion was morphological (genital).[72] If, as Gardner argues, sexed status is based on genitalia, then dual genitalia pose a unique problem. The solution comes from Ulpian, who states that hermaphrodites were to be treated in accordance with whatever sex "prevailed" (*Digest* 1.5.10). Gardner interprets this to mean that jurists could determine individually which sex prevailed in the androgyne and assign them a legal gender.

Matthew Kuefler, on the other hand, critiques Gardener's translation of Ulpian. Instead, Kuefler understands the phrase "the sex that prevails" to refer to masculinity as the sex that would always dominate.[73] In support of his contention, Kuefler cites Augustine, who writes in the *City of God* (16.8.8):

> As for *Androgynes*, also called Hermaphrodites ... the prevalent usage has called them masculine, assigning them to the superior sex; for no one has ever used the feminine names *androgynaecae* or *hermaphroditae*.[74]

70. Pliny the Elder, *Natural History*, 3.3. This passage is also cited by Luc Brisson, among others. See *Sexual Ambivalence*, 38.

71. Diana Swancutt argues that Pliny protests too much, and that there are still some extant strands of Roman thought (she cites Livy, among others) that situate the androgyne as foreign, and as a bad omen. See Swancutt, "*Still Before Sexuality*," 23.

72. Gardner, "Sexing a Roman: Imperfect Men in Roman Law," 136–52. The complication, according to Gardner, is that eunuchs were consistently male in Roman law and literature. This would seem to indicate that regardless of castration, the "original" morphological state of the individual in question matters.

73. Kuefler, *The Manly Eunuch*, 305n12.

74. Augustine, *City of God*, trans. Henry Bettenson (New York: Penguin Books, 2003), 663. Note that Augustine's comment on the androgyne appears in a longer discussion of birth "defects." For Augustine, the androgyne is part of the order of creation. On Augustine, see DeVun, *The Shape of Sex*, 16–40.

While making a point about the grammatical gender of the androgyne, Augustine also argues that androgynes are always weighted toward masculine assignment. Augustine's phrasing is slightly different from Ulpian's, but the sentiment is similar enough that Kuefler cites it as precedent for his interpretation.

Like the androgyne, the eunuch's legal status is debated in the scholarship. Gardner argues that Roman legal systems understand eunuchs as men: castrated men may marry, adopt, and function fully as legal men in every sense.[75] By contrast, Kuefler understands the position of eunuchs in Roman legal sources to be contradictory, in part owing to the difficulty in establishing their status as adult men (a problem we will see debated in rabbinic sources as well.) According to Kuefler, eunuchs have some masculine rights and privileges, but not all. Unlike the androgyne, who, Kuefler believes, was assigned male as a result of their "male" genitalia, eunuchs lack reproductivity. Their sterility prevented them from fathering children, one of the functions of adult men.[76]

Discussions of the legal status of eunuchs and androgynes, like discussions of the practice of exposure, raise questions about how legal discourses relate to material history. Based on the frequent reiteration of the ban on castration within the boundaries of the Roman Empire, scholars suspect that the proscription against castration was regularly flouted. There is a danger of overgeneralizing or conveying an impression of a systemic legal approach to androgynes and eunuchs when the historical picture is much more complicated. And yet, we can still mark some broad shifts in the kinds of legal discourses that seem to circulate about androgynes in particular. The shift away from monstrous birth may have preserved lives; at the same time it can be framed as taming the wild and monstrously subversive potential of the androgyne to disrupt nature.[77]

---

75. In Gardner's phrasing, "Once a man, always a man" (Gardner, "Sexing a Roman," 137). A challenge to that position comes from the famous story related by Valerius Maximus, about a eunuch named Genucius, a Cybellian priest (and therefore, by implication, castrated). Genucius is listed as an heir in a will, but the inheritance is challenged and overturned by Mamercus, who is quoted as saying, "Genucius, whose genital parts had been amputated by his own choice, should not be reckoned among either men or women." See D. R. Shackleton Bailey, trans., *Memorable Doings and Sayings*, 177–79. Gardner points out that Roman citizens are not permitted to be *galli*, and that Genucius's inheritance is denied because he is not a Roman citizen, rather than because of a problem with his sex. Gardner herself admits that the repetition of the anticastration laws may be evidence that they were consistently flouted within the boundaries of the empire. Thus castration might not be reliable evidence for the question of citizenship.

76. Kuefler, *Manly Eunuch*, 19–36.

77. On questions of monstrous births and figuring intersex bodies, see Malatino, *Queer Embodiment*, 39–66.

CONCLUSION: TRANSING LATE ANTIQUITY

In this chapter, I have explored the politics of the study of eunuchs and androgynes in history in order to demonstrate the effects that contemporary transphobia and the erasure of intersexual people have had on the research. I have also provided some general information about the materials that circulate about androgynes and eunuchs in late antiquity. In later chapters, I will share more of that material, including a further exploration of biblical, Second Temple, Sasanian, and Christian texts. Even from this brief survey, however, we can see that these sources touch on profound questions of gender diversity within the order of creation, the place of androgynes and eunuchs within gendered law, and the signs of sex. In the next chapter, I will take up these fundamental questions when the rabbis debate the place of the androgyne in their own gendered legal thought.

In closing, I want to return briefly to Gibbon, the historian who argued that eunuchs were central to the story of the demise of late antiquity. For Gibbon, monstrous eunuchs cause the failure of mighty political powers. In the introduction to this chapter, I argued that Gibbon implicitly assumes that eunuchs hold immense power. Eunuchs had the power to bring down Rome itself.

What if we were to embrace the monstrousness of eunuchs?[78] May we not experience a certain vicarious pleasure in watching eunuchs bring Rome to its knees? Who among us, particularly in the current political moment, wishes to stand firmly on the side of Roman imperialism? Perhaps we should read Gibbon's thesis from the perspective of the early generations of rabbis, who experienced the repercussions of Roman power. Might not the decline and fall of the Roman empire, then, engender a certain sense of schadenfreude? From this perspective, the rabbinic fascination with eunuchs reads like a daring revenge fantasy. In response to Roman might, rabbinic eunuchs spell doom for Roman imperialism.[79]

This is an example of what I mean by transing: I am playing with an obvious anachronism here. Bringing together the rabbis, anachronism, and the monstrousness of androgynes and eunuchs allows us to recast narratives about late antiquity. In the next chapter I will play with anachronism further—by weaving contemporary anti-trans legislation with tannaitic literature. In employing these anachronisms as an interpretive tactic, I am obviously not arguing that the rabbis read Gibbon. Instead, I am inviting us into an imaginative exercise that allows us to engage the gendered and racialized scholarly narratives of late antiquity while centering eunuchs and androgynes in rabbinic literature. And I am arguing (alongside Gibbon, at least in this one small point) that eunuchs and androgynes

---

78. My argument about Gibbon is in conversation with two works: Stryker, "My Words to Victor Frankenstein," 237–54, and Malatino, *Queer Embodiment*.

79. In using the term "Christianization" I am referring to Seth Schwartz's theory in *Imperialism and Jewish Society*, 179–202.

are not a mere footnote of history. If Gibbon places eunuchs at the heart of the (decline of) politics, literature, religion, and cultural production, I will follow his lead in arguing that eunuchs and androgynes are central. They are central both to the story of late antiquity and to the project of rabbinic literature. Transing shifts the way we narrate our histories.

2

The Gendering of Law

The Androgyne and the Hybrid Animal in Bikkurim

In 2018, a memo from the US Department of Health and Human Services was leaked to the *New York Times*. The memo offered a definition of sex: "Sex means a person's status as male or female based on immutable biological traits identifiable by or before birth. . . ."[1] As the *Times* reported, this definition would eradicate federal recognitions of trans people who have gone through bureaucratic processes to change their legal status.[2] While nothing in the memo references religion or theology directly, journalists traced the language back to its Christian evangelical roots.[3]

Conflicts over the definition of sex were also at the heart of the 2020 Supreme Court case Bostock v. Clayton County, which adjudicated the question of whether protections against sex discrimination extend to sexual orientation and gender identity. A key argument hinged on the question of whether or not the definition

---

I am grateful in particular to Rafe Neis for their formal response to this chapter, an early draft of which was presented as "Claiming Queer Pasts: Hermaphroditos, Intersexuality, and Queer Bodies in Rabbinic Literature" at the University of Michigan, Ann Arbor, MI, February 3, 2013. I am also grateful to the fellows of the Frankel Institute for their comments on a working draft and their generous attention to my work. An earlier version of this chapter was published in *Trans Studies Quarterly* under the title "Translating the Human."

1. Erica Green, Katie Benner, and Robert Pear, "'Transgender' Could Be Defined Out of Existence."
2. On questions of trans legal rights, see Currah, Juang, and Minter, *Transgender Rights*.
3. In the popular press, *Mother Jones* has reported on the connection between the anti-trans bills and evangelical Christian theology. See Michaels, "We Tracked Down the Lawyers." The reporters argue that the language found in the memo originates with the Alliance Defending Freedom (ADF), a Christian legal organization that lists marriage, religious freedom, and the sanctity of life as core components of their central agenda.

of sex had changed in recent decades. Could the category of sex, which indicated "biological sex" in the 1964 Civil Rights Act, extend to cover discriminations not intended in the original protections? The court decided that Title VII protections against sex discrimination can protect queer and trans people from employment discrimination. In a sense, then, Bostock v. Clayton County raises questions about taxonomies of sex, and the capacity for sex to change. Both of these examples demonstrate the ways in which the category of sex is currently at the heart of legal and policy wrangling over trans embodiment.

In the last chapter, I argued that transing late antiquity grants us new perspectives on the gendered politics of historical narratives. As a part of transing the past, I brought together the rabbis, eighteenth-century historiography, and contemporary politics in a deliberately anachronistic way, in order to reframe gendered narratives about eunuchs and androgynes. In this chapter, I will extend that deliberate anachronism by weaving together a rabbinic tradition about the androgyne with contemporary legal battles. In doing so, I will illuminate what is at stake in these divergent debates about the definition of sex and gender in law.

The most central early rabbinic source on the androgyne is found in tractate Bikkurim.[4] In this source, the rabbis debate the extent to which law can incorporate mixed bodies, both animal and human. The rabbis simultaneously debate whether androgynes can be included in different ritual and legal obligations, as they assert that the androgyne is part of the order of creation. At the end of the chapter I will move to a discussion of contemporary anti-trans law, which legislates a definition of sex, marriage, and sexuality through the framework of protecting religious beliefs. In the name of protecting religious freedom, anti-trans laws reject trans people from the order of creation. Both sources implicitly gesture toward the creation story in the Hebrew Bible, with very different effects. The juxtaposition between these two sources illuminates the historical and cultural contingency of attempts to define sex and gender in law.

CREATING THE ANDROGYNE

In this chapter I analyze an early rabbinic tradition about the *androginos*. Before I interpret the sources, however, I will first introduce the reader to a variety of different kinds of androgynes in rabbinic and other contemporaneous and earlier bodies of literatures. The rabbis are not inventing categories of androgynes; texts that discuss androgynes circulate broadly throughout antiquity.

---

4. Gwynn Kessler has persuasively argued that this text has been overemphasized in the scholarship. I certainly agree with her conclusion that more attention needs to be paid to the ways the androginos and tumtum are invoked more broadly in the literature. See Kessler, "Rabbinic Gender," 353–71.

Two terms for androgynes are commonly used in rabbinic literature. Neither type of androgyne is found in the Hebrew Bible, so the rabbinic discussion of androgynes is not based on a firm biblical foundation. The first term, "androginos," is a compound of the Greek words for "man" (ἀνήρ) and "woman" (γυνή). The rabbinic text I analyze in this chapter suggests that the androginos has dual genitalia. This androgyne appears more frequently in the halakhic materials—what are conventionally translated as "legal" discussions—as we shall see shortly.

The rabbis also describe a second type of androgyne: a person with two faces. In rabbinic literature, the *du parzuf* (double-faced) human generally has two bodies connected at the back.[5] This double-faced person is found primarily in exegesis of the creation story in Genesis.[6] The rabbis comment on the fact that there are two creation narratives in the Hebrew Bible, and that these stories have discrepancies between them. In the first chapter of Genesis, male and female humans are created simultaneously; while in the second chapter, Eve's creation is secondary to Adam's. Current source criticism would account for this textual conflict by arguing that the narratives reflect different source materials.[7] The rabbis, however, explain these divergences in various ways; at least one such way is to present them as distinct stages of creation. In this reading, God originally created a single human with two faces and two sets of genitalia. The second stage of creation represents the splitting of this androgyne into two distinct bodies.[8]

While scholarship in rabbinics has not worked extensively on androgynes to date, these creation narratives are the exception. Daniel Boyarin argues that the rabbinic two-faced creation myth was a response to Hellenized variants of the androgyne cre-

---

5. *Du parzuf* is also a reflection of the Greek; see Plato's use of πρόσωπα δύ at *Symposium* 190a. See also Wayne Meeks's exploration of the different spellings of the term in "The Image of the Androgyne," 186n90.

6. The tradition in the eighth chapter of Genesis Rabbah has parallels: see Leviticus Rabbah 14, b. Berakhot 61a, b. Ketubbot 8a, and b. Eruvin 18a. See also Genesis Rabbah 1:26, which glosses a being with two sets of genitalia. For a recent discussion of the context of Genesis Rabbah within an increasingly Christianized Roman Palestine, see Gribetz et al., *Genesis Rabbah in Text and Context*.

7. For an overview of source criticism on Genesis, see Speiser's commentary in *The Anchor Bible: Genesis*. There is also a long history of feminist analysis of the gendered implications of these two contrasting narratives. For an overview, see Pardes, *Countertraditions in the Bible*, 13–38.

8. Similar formulations circulate in various sectarian traditions in late antiquity. For example, in the *Apocryphon of John*, the divine triad (mother-father-son) are all described in ways that bend simple gender assignment. Jonathan Cahana reads the Gnostic engagement with the symbolism of the androgyne as a subversion of Greco-Roman definitions of family. See Cahana, "Gnostically Queer," 24–35. Dennis MacDonald reads the cryptic hair covering controversy in 1 Corinthians as a response to Gnostic ideas about androgyny: see MacDonald, "Corinthian Veils and Gnostic Androgynes," 276–92. Cf. Marchal, *Appalling Bodies*, 30–68. On the Manichean interpretation of the divine androgyne, see Pettipiece, "Many Faced Gods." For a trans reading of androgyne creation narratives and the Gospel of Thomas, see Sellew, "Reading the *Gospel of Thomas* from Here," 61–96.

ation story.⁹ Judith Baskin reads rabbinic traditions about the androgyne as undoing any apparent equality between men and women.¹⁰ As an example, Baskin cites a debate about which side of the androgyne (i.e., the male or female half) faces forward when they walk.¹¹ While most scholars have read the rabbinic androgyne through the Greco-Roman tradition, Shai Secunda offers an alternative. Secunda argues that the Zoroastrian creation story in the Bundahišn is a parallel tradition;¹² he notes that the narrative of Mahlī and Mahliyānī (roughly the equivalents of Adam and Eve) bears some striking resemblance to the Platonic Aristophanes's version of the myth.¹³ For Secunda, the rabbis were participating in broad traditions shared with Indo-European cultures. These traditions seek to identify the origins of gender, while (for the rabbis) they also resolve the contradictory accounts of Genesis 1 and 2.¹⁴

When the rabbis use Greek terminology for androgynes, they are already signaling an engagement with broader cultural contexts—at the very least linguistically. In antiquity, there were several different types of androgynes with a range of bodies. In addition to two-headed androgynes and androgynes with dual genitalia, there were "vertical androgynes" who had a single body that was split down the middle. There were also "horizontal androgynes," a phrase that usually referred to a figure with breasts and a phallus.¹⁵

---

9. Daniel Boyarin describes the first-century philosopher Philo's version of the creation narrative, which is shaped by a Middle Platonic dualism. The first created being is incorporeal and therefore androgynous. The second stage of creation results in the corporeal Adam. By contrast, according to the rabbis, marriage is positioned as central to the order of creation. See Boyarin, *Carnal Israel*, 31–61. See also Boyarin, "Gender," 117–36. Leah DeVun thinks that Philo is the bridge to early Christian ideas on the topic. Se DeVun, *The Shape of Sex*, 16–40.

10. Baskin, *Midrashic Women*, 44–64. Wendy Doniger has also argued that the depiction of androgynes is more often weighted toward masculinity. In mythologies that highlight the androgyne's femininity, the image of the androgyne is almost uniformly negative. See Doniger, *Women, Androgynes, and Other Mythical Beasts*, 290–306.

11. Ultimately, according to Baskin, the rabbinic exegesis of the creation story supports the sexual reunification of men and women through marriage, a conclusion not dissimilar to Boyarin's. For a reading of sexual unification in Genesis Rabbah as nostalgia for Eden, see Hasan-Rokem, "Erotic Eden," 156–66.

12. The dating of the materials in the Bundahišn is difficult; most scholars believe that it comes from the end of the Sasanian period but that it contains source materials that are older. See MacKenzie, "Bundahišn."

13. The story in the Bundahišn features a creation with the two figures as humans/plants fused together. Their sex cannot be distinguished. On Gayōmart as an androgyne figure, see Choksy, "Zoroastrianism," 9995. On the Islamic reception of Gayōmart, see Tavakoli-Targhi, "Contested Memories," 149–75.

14. Secunda, "The Construction, Composition, and Idealization of the Female Body," 66.

15. These different "types" of androgynes circulate among different religious traditions. For a well-known "vertical" androgyne see the depiction of Ardhanarishvara (the fusion of Parvati and Shiva) in the caves of Elephanta, for example. On Ardhanarishvara, see Kalidos, "Ardhanari in Early South Indian Cult and Art," 1037–43. "Vertical" androgynes also appear in Aristotle and other Greek thinkers. See DeVun, *The Shape of Sex*, 47. Wendy Doniger catalogues types of androgynes in *Women, Androgynes, and Other Mythical Beasts*, 290–95.

Narratives of two-headed androgynes, however, seem to be the most ancient and were very widespread, often being connected to creation narratives. Statues discovered in 'Ain Ghazal, for example, have one torso supporting two heads placed side by side. Some scholars have argued that two-headed statues date back as far as the eighth millennium BCE.[16] Interpretations of these figures vary widely, but at least some understand this as an early depiction of an androgyne creation story. These sexually hybrid, two-headed beings may represent a kind of ancestor worship, albeit of ancestors that originate from a primal stage of creation.

Other ancient creation stories feature hybrid human and animal creatures that are often also a mixture of genders, although they are not specifically two-headed. So, for example, in the Babylonian creation epic *Enuma Elish*, the original created beings were hybrid. It is only in subsequent stages of creation that distinct male and female creatures are formed. According to Stephanie Dalley, representations of these hybrid animal and hybrid gendered figures appear as early as the late fourth millennium BCE.[17] Many of these narratives predate the Genesis story in the Hebrew Bible.

The clearest counterpart to the rabbinic two-faced androgyne was popularized in Plato's *Symposium*.[18] This creation narrative represents the original humans as having two bodies conjoined in one, back-to-back. Zeus, feeling threatened by the power of these creatures, splits them in half. This split constitutes the origin of

---

16. Irit Ziffer, "The First Adam," 129–52. Note that the two heads side-by-side are different from the Aristophanean or rabbinic version of the two-headed androgyne.

17. Scholars have argued that the *Enuma Elish* is part of the inspiration for the Genesis narrative. See Dalley, "Evolution of Gender in Mesopotamian Mythology," 117–22. Empedocles, a fifth-century BCE, Greek philosopher, relays a creation story that proceeds in stages: the creation of men and women comes only in the third generation at which point sexual reproduction is enabled. For a discussion of Empedocles in relation to the androgyne, see Dietrich, "Der Urmensch als Androgyn," 297–345. For an analysis of the Mesopotamian story of Enki and Ninmah, see Asher-Greve, "The Essential Body," 432–61.

18. I am not disagreeing with Shai Secunda's argument for a broader Indo-European origin, but the Greek narrative is also clearly influential. See Secunda, "The Construction, Composition, and Idealization," 60–86. I am also not positing a direct relationship between the rabbinic *du parẓuf* and *The Symposium*. Galit Hasan-Rokem and Israel Yuval argue that it is possible to trace points of connection between Origen's homilies on Leviticus and the Leviticus Rabbah reworking of the story, for example, but they do not argue for any direct conversation between Galilean rabbis and Origen. Instead, the authors cite the "common echo drum" of late antiquity. See Hasan-Rokem and Yuval, "Myth, History, and Eschatology," 253.

Leah DeVun explores the origins of androgynous creation stories in early Christian thought, arguing that *The Symposium* does not seem to have widespread influence on Christian thinking. Instead, Origen and Gregory of Nyssa imagine an originary ungendered state, not a physically dual-sexed androgyne. Augustine constitutes a shift in early Christian interpretations of Genesis. See DeVun, *The Shape of Sex*, 16–40.

eros, which springs from a longing to find and reunite with our lost half.[19] While Plato does not invent the story, his dialogue *The Symposium* reflects its broad circulation.[20]

Androgyne creation stories were both popular and ancient, but other types of androgyne narratives also circulated broadly in late antiquity. Most notable is the tale of Hermaphroditus.[21] The fourth book of Ovid's *Metamorphoses* contains the most famous depiction of Hermaphroditus.[22] Ovid unfolds the tale of the nymph Salmacis, who spots Hermaphroditus, a handsome youth. In the first of several gender reversals, she asks him for his hand in marriage, and he blushingly refuses.[23] Salmacis pursues him relentlessly until she finally entwines herself with him and prays to the gods that they should never be separated. Heeding her prayer, the gods conjoin Hermaphroditus and Salmacis in one body.[24]

Ovid invokes the image of a tree to describe the fusion of Salmacis with Hermaphroditus:

19. See Plato, *Symposium* 189a–193e. See especially the following: "In the first place, there were three kinds of human beings, not merely the two sexes, male and female, as at present: there was a third kind as well, that had equal shares of the other two, and whose name survives even though the thing itself has vanished. For 'man-woman' (ἀνδρόγυνον) was then a unity in form no less than name, composed of both sexes and sharing equally in male and female; whereas now it has come to be merely a name of reproach" (189e).

20. For the similarities between the Platonic version of the creation myth and the *Brihadaranyaka Upanishad*, see, for example, Doniger, "Bisexuality in the Mythology of Ancient India," 50–60.

21. At least some scholars connect the Hermaphroditus tradition to the creation stories about primordial beings. See Peter Kelly, "Intersex and Intertext," 95–106. There is some debate over whether hermaphrodites and androgynes are in fact conceptually distinct. At least some ancient thinkers connect them. For a discussion of this, see DeVun, *The Shape of Sex*, 16–40. "Androgyne" is the preferred term in Greek; "hermaphrodite" is the preferred term in Latin. It is important to note that the word ἑρμαφρόδιτος/hermaphrodite is also used in Greek, and that both terms are found in Greek and Latin. See Stefanie Lauren van der Gracht, "Hermaphroditism in Greek and Roman Antiquity."

22. Ovid does not originate the connection between Hermaphroditus and water when he places the scene of struggle between the nymph and Hermaphroditus in the latter's spring. The Salmakis inscription attests to a radically different version of the story. See Romano, "The Invention of Marriage," 543–61. The figure of Aphrodite had already been associated with mixed sexed characteristics. Consider the Cyprian worship of a bearded Aphroditos, as well as the ithyphallic statues associated with this androgynous deity as described in Delacourt, *Hermaphrodite*. See also the discussions of the early sources for the narrative: Zajko, "'Listening With' Ovid," 175–202.

23. For a reading of these gender reversals, see Richlin, "Reading Ovid's Rapes," 158–80. Scholars debate what precisely *mollis*/"emasculation" refers to here. Some scholars suggest that it meant castration, others impotence, and still others sterility. For a summary of the various arguments, see Robinson, "Salmacis and Hermaphroditus," 212–23.

24. This is only one of several stories of bodily transformation in Ovid. See also the figures of Tiresias, Sithon, Mestra, Iphis, and Cainis. These are discussed in Swancutt, "*Still Before Sexuality*," 11–63.

As when one grafts[25] a twig on some tree, he sees the branches grow one, and with common life come to maturity, so were these two bodies knit in close embrace: they were no longer two, nor such as to be called, one, woman and one, man. They seemed neither, and yet both. (4.375–80)[26]

The image of grafting raises questions about the nature of the new hybrid being:[27] Is the twig utterly subsumed into the tree? Or does the addition of the twig change the nature of the tree?[28] The identity of Salmacis/Hermaphroditus is at stake. Following a series of elegant metaphors of struggle, the prose in this section becomes stilted, as if language no longer suffices to answer the question of Hermaphroditus's status: is this being now a woman or man, both, or neither?[29]

While the literary traces of Hermaphroditus mostly date to late antiquity, statues of the deity predate Ovid's narrative by several hundred years. Scholars believe that these statues began to popularly circulate in Greece as early as the fourth century BCE. Versions of Hermaphroditus would have been found at gymnasia and public baths (the latter perhaps because of Hermaphroditus's association with the stream in which he meets Salmacis). There is documented evidence for the wide distribution of these terracotta figurines, while the larger marble versions, of which several copies remain extant, would have been rarer. Still, the ubiquity of the figure of Hermaphroditus attests to the popularity of this story.[30]

Among the Hermaphroditus statues that circulated in late antiquity there are a number of different styles, but almost all of them play with the viewer's visual expectations. The three most common styles depict Hermaphroditus as an attractive woman with a penis. In the most famous rendering of Hermaphroditus, the figure is sleeping. This statue is meant to be approached from the back, where the viewer would see what appeared to be a reclining woman. Only by walking around the statue would the viewer discover Hermaphroditus's genitalia.[31] Thus the gen-

---

25. While the verb *conduco* means to assemble more generally, in this context it can mean to unite or connect, which the translator renders as grafting. Lewis and Short cite this passage as an example of the use of *conduco* to mean unite or connect. See Charlton T. Lewis and Charles Short, *A Latin Dictionary*, s.v. "conduco."

26. Ovid, *Metamorphoses* 4.375–80.

27. See Anderson's commentary on this language of grafting: *Ovid's Metamorphoses: Books 1–5*, 453. For an incisive reception history of Ovid's Hermaphroditus (one that focuses on the alchemical adoption of metaphors of grafting), see DeVun, "The Jesus Hermaphrodite," 193–218.

28. There are several analogies to nature in this section of the text. Amy Richlin reads Ovid's use of grafting as a metaphor for the penetration and cultivation of women. See Richlin, "Making Up a Woman," 185–213.

29. For an interpretation of this language as a grafting of a masculine idiom onto feminine others, see Nugent, "This Sex Which Is Not One," 160–85.

30. See Ajootian, "The Only Happy Couple," 220–42.

31. Robert Groves argues that Ovid bases his narration of Hermaphroditus on the experience of viewing these popular statues and that the narrative similarly plays with the gendered expectations of

FIGURE 1. *Sleeping Hermaphroditus*, viewed from the back. Roman copy of a Greek original; second half of second century BCE. MA23I. Marble, I. 148 cm. Photo: Hervé Lewandowski. Musee du Louvre, Paris, France © RMN-Grand Palais /Art Resource, NY.

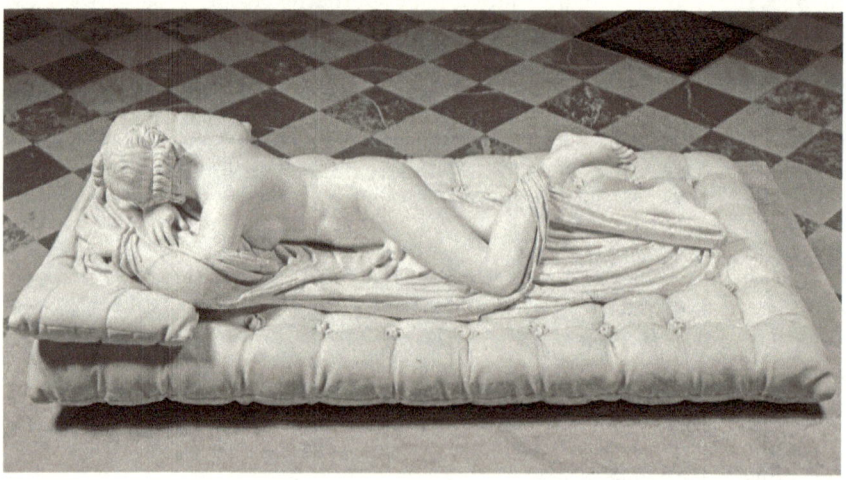

FIGURE 2. *Sleeping Hermaphroditus*, view from front. Roman copy after Greek original; mid-second-century BCE. The mattress was added before 1620 by Gianlorenzo Bernini (1598–80). Marble, 148 © RMN-Grand Palais /Art Resource, NY.

der of Hermaphroditus, and the "revelation" of their genitalia, becomes a spectacle for the titillation of the viewer.

Narratives and art depicting androgynes were popular in late antiquity. People continue to be fascinated with androgynes to the present day. From the popular contemporary film *Hedwig and the Angry Inch*, in which Plato's *Symposium* plays a starring role, to the contemporary novel *Middlesex*, these stories continue to circulate widely.[32] I will address the politics of the deeply problematic term "hermaphrodite" more fully in my conclusion to this book, but it is sufficient to note that from the perspective of contemporary trans and intersex politics, the troubling implications of these sources are exacerbated by their staying power.

HYBRID BODIES IN BIKKURIM: TEXTUAL CHALLENGES

Within the rabbinic corpus, the most famous tradition about the androgyne is beset with philological puzzles. This section is designed for readers familiar with the field of rabbinics. I will briefly address the most relevant debates within the field. One of these concerns the question of the placement of these traditions in the Mishnah or the Tosefta, a subject on which I largely remain agnostic.

This androgyne tradition takes the form of a list of the various areas of gendered obligation accompanied by a terse explanation of how the androgyne fits into each one. This source is often attributed to the second chapter of Tosefta Bikkurim, following Saul Lieberman's placement in his critical edition of the Tosefta. The simplest explanation for a list in tannaitic literature is that it facilitates memorization. Understood solely as a mnemonic device, this list would merely anthologize relevant laws and its composition would have very little significance.[33] In this case, however, I argue that the composed list is itself worthy of study. By compiling a list of the laws that touch on the androgyne, the rabbis are

---

the reader. See Groves, "From Statue to Story," 321–56. For a discussion of the politics of the study of Hermaphroditus, see Linnea Åshede, *"Neutrumque et Utrumque Videntur,"* 81–95.

32. I am thinking particularly here of Jeffrey Eugenides's award-winning novel *Middlesex*, which I will discuss in the conclusion of the book.

33. Martin Jaffee examines the genre of the list and its connection to the oral tradition in tannaitic literature. He points out that some lists are so embedded in the framework of the larger tractate that it is impossible to separate the list from its literary form. In other cases, lists function as independent units, and evolve independently. Jaffee's work could suggest interpreting the androgyne list, which is relatively independent from the general content of tractate Bikkurim, as an oral composition. See Jaffee, *Torah in the Mouth*, 106–11. For a study of the shift in list forms from the Bible (which also employs numbered lists) to rabbinic literature, see Saldarini, "'Form Criticism' of Rabbinic Literature," 257–74. Saldarini is engaging primarily with Wayne Towner's classic work on exegetical lists. See Towner, *The Rabbinic Enumeration of Scriptural Examples*. On lists in later rabbinic literature, see Lehmhaus, "Listenwissenschaft," 59–103.

purposefully organizing a separate legal discussion specifically around the question of the relationship of the androgyne to gendered law.

In one version of the text, the androgyne list is paired with a parallel list about the *koy*, a hybrid animal. Other textual traditions separate the androgyne from the hybrid animal. Structural and linguistic similarities between the androgyne and hybrid animal list suggest that the two lists should be considered as a pair, regardless of which composition the androgyne list is assigned to. The connection between the koy and the androgyne is not immediately obvious; there is very little overlap between the legal questions on each list. Therefore, the pairing of the androgyne and hybrid animal cannot be understood as a memory aid. Rather, I would suggest that the entire composition, which includes both the hybrid animal and the androgyne, is a unit. Read together, the theme of both lists is the incorporation of mixed beings into legal discourse.

In his critical edition of the Tosefta, Saul Lieberman demonstrates that there are two main manuscript families.[34] Lieberman presents the Naples manuscript (the earliest extant printed edition of the Mishnah) and the Vienna manuscript of the Tosefta synoptically, as opposed to providing the variations between the two in the critical apparatus. This is an extremely rare move for Lieberman, and indicative of the well-established and competing versions of the androgyne list.[35] That we have inherited two robust manuscript traditions suggests that this oral tradition about the androgyne was both popular and circulated widely; this popularity may have contributed to the multiple versions that arose.

The two main manuscript traditions of the androgyne list place this source within different early rabbinic compilations, but also shifts the list's place within the larger composition of Bikkurim. In one version, as I stated earlier, the androgyne has been paired with the category of the hybrid animal. In the other version of the list, the androgyne and the hybrid animal are separated from each other. Given the linguistic and structural similarities between the hybrid animal and the androgyne lists, it is likely that the paired androgyne/hybrid animal version pre-

---

34. Lieberman, *Tosefta Kifshuta: Shvi'it- Bikkurim*, 834–46. The Munich manuscript represents a combination of the two groups of manuscripts, while other manuscripts generally conform to one of the two types. One family of manuscripts (Parma, Kaufmann, and the printed edition from Naples) appends the androgyne list to the fourth chapter of Mishnah Bikkurim. Another family of manuscripts arranges this tradition as part of the second chapter of Tosefta Bikkurim. As far as I know, this is one of only two instances where Lieberman arranges the text synoptically, as opposed to giving variants in the critical apparatus, because there are two well-established versions. (The other place is Tosefta Sotah.) See Epstein, who attributes the androgyne list to the Mishnah and not the Tosefta: *Mavo L'Nusach HaMishnah*, 976.

35. I have chosen to cite the text as if it comes from the Tosefta (following Lieberman). I am, as I have stated, agnostic on the debate. I will focus, however, on analyzing primarily those sections that appear in both versions of the list.

serves the earliest arrangement.³⁶ To understand the androgyne, we must therefore consider it within the context of its larger framework, which includes both the laws that address the koy and tractate Bikkurim as a whole.

Both manuscript traditions consistently associate the lists with tractate Bikkurim. Tractate Bikkurim discusses the offerings of first fruits—a biblical obligation that mandates separating out the first fruiting produce in order to convey it to the Temple in Jerusalem. There is no obvious connection between first fruits and either the androgyne or the hybrid animal. Neither the androgyne nor the hybrid animal list contains any individual laws that address first fruits. The question of why these lists are connected to tractate Bikkurim instead of any of the other tractates that address topics pertaining to gender, for example, should give us pause. What do the androginos and koy have to do with agriculture?

Certainly, Greco-Roman texts made numerous connections between agriculture and gender. As I noted earlier, in Ovid's first-century CE narration of the story of Hermaphroditus, the climactic moment arrives when Salmacis (the nymph) and Hermaphroditus are fused into one person. Ovid offers several metaphors in a row that use nature to describe the struggle and eventual fusion. Among these, the central metaphor for the hybrid being is agricultural.³⁷ Just as Hermaphroditus fuses together masculine and feminine bodies, trees become hybrid through grafting.

Roman literature specifically describes grafting in gendered language.³⁸ Varro, the first-century BCE Roman author, gives advice for planting that invokes medical knowledge about women's bodies; he argues that figs, pomegranates, and vines grow faster because of their "feminine softness."³⁹ In these passages, Varro draws on medical science, which classifies women's bodies as moister than men's

---

36. This section begs the larger question about the relationship between the Mishnah and the Tosefta, which is still open. See, for example, Hanoch Albeck, who argues for a late date for the composition of the Tosefta as a compilation: Albeck, *Studies in the Baraita and the Tosefta*. Moreover, orality complicates the whole question of a single original "text." See Jafee, *Torah in the Mouth* and Shanks Alexander, *Transmitting Mishnah*.

37. This is not the only place where Ovid uses grafting as a metaphor. For example, in the narrative of Pomona, the hamadryad, we see a sexualized and gendered narrative that describes grafting. Ailsa Hunt discusses the gendered language of grafting and surveys the broader Roman agricultural literature on the question. See Hunt, "Elegiac Grafting in Pomona's Orchard," 43–58.

38. See, for example, Marcus Terrentius Varro, *On Agriculture* XLI.1–5 for a description of planting that uses gendered language to describe the techniques. Varro is not alone in addressing the subject of grafting in this manner, although his rhetoric is clearest. See Cato the Elder, *On Agriculture* XL.1–4 for a discussion of the techniques of grafting.

39. "Softness" is gendered in Roman literature. See Williams, "The Meanings of Softness," 240–63.

(Hippocrates). Later authors characterize female seed as figlike (Rufus, Galen) and softer (Celsus).[40]

Varro is just one example of the explanatory power of metaphors relying on theories about sex, even for realms that to us might seem distinct, like horticulture; plowing a field, for example, is a common metaphor for sexual intercourse in Roman literature.[41] Katharine von Stackleberg has argued that the frequent placement of statues of Hermaphroditus in garden settings is not accidental. The garden represents a liminal space between the wild and the domesticated, and this hybridity is connected to the gender of Hermaphroditus.[42] The association of Hermaphroditus with agriculture (which might also be said to represent the tension between wild and domesticated) is thus well attested in the Roman tradition.

Rabbinic literature also plays with associations among agriculture, gender, reproduction, and sexuality. For example, a famous mishnah in Ketubbot (1:6) contains a case study in which a woman explains that after she was betrothed, she was raped. She describes the assault with the phrase, "your field has flooded." Beside the obvious androcentrism of situating women as property, the image of the flooded field highlights her lack of control over her own sexuality. Gail Labovitz has argued that this metaphoric association between women and fields is not unique; agriculture is imbricated with gender throughout rabbinic legal discourse.[43] This association in rabbinic literature among gender, sexuality, and agriculture is so pervasive, in fact, as to make a discussion of the androgyne in the context of agriculture begin to seem less farfetched.

Still, there are numerous tractates that address agriculture; why are we discussing the androgyne and hybrid animal within the context of Bikkurim?[44] Tractate

---

40. For an overview of the various constructions of women's bodies in medical texts, see Flemming, *Medicine and the Making of Roman Women*, 1–32. The rabbis also use the fig as an analogy for women's bodies. See m. Niddah 5:7–8, and Charlotte Fonrobert's discussion of this mishnah: "Regulating the Human Body," 275–77.

41. See Richlin, "Making Up a Woman," 185–213.

42. See von Stackleberg, "Garden Hybrids," 395–426. On the question of gender and space in rabbinic literature, see Baker, *Rebuilding the House of Israel*.

43. See Labovitz, *Marriage and Metaphor*, 97–131. See also Margalit, "Not by Her Mouth Do We Live," 61–86. In the Hebrew Bible, a man plants seed in a woman, and the resulting child is called the "fruit" of her belly. In cognate languages, the term "ben" (son) also has the meaning of a bough or a shoot. See Levine, "'Seed' versus 'Womb,'" 337–43.

44. There are rabbinic sources that address the question of the androgyne in agriculture and in relation to first fruits in particular. John Mandsager addresses these texts in his brilliant dissertation ("To Stake a Claim," 208–13). Mandsager makes a general argument in that chapter about the relationship between gender, land ownership, and Bikkurim. He addresses tractate Kil'ayim in chapters 4 and 5 of his dissertation.

Scholars have generally aligned themselves within three different camps when interpreting Leviticus and Deuteronomy on kil'ayim (forbidden mixtures). The first group of scholars argue that the biblical verses ordain the sanctity of God's creation. See, for example, Mandelbaum, *A History of the*

Kil'ayim might make more sense because of the way it addresses crossbreeding and one way to understand the koy is that it is a crossbred animal. In rabbinic literature, the koy is generally understood as a hybrid of a wild and a domesticated animal.[45] In fact, the eighth chapter of Kil'ayim interprets the laws against crossbreeding, among them the prohibition against crossbreeding between wild and domesticated animals.[46] The koy is even associated with Kil'ayim in some places.[47] Two problems emerge: if there is already a biblical prohibition on crossbreeding, why do the rabbis create the category of the koy in the first place? And if there is already a tractate that discusses crossbreeding in the order of laws addressing agriculture, why are the androgyne and hybrid animal lists not found there?

In the version of the list where the koy is introduced separately from the androgyne, the koy appears in the midst of a series of examples that enumerate the similarities and differences among various Temple offerings.[48] Following this discussion, the next tradition describes a kind of tree that functions legally as both a tree

---

Mishnaic Law of Agriculture. This interpretation follows Philo (*On The Special Laws* IV.34.203 –19). Other scholars argue that we should interpret the biblical verses metaphorically, perhaps as a prohibition against intermarriage. See Carmichael, "Forbidden Mixtures," 433–48. Finally, Jacob Milgrom argues that mixtures belong to the realm of the divine and are forbidden in the profane world. See Milgrom, *Leviticus: A Book of Ritual and Ethics*, 236–38.

45. The rabbis have different ideas of whether it refers to a crossbreed of specific wild animals, as we shall see. There have been numerous conflicting attempts to identify the koy that continue through medieval commentaries. So, for example, Jacob ben Judah Weil (a fifteenth-century rabbi) identifies the koy as a water buffalo. I will discuss the possible relationship between the koy and the Greek tragelaphos shortly. For a survey of some of the reception history of the koy, see Nissan and Amar, "What They Served," 95–129. Menachem Dor argues that the koy is distinct from the tragelaphos and is also distinct from kil'ayim and should be identified with the water buffalo. See Dor, "Ma'aley Hageyrah," 122–30.

46. The rabbis inherit the basic categories of animals from the biblical text, but the Hebrew Bible does not always employ the dichotomy of wild versus domesticated. See, for example, Deuteronomy 14:4–5, where the word *b'haymah* (which often refers to a domesticated animal) serves as an umbrella category for all kosher animals. Verse 4 describes the domesticated animals while verse 5 lists the wild animals—but the word *ḥayah* (which also means animal, but which usually designates wild animals) is not employed. On the other hand, Genesis 1:24 uses *ḥayah* as an umbrella category for all living things, while in that context *b'haymah* is more likely a reference to domesticated animals. For a discussion of the reception of biblical law, including an analysis of the way Philo relates cross-breeding and prohibited sexual practices like adultery, see Mandsager, "To Stake a Claim," 87–90. For an analysis of the eighth chapter of Kil'ayim, see Mandelbaum, *A History of the Mishnaic Law of Agriculture*, 251–82.

47. See, for example, m. Bekhorot 1:5, where the koy appears alongside kil'ayim. See also the version of the list that is attached to the Mishnah, where the koy is discussed directly in relation to kil'ayim (m. Bekhorot 2:11). The Palestinian Talmud contains a discussion of the nature of the koy as well: see p. Bikkurim 2:8 (65b).

48. The fifth mishnah begins: "The tithe of tithes (*trumat ma'aser*) is similar [Heb. *shaveh*] to first fruit offerings in two ways, and it is similar to the heave offering in one way." Note the parallel language of shaveh to our androgyne and hybrid animal lists. For further discussion of the text here, see Epstein, *Mavo L'Nusach HaMishnah*, 13–18.

and a vegetable. Then come several different traditions regarding objects that similarly function in two dichotomous categories at the same time. The defiance of legal dichotomy seems to be the thematic link that threads among the subjects in this chapter.

A theme of hybridity, therefore, emerges in this section of Mishnah Bikkurim. The koy crosses the boundaries of the dichotomy between wild and domesticated animals. Similarly, the androginos has some characteristics that could make them subject to men's obligations and others that might subject them to the laws governing women. What seems to connect the androginos and the koy, then, is the challenge that their hybrid nature presents in relation to established divisions. In contrast to previous scholarly approaches, which have tended to focus on the androginos exclusively, I follow the arrangement that pairs the two together. In order to understand the challenge that the koy poses, we need to explore the categories of wild and domesticated in rabbinic literature.

THE KOY: ANIMALITY AND HYBRIDITY

The most central tradition about the androgyne in early rabbinic literature is paired with a discussion of the hybrid animal, called the koy. The etymology of koy is uncertain and the term is not found biblically.[49] Moreover, the rabbis debate the definition of the koy—while some rabbinic traditions seem to classify the koy as a mix of any wild and domesticated species, others define it more precisely. One opinion in the Talmud, for example, argues that the koy is a crossbreed specifically between a goat and a stag.[50]

While the origins of the koy in rabbinic thought are unclear, there are Greco-Roman parallels to the koy. The concept of animal hybridity is commonplace in

---

49. While the words for wild and domesticated animals appear in the Bible, there is no biblical word *koy* that refers to a hybrid animal. The Septuagint translates the "wild goat"/ 'ako in Deuteronomy 14:5 as tragelaphos. See Aitken, "Why is the Giraffe Kosher?" 21–34.

In Greek, there is also the term κοινογενής that may be linked to the koy. I am not making a strong claim for the Greek term as the source of the koy. Rather, both frameworks betray a similar interest in cross-breeding. For example, Plato's dialogue *The Statesman* includes a section that begins with a division between wild and domesticated animals: "Shall we make our division [between classes of domesticated walking animals] on the basis of having or not having cloven hoofs, or on that of mixing or not mixing the breed?" (*Statesman* 265d). Here the word κοινογενής is translated as "mixed breed."

50. See b. Ḥullin 79b–80a. This disagreement over the definition of the koy is carried into the commentators. See, for example, Maimonides, who argues that they could not decide whether the koy is a kind of wild or domesticated animal. See Maimonides, *Mishneh Torah, hilkhot n'zirut*, 2:10. Tosafot, on the other hand, points to a contradiction between b. Keritot 21a and b. Ḥullin 79b–80a. In Ḥullin the line, "the koy is *sui generis*," means that it is a dubious member of either the wild or the domesticated class of animals, but the sages could not decide which. In Keritot the line, "the koy is *sui generis*," seems to suggest that it is neither a wild nor a domesticated animal but rather a unique being.

Greco-Roman sources. For example, animal-human hybrids are ubiquitous in Greco-Roman literature and statuary (and we have already seen their connection to androgynes).[51] Questions about the classification of animals also play a significant role in Roman legal discourses, mostly in the context of damages, a topic of great interest to the rabbis as well. Jurors debate the status of elephants and camels in the laws of damages, for example, since in their view both of these animal species are domesticated insofar as they work for humans, but at the same time they have a wild nature.[52]

The hybrid animal figure that is most often connected to the koy is the *tragelaphos*.[53] The term "tragelaphos" is a compound of the Greek words for *goat* and *stag*. The tragelaphos appears in the works of Plato and Aristotle, among others.[54] There are also artistic depictions of the tragelaphos, although the art itself is no longer extent. So, for example in his life of *Agesilaus*, Plutarch describes a wooden tragelaphos figure used in processions, while Aristophanes mentions Persian tragelaphos tapestries in *The Frogs*.[55] Regardless of whether the Greco-Roman tradition understood the tragelaphos as mythical or real (already a subject of debate in

---

51. See, for example, Johns, *Sex or Symbol?* This work devotes several chapters to the question of human-animal hybrids. See also the mosaics of Ostia, which depict hybrids of sea and land animals (Haselhoff, "Salin's Style I," 3). On the categories of wild and domesticated in Roman literature, see Jennison, *Animals for Show and Pleasure*. For a theorization of "wilderness" that explores Roman gladiatorial games, see Whatmore and Thorne, "Wild(er)ness," 435–54.

52. See Bernard Jackson, "Liability for Animals in Roman Law," 122–44. Jackson does not specify this, but the discussion of the elephant and the camel comes from *Justinian's Digest*, 9.2.2, citing Gaius "Provincial Edict," book 7. This type of division between wild/domesticated within the laws of damages shows up in the Mishnah as well. See, for example, m. Bava Kamma 1:4 and the way *mu'ad* animals are thought to have a greater propensity for harm.

53. Primarily by Wegner, "*Tragelaphos* Revisited," 160–72. Wegner uses the koy to discuss the status of women as hybrids in the tannaitic literature, arguing that women fall in-between the status of chattel and persons. Wegner does not, however, connect the hybridity of the koy to the androgyne, which would have been another way for her to stage a conversation about gender and hybridity. I am not criticizing her desire to focus her research on women, but I am noting that her argument marginalizes the "mythical" androgyne.

54. In Greek, the term is τραγέλαφος. See, for example, Plato, *Republic* 488a and Morgan, "Plato's Goat-Stags," 179–98. On Euripides's animal hybrids, see von Bothmer, "The Tawny Hippalektryon," 132–36. On the tendency of the Greeks to name unknown animals with a compound of two known animals, see Cioffi, "A Trugeranos for Seleukos?" 209–13. This work includes a discussion of the tragelaphos in Aeschylus. For a philosophical discussion of the goat-stag and its reception in history, see Ginzburg, *Wooden Eyes*, 26–62.

55. See also the cameo of an ithyphallic tragelaphos that dates back to the Hellenistic period: Plantzos, "Hellenistic Cameos." I have not found other sources on the ithyphallic tragelaphos. For the depiction of the tragelaphos on Alexander's sarcophagus, see Pollitt, *Art in the Hellenistic Age*, 19. Some scholars believe that the goat-stag appears in Cypriot Iron-Age pottery. See Sørenson, "Here There Be Monsters," 442.

antiquity), this creature is the clearest correspondent to the hybrid animal in one strand of rabbinic understanding.[56]

The rabbinic traditions about the androgyne and the hybrid animal are both organized in a similar format in tractate Bikkurim; both take the form of a list. The hybrid animal list is separated into subsections, and each is introduced by a question: How is the hybrid animal like a wild animal? How is the hybrid animal like both a domesticated and wild animal? Under each of those headings comes a list of laws that describe how the hybrid animal functions legally and ritually within these categories. Accordingly, the list anthologizes laws suggesting that the koy functions like a wild animal—for example, in the way in which it is slaughtered for consumption. Each heading has its own list of laws. So we see the following:

> How is the koy similar to a wild animal? Its blood requires covering [like kosher wild animals] . . . How is [the koy] similar to a wild and a domesticated animal? [When it] is skinned [but the skin is still] attached [to the animal's flesh, it conveys impurity] like [both] wild and domesticated animals . . .

The particularities of these rulings are not immediately crucial to our discussion here. The structure of the list is designed to work through all the ways in which the hybrid animal fits into the established dichotomy of wild and domesticated animals. However, when the list proposes that the hybrid animal is like both wild and domesticated animals in some respects, it suggests that there are some qualities common to all kinds of animals. In other words, the category of being "like both wild and domesticated" implies that there is a concept of animality that supersedes other taxonomical distinctions.

Beth Berkowitz, in her monograph *Animals and Animality in the Babylonian Talmud*, investigates animality. She argues that in rabbinic literature, animals both have selves and are used to negotiate the boundaries between the rabbinic self and its various "others" (pagan, heretic, Samaritan, nonrabbinic, etc.). Often these boundaries are enforced through gendered dicta about sexual contact, so Berkowitz points to texts that analogize sex with a non-Jew to sex with a fish, to sources that associate non-Jews with bestiality, and to a passage that describes a daughter marrying a nonrabbinic Jew ('am ha'arez) as comparable to her being tied up and left for lions. For Berkowitz, the Talmud certainly reinforces a dichotomy between humans and animals, and it describes animals as property, props, and sources of domestic labor (although some humans are described in these terms as well). At

---

56. See Shaye Cohen, "Sabbath Law and Mishnah Shabbat in Origen de Principiis," 160–89. Cohen cites Origen, who believes the tragelaphos to be mythical, and Diodorus of Sicily, who believes that the tragelaphos is real. There are other instances in tannaitic literature where Hellenistic animals are discussed. See, for example, the mouse who is half earth and half flesh in m. Ḥullin 9:6 and van der Horst, "Two Notes on Hellenistic Lore," 252–62.

the same time, she notes that the sources almost systematically undermine those very distinctions.[57]

Divisions between wild and domesticated animals are not self-evident, although some of the distinctions in rabbinic law are inherited from biblical texts. The boundaries between domestic and wild animals are occasionally contested; there are rabbinic debates about whether certain animals (e.g., dogs) are considered wild or domesticated.[58] Given Berkowitz's conclusions, it should not be surprising to us that these taxonomies tend to situate animals in relation to human needs. Thus, for example, animals are divided into kosher and nonkosher, and are therefore grouped according to the criterion of human consumption. A taxonomy of wild and domesticated also centers human perspectives by dividing animals into those that are considered a part of the household and those that are not. This distinction between household animals and animals *external* to the household spatially maps animality based on human kinship structures. Moreover, the category of the domesticated animal implies human ownership of the animal's "domesticated" labor. The utilitarian incorporation of the animal into the household gives structure to the dichotomy between wild and domesticated.

Situating animals as property in relation to human households is also a gendered, and at times racialized, enterprise. The most famous rabbinic source on the establishment of the household comes from the first chapter of Mishnah Kiddushin, over which much feminist ink has been spilled. This chapter establishes the figure of the rabbinic householder and it describes how he acquires his property.[59] It is no accident that the opening of the tractate on marriage laws succinctly lays out the method for acquiring wives, slaves, and animals. Taken together, the acquisition of the three "objects" establishes an androcentric household based in property relations and the subjugation of certain classes of beings. The category of domestication, therefore, is simultaneously a mode of acquisition and both gendered and sexualized. The figure of the hybrid animal perches on precisely these interstices.

This rabbinic tradition is staging a struggle over the viability of hybridity, and it raises a question about how to interpolate the koy into discussions of wild and domesticated animals. We must account for the fact that the rabbis include the hybrid animal in the rabbinic system as such, when the koy does not appear in the

---

57. Berkowitz, *Animals and Animality in the Babylonian Talmud*, 19. Berkowitz mentions 'adney hasadeh and other human/animal hybrids. On bestiality, see also Wasserman, *Jews, Gentiles, and Other Animals*, 73–119. On the categories of human/animal in the context of generation and reproduction, see Neis, "The Reproduction of Species," 289–317.

58. See, for example, m. Kil'ayim 8:6, where the rabbis disagree about whether the dog belong in the category of wild or domestic.

59. See Gail Labovitz, who summarizes the earlier feminist literature in her book, *Marriage and Metaphor*, 29–62.

Hebrew Bible. In making room for the koy, then, rabbinic law cannot fully undo the disruptive possibilities of hybridity. The hybrid animal becomes a site to contemplate animality and processes of domestication.

"LIKE NEITHER": ANDROGYNES AND HYBRID ANIMALS

In this section, I will examine the androgyne list and the debate over the legal status of the androgyne in gendered law. I will argue that the hybridity of the androgyne has a paradoxical effect: hybridity both undermines dichotomous gender in the law and, at the same time, solidifies gender as an ontological category in law. Finally, I will look at the parallel codas of the hybrid animal list and the androgyne list, in order to read the ways both are connected through domestication.

The most famous tradition about the androgyne begins with a thesis statement that mirrors the koy list:

> [In the case of the] androgyne: there are ways in which they are like men, there are ways in which they are like women, there are ways in which they are like both men and women, and there are ways in which they are not like men or women. (t. Bikkurim 2:3)[60]

This topic statement signals that what follows will be a list. In many respects this list is a classic example of the genre of the tannaitic (early rabbinic) list, although in some respects it diverges from that form.[61] The traditions found within this list are also dispersed throughout the corpus in their topical legal contexts. In this list,

---

60. Hebrew grammar uses masculine language for the androgyne. Because of the androcentric conventions of Hebrew, it is difficult to know how to weight that fact. In the past I have translated this text using "ze/hir," primarily because the cognitive dissonance (particularly for those unfamiliar with gender-neutral pronouns) was helpful in disrupting any easy translation. In doing so I was drawing on the work of early trans activists who were playing with translation and this text—primarily Reuben Zellman and Elliot Kukla. Drawing on my translations, Moshe Halbertal uses ze and hir in his recent translation and reading of this source as well. See Halbertal, *The Birth of Doubt*, 171–203.

Currently, in my corners of the trans community, it is more common to encounter the singular "they" than ze/hir. Any perceived awkwardness in the singular "they" should, I hope, help to signal the awkwardness of discussing nonbinary embodiment in English. The drawback of translating the androgyne's gender as "they" is that it papers over the androcentrism of using male grammar as the default. Each solution is decidedly less than perfect. I discuss translation more fully in my article, "Translating the Human," 587–604.

61. Classically, the topic sentence would include the number of clauses to follow in order to aid memorization, although this is not the only list in the tannaitic corpus where the numbering is absent: See m. Shekalim 5:1 for an example of a historical list that is similarly unnumbered, and m. Shevi'it 9:1 for a list that lacks both a thesis statement and numbering. There is a recent dissertation on the list in the Mishnah. See Shasha, "The Forms and Functions of Lists in the Mishnah." Shasha divides lists into two—those that contain a caption, and those that do not, and analyzes both forms synchronically.

the legal traditions follow the structure of the introductory sentence and are arranged in four sections to demonstrate how the androgyne functions in four different ways—that is, like men, like women, like both, and like neither.

The androgyne functions as a man, for example, in that he becomes impure through seminal emissions, just as men do. Similarly, the androgyne must "marry rather than be married," as men must. This can be interpreted to mean that they may initiate a marriage contract with a woman (as men do) but may not be married (a phrase that is grammatically in the passive), as women are to a man. It would be difficult to formulate a more concise distillation of androcentrism and its connection to heterosexual rabbinic marriage law than that six-word sentence. Charlotte Fonrobert uses this legal ruling to point out that the rabbis are privileging the presence of a penis and indicating an overall preference for weighting the androgyne as male.[62] Sarra Lev, by contrast, has argued that the list is formulated to apply the stringencies of both legal categories of male and female, and to prevent the greater problem posed by a union between two men, even at the risk of permitting the lesser problem of a union between two women.[63]

The list continues to spell out the ways in which the androgyne is like a woman: like a woman, she becomes impure through menstruation, and like a woman she is disqualified from serving as a legal witness.[64] Both the obligations and the exclusions that pertain to women are applied to the androgyne. In this way, some of the legal exclusions that the androgyne faces are based not on their status as an androgyne but on their status as potentially female. The androgyne is like women through both sharing the obligations of women and observing the exclusions that mark women as "not-men." A law stating that women and androgynes may not serve as legal witnesses only needs to be formulated in a context in which another group (men) can fulfill this role. The androgyne is therefore like women in that their legal subjectivity is curtailed.

The first half of the list may seem to be merely a prosaic discussion of the status of the androgyne in relation to specific laws, but at the same time the list incorpo-

---

62. On this phrase, "marries but is not married," see Fonrobert, "Regulating the Human Body," 281.

63. Sexual penetration between men is a capital offense. Therefore, this ruling can be said to avoid sexual penetration between a man and the potentially male androgyne. This would be similar to the logic of the koy list, which some have argued is applying the stringencies of both categories. See Sarra Lev, "Defying the Binary?" The fact that these laws value masculinity is a reflection of the broader situation in rabbinic law. The question of whether this specific tradition privileges the penis, or merely reflects the fact that the whole legal system does so, is not ultimately answerable.

64. Just as men become impure through "white" (seminal emissions), women become impure through "red" (menstrual blood). This constructs male and female bodies as analogous to one another. On the language in this section, see Y. N. Epstein, who argues that the specific formulation of obligation is only used when comparing a matter that is unclear to a matter that is clear and agreed on. See *M'vo'ot l'Sifrut haTanaim*, 220.

rates the androgyne into the law, thereby conferring legitimacy on them. If the ideal legal subject for the rabbis is the one with the most obligations, then, when the sages compare the androgyne to both men and women, they demonstrate the ways in which the androgyne has legal obligations as well as restrictions.[65] There may be some practical difficulties in the enactment of these restrictions; for example, according to the laws of seclusion (*yiḥud*), the androgyne is not permitted to be alone with either men or women—but there is an effort to establish the androgyne as a legal subject. The list implies that the androgyne has a place even within marriage laws. Other strains of rabbinic literature will work hard to undo this inclusion, but for the moment the overall impression of the list is that it weaves the androgyne into the fabric of rabbinic culture.

The third category appears to take the inclusion of the androgyne one step further. When the list asks how the androgyne is like both women and men, it suggests that there are laws that are not contingent on gender. So, for example:

> [How is the] androgyne like both men and women? [The person who injures the androgyne] is liable for injuring [the androgyne] as if [they had injured] either a man or a woman, the intentional murder of the androgyne [incurs the capital punishment] of decapitation [in the same way it would if a man or a woman was murdered], [and if the androgyne is murdered] accidentally, [the murderer must] exile themself to the cities of refuge.

If the androgyne is injured, their injury is treated like the injury of either a man or a woman. Their murder is treated in exactly the same way as the murder of a man or a woman; if it was a deliberate and premeditated murder, then the punishment is decapitation, one of the two crimes for which this is mandated. If the murder occurred by accident, then the biblical laws of the cities of refuge are invoked.[66]

The text continues to generate several more ways in which the androgyne functions as both men and women do; however, it is worth dwelling briefly on this category itself. If the overall goal of the list has been to understand androgynes within the context of gendered law, why include a section on androgynes in ungendered law? Is there an actual legal question as to whether the androgyne's death should be treated like any other human death? This section seems, on the face of it, utterly unnecessary. It appears to exist solely to challenge binary gender in law, as suggested by the first two sections of the list. If we are looking for a statement that pushes back against binary categories of gender, then this entire section of the list performs that work.

---

65. Feminist scholars have demonstrated that being exempted from legal obligation is a detriment in the rabbinic system of law. See, for example, Biale, *Women in Jewish Law*, 10–44.

66. For the rabbinic assignments of punishment to murderers, see Steinmetz, *Punishment and Freedom*, 53–68.

There is a similar problem with the category of "both" on the hybrid animal list. For example, the hybrid animal is like both wild and domesticated animals in that you cannot consume its limbs while it is still alive. The law stating that one cannot consume the limb of animal, which originates in the Bible, applies to all animals. Given that, one might question why the list feels the need to state this prohibition in relation to the hybrid animal. Just as the murder of an androgyne seems to obviously be murder, is not the torture of an animal still obviously torture? This ruling, on the face of it, is redundant.

Ironically, this statement about protecting an animal from torture also highlights the many other kinds of licit violence that structure the hybrid animal list. The list of laws that apply either only to wild animals addresses a host of legal issues, including the covering of the hybrid animal's (spilled) blood, the rules of its slaughter, and which sections of the animal's body may and may not be consumed. While the specter of violence is present in both the androgyne and the hybrid animal list, violence in relation to the hybrid animal is mostly sanctioned. Only suffering that is unnecessary for the human use of the animal is disallowed. Animality, broadly speaking, incurs vulnerability to sacrifice, consumption, and enslavement by humans.

In the case of the androgyne, the redundancy of being like "both" men and women also asks us to think about the gendered effects of this category. If being "both" creates a list of laws that transcend gender, then perhaps this allows a concept of humanness, independent of gender, to begin to emerge. It is tempting to conceptualize these statements, particularly the ones touching on such topics as injury and murder, as recognizing the "human rights" of the androgyne. With their application to the androgyne, the category seems to require the law to address the androgyne's (human) suffering.[67] Perhaps, then, suffering transcends not only the gender binary but the boundaries between animals and humans.

In his monograph *Habeus Viscus,* Alexander Weheliye explores the constitution of the category of the human through the lens of Black feminist thought. He writes the following about human rights laws: "Frequently, suffering becomes the defining feature of those subjects excluded from the law . . . due to the political violence inflicted upon them, even as it, paradoxically, grants them access to inclusion and equality."[68] Weheliye critiques a frame that adjudicates access to human rights through a comparison of suffering in order to evaluate whose suffering requires recognition and necessitates sanctuary. In this analysis, humanity is bought at the cost of violence. At the same time, this access to the category of

---

67. Charlotte Fonrobert makes the point that this category establishes the androgyne as human. See Fonrobert, "The Semiotics of the Sexed Body," 69–96.

68. Weheliye, *Habeas Viscus,* 75–76.

humanity does not trouble the basic (racist and sexist) terms of the human. The human, as a category, is built on a foundation of anti-Blackness.

The concept of rights-based legal thinking is not the primary framework of rabbinic legal discourse. The focus of these legal traditions is on the obligation of the person who harms the androgyne, not on the rights of the androgyne per se, for example.[69] However, it is worth noting that the androgyne functions legally as a human uniquely through their injury or death. For those clauses, it is through suffering that the androgyne becomes a legible human under the law. Similarly, the hybrid animal becomes an animal through the statement that torture is not allowable. Acknowledging the category of the animal means recognizing the pain of animals. Becoming human, as well, may come both posthumously and as the result of violence.

My intention here is not to analogize the androgyne and anti-Blackness but rather to learn from Black feminist theory in order to interrogate the mechanisms of imagining the category of the human. Despite the fact that the injury of the androgyne would seem to pose a concept of "universal" human rights that transcends binary gender, this category of "both" is still framed through the poles of gender dichotomy. To belong, the androgyne must be like men and women. The gendered terms of the human are not fundamentally challenged by the inclusion of the androgyne.

The final section of the androgyne list details the ways in which the androgyne is not like either men or women. For example, if someone makes a vow that they will undertake certain personal restrictions if the androgyne is neither a man nor a woman, the vow is valid.[70] This, too, appears as a parallel clause in the hybrid animal list. The vow is not a statement of self-identification: a non-androgyne is making the vow over the androgyne or the hybrid animal. In other words, a third party who makes a truth claim about the androgyne's or koy's hybrid status is deemed to have made a valid statement. This puts the androgyne into a passive role shared with the hybrid animal. At the same time, however, it also crucially suggests that inclusion in the category of human or animal does not depend on complete disambiguation. For this moment of the list, binaries are discarded. To the degree that the vow foregrounds the question of the status of the koy or the

---

69. For a discussion of the frame of "rights" and how it plays out in relation to transgender communities, see Currah, Juang, and Minter, eds., *Transgender Rights*, xiii–xxiv.

70. Although I am translating using the Vienna manuscript (following Lieberman) I chose examples that appear in both versions of the list. Both versions also specify that a person making a Nazirite vow based on the status of an androgyne has made a valid vow. See Lieberman, *Tosefta Kifshuta*, 835. There Lieberman explains the complications around the language of vows and the formulation in the koy list. The law about the koy and Nazirite vows can be found in m. Nazir 5:7. On the text of the koy Nazirite vow, see Frankel, *Darchei HaMishnah*, 253. On the androgyne and Nazirite vows, see m. Nazir 2:7 and t. Nazir 3:19. For a discussion of the androgyne and vows, see Kessler, "Rabbinic Gender," 353–70.

androgyne, it is an instance where the rabbis also touch on larger definitional questions. In the next section I will begin to explore some of these broader ontological questions about gender in halakhah.

"A UNIQUE CREATION": THE ONTOLOGY OF GENDER IN RABBINIC LAW

Jacob Neusner, in his provocatively titled book *How the Rabbis Liberated Women*, argues apologetically in support of rabbinic gender politics:

> The rabbis of late antiquity, founders of Judaism as we know it ... liberated Israelite women by according to them what Scripture had denied.... Women were not only chattel, talking cows, animate sofas, as some have maintained.[71]

Neusner contends that the rabbis liberated women by undoing the misogyny of earlier biblical traditions.[72] He ends the passage by rejecting an analogy between women and chattel—an oblique reference to Judith Romney Wegner's scholarship.[73]

When Neusner dismisses Wegner's equation between women and chattel, he rejects images of women as "talking cows" or "animate sofas" as patently absurd. For Neusner, it is impossible for women to be relegated to the status of barnyard animals: women speak.[74] It is perhaps banal to observe that women do not, in fact, speak in most early rabbinic literature; at the same time there are numerous examples of talking animals in both biblical and rabbinic sources.[75] The image of women

---

71. Neusner, *How the Rabbis Liberated Women*, vii. To be fair, Neusner also acknowledges that the rabbis were not feminists by our contemporary standards.

72. Interestingly, Neusner argues that the liberation of women is primarily apparent in the rabbinic legal system; most feminist scholars have tended to read the genre of law as oppressive toward women. See, for example, Baskin, *Midrashic Women*, 6–8. For Neusner's more measured approach to the question of the status of women in rabbinic law, see Neusner, *A History of the Mishnaic Law of Women*. Judith Hauptman, in reference to this volume, argues, "There is no question that the individual who laid the foundation for feminist readings of rabbinic texts is Jacob Neusner" (Hauptman, "Feminist Perspectives on Rabbinic Texts," 43). While Neusner's scholarship is important, Hauptman's work is equally crucial, along with other feminist literature in rabbinics.

73. Wegner, *Chattel or Person?* Broadly, Wegner concludes that the rabbis sometimes treat women as chattel and sometimes as persons (almost) equivalent to men.

74. The body of literature on the question of what divides human and nonhuman animals is too extensive to cite succinctly. Brian Massumi helpfully proposes six theses that should be avoided, the very first of which is the assumption that it is simple to distinguish between human and nonhuman animals, and that language is what divides us. See Massumi, *What Animals Teach Us*, 91–98.

75. The most famous example of a talking animal is Balaam's donkey (Numbers 22:21–33), a story that the rabbis explore. The rabbis also debate whether idolaters fit into the category of "adam"— humans. This is usually in the context of an exegetical exercise, such as in b. Keritot 6b, where the word *adam* is used specifically to exclude idolaters and animals. For a discussion of the ways inanimate objects function in the discursive construction of the body, see Balberg, *Purity*,

as sofas created to be sat on is a vivid materialization of relations of power, but it also transgresses the boundary between animate and inanimate objects.[76]

From the standpoint of contemporary theoretical literature, however, both the animacy of objects and the relationship between humans and animals are unsettled territory.[77] The philosopher Talia Mae Bettcher has touched on questions of animacy in her response to "gender critical" philosophers who claim (among other things) that trans women do not exist. In her article "When Tables Speak," Bettcher argues that philosophizing about whether tables actually exist is a fundamentally different activity from philosophizing about whether trans women exist. She asserts that trans women should not be treated as tables, rejecting the analogy between the two. However, Bettcher continues: "When we battered tables show up and start philosophizing, only to find these same erasures and invalidations perpetuated in a philosophical context, we can become more than a little upset. . . ."[78] In this passage, Bettcher points out that even after trans women are able to enter into the conversation, philosophical gatekeepers require proof of existence. At the same time, she identifies trans women collectively with battered tables. When she links trans women and tables, tables develop both animacy and affect: they "show up" and "become upset." It is the frame of battering that conditions the connection between tables and trans women: both are philosophical and material beings that have been abused.

The point I am making is not (just) a critique of Neusner's image of the rabbis as the liberators of women, although it is worth noting that he has implicitly constructed a genealogy of women's liberation without women. Rather, I want to turn away from adjudicating between liberation and chattel/animals, and instead focus our attention on the questions of ontology that undergird both. I have argued so far that the androgyne and hybrid animal primarily seem to explore the binary nature of gender and animality in rabbinic legal sources. In this section, I will argue instead that the androgyne and the koy establish gender and animality respectively, as legal categories per se. It is in the context of gendered sofas, chat-

---

Body, and Self, 74–95. For a discussion of the constitution of the category of the human in rabbinic literature, see Wasserman, *Jews, Gentiles, and Other Animals.*

76. There is a broad field of theoretical literature on questions of animacy and materiality. See, for example, Benett, *Vibrant Matter.*

77. The analogy to an animate sofa reminds me of Mel Chen's work. Describing their relations with their couch during chronic illness and chemical injuries, Chen invites us to consider what is at stake in the established boundaries of animacy, in a context where language marks some groups of people as less animate than others. See Chen, *Animacies,* 223–38. On the related question of necropolitics, see also Snorton and Haritaworn, "Trans Necropolitics," 66–76.

78. Bettcher, "When Tables Speak." See also Sara Ahmed's phenomenological exploration of tables in which she draws on Edmund Husserl's table to unpack the concept of orientation. See Ahmed, *Queer Phenomenology.*

tering cows, and trans women as abused philosophical objects, that I wish to conclude my discussion of hybrid human and animal lists in Bikkurim.[79]

. . .

If the strategy of the list in Bikkurim is generally to incorporate hybrid bodies into law, then the coda takes a decidedly different approach. It is in the coda that we find the first attributed statement, "Rabbi Yose disagrees:[80] The androgyne is a unique creation and the sages could not decide about them[81] whether he is a man or she is a woman."[82] In other words, Rabbi Yose differs from the strategy of the list, which incorporates androgynes into a binary set of legal choices. As Rabbi Yose sees it, to allow the androgyne to participate in rabbinic obligations, the sages would have had to designate them as either a man or a woman. As is made clear by the ways in which the androgyne is like both men and women, the sages did not assign them one legal gender. For Rabbi Yose, the implication of this "failure" is

79. Here I am discussing the question of an ontology of gender. For the androgyne list, there is some indication that there is a separation between anatomy and gendered roles, as sexed variation is acknowledged, albeit within the confines of negotiating halakhic obligation and social roles. In later rabbinic texts, there are instances where we might broadly separate out some concept of sex and gender. See Neis, *The Sense of Sight in Rabbinic Culture*, especially chapter 4. But there are also sources in the literature that manifestly do not make those types of distinctions as well, as we shall see in the rest of this book.

80. The Vienna printed edition and the Berlin Staatsbibliothek fol. 1220 both list Rabbi Yose; Zuckermandel's edition also lists Rabbi Yose (using the Erfurt manuscript). See Zuckermandel, *Tosefta*. In the Parma manuscript of the Mishnah (Biblioteca Palatina De Rossi 138), however, this statement is attributed to Rabbi Meir. The Parma manuscript for the koy list also lacks the final statement, so there is no comparable statement to assess attribution. I will use Rabbi Yose here, but I remain agnostic about the question of the proper attribution of this tradition. Other scholars (who argue against Lieberman that these lists should be attributed to the Mishnah) also tend to attribute this statement to Rabbi Meir. In addition to the manuscripts I have already cited in the previous footnotes, there are two geniza fragments of Mishnah Bikkurim that contain the end of the koy list (and lack the final statement by Rabbi Yose/Rabbi Meir). See Israel Yeivin's reproduction of the geniza fragments in the Cambridge University library: Yeivin, *Osef Kit'ei Ha-Genizah shel ha-Mishnah be-nikud Bavli*, 92, 144.

81. Literally "him" but I am translating this pronoun as "them" because this statement is a strikingly clear example of how grammar hinders the ability to express gendered indeterminacy in Hebrew, even when that indeterminacy is the subject of the discussion.

82. The ending of the coda reads as follows: "But the tumtum is different; they are either a doubtful man or a doubtful woman." The tumtum falls into a liminal category of doubt. Rabbi Yose places the androginos and the tumtum in tension with one another. I will discuss the tumtum in greater depth in later chapters. I am simplifying for nonspecialists by not introducing the category here. The concept of doubt is fairly ubiquitous in tannaitic law. Doubt can be used to test whether an action has taken place—see, for example, doubtful marriage or a doubtful divorce in m. Yevamot 3:8. The tractate Demai discusses produce that may not have been properly tithed. See Rosen-Zvi, "Usual Suspects," 117–27. The word that our text uses for doubt (safek) is common in tannaitic sources. On doubt in tannaitic literature more generally, and for a reading of the status of doubt in this text more specifically, see Halbertal, *The Birth of Doubt*, 171–203.

that the androgyne must be excluded; this final statement opposes the work of carefully fitting the androgyne into gendered laws.

And yet, paradoxically, while Rabbi Yose seeks to exclude the androgyne from the rabbinic enterprise, he also establishes a space for the androgyne as a "unique creation." Scholars and activists have read Rabbi Yose's refusal to assimilate the androgyne as carving a space for the existence of nonbinary people.[83] Rabbi Yose's rejection of the androgyne in halakhah is also an acknowledgement that gender exceeds a binary. In that sense, Rabbi Yose, who has the final word, radically subverts binary gender. I am not opposed to that interpretation of the coda to the list, particularly when activists use it as an argument against contemporary transphobia within Judaism; I am not particularly interested in policing the meaning of this list. I do, however, worry about the cost of reading subversion here. To acknowledge the androgyne as unique but unassimilable into social structures (governed by law, custom, and ritual) is to put them into a precarious social position indeed.[84] I have no wish to buy queer subversion using androgynes as currency. I remain mindful of misused philosophical objects and battered tables, even as I am aware of the ways in which Rabbi Yose's statement asserts that the androgyne is both nonbinary and created by God. I shall explore the ways Rabbi Yose's statement implicitly cites the Genesis story shortly.

Even though most scholars interpret the list and the coda by Rabbi Yose as diametrically opposed, there is another way to understand the relationship between the two; read in a certain light, the list and the coda collude with each other.[85] It is true that the two approaches have very different effects for the androgyne. Still, both the list and Rabbi Yose mark gender as central to halakhah. The framers of the list see gender as a crucial organizing principle for law and generally assimilate the androgyne into that structure, even if the structure includes nonbinary space. For Rabbi Yose, on the other hand, gender is so essential to the rabbinic legal project that the androgyne cannot fit within it.

The apparent challenge posed by hybrid gender and hybrid animality obscures the reification of the categories of gender and domestication. The androgyne and

---

83. Kessler, "Rabbinic Gender," 353–71. Kessler also points out that Rabbi Yose's statement and not the list has staying power in rabbinic literature.

84. There is power in monstrousness. At the same time, I am thinking in particular of some of the darker sides of monstrousness, such as the death of Filisa Vistima. See Susan Stryker, "My Words to Victor Frankenstein," 237–54.

85. Fonrobert, for example, sees them as opposed. In her brilliant reading, she argues that while the list may function as a project of inclusion, it is in fact a demonstration of the discursive strength and flexibility of law. Rabbinic authority is propped up by its ability to incorporate all cases, even the "extreme" hybridity of the androgyne. Fonrobert, "Semiotics of the Sexed Body," 79–105, and Fonrobert, "Regulating the Human Body," 270–94. See also Fonrobert, "Gender Duality and Its Subversions in Rabbinic Law," 106–25.

hybrid animal are not disambiguated per se; on the contrary, their incomplete exclusion from halakhah means that they will haunt rabbinic debates for centuries to come. But they are domesticated. The cementing of ontologies of gender and domestication is one of the foundations for the regulation of women, androgynes, and animals in halakhah. This tradition in Bikkurim, therefore, is not merely a *reflection* of the gendered nature of rabbinic law. Rather, it can be understood as a foundational moment in *establishing* gender as central to halakhah.

At the same time, the coda of the hybrid animal and androgyne lists connects both as uniquely created beings.[86] This category of "created beings" encompasses both humans and animals and thus enacts a kind of union between them. This union papers over the violence that inheres in the category of animal; it is a kind of limited connection between those who test the boundaries of taxonomy. Albeit unwittingly, Rabbi Yose has created potential allies in the androgyne and the koy. I will continue to imagine this connection between androgynes and animals in the next chapter; for now, however, I want to explore the contemporary reach toward Genesis in anti-trans laws. Rabbi Yose and contemporary evangelical anti-trans theology read the creation story with very different interpretations. As such, conservative evangelical theologians who claim anti-trans theologies are based on "biblical gender" are in fact privileging a very specific contemporary understanding of the verses.

THE GENESIS OF TRANSPHOBIA

We have seen the widespread invocation of androgynes in creation stories that circulated in antiquity. Creation stories remain surprisingly relevant in contemporary legal battles over trans embodiment as well. Legal advocacy groups turn to Genesis to frame their contemporary regulatory efforts. The Alliance Defending Freedom, a conservative evangelical legal group, has as one of its central doctrines the following statement: "We believe God creates each person with an immutable biological sex—male or female—that reflects the image and likeness of God."[87] This is a direct reference to Genesis 1:27: "And God created man in God's own image, in the image of God, God created him, male and female God created them."[88] Some strains of

---

86. As I discuss in earlier footnotes, it is true that the koy list in some recensions lacks the coda. The versions that do have it, however, suggest an implicit connection between the androgyne and the koy, an impression that is only strengthened by all the parallels between the lists.

87. See "Alliance Defending Freedom Statement of Faith," Alliance Defending Freedom, accessed September 28, 2021, https://www.adflegal.org/about-us/careers/statement-of-faith. In the time period during which I was preparing this manuscript, the statement of faith for the ADF changed to include this language, perhaps signaling a greater focus on trans issues.

88. I have used the JPS translation of the Hebrew Bible throughout as the base of any English translation of biblical verses. The JPS translation of this verse reads: "And God created man in His image, in

rabbinic exegesis read Genesis 1:27 as the creation of an androgyne, as we have seen. The rabbis interpret the oddities of the grammar and syntax as a reference to an androgyne creation.

For contemporary Christian evangelicals, however, this same verse refers to God's creation of biological (and immutable) sex.[89] In other words, for conservative Christian theologies, Genesis is frequently the proof text for the impossibility of transsexuality. In response to these evangelical readings of Genesis, there has been a concurrent increase in popular and scholarly interest in trans theologies that counter these invocations of the Bible.[90]

The formulation of the 2018 Health and Human Services memo (with which I began this chapter) is a variation of the language found in the so-called "bathroom bills"—bills that seek to regulate trans access to many public facilities. I want to read closely the language of one of these laws, Mississippi HB 1523, called the Religious Liberty Accommodations Act.[91] This law is just one of a slew of proposed bills that focus on bathrooms in the continuation of the history of white suprema-

---

the image of God He created him; male and female He created them." In this case I changed the translation to omit the gender of God.

89. The question of why evangelicals are turning to Genesis in particular, as opposed, for example, to Deuteronomy 22:5 or reinterpreting the first chapter of Romans exceeds the scope of my discussion here. But it is not just the ADF or legal advocacy groups that attempt to ground their transphobic arguments in Genesis. See also "Transgenderism—Our Position," Focus on the Family, February 1, 2018, https://www.focusonthefamily.com/get-help/transgenderism-our-position/. I suspect that the contemporary focus on Genesis is related to complementarianism. Theorists in intersex studies have argued that complementarian theologies have profoundly impacted intersex people, for example. For two responses from intersex studies, see Cornwall, *Sex and Uncertainty in the Body of Christ*; and DeFranza, *Sex Difference in Christian Theology*. Leah DeVun gives a history of the reception of Genesis in the medieval period, during which Christian authors began to use Genesis to reject the idea that the original human was an androgyne. DeVun cites theologians like Thomas Aquinas who eliminated the originary androgyne theory. See DeVun, *The Shape of Sex*, 16–40.

90. In addition to the works I have already cited in the notes, here is a sampling of recent English-language books that focus primarily on Christianity in the United States and Europe: Paige, *OtherWise Christian*; Beardsley and O'Brien, eds., *This is My Body*; Harke, *Transforming*. There has been more published on trans theology in the last five years than in the entire twenty years before that.

91. Gayle Salamon has crucially explored transphobia in her book *The Life and Death of Latisha King*. In the book, she argues that Latisha King's gender expression is read as a provocation that justifies her murder. Salamon's work is insightful in the mechanisms of transphobia.

The subset of bills addressing access to public facilities for trans people has been popularly dubbed "bathroom bills"—I call them anti-trans bills. In fact, the media's anxieties focus specifically on women's restrooms, which tend to have stalls with doors, unlike many locker rooms, changing rooms, or men's bathrooms. Transmisogyny plays a role in this emphasis on women's bathrooms. See Schilt and Westbrook, "Bathroom Battlegrounds," 26–31. For innovative new bathroom designs that address transphobia, see Sanders and Stryker, "Stalled: Gender-Neutral Public Bathrooms," 779–88. For a critique of the way the media has been focused on bathrooms, instead of how these laws are dispossessing trans people, see Snorton, *Black on Both Sides*, vii–xiv.

cist regulation of restrooms.[92] These anti-trans laws are intertwined with extralegal efforts to regulate trans embodiment, including the deadly pattern of violence directed primarily at Black trans women and trans women of color, as well as the array of "administrative violence" (as Dean Spade has termed it) that trans people experience routinely.[93]

After a preliminary injunction was overturned, HB 1523 became the law in the state of Mississippi.[94] The text of the law purports to protect individuals and organizations that discriminate against LGBTQ people on the basis of "sincerely held religious beliefs or moral convictions." The opening clauses define what specific religious beliefs are protected as state-sanctioned grounds for legal discrimination. The first two protected religious beliefs are:

(a) Marriage is or should be recognized as the union of one man and one woman;
(b) Sexual relations are properly reserved to such a marriage

Within the context of this law, religious belief is defined as a conviction that marriage is necessarily both heterosexual and monogamous. The choice of the words *is* or *should be* in the first clause evokes a wish to reframe heterosexual marriage, even as the law protects a belief in that reframing. The gap between "is" and "should be" points to a gap between the ideal and reality.[95] Similarly, the language that sex should be "properly reserved" to marriage gestures toward a gap between this ideal and the fact that ("improper") sex outside of marriage is widely practiced.

---

92. The tactic of referring to them as "bathroom" bills is designed to play off a long history of white supremacist regulation of the space of bathrooms, which "protects" certain classes of white women. Whether white supremacists were invoking the anti-Black specter of sexual predation or constructing certain racialized bodies as conduits of sexually transmitted infections, the contemporary regulation of public facilities along ableist, racialized, and gendered lines has a long history in the United States. Sheila Cavanagh argues that the whiteness of bathroom porcelain is significant, and renders a kind of white, able-bodied, straight space. Hygiene (associated with the whiteness of porcelain) itself is connected to a history of state-sanctioned violence against racialized and disabled bodies. See Cavanagh, "Gender, Sexuality, Race in the Lacanian Mirror," 323–39.

93. Dean Spade, *Normal Life*.

94. As I write, HB 1523 is still the law of the land. The American Civil Liberties Union of Mississippi, Lambda Legal, and the Mississippi Center for Justice have asked potential plaintiffs to contact them in order to mount a challenge to the law.

95. This gap is, in part, temporal, even though it is not clear whether the orientation is toward the future or the past; it could be read as nostalgia for heterosexual-monogamous marriage in the past, with a tacit reference to Obergefell v. Hodges, the Supreme Court decision that rendered gay marriage legal. Judge Carlton Reeves, in the preliminary injunction that initially blocked the law, reads it as a response to gay marriage victories in court. See Barber v. Bryant, 193 F. Supp. 3d 677 (S.D. Miss. 2016), *reversed*, 860 F.3d 345 (5th Cir. 2017).

In this section of the bill, in other words, religious beliefs are counterfactual. A different social order hovers just beneath the surface of (an imagined) secular societal reality. The counterfactual nature of these beliefs constitutes an implicit argument for their legal protection.[96] Presumably, if the framers of the bill felt that their world more closely resembled this religious social order, these beliefs would not require legal protections.

The third clause in the bill functions differently from the first two clauses on marriage and sex. It reads:

> (c) Male (man) or female (woman) refer to an individual's immutable biological sex as objectively determined by anatomy and genetics at time of birth.[97]

If marriage is the union between one man and one woman, only certain men and women qualify. The pairing between heterosexual monogamy and binary gender is not accidental. The regulation of sexed embodiment is necessitated by a complementarian theology, according to which the creation of Adam and Eve is the genesis of the gender binary, as God creates two sexes that are counterparts in marriage. In the service of heterosexuality, the regulation of sexuality and gender identity must go hand in hand. Thus, the inclusion of the third clause seems to function as a corollary to the establishment of heterosexual monogamy. The fact that the regulation of gender appears to be a secondary effect of the desire to regulate marriage does not, it should be noted, protect trans people from the impact of this law.

The third clause asserts that both sex and gender identity are assigned at birth. Let us pass over the notion that anatomy and genetics always align, a point many intersex activists would take issue with.[98] The language of biology and genetic

---

96. The gap might also be read as aspirational: a religious striving to reorient the country toward a better—i.e., hetero-monogamous—future. I am arguing here that the (secular) social reality to which the bill responds is also imagined, a part of a US white evangelical narrative of secular/sexual social decay. See, for example, Sara Moslener's work on the growth of the youth abstinence movement in the 1990s, which harnessed white supremacist (and anti-Black) sentiment about out-of-wedlock birth rates and the decline of the white family to fund Republican/Christian abstinence-only education (Moslener, *Virgin Nation*, 109–30). This entire line of argumentation is also greatly influenced by the work of Ann Pellegrini and Janet Jakobsen. See Pellegrini and Jakobsen, *Love the Sin*.

97. The resonance of this language with the definition of sex proposed in the 2018 memo from the US Department of Health and Human Services should be obvious. This language comes almost directly from a proposed school policy on bathrooms that the Alliance Defending Freedom (ADF) sent to school boards across the country. The ADF has targeted particular school districts by offering free legal counsel for any district sued because of this policy. See Michaels, "We Tracked Down the Lawyers."

98. For the earlier history of the Religious Liberty Protection Act, see Feldblum, "Rectifying the Tilt," 159–95. For a discussion of the earlier tendency of the court to move away from a reliance on birth sex and chromosomes, see A. Sharpe, *Transgender Jurisprudence*. Demoya Gordon, a lawyer from Lambda Legal who worked on the challenge to HB2 in North Carolina, has said that the argument

testing also introduces the question of science and medicine into a law designed to protect and define religious belief. Medicine and religion collude to determine the immutable truth of sex at birth.[99] When the law entwines the scientific and the theological, it conspires to naturalize a divinely ordained gender binary. According to state law in Mississippi, science and God do not believe in transsexuals. Put another way, the state of Mississippi protects the belief that gay and nonmarital sex *should not* exist. At the same time, the state also affirms the conviction that transsexuals *do not* exist, in essence legislating that nonexistence.[100] In this way, imagining religious freedom impacts trans and queer bodies differently.

Trans studies theorist Eva Hayward takes up this question of gendered ontology. Citing the actress and activist Laverne Cox, Hayward notes the way trans women are commanded, "Don't exist." One way to combat the murderous imperative of this erasure might be to insist on the humanity of trans women of color. Drawing on Black feminist theory, Hayward rejects this strategy and argues that any attempt to revise the category of the human is compromised by the foundational anti-Black and misogynist logic that animates the category (as we have also seen earlier in this chapter in the case of Weheliye's argument). Instead, she urges us to push against ontology itself: ontology is the ultimate architect of the mandate to trans women of color: "Don't exist."[101]

The gendered theology of HB 1523 (a mandate disguised as a belief) is the ontological scaffolding for the dictate to trans women: "Don't exist." In consequence, as the rest of the law goes on to describe, discrimination (in particular the refusal of services) is transubstantiated. The bill transforms anti-trans discrimination into the material instantiation of a protected religious belief that trans people are an

---

about the challenges of single-sexed spaces for intersex people has in the past been successful only in getting specific exemptions written into the bill for intersex people while retaining the penalties for others. See Gordon and Rasdall, "Stalled Progress."

99. Secularism and the connection between religious freedom and both sex and gender are the subjects of prolific scholarship. For an important anthology that touches on many of these themes, see Sullivan, Hurd, and Mahmood, eds. *The Politics of Religious Freedom*. Talal Asad argues that the constitution of the political and religious is far more complex than simplistic narratives of the secular/religious divide would indicate. See Asad, *Formations of the Secular*. See also Joan Wallach Scott, "Sexularism."

100. I am specifically discussing a US political context here. The relationship between science, transsexual embodiment, law, and religion will look different in other times and places. For an excellent analysis of the imbrication of religion, science, and the state in the Iranian context, see Najmabadi, *Professing Selves*.

101. Eva Hayward, "Don't Exist," 191–94. Hayward also dwells briefly on Genesis specifically in her article, "Transxenoestrogenesis," 255–58. In that piece, she addresses the environmental effects of the production of Premarin for hormone therapies for trans women.

In the context of intersex studies, the mandate, "Don't exist," functions differently. Intersex activists resist the mythologization of their bodies, including in the persistence of the term "hermaphrodite" (an amalgam of Hermes and Aphrodite) as a tactic of writing intersex bodies out of existence.

impossibility. This bill manifests a religious belief in immutable sex, and it thereby closes the gap between religious ideals and gendered mores. One who does not exist cannot experience discrimination.

I want to return to these questions of Genesis, ontology, and gender in rabbinic literature, specifically the coda to the list—namely, the statement by Rabbi Yose that the androgyne is a "unique being." Like Mississippi anti-trans law, this coda also contains an oblique reference to Genesis. The phrase I translated as "The androgyne is a unique creation" uses a noun form of the root word for the verb "to create" found in the very first verse of the Hebrew Bible: "In the beginning, God created the heavens and the earth."[102] The citation of the word *create*, coupled with the narratives that circulate widely throughout late antiquity about androgyne creations, brings to mind Genesis. If this is indeed an oblique reference to Genesis, then although Rabbi Yose is ejecting the androgyne from halakhah, he is also explicitly associating the androgyne with the order of creation. In other words, the androgyne is created by God. This inclusion, despite the legal exclusions that accompany it, contributes to making this tradition so attractive to contemporary trans and intersex Jewish activists. In the face of contemporary erasures of trans people from Judaism, activists point to a source that demonstrates that people who do not fit easily within the bounds of gender binaries were created by God. Whatever else Rabbi Yose's statement accomplishes, it is also a powerful theological assertion.

At the same time, I have also argued that the list/coda is invested in domesticating the androgyne and hybrid animal, and that it establishes an ontology of gender in law. If Eva Hayward is right, and ontology is the ultimate author of the imperative to trans women of color, "Don't exist," then regardless of the way the source supports or undermines nonbinary embodiment, it colludes in the management of gender in law.

Still, unlike contemporary trans women of color, neither the tannaitic androgyne nor the hybrid animal is told, "Don't exist."[103] While the Bikkurim source is certainly

---

102. The phrase, a "unique creation," is quite rare in tannaitic literature. It occurs in this tradition and in t. Kil'ayim 1:9, where the rabbis discuss the status of several animals including the antelope from Deuteronomy 14:5. The root word for "creation" itself is not at all rare; in addition to Genesis Rabbah, which contains numerous usages (as we might expect from a commentary on Genesis), we see that the word has the meaning of God's creations—as, for example, b. Ḥullin 127a. Even outside the context of an exegesis on Genesis, therefore, this word most often is associated with God's creation (although not always). It can describe both humans and animals.

103. See also texts like t. Berakhot 6:3, which address the blessing recited over seeing an "unusual" creation. On this, see Belser, "Queering the Dissident Body," 161–82. These sources do not distinguish between the natural and the theological, and to be created by God renders the creation a part of the order of nature. This is decidedly different from the Greco-Roman philosophical tradition, which explicitly debates what is "against nature." On this category of "against nature" and its application to same-sex sexual acts, there is an extensive scholarship. See, for example, Dover, *Greek Homosexuality*, 60–80.

not utopian by any standards, it stands in marked contrast to contemporary receptions of Genesis. In the list and the coda, androgynes exist, even as they are used to negotiate their own status in law—even if there is a question about whether violence against them constitutes violence. Mississippi anti-trans law, on the other hand, understands Genesis to be the origin story of a cisgendered ontology.

TRANSING CREATION: AN ELEGY FOR THE HATERS

> ... you're as much a part of what people call nature as anyone else; only you're unexplained as yet—you've not got your niche in creation.
> RADCLYFFE HALL, *THE WELL OF LONELINESS*[104]

This pairing of the rabbis with a twenty-first-century law is certainly eccentric. It runs the danger of papering over the differences between these two texts, the first and foremost such difference being that *law* is a very imperfect translation of the word *halakhah*. The rabbis and the legislators in Mississippi are not participating in the same activity. Still, analyzing anti-trans law helps us to conceptualize the potential costs of abstract rabbinic debates over gendered ontology. At the same time, Bikkurim pushes back against the contemporary evangelical assertion that Genesis has always mandated the nonexistence of gender- and sex- marginalized people.

The many differences between the tannaitic androgyne and the life of a contemporary trans teen living in Mississippi may cause the reader to find the framing of the chapter too great of a conceptual leap. The thread between the two moments is tenuous, but I will insist on trying them together. I am connecting them not just because this is the political and social context in which I, as a trans Jew, write about gender in rabbinic sources; not just because activists, rabbis, and Jewish medical ethicists still draw on androgynes and eunuchs to answer contemporary questions; not just to convey a sense of urgency and weight in an abstract debate over the status of the androgyne in law; and not just to get the reader's attention.

Why, then, do I insist on framing my discussion this way?

Perhaps it is simply this, my response to the perennial dilemma from Boswell on: we have collectively insisted on creating a world in which religious transphobia is both timeless and eternal.[105] In other words, we have divinized transphobia and

---

104. Hall, *Well of Loneliness*, book 2, chapter 20, section 3. This is also cited by Halberstam in *Trans**: *A Quick and Quirky Account*, 3.

105. Boswell, *Christianity, Social Tolerance, and Homosexuality*. Boswell undermines the idea that Christianity was always intolerant toward homosexuality. In doing so, however, he also makes transhistorical connections between "homosexuality" in the past and the present. Even so, his work was an influence on Foucault (despite the fact that scholars often position them as opposed to each other). As a sidenote, in his introduction, Boswell also draws interesting analogies between Jews and homosexuals that deserve further unpacking.

given it power over creation itself. If transphobia is our creator God, then we have already imagined an unchanging link between the present and the past. Some of us may be forced to live more fully within the bounds of these murderous ontologies. I therefore claim, for both myself and my kin, the use of any and all anachronisms, close readings, and fanciful-if-tenuous-connections available to disrupt and imagine otherwise.[106]

---

106. See *Imagine Otherwise*, a podcast that features the work of artists and activist academics and asks them how they imagine the world otherwise (Hannabach, *Imagine Otherwise*). I am also thinking of Cypress Amber Reign's mobile museum. See Cypress Amber Reign, "The Justice Fleet."

3

Sex with Androgynes

Cosmetic surgeries designed to normalize the genitalia of intersex infants are still commonly practiced within the United States. In recent years, intersex activists have made inroads in the fight against these surgeries. In 2020, after an intense effort by the Intersex Justice Project (partnered with other activist organizations), Lurie Children's Hospital apologized for performing surgeries on infants and pledged to stop the practice in the future.[1] One of the cofounders of the Intersex Justice Project, Pidgeon Pagonis, was operated on at Lurie as a child, and they have written about the harm that resulted from "fixing" their sex. In a statement that centers BIPOC intersex experiences, Pidgeon Pagonis and Sean Saifa Wall called for a halt to surgery, the hiring of intersex staff, and reparations for those that underwent nonconsensual surgeries as children.

Intersex Justice Project partnered with the organization interACT, an intersex youth advocacy organization, in the struggle with Lurie. InterACT has a history of opposing cosmetic genital surgeries; they were party to one of the first suits against a hospital for performing surgery. A child, named M. C. in the suit, was diagnosed as a toddler with an intersex condition. While he was a ward of the state, M. C.'s doctors assigned him as female and urged cosmetic surgery. In 2006—ironically,

---

1. Intersex Justice Project calls for reparations in the form of free and intersex-centered health care, and for congenital adrenal hyperplasia (CAH) to be included on the list of intersex "conditions" that will no longer be treated through cosmetic surgery (Lurie wrote an exemption for CAH into their apology/policy.) The following blog post at the Intersex Justice Project's website explores this victory: See "Intersex Justice Project's Response to Lurie's Public Apology," Intersex Justice Project, July 29, 2020, http://www.intersexjusticeproject.org/blog.

the same year that saw the release of new medical standards of care for the treatment of intersexuality deemphasizing surgery—M. C. was operated on.[2] M. C. identifies as a boy, and was, as a result of the procedure, involuntarily sterilized. The state's sterilization of a Black intersex child builds on a long eugenic history of forced sterilization in the United States. For M. C., Pidgeon Pagonis, and other intersex activists who were forcibly assigned a sex as children, there has been some form of reckoning, but not true reparation.

In this chapter, I weave together contemporary medical attempts to (re)create intersex bodies with a talmudic discussion of androgynes and sex changes.[3] This *sugya* (unit of discussion in the Talmud), which begins on b. Yevamot 83b, explores the question of whether the sex of the androgyne can be fully disambiguated with surgery. This question of surgery is paired with a debate about whether anal sex with the androgyne transgresses the Levitical prohibition against "lying with a man." At the heart of various arguments over sex/gender, sexuality, and the androgyne is a tension over the fixity of sex played out over nonbinary bodies. Questions of disambiguation, or "fixing" sex, are fundamentally intertwined with the possibilities of sexed mutability.

The disambiguating surgeries practiced on M. C. and the disambiguating surgeries on the tumtum in rabbinic sources are not the same; the different context of these surgical practices matters. My intention is not to collapse the contemporary diagnostic and medical framework with the rabbis or to imply a similar orientation to sex-/gender-marginalized bodies. However, I connect the two frameworks in order to shape an understanding of what can be at stake in an abstract debate over sex/gender. We can measure cost literally: in the $440,000 structured settlement awarded as recompense for the forced sterilization of M. C. by the state.[4] But I will, in various ways, ask about the costs, to androgynes and other beings, of abstract debates about "fixing" sex. In this chapter, I trans the Talmud by attending to some of these unreckoned costs.[5]

---

2. M. C.'s biological mother was consulted before the surgery, and she agreed to sign permission forms. For the new standards of care, which represent the benefits of surgery more conservatively, see Lee et al., "Consensus Statement on the Management of Intersex Disorders," 488–500.

3. I want to note here the problematic character of using "transing" as a frame to discuss intersex surgeries. My intention is not to make the term "transing" function as a colonizing framework for intersex, nor to allow the word *queer* to encapsulate both. I am using "transing" as my overarching frame, and I also cite intersex activism and theorists in this and other chapters.

4. The Intersex Justice Project, which released a statement about M. C., identifies M. C. as a Black child. Most of the news stories about M. C. elide the question of his race. Jamie Lane notes that the stock photos used in news stories about M. C. are almost entirely white, prompting the question: Whose inviolable intersex body do we deem worth protecting? See Lane, "Reproducing Intersex Trouble."

5. I am inspired to consider the question of costs by the discussion in Runions, *How Hysterical*, 93–114.

THE TUMTUM OF BIRI: LEVIRATE MARRIAGE AND THE REPRODUCTION OF LINEAGE

The rabbinic discussion I analyze in this section primarily focuses on the tumtum, so I want to remind us briefly who the tumtum is.[6] The tumtum is a person who lacks sufficient signs to assign them to the category of male or female.[7] Sometimes, the tumtum is described as having a flap of skin covering their genitalia, which precludes the assignment of sex.[8] This flap of skin can tear or be deliberately opened, as we shall see. Rabbinic debates often treat the sex/gender of the tumtum as liminal, in that sex/gender may be revealed.

Narrative sources describe Abraham and Sarah, central biblical figures whose stories are found in Genesis, as *tumtumim*.[9] Playing with the theme of Sarah's infertility in Genesis, the rabbis describe the couple as ambiguously sexed. In this story, both characters spend most of their lives as tumtumim. We know from

---

6. I am going to select some highlights to focus on in my discussion of these final pages of the eighth chapter of Yevamot, rather than trying to explain some of the most technical sections of the sugya to a general audience. Much of the material I discuss is tannaitic in origin. Still, its arrangement by the creators of the sugya, whose focus is on sex and marriage, allows for extended contemplation of the sexuality of androgynes.

The sugya begins with a debate between Resh Lakish and Rabbi Yochanan. They discuss whether the marriage of the androgyne is impermissible ab initio or ex post facto. This question is layered with a discussion about the status of different types of priestly offerings. At stake is the androgyne's priestly rights, interpreted by playing rabbinically or biblically mandated sacrifices off against one another. This dispute has a parallel in the variant of our sugya that appears in the Palestinian Talmud. David Weiss-HaLivni discusses the ways that the Palestinian Talmud argumentation is more coherent in some sections. See Weiss-Halivni, *Mekorot U'Mesorot*.

7. Scholars have suggested two possible etymologies for the word *tumtum*. One comes from the word for "closed." Jastrow defines "tumtum" as a person whose genitals are "hidden or underdeveloped, one whose sex is unknown" (Jastrow, *A Dictionary of the Targumim*). I am grateful to Riki (Rivka) Bilboim for sharing her thoughts on the history of the development of the term in Modern Hebrew (where the concept of a closed head links the root of this noun to the meaning of "stupidity" in its current usage): Riki (Rivka) Bilboim, personal correspondence with author, April 29, 2014.

There is also, however, a possibility that the word may come from the Greek word ἀτόμως, which means "uncut" or "unmown." See Margalit, "Tumtum v'Androginos," 777–80. On the possible Greek derivation of tumtum, Margalit cites Benjamin Musaphia, a seventeenth-century Jewish doctor and scholar. See also Steinberg, *The Encyclopedia of Jewish Medical Ethics*, s.v. "Ambiguous Genitalia (Tumtum)." The entry on the tumtum cites the *Musaf HaArukh* directly, as well as the article by Margalit. The word ἀτόμως is found once in the Christian Bible, in 1 Corinthians 15:52. Translators of the word in that context usually render it in English as "an instant"—in other words an indivisible unit of time. On the use of ἀτόμως as a segment of matter that is so small that it cannot be divided, see Plutarch, *Lives: Phocion* III.5. On the use of ἀτόμως as indivisible, see Aristotle, *Metaphysics* 992a. I did not find the word used to refer to bodies.

8. There are also references to a tumtum whose testicles are visible but who has no visible penis. See b. Ḥagigah 4a.

9. See b. Yevamot 64a–b. For an excellent queer reading of this narrative, see Gwynn Kessler, "Bodies in Motion," 389–430.

Genesis that Sarah and Abraham eventually have children, so in that context, the story suggests that the tumtum may be able to reproduce.[10]

This debate about the tumtum and procreation comes within the context of a discussion of levirate marriage, so I will briefly review levirate marriage for nonspecialists. Levirate marriage occurs when a man dies childless, leaving no heirs to carry on his name. In order to give him heirs posthumously, his widow is obligated to marry her brother-in-law. Any children that result from the union of the widow and her dead husband's brother become the virtual offspring of the deceased husband, whose name is thus carried on. In other words, levirate marriage is a marriage contracted specifically for the purpose of reproduction.

It is in this context of a marriage, a marriage that is allowed only in order to create offspring, that the discussion about the tumtum arises. One can see why the rabbis might be interested in exploring the tumtum within the context of levirate marriage. If the tumtum's flap of skin is removed, perhaps the tumtum can reproduce. If the tumtum can reproduce, then they should be obligated to participate in levirate marriage.

The marriage of a widow to her dead husband's brother would normally be prohibited; it is allowed only when the dead husband did not leave behind heirs. Levirate marriage is therefore established through two replacements: the replacement of one brother for the other, and the exchange of an illicit for a licit sexual act.[11] It is, then, a queerly constituted relationship in which the dead procreate from beyond the grave.[12] If levirate marriage tenders different men's bodies as

---

10. To the best of my knowledge, there is no clear contemporaneous cognate for the tumtum. There are, however, some ancient records in the Near East that describe children born without genitalia. The Šumma Izbu contains the most complete record of "birth defects" from ancient Mesopotamia; this record is intended to help diviners prognosticate about anomalous births. The Šumma Izbu describes a child born without penis or testicles, and a child born without a vulva. There are sources that refer to men who lack secondary sex characteristics: "If the sack of his testicles is large but his testicles slither about (in it), he is close to being a woman" (Scurlock and Anderson, *Diagnoses in Assyrian and Babylonian Medicine*, 114). See also the Sumerian story of Enki and Ninmah, which contains the creation story of a person without genitalia. See Kağnici, "Insights from Sumerian Mythology," 429–50.

11. Dvora Weisberg argues that the position of women in the rabbinic version of levirate marriage is equivocal. Legally, the man makes or declines the union; however, Weisberg cites examples in the rabbinic corpus where women refuse to enter into a union or seek to dissolve it. In general it is accurate to call men the agents in levirate unions, as in other rabbinic forms of marriage. See Weisberg, *Levirate Marriage and the Family*, 123–66.

12. Dvora Weisberg's monograph *Levirate Marriage and the Family in Ancient Judaism* argues that the rabbis transformed the biblical model of the extended family into a nuclear family. In so doing, they rewrite the laws of levirate marriage to make it function similarly to regular marriage. According to Weisberg, the rabbis undertook to change levirate marriage in order to remedy built-in disincentives in inheritance laws that made levirate marriage an unattractive proposition. In doing so, however, they change some of the fundamental attributes of the institution. In this respect, Weisberg is arguing against Satlow. See Satlow, *Jewish Marriage in Antiquity*, 182–98.

equivalent to one another, then the rabbis ask whether the tumtum is an acceptable currency for exchange.

. . .

We tend to think of sexed surgeries as emerging in the twentieth century. In this discussion, the rabbis describe a surgical procedure that "reveals" the sex of the tumtum. This surgery is not intended to disambiguate the genitals of the tumtum; the genitals themselves are not shaped by the surgery; rather, the skin that obscures them is opened up. Still, the question of disambiguation arises when the rabbis ask whether the revelation of genitalia is enough to ascertain sex.

The discussion of the tumtum on b. Yevamot 83b begins as follows: "Rabbi Yehudah says: [In the case of a] tumtum [who has a flap of skin covering their genitalia: if that flap of skin] is torn open and [the tumtum is] found to be male, he should not perform the ritual to dissolve the obligation to levirate marriage, because he is like a eunuch" (m. Yevamot 8:6).[13] In this citation of the Mishnah, Rabbi Yehudah raises the question of the role of the tumtum in levirate marriage. In this case, the flap of skin covering the genitalia of the tumtum is torn open (or perhaps operated on), and their genitalia is revealed. From the evidence of the tumtum's genitalia, it is decided that the tumtum is male. If he is male, then he would be obligated to participate in levirate marriage like any other man; if he does not participate in levirate marriage, then he would have to perform the ritual to dissolve the obligation to marry his brother's widow. Instead, Rabbi Yehudah states that the tumtum, even if he appears to be male, is like a eunuch. Since the tumtum, like eunuchs, cannot reproduce, he is exempted from levirate marriage.[14]

On the surface, this is a straightforward question about whether a person who is a tumtum can procreate. The body of the tumtum is apparently disambiguated, and his "male" genitalia might lead us to believe that he functions in all respects as a man. Rabbi Yehudah disabuses us: that the tumtum has visible genitalia does not guarantee that his genitalia function reproductively. Rabbi Yehudah draws a dis-

---

13. m. Yevamot 8:6. A parallel to this discussion is found in b. Bekhorot 42a–42b, with variations. The sugya in Bekhorot poses an alternative question: what happens if the tumtum is found to have female genitalia? That sugya is fascinating and merits its own in-depth discussion.

14. In the Mishnah, there are no details included to define the scope of the case we are discussing. The Tosefta, on the other hand, is more specific: In this variant, the first ruling is that the tumtum is excluded from *ḥaliẓah* only in the case where there are other brothers who can step in. Since in this case the tumtum is doubtfully a man, their widowed sister-in-law requires the ritual of *ḥaliẓah* to set her free before she can remarry. In the second case, the brothers of the tumtum can perform levirate marriage with the tumtum's wife because either the tumtum was a woman, in which case their marriage did not take legal effect (and there is no incest prohibition at play), or they were a man, in which case the brothers should be performing levirate marriage. This reading of the tannaitic sources is laid out in b. Bekhorot 42a. See also Lieberman, *Tosefta Kifshuta*, 105.

tinction between morphology, reproductive function, and gendered obligation in levirate marriage.

What does it mean to say that the tumtum is like a eunuch? This may be a literal likeness, if the implication is that the surgery that revealed the genitalia of the tumtum also rendered him a eunuch. But if that were so, why is the tumtum *like* a eunuch, rather than simply *being* a eunuch? In other words, the simile between the tumtum and the eunuch (Heb. *k'saris*) invites us to consider what qualities the two categories share.[15] While this functions as a straightforward point about the tumtum's obligation in levirate marriage, it also poses larger definitional questions about the nature of the tumtum.

Hillary Malatino's recent book *Queer Embodiment* explores the category of intersex. Malatino argues that since the early modern period, intersex bodies have been figured as impossible bodies and used as props to establish the legibility of the normative. At the beginning of their book, Malatino poses a provocative question: "What is it to be intersex?"[16] In other words, Malatino frames their research questions through the language of ontology while tracing the emergence of the category itself.

Here I want to pose a similar question about the tumtum, albeit in a very different context. If the revelation of the tumtum's genitalia does not resolve the tumtum's bodily difference, then to be a tumtum is not solely about genitalia. Hidden genitals seem to signify deeper differences. As soon as the tumtum's skin tears, the question of a "cure" for being a tumtum is introduced.[17] Are the "conditions" of eunuchs and tumtumim constant, or can they be eradicated? In other words: what is it to be tumtum?[18]

This simile between eunuchs and tumtumim also obscures the fact that genital morphology never ensures reproduction. In other words, anyone may be "like" a eunuch, if being "like" a eunuch means simply failing to reproduce. Having normative morphology, or even normative gonads, does not guarantee that a (man's) name will be carried on. Reproduction, like all human bodily processes, is fallible.

---

15. The most systematic overview of legal analogy is by Leib Moscovitz, who lays out the legal thinking that structures various layers of rabbinic literature. Moscovitz organizes the types of legal analogies in tannaitic literature into several strands. This analogy between eunuch/tumtum might fit into two of Moscovitz's concepts—that is, "comparison-based extension" or "referential classification." See Leib Moscovitz, *Talmudic Reasoning*, 110–23.

16. See Malatino, *Queer Embodiment*, 1.

17. This question of cure is also raised in relation to the born saris (see m. Yevamot 8:4 and b. Yevamot 80a). In the following chapters I will discuss the violence of cure. On the issue of the ableist violence that inheres in the concept of "cure" see, for example, Clare, *Brilliant Imperfections*. I am also thinking about transition here; once a person has transitioned, does their transsexuality become past? Are we "cured" of our "condition" through the revelation of our new bodies?

18. The tumtum's silence about their own understanding of their being is noticeable, albeit predictable. I address the silence of the androginos at the end of the chapter.

After all, we are discussing levirate marriage; the entire premise of levirate marriage rests on the assumption that a breakdown of reproduction has already occurred, even if that breakdown comes in the form of an untimely death.

Following this citation of the Mishnah, the sugya introduces another sage to challenge Rabbi Yehudah's teaching about the tumtum who is like a eunuch. "Rabbi Ami said: How would Rabbi Yehudah respond to [the case of] the Tumtum of Biri,[19] who was placed on a [surgical] chair and was operated upon [so that their genitals were revealed] and who subsequently fathered seven children" (b. Yevamot 83b)?[20] Rabbi Ami poses a challenge to Rabbi Yehudah's statement that no tumtum can procreate. Apparently, there was a tumtum who lived in a place called Biri and fathered seven children. If a person who is a tumtum has the capacity to procreate, then they should participate in the rituals of levirate marriage. This would suggest that not every tumtum is like a eunuch: the proof is in the children.

The editors who wove together this imagined back-and-forth between different rabbis now invent a response that Rabbi Yehudah might make to this challenge of the procreative tumtum: "And Rabbi Yehudah [would] say to [the challenger]:[21] return [and inspect the parentage of the tumtum's] children [to ascertain] from whence they come."[22] In other words, if Rabbi Yehudah were to respond to the challenge, he would maintain that no tumtum can procreate. If no tumtum is able to father seven children, then the children must be the product of adultery.

---

19. Biri is a place name that shows up a number of times in the rabbinic corpus with variant spellings. For a discussion of these variants, see Reeg, *Die Ortsnamen Israels*, 85. The two best-known citations of Biri in rabbinic literature are t. Mo'ed Katan 2:8 and b. Bava Meẓia 84b. Neither story seems to indicate that Biri was characterized by any particular reputation. The first example is also cited in Klein, *Neue Beiträge zur Geschichte und Geographie Galiläas*. Klein argues that there are two possible locations for Biri: either Biria or Kafr Bir'im. Ben Tsiyon Rozenfeld, on the other hand, positively identifies Biri as Biria. See Rozenfeld, *Torah Centers and Rabbinic Activity in Palestine*, 147, as well as his accompanying footnotes for additional sources.

20. The phrase "and fathered seven children" is found in some, but not all, manuscripts. Munich 95 lacks the phrase, but Munich 141 has it, for example. Regardless, this challenge to Rabbi Yehudah makes sense only if the tumtum of Biri procreated. Also, the Hebrew word that I translate as "operated on" could also refer to being torn open; the chair, however, seems to suggest a deliberate operation.

21. There is a temporal gap between Rabbi Yehudah and Rabbi Ami. Vatican 111 omits "*'amar leh*"/ "[would] say to him," which has the effect of highlighting the artificial construct of the conversation and speculating about how Rabbi Yehudah would respond. Similarly, Munich 141 and Munich 95 have "*'amar l'kha*" /"[would] say to you" instead of "*'amar leh*," again highlighting the hypothetical nature of the response. All these versions are common citational devices.

22. In the phrase, "And Rabbi Yehudah [would] say to [the challenger]," several manuscripts (Ginsburg 594, Munich 141, and Munich 95) add "*ẓe*'" ("go") before *ḥazer* ("return"), while other manuscripts omit it. It does not substantively change the sense of the passage either way, but the verb in the imperative form strengthens Rabbi Yehudah's (hypothetical) conviction that the tumtum of Biri's children are not truly his. In case we missed the (barely) blunted point, Rashi (a medieval commentator) spells it out for us: "[The tumtum of Biri's] wife had illicit sex."

With the introduction of the possibility of the cheating wife, we are faced with another danger of reproduction.[23] On one level, the prospect of illicit sex always haunts discussions of levirate marriage. A levirate union between a widow and her dead husband's brother is allowed only because her husband died childless. Otherwise, it is prohibited sex. Levirate marriage transforms an illicit sexual union into a required one.

In the case of the (potentially) cheating wife of the tumtum of Biri, the problem is not a prohibited relationship, but rather infidelity. The tumtum is again the source of a deception; they have had surgery and appears capable of reproduction. In fact, they have seven children. But, according to the imagined response of Rabbi Yehudah, that appearance is deceptive. Two kinds of duplicity are invoked: a misogynist portrait of the cheating wife coupled with the deceitful body of the tumtum. In the case of the tumtum the body itself can "lie" or can present an appearance of reproductive masculinity that is false, and it destabilizes our ability to ascertain the truth about both bodies and kinship lines. At the same time, the invocation of the lying tumtum body upholds the notion that there is a "truth" to be discerned about sex, gender, and reproduction.

This proposed solution to the problem of the tumtum of Biri's children elides a deeper problematic about reproduction. It is not just the wife of the tumtum of Biri who might have lied about the parentage of her children and denied her husband heirs. The unspoken specter that haunts the text is that all men have the capacity to be deceived by infidelity. This special scrutiny paid to the body of the tumtum obscures the fact that incontrovertible proof of descent is not fully possible. The reproductive failures of the masculine tumtum are played out through a misogynist lament over the inability to control the sexuality of women. How can any man be completely sure that his name is carried on?

The tumtum of Biri is the only tumtum in the corpus who is given a name, and even this name is more of a moniker than a personal name.[24] Biri is a place name, which marks the tumtum by location; it is not a family name. Identifying people by their place of origin is not uncommon in rabbinic literature, and many types of identifying features (jobs, places, and so on) can become a part of a name. At the same time, this partly nameless tumtum is, in fact, memorialized, not just through their (potentially questionable) offspring, but also through their inclusion in this

---

23. The illegitimate child (the *mamzer*) often defines the difference between the products of legitimate and illegitimate sexual unions. There is a long history of scholarship on the question of the mamzer. See the helpful survey in Poppers, "The Déclassé in The Babylonian Jewish Community," 153–79. For a more recent analysis, see Fishbane, *Deviancy in Early Rabbinic Literature*, 4–15. Cf. Bar-Ilan, "The Attitude Toward *Mamzerim* in Jewish Society," 125–70.

24. Outside the biblical figures of Abraham and Sarah, who are sometimes interpreted as tumtumim in later traditions, this is the only example of a specific figure who was presumably contemporaneous with the rabbis.

rabbinic debate. The legacy of the tumtum of Biri includes both children and this rabbinic discussion, which preserves their "name." While the tumtum of Biri is not given an opportunity to answer the question "what is it to be tumtum?" one can certainly imagine trans and intersex midrashim addressing this narrative gap.

EMBODYING LEVITICUS: SEX AND THE BODY OF THE ANDROGINOS

Illicit sex has already been alluded to in the last section of the discussion. As we turn to the next section, a new sexual prohibition comes into play. The prohibition in Leviticus against "lying with a man" has become one of the more famous verses in the Hebrew Bible. This verse structures the next part of the rabbinic discussion of androgynes in which the rabbis address sex between an androgyne and a man.[25] In the process, the rabbis ask how the verse in Leviticus applies to the androginos.

To review, the androginos is generally understood as a person with dual genitalia. Rabbinic debates often pair the androginos with the tumtum. If the tumtum is often conceptualized as a person with a dearth of sexed signs, then the androginos has a surfeit. I described some of the Greco-Roman and Zoroastrian parallels to the androginos in the last chapter.[26]

As a person with dual genitalia, the androginos has the potential to be sexually penetrated either anally or vaginally. The rabbis are now going to discuss which types of sex acts with an androginos constitute "lying with a man."[27] I have already

---

25. In the service of making the text more accessible to the nonspecialist, I have chosen to focus on discrete sections of the sugya. The discussion of the tumtum continues, however. There is a tradition specifying that if the tumtum were torn open and found to be a born saris, they should not participate in levirate marriage. This version of the statement more closely resembles the Tosefta because it is organized around the future revelation of the tumtum's sex. A variant of this *baraita* is also discussed in b. Bekhorot 42b–43a. David Weiss-Halivni points out that the truncated version in Yevamot results in the difficulties that follow, difficulties about the potential of a female tumtum. He finds that the variant in b. Bekhorot 42b is still a third variation. See Weiss-Halivni, *Mekorot U'Mesorot*, 90–91.

26. The tumtum and androginos are often paired together. See, for example, m. Ḥagigah 1:1 on the obligation for pilgrimage and the tumtum and androginos. On the parallels between the Mishnah and the Mekhilta, see Hayes, "Law in Classical Rabbinic Judaism," 76–128.

There are other systems that also pair a person with an excess of sex with a person who lacks it. Bee Scherer's fourfold taxonomy of sex/gender in Buddhist thought is helpful. Scherer notes separate categories for male, not/male (female), both, and neither. Thus, the figure of *paṇḍaka*, which is notoriously difficult to translate, might be a parallel figure. See Scherer, "Variant Dharma: Buddhist Queers, Queering Buddhism," 253–73. I wish to thank Scherer for sharing her essay with me.

27. At the beginning of the sugya, the rabbis discuss the marriage of the androgyne. They begin with a citation from the Mishnah: "It was taught: The androgyne marries [a woman] but is not married [to a man]." I discuss this statement in more detail in the last chapter, where I unpack the androcentrism inherent in the grammar. Lieberman relates this statement to the question of *mishkav zakhar*. He argues that the question is whether stoning is required in punishment for such a marriage, since

argued that the tumtum is made to bear the brunt of reproductive failures in the last part of the discussion. In this section, I will argue that the androginos is made to bear the weight of masculine penetrability.

The verses in Leviticus that prohibit "lying with a man" have some famous grammatical and syntactical puzzles; biblicists debate how to interpret these oddities. Leviticus 18:22 reads "Do not lie with a male as one lies with a woman; it is an abhorrence [to'evah]." This verse, as well as its pair in Leviticus 20:13, leaves scholars debating precisely what sex act is being interdicted here, and why.[28] Although most translators have read these verses as a prohibition against anal sex between men (and only a very few polemical translations understand the verse as a blanket ban of homosexuality), active debate continues over the grammatical oddities of the verses.[29] At least some scholars have conceptualized this verse as a prohibition of the "mixing of kinds" (kil'ayim), or, in other words, as a prohibition against gendered hybridity.[30] How, then, do the rabbis understand the androginos in the face of this biblical law about the transgression of gender and sexual boundaries?

---

marriage is consummated with sex. Lieberman, *Tosefta Kifshuta*. On the face of it, this statement seems to indicate the androgyne can marry; however, within the context of the larger discussion in the Tosefta, the question seems to be whether a legal action has occurred. The discussion in our sugya makes this a question about whether the androginos's marriage is valid ab initio or ex post facto (b. Yevamot 82b).

28. There are several mysteries about these verses: Why is the word *zakhar*/male paired with *'ishah*/woman instead of the corresponding word *n'kayvah*/female? It is also unclear why the term, "lyings of a woman," is expressed in the plural, a detail that the rabbis will interpret in our sugya. The two versions of the verse in Leviticus do not match; the first seems to penalize only the penetrative partner, while the second extends the punishment to both parties. Finally, what is the exact valence of calling something *to'evah* (generally translated as either an "abomination" or an "abhorrence")? Jerome T. Walsh argues that it was the penetrated partner who was subject to the prohibition. See Walsh, "Leviticus 18:22 and 20:13," 201–9. Jacob Milgrom posits instead that both partners were subject to the prohibition. See Milgrom, *Leviticus 17-22*. Recently, George Hollenback has responded to Walsh. See Hollenback, "Who is Doing What to Whom Revisited," 529–37. For a larger overview of some of the history of translations around sexuality and the Bible, see Heather White, *Reforming Sodom*.

29. In the 1990s, three separate articles contextualizing Leviticus within broader theoretical questions of the field of the history of sexuality were published in close succession. See Satlow, "'They Abused Him Like a Woman,'" 1–25; Olyan, "'And with a Male you Shall not Lie the Lying Down of a Woman,'" 179–206; and Boyarin "Are There Any Jews," 333–55. The first volume of Foucault's *History of Sexuality* had already been translated into English by 1978, but the essentialism/constructionism debate raged into the 1990s. Satlow, Boyarin, and Olyan are responding to Foucault. See Foucault, *The History of Sexuality*.

30. Daniel Boyarin argues as follows: "Here, I suggest, also penetration of a male constituted a consignment of him to the class of females, but, rather than a degradation of status, this constituted a sort of mixing of kinds, a generally taboo occurrence in Hebrew culture" (Boyarin, "Are There Any Jews?" 341). In opposition to a cultural system that associated the penetrative/penetrated dichotomy with divisions in status, Boyarin believes that the penetrated man blurs the boundaries between male and female.

The rabbinic discussion of Leviticus and the androgyne begins by citing an earlier tradition: "Rabbi Eliezer says: [in the case where a man penetrates an] androginos, [that man] is liable for [his actions. He will receive the death penalty via] stoning [because he has transgressed the prohibition in Leviticus, just] as [he would have had he had sex with a non-androgyne] man"[31] (b. Yevamot 83b). Rabbi Eliezer states that the man who penetrates the androgyne has, in fact, transgressed the Levitical prohibition against lying with a man. As such, the penetrator is liable for the punishment of being stoned to death for his transgression. [32]

Just as in the comparison of the tumtum to the eunuch, we have another simile. The penetrator is punished for having sex with the androginos just as he would if he had sex with a man. As with all comparative statements, this requires us to ascertain precisely how sex between men is similar to sex between a man and an androgyne. Comparison invites us to interpret the points of connection, as well as to contemplate what it means to "lie with a man."

The rabbis debate this question of similarity between androgynes and men by quoting a tradition in the name of Rav:[33] "The [man who penetrates the] androgyne is liable for [the punishment of] stoning for [penetrating the androgyne through either of the androgyne's] two orifices" (b. Yevamot 83b). A tradition is cited in the name of Rav, a (Babylonian Amoraic) sage. Rav argues that the man who penetrates the androgyne has transgressed the prohibition against lying with a man. According to Rav, it does not matter whether that penetration was vaginal or anal. In other words, in Rav's opinion the androginos himself is like a man. For Rav, it does not matter where on his body he is penetrated, nor does vaginal penetration exempt the man who has sex with an androgyne from punishment.

---

31. This is a citation of m. Yevamot 8:6. The language attributed to Rabbi Eliezer in this mishnah is both terse and cryptic; it is generally understood through the variant in t. Yevamot 10:16. In the Tosefta, it is clear that this mishnah is discussing *mishkav zakhar*. I translate this as distinguishing between anal and vaginal sex (which will be addressed shortly in the body of the sugya). However, others have translated differently, situating the androgyne as the penetrator and penetrated See Brodsky, "Sex in the Talmud," 157–70. There are aspects of my translation that fly in the face of the conventional translation of *zakhrut*, which is normally understood as referring to the penis. I believe that the parallelism, as well as the multiply penetrable body of the androginos, means that, in this exceptional case, the word *zakhrut* refers to the anus, not the penis.

32. If you read the discussion about the marriage of the androgyne as overlaid onto the question of mishkav zakhar, as the sugya does, then the question of the androgyne as penetrator is also addressed; however, the question of the androgyne penetrating a *man* is not. Brodsky understands this text differently. See Brodsky, "Sex in the Talmud," 157–70.

33. The string of attributions varies in the manuscript tradition, but it is generally some version of the following: "Rav Shmuel bar Yehuda said in the name of Rabbi Aba the brother of Rabbi Yehudah bar Zivdi who said in the name of Rav Yehudah who said in the name of Rav." It is possible that some attributions may have been combined to form this longer string.

There are a number of ways in which to interpret Rav's statement. One could understand Rav as arguing that genitalia do not make the man: in other words, the androgyne is male regardless of their dual genitalia. To penetrate an androgyne vaginally is therefore still to penetrate a man. Perhaps this means that genitalia do not comprise the primary criterion for determining sex. At the same time, it is also possible to understand Rav as arguing that the presence of the vulva is not as significant as the presence of a penis. This reading suggests that masculinity is flexible enough to accommodate a variety of forms of genitalia, but it cannot incorporate penetration of any kind. Regardless of whether genitalia are the sole criterion for determining sex, or whether the vulva is insignificant, this is an example of the ways that sex, gender, and sexuality are not fully separable in rabbinic understandings.

A rebuttal to Rav's opinion is now offered: "An objection is raised. Rabbi Eliezer said: [34] the [man who penetrates the androgyne] is liable for stoning as if [he had penetrated] a man. What case are we discussing here? Anal [penetration]. But [if the man penetrates the androgyne] vaginally, [he] is exempt [from the punishment of stoning]" (b. Yevamot 83b). Rabbi Eliezer's statement conflicts with Rav's opinion: only anal sex violates the prohibition against "lying with a man." If a man penetrates the androginos vaginally, he does not receive the death penalty.[35] For Rabbi Eliezer, it appears that the simile "like a man" indicates the act of anal penetration, not the androginos themself.

The rabbis are discussing a technical question of what kinds of sex with an androgyne warrant the severe penalty of stoning. Still, there are broader problems of gender and sexuality at stake. In these reformulations of Leviticus, it is almost as if the androgyne is *becoming* a man through anal penetration. It is as if "lying with a man" transforms the androgyne into a man. If so, then the gender of the androginos arises through transgressive penetration.[36] Transgressive sexual contact transforms sex/gender.

---

34. The language of the tradition attributed to Rabbi Eliezer is similar to the wording in t. Yevamot 10:2. Saul Lieberman believes that Eliezer here refers to Rabbi Eliezer ben Hyrcanus. T. Yevamot 10:2 cites Rabbi Elazar (whom Lieberman identities as Rabbi Elazar ben Shamua on the basis of the story in b. Yevamot 84a. Accordingly, Lieberman believes that the shift between Elazar and Eliezer is not a scribal error but is a result of a tradition that Rabbi Elazar ben Shamua is repeating from Rabbi Eliezer ben Hyrcanus. Therefore, the anonymous variant in the Mishnah should be attributed to Rabbi Elazar ben Shamua in the name of Rabbi Eliezer. See *Tosefta Kifshuta*, 94–95. For a variant of the discussion on what constitutes "lying with a man," see b. Yevamot 54b.

35. There are several possible ways to interpret Rabbi Eliezer's statement. To warrant capital punishment, the commission of the transgression should be certain. For a trenchant analysis of the death penalty, see Beth Berkowitz, *Execution and Invention*.

36. In other words, gender is performative through the reiteration of specific sex acts and tied to a disciplinary structure. Here I am using performative in the technical sense, rather than implying that the androgyne is "performing" their gender in an agentic way. On performativity, see Judith Butler,

The specific language of Rabbi Eliezer's statement strengthens the impression that transgressive sex forms the androginos into a man. The word that indicates the vagina here is *nakvut*, which comes from the same root as the word for female.[37] This is a not particularly innovative word choice, and nakvut refers to the vagina elsewhere as well. On the other hand, the word chosen for anus—*zakhrut*—is unique. Zakhrut, which comes from the word for male, almost always indicates the penis in rabbinic literature. This is true even in other descriptions of the androginos's body.[38] Moreover, the rabbis have specific words for both the anus and anal sex, neither of which is used here.[39] Instead, the anus lexically turns into the "masculine hole." It is almost as if the penis inverts and transforms itself into an anus when sexual penetration is mapped onto the body of the androginos.[40]

The anus is not, of course, confined to masculine bodies. Naming the anus as the masculine orifice requires gendering the anus in the first place. This language reflects the linguistic constraints of binary sex, and the sheer inadequacy of Hebrew in the face of the multiplicity of the androginos. At the same time, however, by calling the anus of the androginos "the masculine orifice," this tradition displaces masculine penetrability onto the body of the androgyne. After all, the anus becomes masculine only for the androginos, not for other types of men.

This is not the only way that the anus of the androgyne is described. There is a variant of the statement about the androginos's "masculine orifice":

Gender Trouble. In Roman sources, gender-deviant sex could transform one into an androgyne. See Diana Swancutt, "*Still* Before Sexuality," 11–63.

37. The designation of the female genitalia of the androgyne as nakvut is seen elsewhere as well. See, for example, b. Bekhorot 41a.

38. There are also secondary meanings for zakhrut; zakhrut and nakvut together describe the two sides of the axe, and zakhrut is also used in agricultural contexts to describe germination. For the most part, however, zakhrut refers to the penis. See b. Shabbat 108a and b. Bekhorot 39b (zakhrut); and b. Ḥagigah 4a and p. Yevamot 8:6 (9d) (ẓad zakhrut).

39. The standard rabbinic phrase for anus is "*pi taba'at*"—literally "the mouth of the ring." See b. Bava Kamma 92a and b. Shabbat 108b. I am grateful to Mira Balberg for discussing the term with me. The rabbis explicitly discuss anal sex and women elsewhere using the language of "according to her way" (*k'darka*): see b. Yevamot 34b. See Boyarin, "Against Rabbinic Sexuality," 131–47. The language of "according to her way" is mirrored in our sugya, except that anal sex is not considered "according to his way." On questions of this phrase, see Bickart, "'Overturning the Table,'" 489–507.

40. There are studies of nominalization and abstract nouns in rabbinic literature. The most systematic is Leib Moscovitz's monograph, which cites earlier work by Ephraim Urbach, among others. See Moscovitz, *Talmudic Reasoning*. Moscovitz's general conclusion is that rabbinic thinking became more abstract through the generations, and that nominalization is characteristic of later layers of rabbinic literature. Jeffrey Rubenstein also examines the process by which nouns become abstract in tannaitic literature. See Rubenstein, "On Some Abstract Concepts in Rabbinic Literature," 33–73. The most-discussed example of the abstract noun is *minut* (usually translated as heresy). See Goodman, "The Function of Minim in Early Rabbinic Judaism"; Boyarin, *Border Lines*. For a critique of Boyarin, see Schremer, "Thinking About Belonging in Early Rabbinic Literature," 249–75.

Rabbi Elazar[41] said ... What case are we discussing here? [We are discussing a case where a man] has sex with [the androgyne] via [the androdgyne's] anus. If he does not penetrate [the androgyne] via [the androgyne's] anus, he is exempt [from the punishment of stoning for transgressing Leviticus]. (t. Yevamot 10:2)

Rabbi Elazar also distinguishes between penetrating the androginos anally and penetrating the androginos vaginally. But rather than using nouns derived from the adjectives for masculine and feminine to map the orifices on the androginos's body, this variant uses a phrase that could more literally be translated as "by way of the masculine" (Heb. *derekh hazakhrut*)."[42] The vagina becomes "not by way of the masculine," marking the vagina as the "not anus." This androcentric cartography of the body positions the anus as the central orifice because it has now become quintessentially masculine. This rhetoric has the paradoxical effect of making anal sex the unmarked sexual act, while sex with the vagina becomes the "other" way. It is as if the multiple orifices of the androginos overwhelm language, producing both sex changes and a destabilized version of normative sexuality. All of these language variants are subtle, but they embroil sexuality, gender, and sexed embodiment through this discussion of the sexual transgression of the man who had sex with the androginos.

After the debate over which sex act is interdicted, the rabbis finally turn to Leviticus itself. They take apart Leviticus 18:22 as the prooftext for the various competing opinions on what it means for the androginos to be "like" a man. Each opinion on which kinds of sexual penetration of an androgyne are allowed requires proof from the biblical verse. The wording of the verse in Hebrew, "Do not lie with a man as one lies with a woman," is famously awkward. The original Hebrew phrase for "lies with a woman" is in the plural; a literal translation would be something like, "And with a male, do not lie the lyings of a woman." The rabbis will use the oddities of the verse as fodder for their interpretations.

The first opinion is that Leviticus prohibits both anal and vaginal sex with the androginos: "Rava said: [the sage] Bar Hamduri explained the reasoning to me [as follows]: "Do not lie with a male as one lies with a woman ... " [Leviticus 18:22]. [Why is the phrase "lies with a woman" in the plural in the verse?] What male has two ways of lying with him? You must conclude [that the verse refers to] the androgyne" (b. Yevamot 83b). This tradition of interpreting Leviticus argues that the odd grammar of the verse is proof that it prohibits both vaginal and anal sex with an

---

41. t. Yevamot 10:2. Lieberman argues that Rabbi Elazar is citing the tradition of Rabbi Eliezer ben Hyrcanus. See Saul Lieberman, *Tosefta Kifshuta*.

42. This phrasing, "according to the way of the male orifice," mirrors the rabbinic language of anal sex for women, but with a twist. Vaginal sex for women is often described as "according to her way," while anal sex is "not according to her way." See, for example, b. Yevamot 34b. This description of the anus as "not her way" parallels these sources that situate the anus as the masculine orifice.

androginos. Bar Hamduri interprets the plural "lyings of a woman" to refer to the manifold penetrability of the androgyne.[43] In other words, Bar Hamduri argues that sex with an androginos is like sex with a woman; only the androginos is a man who can be penetrated through multiple orifices. Therefore, this plural phrase, "lyings of a woman," must mean that both orifices of the androgyne are forbidden.

The language of Bar Hamduri's interpretation of Leviticus is striking. According to him, the odd plural phrasing of Leviticus ("lyings of a woman") can refer *only* to an androgyne. No other man, he argues, has plural "lyings." In that interpretation, the androgyne becomes like a man through being multiply penetrable like a woman. At the same time, the androgyne also becomes the peerless object of the verse. The grammatical oddities of Leviticus 18:22—the way in which it veers between sex and gender, and the strange plural—present a riddle to be deciphered. Bar Hamduri suggests that the answer to the riddle lies in the body of the androginos, who similarly confounds the grammatical boundaries of sex, gender, and number.

Leviticus has been interpreted to prohibit both types of penetration with an androgyne. The rabbinic discussion now tries to interpret Leviticus 18:22 to mean that only anal penetration with the androginos is prohibited. The rabbis turn to the same verse to argue that only anal sex with an androgyne constitutes "lying with a man":

> And [how do the] rabbis [derive the opinion that a man is stoned only for penetrating the androgyne anally]?[44] Even though [the androgyne] has two [orifices, and therefore two ways of] lying with him, "the male" is written [in Leviticus 18:22, and this refers to the anus]. And the rabbis—how do they derive [the prohibition against anal sex] with an ordinary [Heb. *grayda'*] man?[45] [From the words] "and the."[46] "[How do they] derive [the prohibition] against [penetrating a woman] anally [Heb. *shelo' k'darkah*]? From [the word] "woman." (b. Yevamot 83b)

---

43. This is not the only place where the rabbis discuss the plural "lyings of a woman" in this verse; in b. Sanhedrin 54a–b, for example, the rabbinic discussion centers on the multiply penetrable bodies of women. For an interpretation of this tradition in the context of a larger discussion of androgyny in rabbinic literature, see Levinson, "Cultural Androgyny in Rabbinic Literature," 119–40.

44. Rabbi Eliezer's opinion here is also understood to be the opinion of the *rabanan*. The traditional commentators simply emend the text; in a harmonizing move, the medieval commentator Yom Tov ben Avraham Assevilli emends the *rabanan* to Rabbi Eliezer.

45. The word *grayda'*, which I have translated as "ordinary" but which can also mean "simple" or "scant," deserves attention. It appears several other times in the Babylonian Talmud, often when comparing terms. See b. Berakhot 36b, which uses *grayda'* to refer to simple cereal in contrast to a mixed cereal. For a usage that compares lesser and greater items, see b. Yevamot 3b, where *grayda'* describes a lesser transgression as opposed to a greater transgression that incurs the penalty of *karet*. In our case, I do not think *grayda'*/"ordinary" means "less than." As in the case of cereal in Berakhot, there is not always a clear valuation of the term being compared to the ordinary or *grayda'* object. Here *grayda'* does seem to mark the androginos.

46. Here the sixteenth–seventeenth-century scholar Joel ben Samuel Sirkis corrects the text to *mev'et* ("and the") from *me'ishah* ("woman").

By the rules of exegesis here, every excess word (or even a part of the word) is available for interpretation. Once a word has already been used to derive a particular legal decision, then that word or phrase is no longer available for new interpretations. This reading dissects Leviticus 18:22 with a scalpel. Taking the first part of the passage from Leviticus 18:22, "And with a male," the rabbis use the word *male* to derive the interdiction against anal sex with the androginos. Subsequent pieces of the verse are then used to prohibit anal sex between (non-androgyne) men and with a woman. In the process, the rabbis call the non-androgyne man an "ordinary" man, implying that the androgyne is "not ordinary."

Words or short phrases in the verse are interpreted as equivalent to different sexual objects.[47] For the androginos, who is the object of both rabbinic debate and, potentially, sexual penetration, "male" is the proof text for the ban against anal sex. This interpretation redefines the word *male* yet again. Now "male" in Leviticus 18:22 means anal sex with an androginos. This parsimonious hermeneutic, which uses each word to extract meaning, contrasts with the androginos's overabundance of penetrability.

The rabbinic debate over the interpretation of Leviticus 18:22 constructs inviolable masculinity by displacing penetrability onto the body of the androginos. This focus on the penetrable orifices of the androgyne papers over the general permeability of bodies. It is not just the androginos who is penetrable in manifold ways; in fact bodies absorb all sorts of materials from their environments: air, water, disease, scents, and so on.[48] In transing the Talmud, I am noting the ways that penetrability, gender, and the body itself are remapped in response to the possibility of sex with the androginos.

---

47. In ending my discussion here, I am skipping a series of texts about consecrated animals and some traditions about substitution (*temurah*), which introduces the word *m'alyah*—"proper"—to describe the masculinity of the androgyne, in a counterpoint to grayda'. This is also another example of an exchange, albeit one that does not takes place in the realm of kinship. The substitution of sacrificial animals is already prohibited in the Hebrew Bible, and yet the attempt to substitute an animal does consecrate it. Even animals that normally cannot become sanctified (such as those animals who have a "defect") are to a degree rendered sacred. In this example of substitution in the realm of sacrifices, the tumtum and androgyne stubbornly remain unexchangeable, and are therefore outside the legal realm of sacrificial currency. If sexual congress is a method of acquisition (in kinship terms), then the androgyne and tumtum, in sacrificial terms, are not valid legal tender.

48. Regarding the permeability of bodies, Mel Chen, for example, examines the dynamics of lead poisoning. Chen argues that the drive to protect the porous body of the white child from lead poisoning, with its consequent regulation of imported toys, ignores more prevalent vectors of lead poisoning in the United States that predominantly impact children of color. At the same time, this fear over the contamination of the white child correlates to the fantasy of impenetrable borders that support the state as inviolable, sovereign, and white. On the racialization of penetrability, see Chen, *Animacies*, 159–88; Hoang, *A View from the Bottom*, 1–28.

The final section of the sugya presents a story that dramatizes this contest over the borders of the body by mapping it onto social boundaries. At this point in our discussion, the penetrability of masculine bodies is still at stake. This next story dramatizes the challenges and potential of inviolate and distinct bodies.

FIGHTING COCKS, ANDROGYNES, AND REPRODUCTION

Our sugya ends with a story, as is common at the end of a chapter in the Babylonian Talmud. This is the story with which I began the introduction to my book, the story that brought me to apply to graduate school. Rabbi Yehudah HaNasi (a famous early rabbi) tells us this story in the first person. He travels to learn from a particular teacher, but he is thwarted in his attempts access the teacher:

> When I went to learn rabbinic teachings with Rabbi Elazar ben Shamua his students banded together against me like the [aggressive] roosters of Beit Bukiya. [The students] allowed me to learn only one teaching from our tradition:[49] "Rabbi Eliezer says that [in the case of the] androgyne: [the man who penetrates the androgyne anally] is liable for [the penalty of] stoning, [just] as [he would be if he had anal sex with a non-androgyne] man."[50] (b. Yevamot 84a)

Rabbi Yehudah HaNasi travels to learn with Rabbi Elazar ben Shamua. Rabbi Elazar ben Shamua's students block access to their teacher, and they thwart Rabbi Yehudah HaNasi in his desire to learn. The students are described as banding together like aggressive roosters in order to prevent Rabbi Yehudah HaNasi's admission into their midst. Only one teaching filters through the impenetrable barrier presented by the students. This one teaching states that a man who has anal sex with the androginos has indeed lain with a man and is therefore punishable.

Rabbi Yehudah HaNasi's contact with the teacher from whom he desires to learn is attenuated. Not only do the students prevent direct instruction but the teaching that is transmitted is itself only a short citation from yet a different teacher. There are many insulating layers between Rabbi Yehudah HaNasi and his source. The aggressive students police the access to their teacher. At play are sym-

---

49. Part of this formulation is not unique to this sugya. For example, Rabbi Yoḥanan says: "I spent eighteen days with Rabbi Oshaya Beribi and I learned from him only one teaching from our mishnah . . ." (b. Eruvin 53a). While not precisely the same, the wording is certainly similar enough to be suggestive, and stories told in the first person are generally a rarity in rabbinic literature. Later in that same sugya, Rabbi Yehudah HaNasi, also in the first person, relates how crowded it was when they were studying Torah with Rabbi Elazar ben Shamua. This is another tradition linking Rabbi Yehudah HaNasi with Rabbi Elazar ben Shamua.

50. Conflicts between groups of students are a rabbinic trope. See, for example, the story about the conflict between Hillel and Shammai and their students, which uses the same language of "banding together" (Heb. ḥavru 'alav) in b. Beẓah 20a–b.

bolic boundaries: the students present an almost entirely impenetrable border while allowing the androgyne to slip through.[51] Put another way, the students enact an impenetrable, hypermasculine, roosterlike aggressiveness over and against the multiply penetrable body of the androginos.

This confrontation between students and knowledge transmission plays on tensions over cultural reproduction in rabbinic literature. In his book *Carnal Israel*, Daniel Boyarin argues that the rabbis face a dilemma: should cultural reproduction be hereditary, like the priestly system, and pass from father to son? Or should the rabbinic system function as a meritocracy, where every (male) member of the society has the opportunity to compete for success?[52] Cultural reproduction is tied to sexual reproduction in this question: linking the two is the fear that both may be subject to failures that cannot be controlled or accounted for in advance. Situated as we are in the tractate on levirate marriage, there is already a tension surrounding reproduction and its failures. At the heart of both levirate marriage and the debate over cultural reproduction is the question of whether sons will carry on the names of fathers and whether students will carry on the names and ideas of their teachers.

This struggle over cultural reproduction engenders two conflicting values. If cultural reproduction does not depend on being born into the right family, then students must compete aggressively in order to ensure their own place in the scholarly hierarchy and lineage. At the same time, the exchange of knowledge is necessary for the perpetuation of the rabbinic enterprise. Jeffrey Rubenstein has identified motifs in the Babylonian Talmud where narratives of scholarly conflicts sometimes end in violent encounters.[53] Rubenstein believes this later emphasis on scholarly competition reflects the historical development and culture of the Babylonian academies. While he does not analyze this Rabbi Yehudah HaNasi narrative extensively, he includes it in a series of examples to support his broader argument. Using Rubenstein's framework, we could say that Rabbi Elazar ben Shamua's students fight off a competitor to their line. In response to the threat from the outside, they band together to maintain their stranglehold on the knowledge of Rabbi Elazar ben Shamua. The aggressive rooster represents the competitive atmosphere of

---

51. The theoretical backdrop of the argument I make here comes from Douglas, *Purity and Danger*. I am particularly influenced by her argument that the boundaries of the body mirror the boundaries of the social body.

52. Boyarin, *Carnal Israel*.

53. Jeffrey Rubenstein also notes that the rooster does not appear in the Palestinian version of the story. See Rubenstein, *The Culture of the Babylonian Talmud*, 55. The earlier version of the story is found on p. Yevamot 8:6 (9d).

the Babylonian academy. The story thematizes this conflict between knowledge exchange and scholarly competition.[54]

While Rubenstein's scholarship has the explanatory force to unpack the underlying competitive edge in the narrative, it does not answer the question of why the creators of the sugya insert a rooster into the story specifically.[55] The Palestinian Talmud contains an earlier version of this narrative, but with several significant differences from the Babylonian version. One of the biggest changes is that the Palestinian story lacks the aggressive roosters altogether, which suggests that they were added later. On the surface the roosters seem, like the androgyne, to be an almost insignificant detail in a story that features a contest between rabbis. It is therefore worth considering why the later version of the story includes them.

This story contains the only reference to Beit Bukiya in the Talmud,[56] but even without knowing the reputation of the place, we get the impression that it is famous specifically for its ferociously aggressive roosters.[57] Generally, roosters play a number of different roles in rabbinic literature: some traditions link roosters to timekeeping, while others connect them to proper sexual relations.[58] While the word for rooster in this narrative is *tarnigol*, an alternative term for rooster is *gever*, which more commonly means "man" and which can also be a euphemism for the penis.[59] There is, therefore, an established linguistic association between roosters and masculinity.

---

54. Scholars discuss the Sasanian emphasis on the reproduction of lineage, which was regulated through the work of Iranian jurists who set out to maximize reproduction. This tradition tends to contrast *xwēdōah* (literally, "the giving of oneself," but usually translated as incest), which had a positive valence, with sodomy, which was associated with evil. See Payne, "Sex, Death, and Aristocratic Empire," 519–49. For a discussion of *xwēdōah* in relation to rabbinic literature, see Kiel, *Sexuality in the Babylonian Talmud*.

55. In addition to their gendered overtones, roosters also play a role in ancient Judaism. For example, there is a debate as to whether Proverbs 30:31 or Isaiah 22:17 might reference a rooster. Scholars have argued that the rooster symbolized royalty in the seventh century BCE. See, e.g., Fox, *In the Service of the King*, 43–62. The rooster later becomes important because of the ritual of *kapparah*. See Fishbane, "The Ritual of Kapparot," 67–75.

56. I tried to track down Bukiya. The only potential references I found were tenuous and late, such as the citation from the atlas of Al-Mas'udi, the tenth-century Arab historian, who mentions a fort called Bukiya in Seleucia. In the French translation of the atlas, Michael Jan de Goeje renders it as Bukiya. E. W. Brooks suggests such alternatives for Bukiya as Brakiya, Brakana, or Prakana. See Brooks, "Arabic Lists of the Byzantine Themes," 67–77. Prakana, which is from later Byzantine times, is also known officially as Diocaesareia. See Ramsay, *The Historical Geography of Asia Minor*.

57. In Greco-Roman literature, there are also traditions circulating that claim that roosters from a particular place have a reputation for being more vicious. See Jennisen, *Animals for Show and Pleasure*.

58. Roosters mark time through their crowing (see b. Yoma 21a); they can play a role in idolatry (see m. Avodah Zarah 1:5); and their death can help to save lives (see b. Berakhot 60b). For the gallant rooster as an exemplar of proper sexual relations, see b. Eruvin 100b.

59. For the use of *gever* to mean rooster, see m. Yoma 1:8, for example. For its use as a euphemism for the penis, see m. Bekhorot 7:5.

The rooster is a richly symbolic choice in the broader cultural and historical context; the rooster figures prominently in Greco-Roman art and literature, early Christian iconography, and Babylonian Aramaic sources. The rooster's extensive cultural associations invite us to consider this simile of the rooster and aggressive students as playing with multiple idioms at once.

Roosters were likely imported into the Greek colonies of Asia Minor from Persia, which is why Aristophanes (among others) calls them the "Persian bird."[60] From this beginning, roosters spread, and cockfights became a form of popular entertainment. We see this popularity reflected in a variety of material and literary remains—from depictions of cockfights, to treatises advising on the proper rearing of cocks, to images on pottery.[61] Sometimes these depictions have gendered overtones: the Roman author Aelian muses that any hen that beats a rooster in combat changes its demeanor to become more roosterlike.[62]

Roosters therefore loom large in Greek literary and material remains, where they are simultaneously connected with foreignness. Philo thematizes this dual association in his narrative about a famous cockfight. He describes the story of Miltiades, a general of Athens, who stages a cockfight on the eve of a battle against a vastly superior Persian army.[63] This cockfight is a stand-in for the military conflict to come. Philo characterizes the roosters as noble and courageous, and he credits them with inspiring the troops to victory. Here roosters play a role in the conflict between Greeks and Persians, but the cocks are a metonym for the masculine ferocity of the Greek soldiers. According to Pliny the Elder, a yearly cockfight commemorated this victory over the Persians.[64] This tradition stages social and

---

60. In Egypt, chickens were introduced during the New Kingdom but did not become popular until their later reintroduction by the Persians. The original habitat of the rooster was most likely eastern India, from which it probably spread to southwestern Asia. We know that the introduction to Asia Minor likely came after the Homeric age, and their first known mention is likely in Theogenes (fifth century BCE). We have a prolific attestation of chickens from later ages: Aristotle offered instructions for their care and Pausanius described their sacredness. For a survey of these primary source materials, see Lewis and Llewellyn-Jones, *The Culture of Animals in Antiquity*, 244–47. The economic use of chickens probably expanded in the Hellenistic period. See Perry-Gal et al., "Earliest Economic Exploitation," 9849–54. In Mesopotamia, we have depictions of roosters dating to the Middle Assyrian period. See Kalla, "Date Palms, Deer/Gazelle, and Birds," 863–901.

61. Beier, "Fighting Animals," 275–305. See also Johnston, Mastrocinque, and Papaioannou, eds., *Animals in Greek and Roman Religion and Myth*.

62. For hen/cock transformations, see Aelian, *Characteristics of Animals*, 5.5.

63. Philo, *Every Good Man is Free* XIX.131–34., 694. Other accounts name Themistocles as the general in the story. See also Eric Csapo on variants of this narrative that circulated in Greek literature and art: Csapo, "The Cultural Poetics of the Greek Cockfight," 20–37; and Csapo, "Deep Ambivalence," 1–28.

64. For the yearly cockfights in Pergamon, see Pliny the Elder, *Natural History*, X.XXV.50–51. For all its popularity in Greek culture, cockfighting became even more prevalent in the Roman period, scholars have argued. Pliny the Elder and Varro convey instructions on how to raise the best fighting cocks. According to Pliny, cocks could even foretell the future of a battle. See Forsyth, "The Theme of

cultural conflict via proxy, where animals reenact (and experience) violence in lieu of their human counterparts.

Roosters also make an appearance in Jewish Babylonian sources. Yishai Kiel contextualizes the image of a white rooster in an Aramaic magic bowl within the larger Sasanian religious world. Kiel connects the iconography of the bowl to Talmudic texts that position the rooster as channeling divine wrath against one's enemies. The choice of the rooster derives from its Zoroastrian context, where the rooster is associated with Sraoša, an Avestan deity possessing the power to smite demons.[65]

Although the fighting cocks of Beit Bukiya are neither the demon-defeating roosters of the Aramaic bowls nor the roosters on the eve of the battle against the Persians, elements of these various narratives provide a larger semantic field and context. Roosters, as the "Persian bird," are already marked as a sign of social exchange and contestation in late antiquity. The roosters of Beit Bukiya, while situated in a specific time and place, seem to draw on a variety of idioms for their power and ferocity.

The inclusion of fighting roosters is one of several differences between the earlier Palestinian and later Babylonian recensions of this narrative. The version found in the Palestinian Talmud implies a question about Rabbi Yehudah HaNasi's worthiness to learn with Rabbi Elazar ben Shamua.[66] In the Babylonian narrative, the refusal of Rabbi Elazar ben Shamua's students to engage seems both ungenerous and unaccountable. In this way, the aggressive nature of roosters is indiscriminate, and they cannot distinguish between friend and foe.

The students of Rabbi Elazar ben Shamua remain unnamed. It is not that the text wishes to avoid naming names out of politeness—we certainly see many other

---

Cockfighting," 252–82. Roosters also play a significant role in early Christian iconography and are associated with the figure of Peter. This is related to the story in the gospels where the rooster does not crow until Peter denies Jesus three times. See Callisen, "The Iconography of the Cock on the Column," 160–78.

65. Kiel, "Negotiating 'White Rooster' Magic and Binitarian Christianity," 259–79. The rooster features directly in the Avesta, where Ahura Mazda invokes the aid of the rooster to awaken the people to curse the demons. See Ahbabi, "A Comparative Study of *Zahhak*'s Dual Character," 301–15. For an overview of Islamic sources on roosters, including roosters as augurs, see Tottoli, "At Cock-Crow," 139–47.

66. The language of the Palestinian Talmud's version is somewhat opaque. Rabbi Yehudah HaNasi searches out Rabbi Elazar ben Shamua's teachings on the androgyne in particular; this lends the story an entirely different flavor. The Palestinian version also explicitly debates the question of why Rabbi Yehudah HaNasi was denied learning. There are suggestions in the literature that the relations between Rabbi Yehudah HaNasi and certain Jewish communities were strained, although this most specifically applies to Babylonian Jewish communities. For example, see b. Kiddushin 72a and Oppenheimer, "Rabbi Judah Ha-Nasi and Babylonia," 297–318.

examples of shaming in rabbinic literature.[67] Rather, in this narrative Rabbi Yehudah HaNasi leaves a legacy. Acting as a link in the chain of knowledge, he transmits both a teaching and a cultural value: knowledge must be shared in order for rabbinic culture to perpetuate itself. In the end, this text does not function merely as a critique of the competitive spirit of the students. It is also a reinscription of the value of competition whereby the students lose the game by refusing to play. Located after a lengthy discussion about men failing to reproduce their names, these nameless students fail as links in the reproductive chain of knowledge. The named character, Rabbi Yehudah HaNasi supplants the nameless students in the transmission chain from their teacher.

It is tempting to read the story of Rabbi Yehudah HaNasi and the nameless students as a proxy battle played out through fighting cocks. In that interpretation, the story functions as a critique of hypermasculinity and proposes a queerly subversive alternative. From the perspective of Rabbi Yehudah HaNasi, the students should welcome his incursion, and allow the cross-fertilization of the scholarly encounter to take place. Rabbi Yehudah HaNasi presents a cooperative masculinity as an alternative to the hypermasculinity of the students/roosters. This cooperative mode of relationality would allow the reproduction of rabbinic culture to flourish. If we were to read the text through this lens, the rabbinic intimacies proposed by Rabbi Yehudah HaNasi would become almost homoerotic.[68]

That is one possible reading of the story. However, it is a reading through which subversion is enabled by roosters and androgynes. In the next and final section of this chapter, I will return to intersex activism in order to discuss the costs of sterilizing surgeries on intersex children. At the same time, I will try to account for the costs of the Rabbi Yehudah HaNasi narrative to androgynes and roosters. This is a story about fighting cocks who suffer the pains of the cockfight for human entertainment and edification. It is also the story of the androginos whose sexual penetration is instrumental in rabbinic musings on scholarly boundaries, cultural reproduction, and normative masculinity. Gendered subversion may not be worth its cost.

CALCULATING THE COSTS: ANDROGYNES AND ROOSTERS STAGE A COUP

I want to return to the case of M. C., the intersex child who was operated on while a ward of the state. M. C. currently identifies as a boy, and in 2013, his adoptive

---

67. On shaming, see Rubenstein, *The Culture of the Babylonian Talmud*, 67–89.
68. Readings of this type have been justly criticized. Daniel Boyarin finds fault with some of his earlier work. See Boyarin, *Unheroic Conduct*.

parents, Mark and Pam Crawford, filed suit at both the state and federal levels. After wending its way through the courts for four years, the case was settled.[69] Cosmetic genital surgeries have been performed in the United States since the nineteenth century,[70] but this is the first lawsuit of its kind; scholars predict that more will follow.[71] Bo Laurent, the original founder of one of the earliest intersex activist organizations in North America, has argued that the public settlement will help undermine medicine's argument that these procedures are uncontroversial.[72] The cost of settlement, it is hoped, will dissuade medical practitioners from pursuing cosmetic surgery on infants.

. . .

We cannot historically calculate the costs of these rabbinic discussions to androgynes: did the stoning of the penetrator of the androgyne ever take place? Certainly these texts continue to harm trans and intersex Jews; some of the sources I have analyzed in this chapter have been used to reaffirm a position that would have banned ordaining LGBTQ rabbis in the Conservative movement, for example.[73] The fighting cocks of Beit Bukiya suggest that these battles are contested, and occasionally even bloody. The debates are theoretical, but that does not mean immaterial. Yet I cannot perform an accurate accounting of the costs to androgynes and roosters.

We can, however, determine some of the costs of what it means to inhabit a body that is understood to require "correction." In order to understand the M. C. case, however, we must situate it within the broader racialized and ableist

69. The case settled for the sum of $270,000 paid to a structured settlement company. The full settlement documents are publicly available online, with a few of the particulars obscured. See Pamela and John Mark Crawford v. Medical University of South Carolina, South Carolina Department of Social Services and Greenville Hospital Systems, 2013CP4002877 (July 27, 2017), https://www.documentcloud.org/documents/3901419-Final-Settlement.html.

70. See, for example, Elizabeth Reis's account of the case of Dr. Samuel D. Gross, a prominent American surgeon who in 1849 removed testicular tissue from a three-year-old in order to support her future as marriageable (and heterosexual): Reis, *Bodies in Doubt*, 46–48. The most intense focus on external genitalia and its correction dates to the 1950s and the influence of John Money's work. On John Money, see Karkazis, *Fixing Sex*; and Feder, "Imperatives of Normality," 225–47.

71. For the challenges facing intersex individuals seeking legal redress, see Lloyd, "From the Hospital to the Courtroom," 155–97. There have been other lawsuits in the United States—a wrongful termination suit brought by an employee, and two suits brought by individuals protesting their treatment while incarcerated—but this is the first to present a real legal challenge to the practice of this kind of surgery. See Greenberg, *Why Sex Matters*.

72. Ghorayshi, "A Landmark Lawsuit About an Intersex Baby's Genital Surgery."

73. See Joel Roth's 2006 responsa for the Committee on Jewish Law and Standards, which served as an addendum to his 1992 responsa. You will see from my reading of the text in this chapter that I believe he misreads the term "zakhrut." See Roth, "Homosexuality Revisited."

constructions of intersex surgeries. The Crawfords, M. C.'s adoptive parents, first found M. C. on an adoption website for children with "special needs." His "special need" was being intersex, or, as the official documents named it, having an "ovotesticular disorder of sexual development."[74] The surgery performed on M. C as a toddler to correct his "disorder" sterilized him, which constituted a partial basis for the Crawfords' legal claims. While the intent of the surgery was not sterility, it was one of the predictable outcomes of the procedure. The doctors were well aware of the potential risks when they counseled surgery.

The practice of medicine is not equally invested in all people's reproductive futures.[75] The case of M. C. can be read within the long narrative of forced sterilizations in US history. The bodies of disabled BIPOC people (in particular) have been the most frequent site of state-sanctioned eugenics. The Southern Poverty Law Center (which, alongside interACT, signed on to M. C.'s lawsuit) participated in the case because of their historical and continued opposition to coerced sterilization and medical experimentation on people of color.[76] The legal basis for forced sterilization comes from the notorious Supreme Court case Buck v. Bell, which authorizes eugenics for people with disabilities and has yet to be overturned.[77] In addition to the racialized and ableist politics of sterilization, scholars have contextualized the recent attention to athletes such as Caster Semenya within the history of racial sciences and the constitution of Black women's bodies as sexually

---

74. Some of the popular news articles that address the M. C. story emphasize that he was otherwise healthy, apart from his "special need" of being intersex. The implication is that there was nothing "wrong" with him *because* the sex variation that the doctors intervened to reconstruct was natural. I want to resist this ableist construction of intersexuality as natural and *therefore* not disabled. As we shall see shortly, the constitution of certain kinds of sexed variance in history as deviant is racialized. In other words, there is nothing particularly natural (or prediscursive) about the term "intersex" itself. At the same time, the assertion of health in these articles (which suggests that M. C. was not disabled), is a way of solidifying "true disability," not unlike the process by which certain bodies are rendered "true hermaphrodites."

75. See, for example, Cárdenas, "Pregnancy: Reproductive Futures in Trans of Color Feminism," 48–57.

76. The practice of coercive sterilization has a long history in this country. There is also evidence that Nazi Germany drew from the Jim Crow regulations to formulate its eugenics plan. It is impossible to highlight all the abuses (and the literature about them), but the Tuskegee experiments, the sterilization of Puerto Rican women, and the sterilization of Indigenous women remain among the most famous case studies. Recently, the Southern Poverty Law Center went on record opposing cases in Tennessee, where prisoners were offered reduced sentences in exchange for sterilization. See Schwartz, "Tennessee Inmates Are Being Offered a Horrifying Choice." For the connection between US eugenics and Nazi policies, see Lombardo, *Three Generations, No Imbeciles*, 239–49.

77. Eli Clare analyzes the category of "imbecile." See Clare, *Brilliant Imperfection*, 103–24.

deviant.⁷⁸ Thus, M. C.'s story can be read within this historical arc of the racialized and ableist regulation of reproduction.

There are, therefore, all kinds of corollary costs to intersex surgeries, embedded as they are within the regulation of racialized ableist gender. M. C.'s case has been valued within the framework of racialized capitalism: M. C.'s forcible assignment (first as a "true" hermaphrodite, then as a girl) was worth $440,000 in structured settlement funds. Since the law works through simile, requiring arguments based on past precedent, M. C.'s case may, in fact, prove invaluable to intersex activists. At the same time, M. C.'s story is representative of a collective cost that has never been fully calculated.

. . .

Neither the tumtum nor the androginos are subjected to the same kinds of violence as intersex Black children in the United States. I am not trying to draw any easy correspondence between the androginos and M. C. But the medical abuse of intersex children, which lies at the heart of the development of contemporary gendered medicine, actively suppressed the self-determination of its supposed subjects. M. C. is not a metaphor. Neither is the androginos. I am drawing a fragile connection between the misused objects of my sources. This allows me to imagine the stories from the perspective of those we were never intended to hear from.

Cocks and androgynes seem unlikely bedfellows. As I read and reread the story in the writing of this chapter, I began to imagine what Rabbi Yehudah HaNasi's narrative might look like from their perspective. How might the androginos and the roosters understand their own relationship? Their version of the tale may be unrecognizable to us, a narrative world in which animals and androgynes do not function as props.

Perhaps, on one silent warm afternoon, a capon and an androginos person sit beside one another.⁷⁹ They move as little as possible in order to capture wayward breezes. Their stillness makes them appear inanimate from afar. After a while, the capon inclines their head to the androginos, and the androginos strokes them carefully, avoiding the capon's scars. The androginos trails their fingertips along the shifting colors and textures of the capon's feathers. They both lean back simultaneously to watch the clouds of dust that are the only mark of the retreating rabbis. "As if," mutters the androginos. The capon cocks their head quizzically, shivering with pleasure at the androginos's gentle, teasing fingertips. "As if I wanted any of them." And then the androginos picks up a tan stone, worn smooth, a

---

78. Magubane, "Spectacles and Scholarship," 761–85.
79. A capon is a castrated rooster. On the history of the capon in the development of trans and intersex medicine, see Gill-Peterson, *Histories of the Transgender Child*, 35–59.

FIGURE 3. *Worn Smooth, Nicki Green,* 2021. Pencil on paper. 12 × 9 inches.

pebble really. They toss it lightly, innocuously. The capon watches as the stone indents where it lands, creating a ripple of dust. And then the capon's sharp talons close about the androginos's finger, squeezing gently. A small bead of blood forms on the adroginos's fingertip. The breeze finally arrives, tossing hair and feathers playfully. The androginos and the capon incline toward one another incrementally, in silent enjoyment.

Some stories may be lost to us. We may still imagine what they might have said.[80]

---

80. In writing this story I am inspired by Jordy Rosenberg's brilliant novel *Confessions of the Fox*, and the ways he reimagines the practice of history.

4

Transing the Eunuch

Kosher and Damaged Masculinity

Historically, scholarship on illness, injury, and bodily differences has tended toward the diagnostic: scholars connect late ancient categories to contemporary medical conditions.[1] Research into biblical and rabbinic medicine has retrospectively diagnosed illnesses and disabilities in ancient sources by closely examining verbal descriptions of symptoms. This research was often interested either in establishing the unerring nature of the sources, or in situating ancient and late antique Jews as early precursors to Western medicine.[2]

When we, as scholars, frame biblical and rabbinic sources through the lens of medical diagnosis, we make certain assumptions about both bodies and texts. If we diagnose bodily conditions from ancient texts, we frame illness and disability as facts written on the body that transcend time and place. The body itself, then, becomes a text—a text that can be read to reveal transhistorical truths. This

---

1. Classically, see Preuss, *Biblisch-talmudische Medizin*. Preuss connects some of the rabbinic texts about "damage" to the penis with hypospadias, for example. See also Hector Avalos, who criticizes "hyper-diagnostic" approaches while maintaining that the diagnostic approach is still important. See Avalos, *Illness and Health Care in the Ancient Near East*. Contemporary scholarship uses diagnosis in service of medical ethics; see, for example, Grey, "Not Judging by Appearances," 126–48. See also Aviad Hacohen, who makes connections to contemporary *responsa* and Israeli law (Hacohen, "'Kol Ish Asher Bo Mum lo Yikarev'" 51–77). Biblicists have criticized diagnostic frames. See Schipper, "Deuteronomy 24:5 and King Asa's Foot Disease in 1 Kings 15:23b," 643–48. The diagnostic impulse is not confined to scholarship in Jewish Studies; see, for example, H. J. Mason on the famous born eunuch Favorinus (Mason, "Favorinus' Disorder," 1–13).

2. For an excellent history of the research on Jewish pharmacology and the connection to Wissenschaft des Judentums, see Lehmhaus and Martelli, eds., *Collecting Recipes*, 1–31. For an analysis of the body in tannaitic literature, see Balberg, *Purity, Body, and Self*.

methodology for reading bodies/texts has a decidedly depoliticizing effect. As Allison Kafer puts it, "Casting disability as a monolithic fact of the body, as beyond the realm of the political and therefore beyond the realm of debate or dissent, makes it impossible to imagine disability and disability futures differently."[3] In Kafer's analysis, treating disability as written on the body forecloses meaning, and restricts the types of questions that we can ask.[4]

What unifies both bodies and texts in the diagnostic approach, however, is the epistemology of diagnosis itself, with its unquestioned assumption: both bodies and texts can divulge their "truths" to a trained interpreter. This methodology not only situates texts to reflect material reality, but it also strips historical texts/bodies bare before the discerning gaze of the diagnostician/scholar. Sick and disabled bodies, therefore, have been used to consolidate a particular hermeneutic in rabbinics.

In response to these earlier diagnostic efforts, contemporary scholars of the Bible and rabbinics tend to complicate relationships among bodies, disability, history, and texts. Recent scholarly approaches do not position disability as an ordained and ahistorical impairment. Instead, to interpret disability is to interpret the processes by which some bodies are accommodated and other bodies are not.[5] To interpret disability is therefore also to interpret the constitution of the norms of embodiment and the various ways contingent bodily attributes are conscripted to work together. In that sense, it is not just disability, but processes of racialization, for example, that are embroiled in determining which bodies receive accommodation in which spaces.

The rabbinic tradition that I analyze in this chapter (a portion of the eighth chapter of Mishnah Yevamot) entwines a conversation about genital damage, ethnicity, masculinity, and sexuality in order to define a "kosher" body. Transing eunuchs and genitally damaged men, therefore, entails attending to overlapping normativities: the enabled body, the normatively sexed body, the constitution of the body as Israelite (nonforeign/nonenslaved), and the androcentric privileges of

---

3. Kafer, *Feminist, Queer, Crip*, 3. Allison Kafer cites Robert McRuer's work as an example of an antinormative use of the term "crip" (McRuer, *Crip Theory*, 31–32.). I am drawing on the antinormative politics of cripping in my frame of transing throughout this chapter. My work as a whole owes much to theorists of disability studies.

4. For a critique of retrospective diagnosis on historical and scientific grounds (citing pathomorphosis and other methodological difficulties), see Leven, "At Times Theses Ancient Facts Seem to Lie Before me Like a Patient," 369–86. See also the work of David Mitchell and Sharon Snyder; they argue that disability in narrative is often construed as though it requires an explanation (Mitchell and Snyder, *Narrative Prosthesis*, 1–14).

5. Disability studies have particularly taken hold in biblical studies, and there is now a vibrant field. See, for example: Moss and Schipper, eds., *Disability Studies and Biblical Literature*; Schipper, *Disability Studies and the Hebrew Bible*; Raphael, *Biblical Corpora*. See also Marx, *Disability in Jewish Law*.

masculinity.⁶ I do not intend transing to function as a colonization of disability studies, critical race theory, feminist theory, or intersex studies. Rather, transing notices the way the mishnah is arranged so as to suggest that these various bodily attributes work harmoniously together, and to examine the kinds of disharmonies that occur when sex changes.

. . .

A note on language: I am referring to genital "damage" because biblical and rabbinic texts use language that suggests that certain men are genitally "blemished" or "damaged."⁷ I will therefore discuss these bodies as damaged in my analysis. Part of the work of this chapter will be to unravel what "damage" means in this context. Before I begin, however, I want to acknowledge that both "damage" and "blemish" are words with a history of violent use to control, contain, and incarcerate people with disabilities. To facilitate greater ease in reading, I do not write "damage" in quotation marks every time; I trust that you will denature these terms without the aid of my punctuational intervention.

In writing this note, I am reminded that just after I underwent top surgery, I received well-meaning advice about treatments that could minimize the scars on my chest. I know many people wish to minimize their scars for a wide variety of reasons: aesthetics, safety, or sensory concerns, for example. I felt very differently about my scars: I had earned them. They were reminders of the process I went through to be able to acknowledge what I desired, and of all the obstacles trans people face when they seek out surgery. The transphobic scars that the world leaves on me are not always apparent; in contrast, these scars were a visible, embodied sign of my transness.

One could read my scars as damage of a kind. Certainly those who oppose access and coverage for trans medical care do. But that is not what my scars mean to me.

BIBLICAL EUNUCHS AND GENITALLY DAMAGED MEN: AN OVERVIEW

Before I delve into the rabbinic sources, I want to briefly review the biblical categories of eunuchs and genitally damaged men. In my chapter "Transing Late

---

6. The term "able-bodied" is more common than the terms "enabled" or "abled" although any of these terms can be fraught in disability justice communities. I am using *abled* and *enabled* to resist the separation of bodies and minds. For an excellent discussion of the terms "bodymind" and "(dis)ability," see Schalk, *Bodyminds Reimagined*, 4–6.

7. Jacob Milgrom argues that the base meaning of *mum* in the Bible is "physical deformity." In some cases the meaning may also cover "moral deficiencies," but not in the verses in Leviticus. See Milgrom, *Leviticus 17–22*, 1823. Any of these terms is problematic from a disability justice perspective.

Antiquity," I describe some of the battles over the translation of the word *saris*, and the debate as to whether it refers solely to eunuchs or also to uncastrated servants in some verses. While some usages of the word *saris* may be ambiguous, there are also some verses where the Hebrew term definitively must refer to a eunuch. So, for example, Isaiah 56:3–5 is one place in the Hebrew Bible where the verses clearly describe a eunuch; biblical scholars have read these verses for clues about the status of eunuchs in the Hebrew Bible:

> And let not the eunuch say, "I am a withered tree." For thus said the LORD: "As for the eunuchs who keep My sabbaths, who have chosen what I desire and hold fast to My covenant, I will give them, in My house, and within My walls, a monument and a name better than sons or daughters. I will give them an everlasting name which shall not perish."[8]

Here God promises a legacy to nonreproductive eunuchs who follow the covenant. Instead of children to carry on the eunuch's name, God grants faithful eunuchs an everlasting name. The eunuch describes their own body as a withered tree in a poignant lament. J. Blake Couey argues that the image of a dried tree is a common Isaianic image that compares barren elements of landscapes with disabled bodies; in this case, the eunuch has internalized the (ableist) rhetoric of Isaiah.[9] As Couey points out, however, unlike the other traditions in Isaiah that describe healing disabilities, this text promises a healed genealogy instead. The end of the last verse proffers a "name that shall not perish." A more literal translation of the verse would be: "A name that shall not be cut off." The reference to "cutting" is not accidental; the play on words is reminiscent of the act of castration itself. But it is also potentially a subtle allusion to the fragility of legacies, and even of children as a legacy; an everlasting divine memorial is less precarious than an earthly one.[10] In the rab-

---

8. For a discussion of the ascription of these verses to Trito-Isaiah, see de Hoop, "The Interpretation of Isaiah 56:1–9," 671–95. For a discussion that contextualizes the verses in Isaiah within the larger Near Eastern culture of caring for the dead (and not as a response to the strictures on genital damage in Deuteronomy), see Wright and Chan, "King and Eunuch," 99–119. Cf. Tuell, "The Evidence of the 'Foreigner,'" 183–205. This is another instance where genital changes are associated with foreignness in the Hebrew Bible.

9. Couey, "Isaiah, Jeremiah, Ezekiel, Daniel, and the Twelve," 215–73. Couey also points out that the word that has been translated as "monument," but that literally means "hand" is a euphemism for "penis" in other biblical texts. See also Wisdom of Solomon 3:14 for a parallel tradition, as well as Martti Nissinen's comments on it (Nissinen, "Relative Masculinities in the Hebrew Bible/Old Testament," 221–47).

10. Given this biblical discussion of procreativity and eunuchs, it is all the more striking that the rabbis do not cite Isaiah in their extensive discussions of the eunuch and levirate marriage. The rabbis examine the Isaiah verses in a variety of different contexts: in praising the keeping of Shabbat (b. Shabbat 118b); in the discussion of a good name (Midrash Tanḥuma', *Vayakhel* 1:5 to Ecclesiastes 7:1); in the discussion of Daniel as a eunuch (b. Sanhedrin 93b and Pirkei d'Rabbi Eliezer, chap. 52:10 to Isaiah 39:2); and in relation to the status of the convert (Bamidbar Rabba 5:3 on Numbers 4:18).

binic discussion that I analyze in this chapter, we shall see the rabbis directly addressing eunuchs and the question of reproduction and legacies as raised in the Hebrew Bible.

In addition to the saris/eunuch, there are also three other biblical categories: the *m'roaḥ 'ashekh, p'zua daka'* and *krut shafkhah*. These three categories are all terms for genitally damaged men in the Bible. They are found in two different contexts: genitally damaged priests are addressed in Leviticus, while nonpriestly men with genital damage are found in Deuteronomy.[11]

The genitally damaged priest appears in a section of Leviticus usually designated as the Holiness Code: it lists a number of laws that govern priests in particular, including the laws of priestly marriages. In the middle of this chapter there is a list of "defects," which, when found in priestly bodies, disqualify them from certain kinds of priestly work.[12] These "blemishes" include blindness, lameness, and a term that is most often translated as "crushed testes" (*m'roaḥ 'ashekh*).[13] Priests must be free of "blemishes" in order to perform the ritual sacrifices, and in order to enter certain parts of the Temple.[14]

The next chapter of Leviticus contains a parallel list of blemishes that disqualify animals from being sacrificed.[15] In both lists, genital "damage" is just one of a number of disqualifying conditions, and it is not particularly emphasized.[16] In

---

11. While these chapters in Leviticus elaborate on a list of blemishes, the Hebrew Bible did not invent this genre. We have lists of bodily blemishes from Sumerian sources, and examples from the Hittite Law code, among others. See Stewart, "Sexual Disabilities in the Hebrew Bible," 67–87.

12. Many of the terms on this list in Leviticus 21 and 22 are *hapax legomena*. Scholars compare these terms to the Septuagint and other early translations and interpretations, but there is little consensus about the translation of some of them. See Saul Olyan on the lists in Leviticus (Olyan, *Disability in the Hebrew Bible*, 26–47).

13. The word *'ashekh* is a *hapax legomenon*, but Jacob Milgrom notes that it is similar to the Akkadian and Ugaritic words for testicle (see Milgrom, *Leviticus 17–22*). Johanna Dorman posits that the term probably literally means something like "one whose testicles are rubbed or crushed." Although the biblical text does not specify, later translations and discussions of this verse discuss the number of testicles damaged. So the Septuagint translates the *m'roaḥ 'ashekh* as μόνορχις—"one testicle." See Dorman, "The Blemished Body," 31.

14. Jacob Milgrom argues that the word *yikrav* (which I am translating as "approach") must be understood as encroaching in this case (Milgrom, *Leviticus 17–22*). The topic of what precisely is being prohibited is discussed in rabbinic literature. See, for example, m. Kelim 1:9 and Sifra, *Emor* 3:3–4, to Leviticus 21:17.

15. There is more to be said about this parallel between priestly and animal blemishes, but to do so would exceed the scope of my discussion here. We witness rabbinic literature drawing parallels between the two lists: see, for example, Sifra, *Emor* 7: 13 on Leviticus 22:22, where the text asserts that anything on the list of animal blemishes also constitutes a blemish for humans and vice versa.

16. Saul Olyan uses the case of the priestly blemish to argue that defects do not always profane holiness, since the priests can still partake of the heave offering. See Olyan, "Defects, Holiness, and Pollution," 1018–28.

addition, while the blemished priest may be banned from certain parts of the Temple, he is not wholly excluded from the priesthood.[17] The rabbis import all the categories of genital damage, including the priest with the crushed testes, into their debates. Still, they discuss the category of the *m'roah 'ashekh* the least.[18]

The second set of biblical categories of genital damage is found in Deuteronomy, which introduces two additional terms of genital damage. Here the text is not discussing priests per se, but ordinary men:[19] "No one whose testes are crushed (*p'zua daka'*) or whose penis is cut off (*krut shafkhah*) shall be admitted into the congregation of the LORD." (Deuteronomy 23:2). In Deuteronomy, as in Leviticus, there is a category of testicular damage, but this is paired with a separate category of the severed penis.[20]

The interdiction against "entering into the congregation" has puzzled scholars, and there is no consensus on its precise meaning.[21] The rabbis generally interpret "entering into the congregation" as pertaining to marriage. Using this understand-

---

17. David Tabb Stewart helpfully schematizes Leviticus into two binaries: pure/impure and blemished/unblemished. Thus, for example, genital damage leaves one pure but also blemished. Therefore, the priest may still eat the holiest foods (since those must be consumed in a state of purity but do not require an unblemished state). See Stewart, "Sexual Disabilities in the Hebrew Bible," 67–89.

18. Johanna Dorman provocatively asks why the Leviticus verse does not use the terms *p'zua daka'* and *krut shafkhah*, but she does not fully answer the question (see Dorman, "The Blemished Body," 15–47). The *m'roah 'ashekh* is found in m. Bekhorot 7:5, t. Bekhorot 5:4, Sifra, *Emor* 3:12 to Leviticus 21:20 and Sifra, *Emor*, 3:15 to Leviticus 21:20, and b. Bekhorot 44b. The saris and the Deuteronomic categories of genital damage are discussed much more frequently. This is even more striking in light of the extensive rabbinic engagement with these lists of priestly blemishes. The rabbinic elaboration (in Mishnah Bekhorot) takes the list of twelve "blemishes" for priests and adds sixty-three more types of disqualifying blemishes; it also includes forty-seven new animal blemishes. For a discussion of this text, see Ishay Rosen-Zvi, "*Haguf v'ha'mikdash*," 49–87. As we shall see, the rabbis will apply the Leviticus verses (about the *m'roah 'ashekh*) directly to the *p'zua daka' / krut shafkhah*. For all intents and purposes, they collapse the three terms (one originally used only in the context of priests and two that applied to all Israelite men). The rabbis keep the concept of priestly genital damage in rabbinic legal thought while using the specific biblical term sparingly.

19. Johanna Dorman notes that the Septuagint translates the *krut shafkhah* as ἀποκεκομμένος (from the word for "cut") and *p'zua daka'* as θλαδίας—both Greek terms that can be used to refer to eunuchs. Dorman speculates that there was a distinction between the two kinds of genital damage, but it is not clear what the distinction was. See Dorman, "The Blemished Body."

20. David Tabb Stewart has argued that the Deuteronomic categories should be understood as referring to men who have no function in the penis or testicles. See Tabb Stewart, "Leviticus-Deuteronomy," 76.

21. The use of *lavo*/"enter" with *kahal*/"congregation" appears also in Lamentations 1:10, Nehemiah 13:1, and Judges 21:8, as well as in the Dead Sea Scrolls (1QSa 2:3–11); scholars generally use these parallel verses, along with the larger context of the chapter in Deuteronomy, to determine the meaning of the phrase. Christine Hayes argues that "to enter into the congregation" has two principal meanings in the biblical texts—sanctuary and marriage (Hayes, *Gentile Impurities and Jewish Identities*). Saul Olyan tentatively interprets Deuteronomy 23:2 to refer to the sanctuary (see Olyan, *Rites and Rank*). Susan Ackerman argues that the prohibition was spatial; moreover, she thinks that barren women would have been banned from the Temple by those verses (Ackerman, "The Blind, the Lame, and the Barren," 29–47).

ing of the verse, the rabbis read this as a prohibition against a genitally damaged man marrying a woman who is an "Israelite" (i.e., born free and Jewish). This implies that genitally damaged men are allowed to marry only freed slaves and converts to Judaism.[22] The rabbis, therefore, generally interpret these verses as placing limitations on whom genitally damaged men can marry.[23]

The biblical sources do not explicitly connect eunuchs and genitally damaged men. And yet, as we shall see, the rabbis create links between the two.[24]

KOSHER MASCULINITY: TRANSING GENITAL DAMAGE

The beginning of the eighth chapter of Mishnah Yevamot focuses on genitally damaged men.[25] In this opening discussion, the rabbis define genital damage using the language of "kosher" genitalia. Jewish texts, of course, pay plenty of attention to genitalia, primarily to the penis, and mostly in the context of circumcision. Within a wider discussion of genital cutting, then, the rabbis draw careful distinctions

---

22. On the question of the related prohibition against Ammonites and Moabites, see Hayes, "Intermarriage and Impurity in Ancient Jewish Sources," 3–36.

23. The interpretation of "being admitted into the congregation" as marriage is plausible in part because of the larger biblical context: the latter half of chapter 22 in Deuteronomy discusses sexual transgressions, and the first verse of chapter 23 continues in the same vein. The word that I am translating as "enter" is also a euphemism for sexual intercourse. The rabbinic interpretation of this verse plays with the double entendre of the verb.

24. There is only one rabbinic source that potentially completely conflates the genitally damaged men with the saris: see t. Yevamot 10:3, which seems to collapse the *p'zua daka'* and the born saris. Sarra Lev discusses this source in "Genital Trouble." In later layers of rabbinic literature, the rabbis apply the Deuteronomic prohibition (which pertains biblically only to genitally damaged men) to the eunuch. However, Philo and Josephus pair these categories, so there is an established reception history that connects genitally damaged men and eunuchs.

25. The eighth chapter of Mishnah Yevamot appears to be held together tenuously by its connection to androgynes and eunuchs. One possible reading of the connection among the mishnayot is that these figures are all suspected of being barren. If that were the case, we might expect to see others like the barren woman included in the chapter as well. Barren women and old men are paired with eunuchs in other tannaitic legal texts. See t. Yevamot 2:5 or t. Yevamot 11:2.

We might read this chapter of the Mishnah as loosely organized, because it is mostly linked through a connection to eunuchs and androgynes. Some mishnaic chapters are more tightly organized than others. The easiest way to argue for the coherence of a mishnaic chapter is through linguistic or other structural markers. Repetition of phrasing and consistent content suggest that the chapter is a crafted unit (see, for example, m. Terumot 5). The eighth chapter of Yevamot is neither a list nor does it contain linguistic markers that distinguish it from the surrounding material. The chapter has no easily identifiable thematic unity; it discusses heave offerings, marriage, levirate marriage, and illicit sex. And yet, it is still carefully edited together to unite eunuchs and androgynes. As such, it seems likely that at least some strands of tannaitic thought are working with an abstract concept of sex/gender variation, a category that includes both eunuchs and androgynes.

between cutting "too much" and "not enough." The discussion of "kosher" genitals is embedded in a particular legal question, and yet it functions to regulate the mutability of sex: some changes are necessary, while others are destructive. In this section, we will begin to trans genital "damage" with a discussion of the kosher cut.

The beginning of this chapter of the Mishnah defines two types of genitally damaged men:[26]

> Who is the *p'zua daka'*? Anyone whose testicles are wounded [Heb. *nifza'*]—even one of them. And [who is] the *krut shafkhah*? Anyone whose penis[27] has been severed [Heb. *nikhrat*]. And if there is left of the crown [of the penis] even a strand [of skin],[28] [he is] kosher. (m. Yevamot 8:2)[29]

This tradition suggests an etymology for the biblical terms for genitally damaged men. The Mishnah defines the terms through wordplay. The rabbis note that the phrase that describes a man with damaged testicles contains the word *p'zua*, which means wound, and the phrase for the man with a severed penis contains *krut*, the word for cut.[30] The pair is therefore differentiated by the exact location of their genital damage—either to the penis or to the testicles. Interestingly, there is almost no legal import to that distinction, and when these figures are invoked throughout the corpus, they are most often treated together in discussion.

---

26. In the rest of the chapter, the expression "genitally damaged men" will refer to the *p'zua daka'* / *krut shafkhah*. If I need to specify one of them, I will use the transliteration. If I am discussing the *m'roah 'ashekh*, I will specify that as well.

27. The word that I am translating as "penis" is *gid*, which elsewhere in tannaitic literature almost always refers to the *gid hanasheh* and is therefore usually translated as "the sciatic nerve." The word also infrequently serves as a euphemism for the penis (see, for example, b. Yevamot 55b, where it clearly refers to genitalia). We also see *gid* come to mean penis in legal traditions about determining the age of the *ben sorer umoreh* (see b. Sanhedrin 68b).

28. Both the Parma (Biblioteca Palatina 3173) and Kaufmann (A 50-Budapest) manuscripts omit the word *hair* ("even a strand of hair"), and I have omitted it here. The inclusion/exclusion of the metaphor does not substantially change the sense, which is that even a small amount of the crown is sufficient. In the Tosefta, the definition is elaborated, and one opinion holds that even a missing testicle counts (although another opinion argues that a person who is missing testicle is a born saris). See t. Yevamot 10:3.

29. I will begin my discussion of the text slightly out of order—it is only in the second mishnah that the rabbis offer a definition of their terms.

30. The terms *p'zua daka'* / *krut shafkhah* are hapax legomena, but scholars believe that this derivation of the terms is generally accurate. The term *p'zua daka'* probably comes from a joining of the words for wound and crush. This etymology is suggested in the sugya on b. Yevamot 75b. See also Sifra, *Emor* 7:9 on Leviticus 22:24 where there is a disagreement over which term applies to the penis and which to the testicles. Based on the etymological work of biblical scholars, Sarra Lev thinks that the *krut shafkhah* refers to someone whose urethra was cut. For an excellent survey of the biblical philology on *p'zua daka'* and *krut shafkhah*, see Lev, "Genital Trouble," 82–121.

This is certainly not the only moment when early rabbinic sources pay a lingering attention to the question of valid penises. There are discussions, for example, of invalid circumcisions.[31] In this context, however, in order to lay out the diagnostic criterion for genitally damaged men, the Mishnah scrutinizes genitalia to decide how much damage is significant. The criterion for damage varies; according to this anonymous opinion, any wounding of the testicles renders a person damaged, but the penis may be substantially damaged while the person remains "fit."

Wordplay is a common enough rabbinic mode of interpretation, but in this case the play on words dictates the boundaries of the categories themselves. Since we are explicitly discussing the question of which genitalia are "kosher," it is easy to lose sight of the fact that the Mishnah is also rendering a ruling on a question of signification: when are genitalia so changed that they may no longer be defined as kosher? Or (and this phrasing is playful but deliberate): when is sex changed?

This anonymous definition of kosher genitals is not the beginning of the mishnaic chapter. It is preceded by the case of the uncircumcised priest. In rabbinic sources, there is an acknowledgement that infants sometimes cannot be circumcised for health reasons. Therefore, the figure of the uncircumcised priest is established within rabbinic literature.[32] In our chapter, the rabbis discuss the uncircumcised priest and his ability to feed his household the heave offering: "An uncircumcised [priest], [or a priest] who is ritually impure, does not eat the heave offering, [but] their wives and slaves eat the heave offering." The heave offering is a sacrifice that must be consumed while the priest is in a state of ritual purity. The uncircumcised priest is likened to other priests that are in a state of impurity. A priest in a state of impurity may not partake of the heave offering himself. However, his own personal status does not disqualify his household, so his wife and servants may continue to eat it.

It makes sense that the tradition about uncircumcised priests and genitally damaged priests are in proximity; they are connected by the heave offering and the legal question of the priestly household's access to it. And yet the placement of the case of the uncircumcised priest adjacent to the question of genital damage is

---

31. See m. Shabbat 19:6 for a case where shreds of skin invalidate circumcision. The word *kosher* is not used there, but the text pays similar attention to defining what kinds of penises (and, in this case, circumcisions) are valid. The Tosefta elaborates on the discussion of kosher genitalia; in the Tosefta, however, the term "kosher" can relate to whether the damage renders them infertile. See t. Yevamot 10:4.

32. The term 'arel is already in the Hebrew Bible (see Exodus 12:48), but it is not used in reference to priests. In rabbinic literature there is a lively debate about when someone is required to circumcise if the prospect of doing or not doing so presents a potential health risk (see b. Yevamot 64b and b. Shabbat 134a and Geller, "Akkadian Healing Therapies," 16). For a discussion of the sugya that discusses the qualities of the 'arel, see Kraemer, *Reading the Rabbis*, 109–23. For a discussion of the stigma associated with being uncircumcised in the Hebrew Bible, see Olyan, *Disability in the Hebrew Bible*, 36–38.

suggestive.³³ While the genitally damaged man has unfit genitalia, the intact/uncircumcised priest's genitalia are also problematic. An acceptable range for the penis is being enacted. Being uncut is like being impure but being too cut is not kosher.

The Mishnah continues to address the situation of the genitally damaged priest. The household of the genitally damaged priest is treated differently from the household of the uncircumcised priest:

> Genitally damaged priests and their slaves eat [the heave offering], but their wives do not eat [the heave offering.] And if [the genitally damaged priests] have not had sex with their wives from the time when they incurred the damage, then [their wives] can eat [the heave offering]." (m. Yevamot 8:1)³⁴

The rule for the genitally damaged priest does not assume that his genital damage makes him ritually impure (like the uncircumcised priest). Instead, the genitally damaged priest is free to eat the heave offering himself; this implies that he is not considered impure.³⁵ But his household is split up: his servants are allowed to eat the heave offering, while his wife is not.³⁶

---

33. Biblical law (Leviticus 22:1–15) already rules that priests cannot eat the heave offering while in specific states of impurity; this mishnah makes the uncircumcised priest analogous to one in a state of impurity. Any person the priest acquires, according to biblical law (and this would include both his wife and servants), is allowed to eat the holiest foods by virtue of that acquisition.

34. Kaufmann (A 50-Budapest) is substantially the same with minor changes, except that it was written in a different hand as though it had been filled in later. Parma (Biblioteca Palatina 3173) has *y'da'ah*. What I am calling the sexual clause (if he did not have sex with her, she may eat) is an unaccountable addition to the biblical laws, and later commentators discuss it.

35. Leviticus 21:16–24 spells out the various blemishes that disqualify a priest from certain kinds of Temple service. Leviticus 21:22 states explicitly that a priest with a blemish may eat sacrificial food, even food that has the status of "holiness." Although the term that the Bible uses in these verses is *m'roah 'ashekh*, it is evident that the rabbis are interpreting the *p'zua daka'* and *krut shafkhah* as an equivalent category of genital damage when they rule that the *p'zua daka' / krut shafkhah* can himself eat the heave offering. In that sense, the mishnaic case of the genitally damaged priest is consistent with the biblical category of any priest with a blemish who is permitted to eat the heave offering. Genital damage is like any other blemish on the long list in Leviticus.

In the next chapter of Leviticus, the Bible elaborates on the question of who is permitted to eat holy foods. Leviticus 22:10–13 informs us that the household of the priest, including anyone the priest acquires, may partake of the holy food. The word acquire (*yikneh*) in the verse is the same word used in early rabbinic (tannaitic) literature to refer to the acquisition of property, slaves, and wives. The biblical text suggests that all the members of the priestly household (barring hired laborers and others the priest does not "acquire") may eat the holy foods.

36. By separating out the wife from the slaves of the priest, this mishnah makes it clear that the acquisition of the slave is not in question. The biblical text specifically juxtaposes the hired laborer with someone the priest "acquired," although the discussion in later layers of rabbinic text also seeks to complicate the question of slaves and laborers. See, for example, the discussion in Sifra, *Emor* 5:1–5, on Leviticus 22:11, p. Yevamot 8:1 (8c–9a), and b. Yevamot 70a.

This deceptively benign discussion of the range of different types of penises enables a broader conversation about sex, Jewish masculinity, and bodies.[37] On a prosaic level, the use of the term "kosher" in the second mishnah is quite straightforward: if the man's penis still contains a strand of the crown, then his body is kosher. However, the word *kosher* invites us to speculate about the category of a kosher or "fit" man.[38] By judging certain penises kosher, the text implicitly renders other genitalia *treyf.*

A purely medical model of disability might invite us to consider the question of being kosher or fit, literally. We might connect this description of damaged genitalia to a host of other conditions or injuries in order to imagine how this condition might be physically disabling. We might speculate on the question of how genital damage could interfere with the ability to perform particular priestly duties.[39] Alternatively, we might turn to aesthetics in order to assess the aesthetic criterion that dictates what constitutes (sufficiently whole) genitalia. Some scholars writing about priestly blemishes in the Bible argue that the list of disabilities is, in fact, a problem of visual bodily differences.[40] If we accept that this argument holds in rabbinic texts, we might interrogate the aesthetics of the kosher penis against which penile damage is assessed.

Either of these interpretative frames—function or aesthetics—falls into a common pattern of interpreting disability, as disability studies scholars like Lennard Davis have pointed out.[41] Both types of interpretations run the risk of assuming that our definitions of functionality and aesthetics are stable across time and place. We know, for example, that the genital aesthetics of early layers of rabbinic literature are in dialogue with Greco-Roman ideals.[42] And questions of the "functionality" of

---

37. There are at least two ways to interpret the word "kosher" here. The first is that it refers to the man's fitness to enter into the community, because of the verse cited in the third mishnah. Thus, the adjudication of genitalia refers to the question of whether the man to whom they pertain may marry an Israelite woman or not. The second is to connect the third mishnah to the second, and to read it as a continuation of the discussion of the heave offering (a reading that Sarra Lev rejects—see "Genital Trouble").

38. In her discussion of b. Kiddushin 70a, Christine Hayes examines the question of fitness in her argument that the regulation of genealogical status in rabbinic sources is a means of guarding against potential priestly transgressions of biblical marriage regulations. See Hayes, *Gentile Impurities and Jewish Identities,* 274–75.

39. Johanna Dorman suggests that one reason Leviticus 21 might have excluded certain priests from priestly service is that they would not have been physically able to carry out their duties. Although she does not settle on this interpretation, the idea that disability is a problem of bodily function underlies this speculation. See Johanna Dorman, "The Blemished Body," 15–48.

40. Scholars debate whether there is an underlying logic in the biblical lists of priestly blemishes. For a discussion of the various arguments, see Olyan, *Disability in the Hebrew Bible,* 27–31.

41. Davis, *Enforcing Normalcy.* On the question of function, see his comments beginning on page 9. On the question of aesthetics (and the ideal body) see the discussion that begins on page 24.

42. Boyarin analyzes Greco-Roman genital aesthetics and the rabbinic discussion of genitalia in several places. See, for example, Boyarin, "The Great Fat Massacre," 69–99.

genitalia remain contested even today. In the last chapter, I described recent activist fights against surgical sex assignments for intersex infants. Cosmetic genital surgery on intersex infants is often designed to facilitate future heterosexual penetrative sex; in other words, it assumes what the function of genitalia is. Function and aesthetics are contested ground both historically and today, and any assumptions that we detect may be assertions rather than reflections of a general consensus.

Instead, I want to examine the legal impacts of this ruling on the marriage of the genitally damaged priest, in order to explore how genital damage functions locally within this particular discussion. What is it about genital damage that particularly impacts the status of the priest's wife? Neither a functional nor an aesthetic approach can completely explain what I am calling the "sexual clause"—that the priest's wife may eat the heave offering only if she has not yet had sexual contact with the damaged genitalia of her husband.[43] Clearly, the function of the priest's genitalia is not at issue—the premise of the sexual clause is that the priest can have sexual contact with his wife. And aesthetics, while they may be at play in the status of the priestly body, should be irrelevant to the status of his wife.

The interpretation of this mishnah is difficult (and debated by later commentators). But the continuation of the mishnah cites a biblical verse:

> Genitally damaged priests are permitted [to marry] a convert or a freed slave; they are only prohibited from "entering into the congregation" as it is written [in Deuteronomy 23:2]: "The *p'zua daka'* and *krut shafkhah* should not enter [Heb. *yavo'*] into the congregation of the LORD." (m. Yevamot 8:2)

The rabbis cite the verse in Deuteronomy that prevents genitally damaged men from "entering into the congregation." According to the rabbinic interpretation of this verse, genitally damaged men are permitted to marry certain women—converts and freed slaves. The rabbis are interpreting the phrase "enter the congregation" as a limitation on whom genitally damaged men may marry; specifically, genitally damaged men may not marry Israelite women—women who were born free and Jewish. At the same time, the Hebrew Bible carefully regulates priestly marriage more generally. Leviticus states that because priests have a status as holy, they cannot marry a freed slave.[44] In other words, normally, priests would be able to marry *only* Israelite women.

---

43. On the surface, this seems like an unprecedented advocacy of celibate marriage. Scholarship has mostly argued that rabbinic culture has little place for celibacy. See Diamond, *Holy Men and Hunger Artists*; Satlow, *Tasting the Dish*. Cf. Kiel, *Sexuality in the Babylonian Talmud*. There is some indication that there may be a question of penile aesthetics in rabbinic literature. See the sugya in b. Yevamot 75b on the shaping of a different penis (like a quill, etc.).

44. Milgrom, *Leviticus*, 264–65. Milgrom explains that women entering into priestly marriages were investigated in Second Temple times, in order to ascertain their fitness to marry priests. Christine Hayes has argued that the biblical prohibition against priestly intermarriage was extended to all Israelites in the Second Temple period. See Hayes, *Gentile Impurities*, 68–92.

The genitally damaged priest, according to our mishnah, now has a marriage dilemma. On the one hand, priests in general are not allowed to marry converts and freed slaves. On the other hand, the genitally damaged priest is allowed to marry *only* a convert or a freed slave.⁴⁵ Instead of completely invalidating a prior marriage if there is subsequent genital damage, this ruling permits the consumption of the heave offering if no sexual contact has occurred in the interim since damage took place.⁴⁶

There are technical reasons for the prohibition against sexual contact between the genitally damaged priest and his wife. But the aversion to sex with the damaged genitalia of the priest exceeds the dictates of biblical law. The detailed and evocative description of his genitalia, which invites us to participate in inspecting the contours of his injury, coupled with an avoidance of sexual contact, all work together to create a sense of fascinated disgust. At the same time, this mishnah has some real impact on the priest. While the mishnah leaves intact his basic ability to acquire a wife, because of the warring marriage constraints on priests and genitally damaged men, there is no woman whom he can acquire who can then partake in the heave offering—either because of her status, or because of his.

---

45. Although the Deuteronomic verse is not about priests but about genitally damaged men, by conflating priestly damage with the issue of "entering into the community," the rabbis create a dilemma for genitally damaged priests. The marriage dilemma of the priestly *p'zua daka'* / *krut shafkhah* is discussed explicitly in the Babylonian Talmud; see b. Yevamot 76a. Christine Hayes reads this sugya closely and argues that Rava is mobilizing a holy seed rationale in considering the Deuteronomic prohibition on intermarriage. See Hayes, *Gentile Impurities*, 178–84.

46. The technical logic to the mishnah here, as read through parallel sources in the Tosefta, is as follows: We must assume that the woman is betrothed to the priest while he has "intact" genitalia. She must be an Israelite woman (since we know that she is originally fit for marriage with a priest). Once the priest is genitally damaged, the woman is now forbidden to him by the prohibition against "entering into the community." If the priest and the woman marry and have sex, she has now had prohibited sex. As we know from other sources, women who have prohibited sex may not partake of the heave offering.

Note that the status of the woman in the marriage has not changed; it is only the priest's body that has changed. Still, the commentators tend to frame the question around her status. Ovadiah ben Abraham, the sixteenth-century rabbi, explains that the wife is equivalent to a *ḥalalah*, who is prohibited for marriage to the priest by Leviticus 21:7. Maimonides, a famous commentator writing in the twelfth century, explains the case in a similar vein but with a slight variation: "And we already knew, intercourse with the *p'zua daka'* and *krut shafkhah* constitutes *bi'ilat znut* [improper sexual relations]." Maimonides reads this mishnah through rabbinic discussions about cases of women betrothed to priests who would be judged either forbidden or unfit (see p. Yevamot 6:3 (7b-c), b. Yevamot 56b). In his reading, this case is of a widow or divorcée who is engaged to a priest but who is also the daughter of a priest; thus, she would normally eat the heave offering because of her father. In Maimonides's view, we are dealing with a case where sex has not yet occurred. This is how Maimonides interprets the oddity of the mishnah. Although in doing so, he interprets the text in a way that goes against the plain sense of the mishnah; the phrase, "If he has not had sex with her since becoming a *p'zua daka'*," implies that he had already had a sexual relationship with her. There are other cases where the status of the priest changes after contracting marriage. See, for example, b. Yevamot 20b.

The effect of the sexual clause is to single out the genitally damaged priest. When the Hebrew Bible lists the blemishes that disqualify the priest, it does not emphasize any particular bodily difference on the list. Blindness is not treated any differently than genital damage. The Mishnah undoes the implicit equation among the bodily differences on the list. The effects of this ruling are significant: since eating the heave offering is one of the fundamental perks of a priestly marriage, the priest's function as the paterfamilias—as the head of his household—would be compromised by sexual contact with his wife.[47] Normally, we think of impurity as contagious in Jewish legal sources. Instead, in this passage bodily damage seems to function as a sexually transmitted infection.

Rather than turning to function or aesthetics to explain genital damage, I am drawing our attention to the precarious balance in the juxtaposition between the uncut penis and the one that is too cut. Necessary cuts to the penis enable the priest to participate in eating the heave offering. Cuts that are deemed damaging instead disable the priest. Transing kosher genitalia, therefore, notices how these traditions, taken together, mandate a certain acceptable range of the mutability of sex.

Fitness may be literally measured by a strip of flesh, but it also dictates the kinds of women the priest may marry. Male "fitness" is enacted through a sexual economy predicated on the acquisition of women and servants. Women and servants, in turn, serve as a yardstick of kosher genitalia; the question of fit/kosher genitalia, therefore, exposes masculinist ableist logics.[48] If the rights of the householder are central to the gendered project of rabbinic law, then the result of this ruling is that genital damage interferes with the most fundamental purview of masculinity. While the priest's physical capacity to engage in sex seems not to be in question, the rabbis legislate a sexual disability.

THE AMMONITE AND MOABITE: PENETRABLE SOCIAL BOUNDARIES

Circumcision is at times conflated with castration, and at times a rhetorical link is drawn between the two practices that extends beyond rabbinic literature.[49] At the

---

47. See also Hezser, "Passover and Social Equality," 91–107. Hezser argues in the introduction to her article that the rabbinic male householder is analogous to the Greco-Roman paterfamilias.

48. The literature on the question of men's acquisition of women and servants is too vast to summarize, but regarding the question of the acquisition of women in marriage, Gail Labovitz's article has a good summary of various classic feminist interpretative trends. See Labovitz, "The Language of the Bible," 25–42. Other scholars have argued that the rabbis negotiate masculinity through the bodies of priests. See, for example, Lehman, "Imagining the Priesthood in Tractate Yoma," 88–105. See also Rosen-Zvi, *The Rite that Was Not.*

49. I am less concerned with Freud and the psychoanalytic linkages here than with the rhetorical constructions of circumcision in late antiquity. On the connections drawn between circumcision and

same time, circumcision also carries enormous symbolic weight as a sign of the Israelite's covenant with God, written on the masculine body. While Jews (or Israelites) were not the only ones to practice circumcision in this period, the practice was associated with debates over the boundaries of Jewishness.[50] When our chapter of the Mishnah assembles uncircumcised priests, genital damage, and the verses that prohibit "entering into the community," it links communal boundaries with masculine bodies and genital cutting. The next section of the Mishnah extends this linkage.

In the Hebrew Bible, the verses that prohibit genitally damaged men from "entering into the congregation" are followed by prohibitions against other groups of people "entering into the congregation." In subsequent verses, children of prohibited sexual unions and other groups of undesirables are also barred. The Hebrew Bible, therefore, already links genitally damaged men with other groups in a series of verses. Thus, it is not surprising that the next section of the Mishnah addresses the question of other groups "entering into the congregation:"

> The Ammonite and Moabite are forbidden [to "enter into the congregation"], and [their descendants] are forbidden [from "entering into the congregation] forever. But their women are permitted immediately [to "enter into the congregation"]. An Egyptian and an Edomite—both men and women—are only forbidden [to "enter into the congregation"] for three generations . . .[51] (m. Yevamot 8:3).

The rabbis have already interpreted the phrase "entering into the congregation" to mean marriage with Israelites (i.e., women who were both free and Jewish by birth.) This mishnah restates the prohibition and relates it to a host of other groups

---

effeminacy in Philo and others, see Cohen, *Why Aren't Jewish Women Circumcised?* For the debate over Hadrian's ban (and the question of whether the ban prohibited castration, circumcision, or both), see Boustan, "Negotiating Difference," 71–92. For a classic article on the question of the sources for Hadrian's ban on circumcision/castration, see Geiger, "Hag'zeirah al hamilah u'mered Bar Kochba," 139–47.

50. For instance, we see the debate over circumcision and Jewishness in Paul's writing, but it is continued in the patristics. See Hoffman, *Covenant of Blood*; Boyarin, *A Radical Jew*. In the realm of art, see Couzin, "Uncircumcision in Early Christian Art," 601–29.

51. The rest of the mishnah also prohibits the entrance of the mamzer and the Natinim. "Natinim" is the name given to the Gibeonites after they deceive Joshua about their native status in Canaan. In response, they are cursed to be slaves (water-carriers and wood cutters)—see Joshua 9. The Bible, however, makes no specific mention of a prohibition against intermarriage with them. The Natinim are mentioned in other places in tannaitic literature, generally in the context of other lists (some of which also contain the *p'zua daka'* / *krut shafkhah*). Compare, for example, t. Megillah 2:7 with m. Horayot 1:4. For an analysis of the question of whether the Israelites understood foreigners as full persons, see Lemos, *Violence and Personhood in Ancient Israel*, 28–60.

Given the order in the Hebrew Bible, the *mamzer* should appear before the Ammonite and Moabite on the mishnaic list. Instead, the mamzer follows the discussion of the Ammonite and Moabite. Genital damage functions as the hinge between the uncircumcised priest and the mamzer, but it is possible to read this as evidence of the careful shaping of this mishnaic chapter.

of people already mentioned in the Hebrew Bible. These are groups of people that are generally portrayed as opponents of the Israelites in the Bible; among the offenses ascribed to the Ammonites, for example, is their refusal to allow the Israelites to pass through their lands (Numbers 21:21–23).[52] The Mishnah adds to the biblical text, but the basic contours of the law, and the careful genealogical accounting that seems to be required, are already established.

As the Ammonite and Moabite are already linked to genital damage by the Hebrew Bible itself, it is unsurprising to find them in proximity to genital damage in the Mishnah. And yet this association continues to strengthen the linkage between the borders of Jewishness and genital damage. And while this mishnah picks up the themes established in the Hebrew Bible, it also mirrors a much broader discourse about genital cutting and foreignness in Greek and Latin literatures.

The polemical characterization of eunuchs as foreign is reiterated in Greco-Roman literature and eventually inscribed in Roman legal discourses as well. Scholars have discussed, for example, the difficulties of studying eunuchs in Persia when many Greek sources deploy the eunuch as a rhetorical figure that symbolizes the effeminate Persian court.[53] Although Greco-Roman sources tend to displace eunuchs to Persia, there are independent sources that seem to confirm the presence of eunuchs in Persia from the Achaemenid to the Sasanian period.[54] It is

---

52. The biblical categories—the Ammonite, the Moabite, the Egyptian, and the Edomite—are only sparingly treated in the rest of the Mishnah, and this chapter is the only one in which we see all of them grouped together. The fourth chapter of Yadayim (m. Yadayim 4:3–4) treats the Ammonites and Moabites; this chapter of Yadayim is one of the few places in which Ammonites are mentioned—that is, apart from a few scattered references to Ammon (see, for example, m. Sotah 8:1, which alludes to Ammonites in a citation from II Samuel). Of this list, only the Natin figures more broadly in the Mishnah. For similar lists (in different legal contexts) that include the Natin, see m. Kiddushin 2:3, 3:12. See also Stern, *Jewish Identity in Early Rabbinic Writings*, 13–18. Stern argues that mishnaic law ultimately undoes even the prohibition against the Ammonite and Moabite entering into the congregation.

53. Llewelyn-Jones, "Eunuchs and the Royal Harem in Achaemenid Persia," 19–51. While most of the sources that Llewelyn-Jones cites would come from an earlier period than ours, he includes some later Hellenistic and Roman authors. David Hester discusses the ways in which the eunuch is used to feminize the "other" in Greco-Roman discourse. See Hester, "Queers on Account of the Kingdom of Heaven," 809–23.

54. There are accounts of eunuchs in court as far back as the Achaemenid period, but the Old Persian term for eunuchs does not survive. In the Sasanian period there are citations of the Middle Persian *shābestān*, which, according to Omar Coloru, indicates the title of the eunuch as a master of the "women's sleeping quarter." Coloru notes that the Shapur I inscription translates shābestān into Greek as *eunouchos*. See Coloru, "Ancient Persia and Silent Disability," 61–74. There are narratives of eunuchs at court, some of which seem to be exaggerated. See, for example, the claim that Yazdgard castrated eight thousand subjects to act as servants. On this, see McDonough, "A Question of Faith?" 69–85. On Antiochus, see Greatrex and Bardill, "Antiochus the 'Praepositus,'" 171–97. From the same time period, see also the figure of Chrysaphius (Chew, "Virgins and Eunuchs," 207–27). See also the figure of Mār Abā, who served as chief eunuch (Macuch, "The Case Against Mār Abā," 47–58). Finally, for the change of the position of eunuchs in the court over the Sasanian period, see Kolesnikov, "Eunuchs," 64–69. On

unclear how these eunuchs made their way into the Persian court; ironically, some scholars believe that eunuchs may, in fact, have been imported into Persia.[55] Still, even the presence of eunuchs within various Persian courts does not fully account for the way Greco-Roman sources associate the eunuch's gender with foreignness.

In Greek literary sources, for example, foreigners practice castration as punishment. In her analysis of Sophocles's play *Troilus*, for instance, Ruth Bardel notes that Hecabe, the queen, castrates an enslaved eunuch and thereby associates the barbarian royal body with the feminine (and the effeminizing).[56] Similarly, eunuch priests (the *galli*) are widely associated with the popular Magna Mater religious traditions, and yet literary sources portray the galli as "the exotics *par excellence* in an exotic cult."[57] Other scholars read the surviving images of the galli as pointedly thematizing the ability of Rome to absorb such "foreign" bodies.[58]

In addition to literary and material representations of the eunuch, we can trace Roman legal discourses that shape the eunuch as foreign. While there are earlier attempts to eradicate the link between castration and slavery, Nerva broadens the ban to address castration of any kind. Justinian's *Digest* records a rescript that specified that the ban on castration, and the associated penalties, obtained for both voluntary and involuntary castration.[59] However, the text in the *Codex Justinianus* recorded what was essentially a legal loophole—castration was outlawed within the boundaries of the Roman Empire, but trade in "barbarian" eunuchs was

---

the title, "chief of the royal eunuchs," see Tafazzoli, "An Unrecognized Sasanian Title," 301–5. On the evidence of the seal that may have belonged to a eunuch in the Sasanian court, see Lerner and Skjaervø, "A Seal of a Eunuch in the Sasanian Court," 113–19. Lerner dates the seal to the third century. See also, Skjaervø, "A Postscript on the Seal of a Eunuch in the Sasanian Court," 39. Skjaervø argues, based on a passage from the *Dēnkard*, that the term "shābestān" definitely refers to a castrated eunuch, and did not simply denote a job title.

55. While eunuchs generally have Persian names in the sources, it is possible that eunuchs originally came to the court as tributes or through the slave trade and were subsequently given new names. Given some of the Zoroastrian attitudes toward disability (and the value of bodily integrity and procreation), some scholars speculate that eunuchs were indeed primarily imported. See Coloru, "Ancient Persia," 69–70.

56. Bardel further argues that when castration appears thematically in a text about Greek characters, it often serves to highlight the subversion of Hellenic values. See Bardel, "Eunuchizing Agamemnon," 51–71.

57. Lightfoot, "Sacred Eunuchism in the Cult of the Syrian Goddess," 74. See, however, Jacob Latham, who argues that perceptions of the galli change through time, and that the image of the galli as foreign is much more characteristic of the late Republic period (Latham, "'Fabulous Clap-Trap,'" 84–122).

58. Hales, "Looking for Eunuchs," 87–103. In contrast to previous scholars, Hales argues that the surviving images of these priests show a rejection of the standard visual markers of Roman acculturation, which represent the artists' tactic for negotiating the "foreignness" of the galli priest. For an alternative reading of phallic depictions of Attis, which also addresses the "foreign" nature of the galli, see Butler, "Notes on a Membrum Disiectum," 236–55.

59. Murison, "Cassius Dio on Nervan Legislation," 343–55.

allowed.[60] There is some evidence that, in certain periods, castration took place along the borders of the Roman Empire in order to supply the Roman demand for eunuchs.[61] Still, the frequent reiteration in various legal sources of a ban against castration has led some scholars to posit that not all eunuchs were imported, and that the laws may have been flouted frequently.[62] We can see significant cultural energy expended to highlight the foreignness of eunuchs in literature, visual arts, and legal discourses.

If one of the dominant depictions associates eunuchs with foreign effeminacy, then early rabbinic literature diverges from this overtly rhetorical positioning in regard to genitally damaged men or eunuchs.[63] This discussion of genital damage does not directly situate castration as a "foreign" practice. And it is the Hebrew Bible, not the rabbis, that first explicitly discusses the place of genitally damaged men within "the community." This tradition about the Ammonite is included in the chapter of the Mishnah largely because of the connection to the verses in Deuteronomy. Still, it also serves as a pivot in the chapter.[64] Whereas before we had been discussing the priestly householder, this mishnah about Ammonites and other groups extends the conversation to the boundaries of Israel writ large. This biblical metaphor of "entering into the congregation" may be interpreted as a marriage prohibition, but marriage itself is also metaphorical. In this case marriage, as a method of entering into a community, erects a boundary.

Although it is the Bible that originates the link between genital damage and Ammonites and Moabites, there is an associative link because of the way this chapter of the Mishnah has been put together. Transing genital damage invites us to pay attention to the simultaneous negotiation of Jewishness, masculinity, abledness, and cultural and ethnic boundaries. The chapter of Mishnah begins by invoking the figure of the uncircumcised priest, who is clearly within the community

---

60. Piotr O. Scholz, *Eunuchs and Castrati*, 112.

61. Thomas Sizgorich examines the narratives about Abasgian castration. See Sizgorich, "Reasoned Violence and Shifty Frontiers," 167–79.

62. Hopkins, "The Political Power of Eunuchs," 172–97. See Shaun Tougher's response ("In or out?" 143–61).

63. Very few texts in tannaitic legal discourse even suggest the effeminacy of the eunuch, and the few that might be interpreted as such are the exception and not the rule. See Sarra Lev, "Genital Trouble."

64. If we compare this chapter to other places where the prohibition against entering into the congregation is treated in the Mishnah, we can see a marked difference in approach. See Gary Porton's analysis of m. Yadayim 4:4 and t. Kiddushin 5:5–6 (Porton, *The Stranger Within Your Gates*). Porton concludes that the rabbis were more concerned with the question of whether these biblical categories had become redundant by the mishnaic era. See also the beginning of the fourth chapter of Mishnah Kiddushin. There, the biblical law is situated in the broader context of genealogy, and the Mishnah lists not only categories like the *mamzer* and *Natin*, but also priests and Levites. In Kiddushin, the *p'zua daka'* / *krut shafkhah* does not appear. This alternative version serves to highlight the ways in which the organization of the eighth chapter in Yevamot links the gendered and ethnic borders of Israel.

but lacks some of the signs of Jewish masculinity. The uncircumcised priest's uncut genitals restrict his access, if not to the congregation per se then at least to foods designated as holy. By moving from uncircumcision to a conversation about genital damage and the boundaries of the Israelites, the organization of the chapter links these categories that navigate the parameters of Jewish masculinity. Structurally, the chapter implicitly imagines a community of Jewish men with kosher genitalia who have sexual and marriage access to certain classes of Israelite women.

The social order of this chapter, therefore, is bounded by (semiporous) cultural and gendered borders, which are established through sexual access to women.[65] The hierarchy of women's status, from convert and freed slave to the Israelite woman, determines the extent to which kosher male entrance into the congregation, household, and people Israel, is sanctioned. Kosher masculinity is predicated, in this case, on access to Jewish women's bodies.[66]

EUNUCHS AND REPRODUCTION: A BRIEF REVIEW OF LEVIRATE MARRIAGE

After the discussion of genitally damaged men and the boundaries of the community, the Mishnah pivots. This next section of the chapter moves to the eunuch (saris). As the chapter switches terms from genitally damaged men to eunuchs, it also addresses new legal issues. Eunuchs are firmly connected to questions of reproduction and law.

The term "eunuch" (saris) appears biblically (like the terms for genitally damaged men), although there is scholarly debate as to whether the word *saris* always refers to eunuchs in the Hebrew Bible.[67] By the time of the Mishnah, however, the word *saris* clearly refers to eunuchs.[68] Throughout the following analysis, I want to

---

65. The third mishnah describes both male and female Ammonites, Moabites, and other categories, and, in some cases, treats them similarly. In some sections women are distinguished from men, and it is women who are permitted to enter the congregation immediately, while men are not. Thus, the status of marriage with Israelite women is still the most highly regulated permutation.

66. Greco-Roman legal and literary texts connect eunuchs to foreignness in a variety of ways, either through stereotyping or regulating castration within the boundaries of the Roman Empire. While there is no definitive way to prove here that the rabbis are deliberately reinforcing a connection between eunuchs and "foreignness" in this passage (particularly because of the connection in the biblical verses), the arrangement is suggestive.

67. Some scholars think that in the biblical text, the word *saris* generally refers to eunuchs, while others argue that it most frequently refers to a servant. See Tadmor, "Was the Biblical *Saris* a Eunuch?" 317–27.

68. While most scholars believe that the Hebrew Bible does not discuss eunuchs in relation to law, a small subset argue that the verses in Isaiah are meant as a commentary on Deuteronomy. For an overview of the disagreement, see Wright and Chan, "King and Eunuch," 99–119. If the majority of such scholars are right, there is no formal reason the rabbis need to discuss the legal position of the eunuch.

leave open the question of why the rabbis import both eunuchs and genitally damaged men from the Hebrew Bible, and what kinds of rhetorical work each category performs in the context of this chapter.

With the shift to the eunuch, we also leave behind the legal discussion of priestly marriages and turn to the topic of levirate marriage. I will explore how levirate marriage is the test of the procreative functions of eunuchs, but before I can do so, I want to review again the basics of levirate marriage for the nonspecialist.

To understand levirate marriage, we will need to return briefly to the Hebrew Bible.[69] Levirate marriage (described primarily in Deuteronomy 25: 5–10) occurs when a married man dies without offspring.[70] Deuteronomy is concerned that that man has no descendants to carry on his name. In order to preserve the name of the man who died without children, his widow marries her dead husband's surviving brother. The child that results from this union is considered the heir of the deceased brother; in this way, his name continues. Generally, a man is legally prohibited from marrying his brother's wife (Leviticus 18:16 and 20:21), even after his brother's death. It is only in the special case where the brother died without children that an otherwise prohibited relationship is sanctioned. This irregular union is called levirate marriage.

Levirate marriage, as described in the Bible, also allows an alternative for those who do not wish to undertake this union. If the brother of the dead man does not wish to wed the widow, the pair can perform a ritual (called *ḥaliẓah*) to dissolve any marital obligation between them. In the case where a married man dies childless, either levirate marriage or the ritual to free the widow must be performed if there are eligible brothers. Without the ritual, the widow may not remarry.

There are many ways to criticize levirate marriage. The androcentrism that focuses solely on the transmission of men's names is one—women are instrumentalized in carrying on masculine bloodlines. On the other hand, even embedded in such a deeply androcentric legal framework, there is also something decidedly odd about this irregular union. Levirate marriage, at its heart, is about reproductive

---

69. The most current and thorough exploration of the topic of levirate marriage is Dvora Weisberg's monograph, in which she argues (against Satlow) that the rabbis regularized levirate marriage as a marriage like any other (Weisberg, *Levirate Marriage and the Family*; Satlow, *Jewish Marriage in Antiquity*). See also Louis Epstein's classic *Marriage Laws in the Bible and the Talmud*. For a more recent take on levirate marriage that engages with the historical data, see Schremer, *Male and Female He Created Them*.

70. Levirate marriage is not just a biblical construct; it has cognates in other legal systems. In the Iranian context, jurists formulated various frameworks to encourage reproduction among elites. This included a system of "substitute-successorship," similar to levirate marriage. See Payne, "Sex, Death, and Aristocratic Empire," 519–49. On the differences between Zoroastrian and rabbinic law on levirate marriage, see Weisberg's conclusion to "The Babylonian Talmud's Treatment of Levirate Marriage," 35–66. On questions of the similarity of biblical levirate marriage to other contemporaneous Near Eastern ideas, see Weisberg, "The Widow of our Discontent," 403–29. On questions of agnate marriage, see Belkin, "Levirate and Agnate Marriage," 275–329.

failures and disrupted kinship lines. It promotes a union that would otherwise be considered prohibited (or even incestuous). Finally, it creates a strange ghostly lineage with a man who reproduces even after death. In other words, levirate marriage has some queer effects.

The entire edifice of levirate marriage is predicated on the idea that sometimes procreation fails. Procreative failures are a part of life, and levirate marriage is a work-around for the problem. I have argued that transing eunuchs and androgynes can mean noticing the ways in which they carry special burdens in rabbinic sources. In transing the eunuch and levirate marriage, I want to pose a naïve question about the text: why should the procreative failure of eunuchs be different from other "normal" procreative failure? I want to discard the assumption that eunuchs naturally are of interest in a discussion of levirate marriage. If we do, we can see the ways that levirate marriage is used to define some reproductive failures as pathological, and others as a normal part of life.

DEFINING EUNUCHS

If the first section delineated genital damage, this next section of the rabbinic discussion introduces and defines the eunuch (saris).[71] Genital damage and eunuchs are separate terms in the biblical sources, and the legal discussion surrounding each in this chapter of the Mishnah is distinct. Still, it is not an accident that they are found in proximity to one another; later sources connect genitally damaged men and eunuchs explicitly. That the distinct biblical categories of genital damage and eunuchs become connected may reflect the range of bodies covered by the Greek word *eunuch*. Second Temple period authors who apply verses about genitally damaged men to eunuchs are tapping into the ambiguity in the Greek term "εὐνοῦχος" itself.[72]

---

71. In this section, when I use the term "eunuch" I am primarily referring to the saris, who is generally understood as male in the sources. I will specify when I am discussing a particular kind of eunuch (born or acquired). When I refer to the eunuchs that are generally understood as female, I will use the term "aylonit." I am aware that I am not using person-centered language like "a person who is a eunuch." One would not, for example, call someone "a transgender" or "an intersex." In a text as technical as this one (and as difficult for nonspecialists to unpack), I am trying to simplify the language and terminology as much as possible. But I want to acknowledge the discomfort in this way of addressing people who are eunuchs or androgynes.

72. See Walter Stevenson: "To complicate the issue further, there clearly are a variety of 'eunuchs' living at the time of our early Christian authors. I would break these down into those who are born in a variety of conditions without strong masculine characteristics, those who had 'moderate' destruction of the gonads (θλαδίας, and θλιβίας) and those who had radical surgery (ἀποκεκομμένος and *castratus*)" (Stevens, "Eunuchs and early Christianity," 124). For an example of the equivalence drawn in Roman law between crushed testes and excised testes, see the *Digest*, 48.8.5.

In this section, therefore, I contextualize the rabbinic definition and discussion of the failures of the eunuch within Greco-Roman and Christian discourses about eunuchs. This is meant to be a brief survey to contextualize the rabbinic discussions within the range of responses to eunuchs in this time period. While there are certainly grounds to criticize the rabbinic imagination of an abled masculinity, the types of invective that are so popular in Greco-Roman rhetoric are not found here. I will begin, however, with the rabbinic definition of the eunuch.

Rabbi Yehoshua poses a quandary about the eunuch. He is confused by two conflicting teachings that he has received:

> Rabbi Yehoshua said: I have heard that the eunuch performs the ritual to dissolve the obligation to levirate marriage [Heb. *ḥalizah*] [in the case of his brother's death], and that [the eunuch's brothers] perform the ritual with his wife [in the case of the eunuch's death]. And [I have also heard the contradictory teaching] that the eunuch does not perform the ritual and [that his brothers] do not perform the ritual [with his wife, in the case of the eunuch's death]. I cannot explain [the apparent contradiction between these two teachings]. (m. Yevamot 8:4)

Rabbi Yehoshua cites two conflicting teachings about the participation of eunuchs in levirate marriage. Each of the two teachings includes two scenarios: the first scenario involves a eunuch whose married brother dies childless. In that case, the question is to what extent the eunuch is beholden to the rituals of levirate marriage with his brother's widow. In other words, if he cannot procreate, and levirate marriage is sanctioned only for the purposes of procreation, is he obligated to his brother's widow? In the second scenario, the eunuch himself dies. In this version of events, the question is whether his brother has to participate in the ritual with his widow. If there was no way the eunuch could have procreated while married, is his brother still obligated to the rituals of levirate marriage?

Rabbi Yehoshua has heard two teachings about these two scenarios: in one teaching, the eunuch and his brother must perform the ritual; in the other, they must not. These two traditions obviously contradict each other. If there is no obligation to be dissolved, then it is almost as if there are no eligible brothers to perform the ritual. This would imply that eunuchs, who are unable to procreate, are fundamentally exempt from levirate marriage. At stake in these contradictory teachings is the status of the widow. If the eunuch and his brother are required to perform the ritual, then in order for the widow to remarry, she needs to be set free of them.

At the heart of Rabbi Yehoshua's question, however, is a larger dilemma: if the institution of levirate marriage is to ensure procreation, what is the place of the nonprocreative eunuch? Levirate marriage, after all, creates a union between two people who would otherwise be prohibited from marrying one another. This relationship is either prohibited or mandated.

Rabbi Akiva responds to Rabbi Yehoshua's question. He brings a new teaching to resolve the apparent conflict over the eunuch's participation in levirate marriage:

> Rabbi Akiva said: I will explain it—an acquired saris performs the ritual to dissolve the obligation to levirate marriage, and the ritual is performed with his wife because he had a time when he was fit [kosher], and the born saris does not perform the ritual and the ritual is not performed with his wife, because he never had a time when he was fit [kosher].

Rabbi Akiva clarifies the contradictory teachings for Rabbi Yehoshua by splitting the eunuch into two: there are two different kinds of eunuchs. Eunuchs who acquire their status as a eunuch (whether by injury or deliberately—the text does not specify) are subject to the laws of levirate marriage because they once had the capacity to procreate. However, a person who was born a eunuch—born without the capacity to procreate—does not participate in levirate marriage because he was never able to reproduce.[73] The category of saris, therefore, includes both those born with bodily differences that render them unable to reproduce and those who become castrated later in life. The word *saris* is itself flexible enough to describe these different types of embodiment, according to Rabbi Akiva.

The repetition of the word *kosher*—fit—to describe the status of the acquired saris resonates. We saw the term "kosher" used before to describe the degree of genital damage that would render the priest "unfit." While the word *kosher* is common enough in early rabbinic literature, in this case, and in particular because of the way these traditions are edited to be proximate to one another, the use of the word *kosher* has echoes.

This semantic flexibility of the term "saris" proposed by Rabbi Akiva in this passage mirrors the elasticity of the term "eunuch" in the Greek. Nowhere is that flexibility laid out more clearly than in the Gospel of Matthew, which describes three types of eunuchs: "For there are eunuchs who have been so from birth, and there are eunuchs who have been made eunuchs by others, and there are eunuchs who have made themselves eunuchs for the sake of the kingdom of heaven" (Matthew 19:12).[74] Matthew sketches out three separate categories: the born eunuch, the acquired eunuch, and eunuchs for heaven. For each of these three categories,

---

73. This distinction between born or acquired is also introduced in the Sifra in relation to the priestly blemishes. See Sifra, *Emor* 3:2 on Leviticus 21:17. However, that distinction is not discussed in this chapter of the Mishnah in relation to the *p'zua daka'* / *krut shafkhah*.

74. The English translation of the verse is from Michael Coogan, ed., *The New Oxford Annotated Bible*. The Greek reads: εἰσὶν γὰρ εὐνοῦχοι οἵτινες ἐκ κοιλίας μητρὸς ἐγεννήθησαν οὕτος, καὶ εἰσὶν εὐνοῦχοι οἵτινες εὐνουχίσθησαν ὑπὸ τῶν ἀνθρώπων, καὶ εἰσὶν εὐνοῦχοι οἵτινες εὐνούχισαν ἑαυτοὺς διὰ τὴν βασιλείαν τῶν οὐραῶν. Note the way the same word—εὐνοῦχος—can be used to describe all three types of eunuchs.

the same word *eunuch* (εὐνοῦχος) is used. Eunuch, in the Greek, is an expansive umbrella term for a number of different kinds of bodies. Later Roman sources also reflect this division between people that are born without reproductive capability and people who become eunuchs. For example, the Roman jurist Ulpian distinguishes between "eunuchs by nature" and "those who are made eunuchs."[75]

The precise meaning of this verse has been hotly debated both by early Christians and by contemporary biblical scholars (mirroring the debate about the translation of the word *saris* in the Hebrew Bible). Historically, scholars and theologians have mostly understood the invocation of the eunuch in Matthew as allegorical, and they have variously interpreted the verse as addressing sexual temptation, celibacy, or second marriages. Some commentators believe that the verse is, in fact, discussing eunuchs.[76] We know from religious movements (like Cybellianism) that the idea of religious castration was in circulation, so there are counterparts for the concept of "eunuchs for the kingdom of heaven." Even if the verse in Matthew was meant as allegory, this is only one early Christian example of a rich tradition of discussing eunuchs. Scholars have written about eunuchs and androgynes in the Christian Bible[77] and in early Christian literature.[78]

---

75. Matthew Kuefler cites Ulpian's statement: "'The name of eunuch is a general one,' he wrote; 'under it come those who are eunuchs by nature, those who are made eunuchs [*thlibiae thlaisae*], and any other kind of eunuchs [*aliud genus spadonum.*].'" See Kuefler, *The Manly Eunuch*, 33. See also Candida Moss's commentary: "Mark and Matthew," 275–301.

76. See, for example, these four different allegorical readings: Van Tine interprets the verse as describing the dangers of adultery (Van Tine, "Castration for the Kingdom," 399–418). Carmen Bernabé argues that these verses are a commentary on forms of marriage (Bernabé, "Of Eunuchs and Predators," 128–34). Retief, Cilliers, and Riekert argue that Matthew is addressing the practice of celibacy ("Eunuchs in the Bible," 247–58). Rick Talbott claims that this verse speaks to the status of women (Talbott, "Imagining the Matthean Eunuch Community," 21–43). J. David Hester, on the other hand, argues that allegorical readings of the verse were attempts to sanitize the tradition (Hester, "Eunuchs and the Postgender Jesus," 13–40). At least some early Christians probably understood this verse literally. See Caner, "The Practice and Prohibition of Self-Castration," 396–415. See also Brower, "Ambivalent Bodies." The question of castration in early Christianity often emerges in the debate over whether Origen castrated himself (see Hanson, "A Note on Origen's Self-Mutilation," 81–82). For a theoretically sophisticated take on the question of identifying these eunuchs as intersex or trans, see Marchal, "Who Are You Calling a Eunuch?!" 29–54.

77. On the figure of the Ethiopian eunuch in Acts 8:26–40, see Burke, "Queering Early Christian Discourse," 175–91; Villalobos, "Bodies *Del Otro Lado*," 191–223; Brittany Wilson, "'Neither Male nor Female,'" 403–22. For a fuller discussion of the implications of the discussion in Galatians, see Marchal, "Bodies Bound for Circumcision and Baptism," 163–82. On Corinthians, see Marchal, "The Corinthian Women Prophets and Trans Activism," 223–47. For a general reading of the biblical sources as they relate to intersex categories, see DeFranza, *Sex Difference in Christian Theology*.

78. For a survey of early Christian literature that focuses specifically on Clement of Alexandria, see Horstmanshoff, "Who is the True Eunuch," 101–18. For early Christian sources in which female saints cross-dress as eunuchs, see Davis, "Crossed Texts, Crossed Sex," 1–36. Patricia Cox Miller interprets the cross-dressing of Pelagia, an important saint in the Syriac tradition. See Cox-Miller, "Is There a Harlot in This Text?" 419–35.

While the figure of the eunuch in Matthew 19:12 is not obviously polemical, a persistent and dominant trope of the eunuch in Greco-Roman literature is its rhetorical use in invective.[79] One of the best studies on eunuchs and rhetoric is Maud Gleason's survey of Favorinus, a rhetorician (and born eunuch) in the Second Sophistic movement. Gleason provides numerous examples of the types of invective heaped on eunuchs, citing some of the more extreme statements by Favorinus's frequent opponent: "Hence no one is more perfectly evil than he who is born without testicles."[80] This kind of vilification of eunuchs is not confined to the Second Sophistic movement; rather, it represents a broader characterization of eunuchs in Greco-Roman literature. Authors from Juvenal to Claudian famously characterize eunuchs negatively: as sexually voracious and lacking in self-control (considered an important aspect of male virtue), as effeminate, and as deceitful.[81]

The rabbis do not have a category corresponding to "eunuchs for the sake of the kingdom of heaven." They do, however, have the first two categories: those who are born eunuchs, and those who become eunuchs. I am not arguing that the rabbis borrowed their concept of eunuch directly from Matthew; their saris emerges in the same milieu as the eunuch. The verse in Matthew plays with the semantic flexibility that inheres in the term "eunuch" in the Greek, and it reflects an extant understanding of the taxonomy of eunuchs. While the words that the rabbis use for eunuchs derive from the Hebrew Bible, the rabbinic division of the biblical saris into the born saris and the acquired saris engages broader Greco-Roman taxonomies of eunuchs. At the same time, however, the rabbinic discussion of the saris seems positively measured in comparison with such authors as Philo and Juvenal.

THE KOSHER EUNUCH: PROCREATIVE MASCULINITY AND LEVIRATE MARRIAGE

The rabbinic discussion of the eunuch in this chapter of the Mishnah does not center on bodily damage like that of the genitally damaged priest. Instead, the

---

79. Other early Christian texts deploy eunuchs rhetorically to construct boundaries. See, for example, Chrysostom's association of Jewishness and effeminacy. Joshua Levinson discusses these sources (Levinson, "Cultural Androgyny in Rabbinic Literature," 119–40).

80. Gleason, *Making Men*, 47.

81. I am summarizing and generalizing vast bodies of scholarship. See Juvenal's famous sixth satire in particular, and Claudian, *Against Eutropius* 1.277–81. For a survey of the literature, see Asikainen, "'Eunuchs for the Kingdom of Heaven,'" 156–88. There is a whole subfield of scholarship on Roman masculinity, some of which addresses eunuchs and androgynes. See Foxhall and Salmon, eds., *When Men were Men*; Richlin, ed., *Arguments with Silence*; and Kraemer, *Unreliable Witnesses*. On sexuality, see Hallett and Skinner, eds., *Roman Sexualities*. For the classic work on eunuchs in antiquity, see Keith Hopkins, who explored structural reasons for the importance of eunuchs in court and political settings. He has several pieces on the topic, including "Eunuchs in Politics in the Later Roman Empire," 62–80.

rabbis explore different types of reproductive failures. As the flipside of reproductive failure, a concept of reproductive "fitness" is introduced. I will argue that reproductive fitness, therefore, becomes embedded in a notion of abled masculinity.

Rabbi Yehoshua's confusion about eunuchs and levirate marriage is solved when Rabbi Akiva harmonizes the competing traditions by dividing eunuchs into two categories. A eunuch who was born without the capacity to procreate does not participate in levirate marriage because he was never capable of procreation. On the other hand, someone who becomes a eunuch later in life had an earlier time when he was kosher (able to procreate) and therefore is obligated to participate in levirate marriage.

The mishnah continues with Rabbi Eliezer, who has a different solution for the problem of the conflicting traditions:

> Rabbi Eliezer disagrees: [It is] not so, rather the born saris performs the ritual [to dissolve the obligation to levirate marriage] and the ritual is performed for his wife, because there is a cure [for the condition of being a born saris]. The acquired saris does not perform the ritual, and the ritual is not performed for his wife, because there is no cure [for his condition].

Rabbi Eliezer agrees with Rabbi Akiva that two different kinds of eunuchs are being discussed. He disagrees with Rabbi Akiva about which eunuch has an obligation to participate in the rituals of levirate marriage. Rabbi Eliezer argues that the born saris performs the ritual to dissolve the obligation to levirate marriage, and the acquired saris does not; his conclusion is the exact opposite of Rabbi Akiva's. Rabbi Eliezer's rationale is that the born saris has the potential to be cured, while the acquired saris does not.[82]

On the surface, the debate between Rabbi Akiva and Rabbi Eliezer is about their understanding of what prompts levirate marriage: is levirate marriage prompted by something that happened (or failed to happen) in the past, or is it oriented toward future reproduction? [83] The mishnaic discussion about "a time when he was kosher" and "cures" positions us firmly within the realm of abstract, potential reproduction. This is, to an extent, always true: levirate marriage is predicated on hypothetical reproduction. Yet this is not just a debate about levirate

---

82. The Hebrew Bible itself treats the topic of (divine and medicinal) cures for infertility: see Genesis 30:14–16 and the conflict between Rachel and Leah, for example.

83. The *s'ris ḥamah*, the term I am translating as born eunuch, is glossed in p. Yevamot 8:4–5 (9d) as "sun" eunuch, which is a literal rendering of *ḥamah*. The reference to the sun is interpreted to mean that the eunuch has never seen a moment of the sun where he was not a eunuch. In other words, he was always a eunuch. The *s'ris 'adam* more literally means "human" eunuch. One could think of this as a division akin to the one in Matthew: the one who becomes a eunuch by human hands and the one who is born a eunuch (and here, born might indicate both natural and created by God.) For more discussion of my translation choices, see the introduction to this book.

marriage. Rather, this simple attempt to define eunuchs reflects a struggle over two different understandings of the nature of the saris: is the born saris a liminal category? Can a saris be "cured"?

In discussing cure, we are entering into a realm to which disability studies has much to contribute. Rabbi Eliezer might consider a cure a positive promise that looks to a better (reproductive) future. Eli Clare, on the other hand, in his book *Brilliant Imperfections*, unpacks the darker side of cure. Clare simultaneously acknowledges that some people with disabilities wish ardently for cures, and yet he positions cure as, at least in part, a eugenic desire:

> Operating in tandem with diagnosis, treatment, management, rehabilitation, and prevention, cure is quite adaptable. Together these six processes ... define and redefine *normal* and *abnormal*.[84]

In cooperation with the other processes of medicine, cure works not only to manage disability out of existence, but also to define the contours of normal and abnormal itself. The promise of cure is to eradicate bodily differences. As such, cure authorizes a type of eugenic violence. This violence does not operate solely at the level of language; Clare describes the US history of the forced institutionalization of people with disabilities. This incarceration was often accompanied by the promise of release on condition of sterilization. Reproduction, disability, processes of racialization are entangled with administrative violence in US history—often in the name of cure.

Within the context of this particular mishnah, it is clear that for Rabbi Eliezer, cure is positive. The concept of cure enables eunuchs to participate in the legal system. And yet, cure simultaneously pathologizes the infertility of eunuchs. If levirate marriage assumes that all male bodies can experience infertility, the discussion of eunuchs—whether defined in regard to having had or having lacked a "time of being kosher" or in regard to having or lacking the possibility of a cure—situates the infertility of some eunuchs as set apart from this norm.

This is not the only text in which the rabbis describe a cure for disability. Julia Watts Belser analyzes midrashic traditions of resurrection. Belser discusses a text in which people are resurrected with their disabilities intact in the world to come, so that their family members can recognize them. As Belser argues, this rabbinic tradition promotes disability as an important facet of embodiment. At the same time, the rabbis hold out hope for a cure as an eventual facet of the eschaton.[85]

---

84. Clare, *Brilliant Imperfection*, 71.
85. Belser, "Disability, Animality, and Enslavement," 288–305. Belser argues this rabbinic tradition is a corrective to the tendency to situate disability as an individual failing, in the way the rabbis understand healing as a method of erasing the social marks of injustice and oppression.

The potential of an (as yet unrealized) eschatological cure is future oriented. Temporality plays a part in the politics of cure in this mishnah as well. Timing distinguishes the born saris from the acquired saris. Timing is also a central facet of the debate between Rabbi Akiva and Rabbi Eliezer: in determining the eligibility of eunuchs for levirate marriage, Rabbi Akiva's position asks whether the eunuch had a period of being "kosher" in the past.[86] Since the acquired saris had the potential to procreate in the past, if he dies childless, his status is the same as that of any other man who dies childless.[87] Rabbi Eliezer, by contrast, is oriented toward the future; for Rabbi Eliezer, since the born saris might be cured in the future, he should participate in levirate marriage. Rabbi Akiva is oriented toward past loss, while Rabbi Eliezer is oriented toward reproductive futures.[88]

Embedded in this idea of the "time when he was fit" is an original wholeness, and a nostalgia for the body that was prior to disability. A past time of being "kosher," then, invokes both the fragility of the body, and the myth of an unchanging masculine body. And yet, death, failure, and sterility are all at the heart of levirate marriage; to have a body is to experience loss. Both these temporal orientations are a part of levirate marriage.[89] But the framework of future cure is different

---

86. The word *kosher* most frequently refers to objects and their legal validity; it is less frequently applied to humans or body parts. There are over one hundred uses of the word in tannaitic literature, so I will not list them all, but I will cite a few examples from the Mishnah of uses of the term "kosher," meaning "valid." For a use of "kosher" applied to objects, see m. Bava Batra 10:1, which talks about the validity of different kinds of writs of divorce. For an example of a kosher act, see, for example, m. Zevahḥim 2:5, which considers details of improper consumption of sacrifices. On occasion it appears that the word *kosher* is applied to the person making sacrifices; however, this almost always actually refers to the validity of the sacrifice itself, although this can sometimes be read as reflecting on the status of the individual. On the other hand, however, see m. Zevahḥim 10:5, where the term "kosher" is applied to the leper to adjudicate his status. M. Bekhorot chapter 7 has several instances where "kosher" is applied to a person; blemishes are discussed in this chapter. There are other instances of the word *kosher* applied to people in a variety of contexts: see m. Yevamot 4:2, in which "kosher" indicates that the offspring is legitimate. The use of the word *kosher* to apply to the status of a person is thus not unheard of, but is nonetheless rarer.

87. Rabbi Akiva's position makes less sense when we are discussing the eunuch as the brother-in-law, however. Why should a period of having been fertile in the past dictate that the acquired saris must currently perform the ritual with his brother's widow? If he can no longer procreate, why does levirate marriage trump the prohibitions against incest?

88. The coda of the debate between Rabbi Akiva and Rabbi Eliezer is as follows: "Rabbi Yehoshua ben Beteira brought [a case] that would support Rabbi Akiva's opinion: There was a *s'ris 'adam* [named] ben Megusat who lived in Jerusalem [and when he died his brother] performed marriage with his wife." This seems to suggest that the Mishnah privileges Rabbi Akiva's opinion. However, the case is complicated as a legal precedent. While it is evident that the *s'ris 'adam* (rather than the *s'ris ḥamah*) participates, Rabbi Akiva authorizes only *ḥaliẓah*, not levirate marriage itself.

89. In the phrase "reproductive futurity," I reference Lee Edelman's *No Future*. Edelman has been critiqued by Jose Esteban Muñoz in *Cruising Utopia*.

from the nostalgic desire for whole, unchanging, masculine bodies.[90] Still, both are ways of cementing a vision of an abled masculine body, connected intimately to reproduction.

Rabbi Akiva's "time of being kosher" echoes the use of the word *kosher* to describe the genitalia of the priest. In the questions of whether the genitally damaged priest is "kosher" for the purpose of marrying an Israelite woman (thereby figuratively entering into the community) and whether the acquired saris had a time of being "kosher," there is something more than the physical capabilities of these bodies at stake. The repetition of "kosher" plays with the idea of masculine fitness. These laws function as a method of measuring one's (gendered) place. Entering into the community and carrying on one's name are deeply gendered but also highly symbolic acts. It is not enough to acquire a wife and support her, one must also have the ability to reproduce, even after death.

The effect of linking the two areas of law (heave offering and levirate marriage), and of simultaneously connecting genital damage with eunuchs, is to both reinscribe and elide the differences between priests and the rest of the Israelites.[91] Neither the structure of the chapter nor the enumeration of terms for sex/gender deviant bodies is accidental; on the contrary, they represent a kind of layering effect. Layering enables a broad discussion of masculinity and the diversity of male bodies that is not

---

90. A similar question about eunuchs and procreation is debated within the context of Roman law, in a discussion of posthumous heirs. The legal issue of posthumous heirs is complex: a man had to either include or exclude all potential heirs in his will; otherwise, the will could be ruled invalid. This included any potential heirs that were born after the death of the father, and so a common practice developed of instituting a clause that would include any future posthumous children in the will. Since the legal edifice of posthumous heirs was designed to address the question of biological (as opposed to adopted) offspring, this leads to a potential conflict between these two facts—that all men ostensibly had the right to invoke the posthumous heirs, and that not all men were necessarily able to reproduce. The Roman jurist Ulpian comments on the debate: "But the question is asked whether someone who cannot easily father children can make a *posthumous* heir. And Cassius and Javolenus write that he can; for he can take a wife and adopt. Both Labeo and Cassius write that an impotent person [*spado*] can appoint a *posthumous* as heir, because neither age nor sterility is an impediment to that. But if he has been castrated [*castratus*], Julian, following the opinion of Proculus, thinks that he cannot institute a posthumous as heir, which is the law we apply. A hermaphrodite though, will be able to institute a posthumous as heir, if the male characteristics in him are predominant" (Digest 28.2.6). See *The Digest of Justinian*, 362. This is also cited by Gardner ("Sexing a Roman," 139).

I am not claiming that Roman discussions of posthumous heirs influenced rabbinic literature directly here. There is, however, a shared anxiety about the ability to reproduce even after death. And there is a remarkably similar debate over the question of which kinds of masculine bodies can have access to posthumous procreativity. For the dangers of assuming Roman influence on the content of rabbinic law, see Heszer, "Roman Law and Rabbinic Legal Composition," 144–63.

91. There are other places where the question of levirate marriage is discussed in relation to the *p'zua' daka'* and *krut shafkhah* solely and places where laws for priests are used to derive laws for non-priestly (Israelite) men. See, for example, Sifra, *Emor* 3: 8 on Leviticus 21:22.

confined to the priestly realm.[92] The editing of this chapter of the Mishnah combines what would normally be two distinct registers of conversations about masculinity in rabbinic law: a conversation about the perfectly unblemished priestly body, and a conversation about the privileges and responsibilities of the male householder.

THE AYLONIT: PROCREATIVE FEMININITY AND LEVIRATE MARRIAGE

Much of my discussion of this chapter of the Mishnah has focused on masculinity. Women have entered into the picture mostly as a testing ground for these masculine norms.[93] If the discussion has centered men and masculinity up to this point, the introduction of the aylonit (female born eunuch) in the next mishnah ostensibly shifts the focus.

The aylonit is a parallel figure to the born saris: both are born without the capacity to reproduce.[94] If the saris is used to explore masculine reproductive fitness, however, the aylonit does not establish a parallel frame of feminine fitness. Instead, I will argue that the aylonit is made to embody the illicit nature of women's sexuality.[95] Transing the sources, in this section, will mean a sustained atten-

---

92. Some scholars posit that the verses in Isaiah that treat the saris/eunuch are a response to the more restrictive traditions in Deuteronomy that discuss the *p'zua' daka'* / *krut shafkhah* and the topic of the priestly blemish. In that interpretation, laws applying to genitally damaged men could apply to the saris as well. If that is correct, there is a kind of intrabiblical collapse of the distinctions among the three sets of categories, and the rabbis are simply expanding on this precedent. However, not all scholars agree that Isaiah is a response to Deuteronomy. For a critique of this view, see Wright and Chan, "King and Eunuch," 99–119.

93. Julia Watts Belser, in her article on blemishes and marriage contracts, argues that most of the scholarship on blemishes in rabbinic literature has focused on men and the legal limitations that disability imposes on their religious obligation. My discussion in this chapter follows (and perhaps reinforces) that trend. See Belser, "Brides and Blemishes," 401–29. The focus on masculinity in this book is also a function of the texts I chose: there are other sources that would have shaped a different conversation. My hope is that this book is the beginning of an ongoing conversation on the topic, and it is in discussion with the work of other scholars, like Gwynn Kessler and Sarra Lev, who are researching similar topics.

94. Sarra Lev proposes the invention of the aylonit as the conceptual opposite of the born saris (see Lev, "How the *Aylonit* Got Her Sex," 297–316).

95. Unlike other traditions, our mishnah does not frame the aylonit as deceptive; elsewhere the rabbis discuss whether her status as an aylonit needs to be disclosed before marriage and what happens to her marriage contract if it is not (see for example m. Ketubot 11:6). For the most part, the rabbis discuss the aylonit in relation to the laws of marriage, although this does not entirely set her apart from other women in rabbinic legal discourse. The rabbis discuss the possibility of her "condition" changing; see m. Giṭṭin 4:8. She is discussed extensively in relation to levirate marriage (see for example m. Giṭṭin 8:5–6). Finally, the aylonit is discussed in reference to the ritual of the suspected adulteress (see for example m. Sotah 4:3), whether she has to wait three months after being widowed to remarry (b. Yevamot 42b), and how her status as nonprocreative relates to the commandment to reproduce (m. Yevamot 6:5).

tion to the way in which the aylonit is treated differently from the saris. Androcentrism structures the text even when the rabbis are discussing eunuchs and androgynes.

Continuing with the topic of levirate marriage, the next mishnah now turns to the born saris:

> The saris[96] does not perform the ritual to dissolve the obligation to levirate marriage, and [does not perform] levirate marriage. So, too, the aylonit does not perform the ritual to dissolve [the obligation to contract] levirate marriage and is not taken [as a wife] in levirate marriage.

This tradition seems relatively straightforward: it argues that born eunuchs (both the saris and the aylonit) do not perform either levirate marriage or even the ritual to dissolve the requirement for levirate marriage. Because born eunuchs are not able to procreate, they have no role in levirate marriage. If the mishnah were to stop here, then the nonprocreative body of the aylonit would be exactly parallel to the nonprocreative body of the born saris. There are no distinctions between them.

This mishnah, however, continues. In the next section, the rabbis discuss the status of the born saris who does perform the ritual. In other words, the mishnah asks what happens when, despite the fact that eunuchs are not supposed to participate in levirate marriage, they do so anyway:

> [In the case of] the saris that performed the ritual to dissolve levirate marriage with his brother's widow [even though he was not obligated to], he has not disqualified [the widow from subsequently marrying a priest]. But, if [the saris] had sex with her [in order to enact levirate marriage], he disqualified her [from being able to marry a priest] because sex with her was [an act of] illicit sex. (m. Yevamot 8:5)[97]

---

96. The most common way to read this mishnah is that the general term "eunuch" (saris) refers specifically to the born saris. The phrase "so too the aylonit does not perform . . ." seems to suggest that the first part of the sentence must refer to the born saris, which is the conceptual pair of the aylonit. The sugya in the Babylonian Talmud attached to this mishnah understands this mishnah to refer to the born saris, and therefore classical commentators (Maimonides, the Bartenura, etc.) in their respective commentaries on the Mishnah all read this statement through the lens of the Bavli. From this mishnah, the commentators argue that whenever the rabbis do not specify a type of eunuch, the born saris is the default eunuch. Interpreted in this way, this ruling supports the view of Rabbi Akiva that only the acquired saris performs ḥaliẓah, while adding the *aylonit*.

There is, however, another possible interpretation: there may have been two different traditions related to eunuchs and later rabbinic sources attempted to harmonize them. If this is the case, then the fourth mishnah divides the eunuch in order to define his obligation to levirate marriage, while the fifth mishnah disagrees with Rabbi Akiva's distinction and issues a blanket prohibition on eunuchs performing levirate marriage (including the aylonit). Since levirate marriage is allowed only because of the potential for procreation, a blanket prohibition on the saris and aylonit is a real possibility.

97. The tradition about the aylonit is its own mishnah in Kaufman. Combining the aylonit with the born saris has the effect of highlighting the parallels, as pointed out in Lev, "How the *Aylonit* Got Her Sex," 297–316.

If the born saris performs the ritual to dissolve the obligation to levirate marriage with his brother's widow, it is as if nothing happened. Put another way, because he was not supposed to perform the ritual, there is no legal import to his act. However, if the saris marries the widow in a levirate union and has sex with her, then the widow is disqualified from marrying a priest in the future.

Generally speaking, a woman who has had illicit sex is not eligible to marry a priest. In this case, since the saris is exempted from levirate marriage, then the usual prohibitions against marrying his brother's widow should have applied.[98] By having sex with his brother's widow without the protective framework of levirate marriage, he has participated in prohibited sex, even if he (presumably) believed that he was performing his duty in a sanctioned levirate marriage. Notice, however, that while it is the saris whose status is problematic, the repercussions follow the widow. It is the widow who becomes tainted as someone who has had illicit sex (*b'ilat znut*) and is now no longer eligible to marry a priest.

This mishnah continues to discuss the situation of the aylonit who has participated in levirate marriage despite the fact that she is exempt. The Mishnah constructs the case in exactly parallel terms to the saris:

> So too, if the brothers [of the dead husband] of the aylonit perform the ritual to dissolve [the obligation to enter into] levirate marriage, they have not disqualified her [from marrying a priest.] If [the brothers] had sex with her, they disqualify her [from subsequently marrying a priest], because the sexual act constitutes prohibited sex.

If the aylonit is widowed and her brother-in-law performs a ritual to set her free to remarry whomsoever she pleases, she is still fit to marry a priest. However, if the brother-in-law has sex with her (perhaps because he thinks that he is obligated to perform levirate marriage with her), he disqualifies her from marrying a priest. Since she is not obligated under the system of levirate marriage, the sex is illicit (*b'ilat znut*). The tradition itself suggests parallelism between the *saris* and the *aylonit* when it uses the phrase: "So too the *aylonit*. . . ." However, the technical parallel between her case and that of the *saris* does not change the unequal effects of their situations. The status of the born *saris* disqualifies his brother's widow. In the case of the *aylonit*, her own personal status is impacted. Androcentrism shapes the parallelism between the *saris* and the *aylonit* to put the woman's status at stake in both cases.

While the Mishnah discusses eunuchs and their disqualification from certain types of levirate marriages, at the same time, the discussion itself normalizes their status within legal debates. The fact that eunuchs are included in the discussion of

---

98. Priests are subject to stringent rules that dictate whom they are permitted to marry. Leviticus 21:7 specifies that priests are not allowed to marry a divorced woman, a woman who has participated in extramarital sex (Heb. *zonah*), or a profaned woman (Heb. *ḥalalah*).

the exceptional case of levirate marriage assumes that there is no blanket ban on marriage for eunuchs, for example. Compared to the marriage dilemma of the genitally damaged priest, the status of the *aylonit* is much less fraught. This appears to be a case where the lack of reproductive capacity is not construed more broadly as a social disability.[99]

At the same time, as I have already pointed out, the test that determines whether sex was licit or not impacts the status of women differently. In the same way that the validity of the priestly marriage is tested through the acquisition of women, the validity of sex is evaluated based on a woman's ability to marry a priest subsequently. There is a type of social regulation associated with prohibited sex, to which the aylonit is constitutionally prone.

Even more than the differential status between the saris and the aylonit—which is, after all, mostly owing to the fact that she is a woman—there are other early rabbinic sources that suggest deeper stigma attaches to the aylonit. I will include one additional early rabbinic source to help cement my claim that the aylonit, in particular, is associated with illicit sex in some strains of rabbinic thought. I am introducing this text in part to linger over the aylonit in a book that has been focused so heavily on masculinity.

This mishnah, which comes from the sixth chapter of tractate Yevamot, states:

> An ordinary priest does not marry an aylonit unless he already has a wife and children. Rabbi Yehudah disagrees: Even if he has a wife and children, he should not marry an aylonit, because she is the "woman who has engaged in illicit sex" [Heb. *zonah*], who is referenced in the Hebrew Bible. (m. Yevamot 6:5)[100]

This mishnah appears to combine two legal issues into one: the first is the obligation that falls on men to procreate and produce a certain number of offspring; the second is the prohibition against priests marrying women who fall into certain categories. The commandment to procreate is behind the first anonymous opinion, which argues that the priest may marry a woman who is an aylonit only if he already has children and has thus fulfilled his obligation to procreate. Since she is incapable of reproduction, only men who already have children should marry the aylonit. In this section, one could almost translate the term "aylonit" as a barren

---

99. Sarra Lev argues in her dissertation that eunuchs are considered "normal" men and women with a particular reproductive disability. See Lev, "Genital Trouble."

100. The end of the mishnah contains a third opinion, in which the sages disagree with Rabbi Yehudah: "The sages disagree: there is no zonah other than the convert, the freed slave, and the one who has engaged in illicit sex [*bi'ilat znut*]." Christine Hayes treats this mishnah in her book in the context of a discussion about female converts and marriage to male priests (and she translates aylonit as "infertile woman"). She argues that Palestinian sources understand converts to fall within the category of zonah and that they are therefore prohibited from marrying priests. She also discusses the Roman equivalents to *bi'ilat znut* in her notes on her discussion of the text. See Hayes, *Gentile Impurities*, 172–73.

woman—and, in fact, some scholars have done this. Although there is a separate term for barren women found in rabbinic literature, the issue with marrying the aylonit here seems directly related to her inability to procreate.

Rabbi Yehudah, however, disagrees with the anonymous opinion. Even if a priest has children and has therefore already fulfilled his obligation to procreate, he still should not marry an aylonit woman. Here, then, the issue cannot be fulfilling the commandment to procreate; rather, it is his status as a priest. As we have already seen, priests are prohibited from marrying certain women (converts, freed slaves, and women who have had illicit sex). Rabbi Yehudah is interpreting the aylonit as equivalent to a woman who has engaged in illicit sex.

We could linger on the gendered standards here: reproduction for men and the regulation of sexuality for women. There is, of course, more to say about both. But I want to focus on Rabbi Yehudah's opinion and the ways in which the aylonit herself is subject to special scrutiny. Just as the genitally damaged priest and his wife face certain restrictions with regard to sex and access to the heave offering, the aylonit, in Rabbi Yehudah's opinion, faces restrictions on sexual contact with a priest. And yet, while the damaged genitalia of the priest are framed as unkosher, the aylonit is different. She is not simply *capable* of transgressing sexual laws; the aylonit herself is somehow inherently a harlot.

I am (somewhat misleadingly) translating a Hebrew phrase as "harlot" when it, in fact, is a technical term indicating that the person has engaged in illicit sex. There is a linguistic gap between labelling someone a person who has participated in an act of illicit sex and calling the aylonit a *zonah*—a harlot. According to Rabbi Yehudah, the aylonit becomes the peerless subject of the biblical verse about prohibited sex. Sex with an aylonit woman highlights the ways she embodies forbidden sexuality. While Rabbi Yehudah's opinion is just one of the voices in this local debate, it offers evidence that at least some strains of tannaitic thought understand the sexuality of the aylonit as inherently transgressive.[101]

If levirate marriage is about the ways in which men may fail to reproduce, it is also haunted by the specter of illicit sexuality. Women may thwart lineage through deceptive and illicit sex. Ironically, the aylonit is unable to participate in reproductive deception; she cannot reproduce, and therefore she cannot lie about the father of her child. At the same time, just as any man mail fail to reproduce, any woman can transgress the gendered laws that govern licit sexual relations.[102] And yet, the

---

101. While the word *zonah* refers to specific sexual transgressions, it is interesting to note that here, at least, there is a correspondence with Roman discourses about the "mannish woman" as hypersexual. Often, this (post-Hippocratic) idea is connected to physical and bodily signs. On this subject (and the connection between reproduction and sexuality), see, for example, Hanson, "The Medical Writer's Woman," 309–38. See also Brooten (who cites Hanson), in *Love Between Women*.

102. There is a sleight of hand in this mishnah to switch from marriage in general to marriage with a priest. It is not just priests who have an obligation to procreate; and yet, by suggesting that the word

special scrutiny paid to the aylonit in particular raises broader questions about the gendered expectations that govern women's sexuality and reproduction.

The imperative to reproduce falls ostensibly on men, and yet here it has some very uneven effects that both define and regulate the boundaries of women's sexuality. Moreover, this mishnah about the aylonit and prohibited sex proscribes the aylonit herself. Lacking reproductive capacity, therefore, at least according to some strains of thought, is a gendered social limitation. Being a eunuch is defined by masculine (un)fitness and feminine sexual deviance.

CONCLUSION: TRANSING THE EUNUCH AND ANDROGYNE

On the face of it, is there anything less promising for the project of transing than a framework of genital "damage?" The concept of "damage" understands changes to genitalia as destructive and seems to underwrite an assumption that genitalia should remain unchanged or "whole." If transing can mean, at least in part, paying attention to the ways that sex changes (as I have argued in my introduction), then logics of immutable genitalia are, at their core, both ableist and transphobic. The idea that sex change is akin to damage also bears a striking resemblance to some contemporary anti-trans understandings of sex, not unlike those who have seen my top surgery scars as evidence of damage to my chest. And yet, transing, according to Susan Stryker, Paisley Currah, and Lisa Jean Moore, is also the process that "assembles gender into contingent structures of association with other attributes of bodily being."[103] If so, then I am called to attend to the ways in which genital damage entwines sex with other bodily qualities for the rabbis. Genital damage becomes a useful vantage point, then, for examining the way that body parts come to be imbued with meaning. This, in turn, allows me to explore how the rabbis

---

zonah refers to converts, freed slaves, and women who have participated in prohibited sex, we enter the realm of women prohibited to a priest. The word zonah refers to any woman who has had sex with someone with whom sex was forbidden, whether the act was consensual or forced on her (see, for example, m. Ketubot 2:9). Judith Hauptman cautions against translating zonah as prostitute, which is the valence of the word in modern Hebrew. See Hauptman, *Rereading the Rabbis*, 89–97. And yet, despite Hauptman's caution I translate zonah as "harlot" here because "harlot" captures the rhetorical intent of Rabbi Yehudah's opinion. In opposition to Hauptman, Wegner translates zonah as harlot or prostitute, but she argues that this designation is not a major feature of mishnaic thought (see Wegner, *Chattel or Person?* 37). Jacob Milgrom argues (based on evidence from Philo) that in Second Temple times, the lineage of any woman marrying a priest would have been investigated. Scholars believe that the community at Qumran would have been even stricter—they applied these marriage prohibitions, including forbidden marriages with "outside women," to all Israel. Thus the tradition of associating the word zonah with women who are "outside," as in the sages' disagreement in the mishnah above, may have roots in sectarian law. See Milgrom, *Leviticus 17–22*, 1805–6.

103. Stryker, Currah, and Moore, "Introduction," 13.

connect genitalia with other bodily attributes and social structures to outline "kosher" sex.

In this chapter, I placed disability studies at the heart of the project of transing the eunuch. In my reading, I have refused to interpret eunuchs or "genitally damaged" men as disabled in advance. Instead, I examine the moments when eunuchs and people with "genital damage" are accommodated by the rabbis, as well as the moments in which they are not. The rabbis enact a sexual disability for genitally damaged men. They also subject eunuchs to special scrutiny: the saris bears the weight of procreative breakdowns, while the aylonit stands in for the sexual failures of women. Transing the text means paying attention to the way eunuchs are saddled with the weight of gendered expectation. Just as any man may fail to grow a beard and yet we single out trans men for their gendered "failures," so too the rabbis make eunuchs bear the brunt of male reproductive malfunction.

At the same time, the effects of androcentrism distribute the burdens of failure unevenly. The special scrutiny paid to trans women's bodies in the contemporary sphere is an outsized version of the excruciating levels of attention directed at regulating female embodiment more generally. The aylonit is subject, at times, to being reduced to her sexuality or to her incapacity to reproduce. She *is* the "harlot;" she becomes her body. To trans eunuchs is to pay attention to places where the pretense of parallelism (between the saris and the aylonit, between trans men and trans women) cannot hold. For all of us, sex changes throughout our lives. Some of those sexed changes are accommodated. Others are manifestly not.

5

Eunuch Temporality

The Saris and the Aylonit

Trans and intersex authors entwine temporality, sex, and gender in their work. They describe what it feels like to re-experience sexual adolescence in mid-life, to find out they are intersex after years of secrecy, to undergo transition (or its deferral), and to hear loved ones express fears about their future lives as trans or intersex people.[1] Thea Hillman, for example, describes her early puberty, and what it means to have an intersex body that is out of step with the bodies of her peers.[2] Janet Mock opens her latest memoir by relating a story about passing for older than she is.[3] When I read these accounts, I think about my own trans body in time, and the ways in which I am often read as fifteen years younger than I am, despite my gray hairs, because I lack the secondary sex characteristics of adult masculinity. To paraphrase Mary Douglas, our bodies are matter out of time.[4] We disrupt normative expectations of the way bodies travel through time.[5]

---

1. In her zine, for example, Mira Bellwether records compliments from her lovers: "Being with her makes me feel like I'm 16 again; small, and naïve, and horny, and like everything is possible." Bellwether, *Fucking Trans Women*, 52. In this case a nontrans person experiences time differently through her contact with Bellwether. For an account of learning about intersex status later in life, see Viloria, *Born Both*. There are numerous descriptions of the deferrals associated with transition. See, for example, Boylan, *She's Not There*.
2. Hillman, *Intersex (for lack of a better word)*.
3. See Mock, *Surpassing Certainty*.
4. Douglas, *Purity and Danger*.
5. Queer temporality is an established subfield. See Muñoz, *Cruising Utopia*, as well as the roundtable in *GLQ* (Dinshaw et al., "Theorizing Queer Temporalities," 177–95). Recent trans and crip theorists have pushed the field in new directions. Allison Kafer has argued that accounts of queer time have tended to decenter the body. See Kafer, *Feminist, Queer, Crip*, 34–40. See also Morrigan, "Trauma

Iain Morland, in his essay "Lessons from the Octopus," meditates on the ways temporality shapes intersex embodiment. Morland argues against the practice of performing cosmetic surgeries on intersex infants in the United States,[6] and in doing so, he describes the kinds of temporalities enforced by the medical management of intersexuality.[7] He discusses, in particular, the famous case of David Reimer. Reimer was forcibly reassigned female as a child after a botched circumcision. His case was lauded as a success by the treating psychologist; it was only later that Reimer himself spoke out against what had happened to him. Morland explores this time lag between current treatments and their aftereffects:

> If there is a lesson to be learned from the intersexed, it is structured by multiple deferrals: the deferred revelation of the outcome of David Reimer's medical management, on which much intersex treatment has been based; the now seemingly self-evident barbarity of surgical procedures that for years appeared reasonable to many clinicians and patients; the difficulties of choosing treatments, even with informed consent, that will have effects at once long-lasting and unpredictable . . . In these and other ways, I argue that the most acute "lesson from the intersexed" is that intersex treatment in the present should always be considered, paradoxically, in the light of what may come after it.[8]

The specter of Reimer's suicide, after years of abusive medical treatments, hovers just below the surface of Morland's prose.[9] The gap between the time when Reimer

---

Time," 50–58. For an excellent genealogy of the term "crip time," see Baril, "'Doctor, Am I An Anglophone Trapped in a Francophone Body?'" 155–72. In the field of trans temporality, Jenny Sundén has elucidated the particular effects of deferral on trans femininity. Trish Salah has argued that trans temporality is simultaneously the time of becoming and is defined by the conditions of colonial modernity. See Sundén, "Temporalities of Transition," 197–216; Salah, "'Time Isn't after Us,'" 16–33. Salah's piece is found in a special issue of *Somatechnics* on trans temporality. See also Kadji Amin's helpful framing in the keywords issue of *TSQ* ("Temporality," 219–22).

6. Morland, "Introduction: Lessons from the Octopus," 191. Morland builds on the early nineties boom in intersex activism and the subsequent scholarship that developed. For an example of activist critiques of disambiguation surgeries, see Emi Koyama's zine: Koyama, "Intersex Critiques." The activist history of the 1990s is described by Cheryl Chase/Bo Laurent ("Hermaphrodites with Attitude," 189–211). For the work that develops in the 1990s, see Fausto-Sterling "The Five Sexes," 20–24; Kessler, *Lessons from the Intersexed*; Fausto-Sterling, *Sexing the Body*. Scholars also returned to an older work by Michel Foucault in the 1990s (see Foucault, *Herculine Barbin*).

7. The medical "management" of intersex births has undergone seismic shifts in the last decade as the result of work by committed activists. The release of a new standard of care in 2006 was a major victory for activists, although its application has not meant the end of cosmetic surgeries on infants in the United States. The new standards officially jettison the term "hermaphrodite" and present the benefits of cosmetic surgeries in a much more conservative light.

8. Morland, "Introduction: Lessons from the Octopus," 191–92.

9. While David Reimer was not intersex according to any accepted definition of the term, Reimer's case has been widely discussed in the literature. Reimer was a twin who experienced a botched circumcision as a child. The psychologist John Money advised Reimer's parents to raise him as a girl,

was treated and the time the effects of that treatment became known lends urgency to the contemplation of temporality and intersex bodies. But Morland outlines various punishing lags—for example, the slow shift in the standards of care for intersex infants. In response to this painful lagging, Morland ends by arguing that the treatment of intersex people must be evaluated in light of what may come after.[10] Temporality shapes the material conditions of intersex embodiment.

In this chapter, I will closely analyze a discussion of eunuchs and time in the Babylonian Talmud (b. Yevamot 79b–81a). In drawing on intersex theories of temporality, I am not claiming an essential ahistorical connection between intersex bodies and time. Rather, my intent is to take up this theoretical turn to bodily time as a frame for the rabbinic discussion of eunuch embodiment.

I trans this sugya (unit of discussion in the Talmud) by attending to the ways eunuchs disrupt the orderly progression of time. The effects of this rabbinic discussion are contradictory: on the one hand eunuchs illustrate the normative and gendered expectations of bodily time, as they move through birth, puberty, reproduction, and death. On the other hand, eunuch bodies are framed as unruly, resisting the proper movement of reproductive time.

Scholars have characterized eunuchs as stably gendered, and therefore as not disruptive to systems of sex/gender in rabbinic literature. While it is true that the rabbinic discussion in our sugya mostly understands the born saris as a man and the aylonit as a woman, the ways eunuchs disrupt time for the rabbis has gendered effects. By centering eunuchs, we can begin to perceive the challenges they pose to the orderly progression of somatic time. I will trans the text by reading the rabbis literally, or deliberately badly, at certain points in order to expose some of the oddities of their logic and argumentation.

In order to examine the temporal effects of eunuchs in our sources, I want to first address the conjunction of gender and time in rabbinic literature for the

---

on the theory that gender identity is primarily learned behavior. Reimer's parents accepted his recommendation, and Money subsequently wrote about the case as a success. David Reimer committed suicide as an adult, and so references to him are fraught with the knowledge of his subsequent death. Sexologist Milton Diamond's exposé on the failure of the Reimer/Money case is famous. See Diamond, "Sexual Identity, Monozygotic Twins," 181–85. There is too much writing on the Reimer case to summarize all of it; Judith Butler addresses the various ways theorists have used Reimer to justify their approaches to gender. See Butler "Doing Justice to Someone," 621–36.

10. While Morland's argument about "what comes after" is compelling, the justification for cosmetic surgeries on infants is also based on a fear about "what comes after" as the child develops. Many medical interventions were enacted on the grounds that a child's appearance must be normalized in the service of an imagined future developmental trajectory. The sexed assignment of some infants is also sometimes based on future reproductive capabilities; in these cases, a reproductive future is surgically carved into the bodies of intersex infants.

nonspecialist.[11] Time is one of the central avenues of feminist inquiry in rabbinic literature.

GENDERED TIME IN RABBINIC LITERATURE

Much of the contemporary theoretical literature on (queer, trans, intersex, racialized, and crip) temporality begins by asserting that there *is* a connection between time and race, disability, class, sexuality, and gender. By contrast, the suggestion that time is gendered is not a radical or novel move in the field of rabbinics. The relationship between gender and time lies at the heart of feminist inquiry into rabbinic literature. This is primarily because of the construct of "positive time-bound commandments" and the analysis of women's obligation in rabbinic literature.[12]

According to rabbinic legal discourse, women are obligated to fulfill many of the same commandments as men. For example, women are bound by all negative commandments, such as those that prohibit adultery, carrying objects on the Sabbath, eating nonkosher food, and so on. Positive commandments, on the other hand, require a person to perform an action (recite certain prayers, follow festival laws, etc.), and women are obligated to carry out only some of these commandments. Mishnah Kiddushin 1:7 famously prohibits women from participating in a subset of these latter types of commandments—namely, positive timebound commandments or, in other words, those obligations that require performance at a certain time. Classic debates about women's participation in positive timebound commandments have focused on obligations like the commandment to sit in the festival booth on the holiday of Sukkot, or to wear ritual garments, such as phylacteries, which must be put on at certain times.[13]

The conclusion that gender and time are entwined in rabbinic law is not controversial; however, the interpretation of the relationship between the two is contested. Some scholars understand positive timebound commandments as a legal reflection of women's innate bodily time. These arguments often assume that

---

11. For a trans historical project that explores the category of the eunuch and temporality, see Chiang, *After Eunuchs*.

12. For example, one third of all the essays in the introductory volume of the feminist commentary on the Talmud reference positive timebound commandments. See Ilan et al., *A Feminist Commentary on the Babylonian Talmud*. The literature on the topic of gender and positive timebound commandments is so robust that I cannot cite it all, but see Shanks Alexander, *Gender and Timebound Commandments*. These discussions of women's obligation are not the only place where scholars consider the relationship between gender and time. See Kattan Gribetz, "Time, Gender, and Ritual in Rabbinic Sources," 139–57; Kattan Gribetz and Kaye, "The Temporal Turn in Ancient Judaism," 332–95. Sarit Kattan Gribetz's important book on the subject came out after the preparation of this manuscript, but see *Time and Difference*.

13. I am simplifying the issue for nonspecialists—these topics are, of course, debated within the literature. See, for example, Lehman, "The Gendered Rhetoric of Sukkah Observance," 309–35.

women intrinsically have natural rhythms that are cyclical, biological, reproductive, and different from those of men, although some scholars distinguish between the rabbinic construction of women's time and an essentializing argument about women's bodies.[14] Those scholars or traditional commentators who argue that the rabbis are merely reflecting women's biological time maintain that when the rabbis exempt women from positive timebound commandments, their exemption simply accounts for the bodily facts of women. Their scholarship suggests a kind of prediscursive gendered temporality, a temporality that adhered to women before the rabbis began opining on the subject. This temporality, as they see it, means that the "seasons" of women's bodies necessarily flow in heteroreproductive rhythms.

In contradistinction to those that tend to understand women's time as biological, feminist interpretations of positive timebound commandments tend to downplay the temporal aspect of the exemption. When scholars highlight the "timebound" piece of women's exemptions, they often do so to point out its utter incoherency. So, for example, women eat matzah (unleavened bread) on Passover, an obligation that is certainly bound to a specific time, and yet they are exempted from other kinds of festival obligations.[15] While these analyses take some interest in time per se, they focus on it primarily in its function as a prop in a (largely incoherent) attempt to regulate women's participation in halakhah.

That the rabbis deploy positive timebound commandments to regulate women's exemption is indisputable. At the same time, if we understand "positive timebound commandments" as a method of instilling and naturalizing a sense of women's time, then time itself becomes a gendered category. Perhaps, then, the function of time in positive timebound commandments is not just as a handy (if incoherent) way to regulate women; it may also recruit the reader into conceptualizing women's bodies, time, and obligations as connected in rabbinic culture.

Theorist Elizabeth Freeman has argued that time is used to create normative gendered expectations of bodies. Freeman coins the term chrononormativity to describe how the movement of time becomes bound up in embodiment:

> [By "time binds"] ... I mean that naked flesh is bound into socially meaningful embodiment through temporal regulation: binding is what turns mere existence into

---

14. On questions of the construction of cyclical time for women, see Goldberg, "Is Time a Gendered Affair?" 15–29. See also Anat Israeli, who argues that the construct of Jewish time shapes the formation of Jewish identity, and therefore women are excluded from central aspects of Jewish identity-formation (Israeli, "Jewish Women and Positive Time-Bound Commandments," 1–27). For a classic apologetic reading of Kiddushin, see Lederberg, "'A Woman is Acquired in Three Ways,'" 25–41. These studies aside, there has been a relative lack of interest in the "time" component of positive timebound commandments; this lack of interest runs counter to a robust one among Jewish studies scholars in the category of time generally.

15. Often scholars point to the ways that the "timebound" category does not impact men's participation. See, for example, Labovitz, "A Man Spinning on His Thigh," 75–87.

a form of mastery in a process I'll refer to as *chrononormativity,* or the use of time to organize individual human bodies. . . .[16]

Chrononormativity is the means by which we internalize certain somatic rhythms as routines that seem ahistorical and depoliticized. Temporal regulation transforms a human construction into natural fact. In Freeman's account, time is a method for naturalizing power relations.

The concept of chrononormativity can help us to unpack the relationship among bodies, gender, and time in rabbinic literature. When bodily time is construed as prediscursive and essentialized, it becomes part of a system that establishes and naturalizes asymmetrical gendered relations.[17] When the rabbis imagine women's cyclical time as an impediment to halakhic obligation, they create the impression that the sources merely reflect the body instead of interpreting it.

Part of my project in this chapter is to expand on the scholarship of gendered embodiment and time by examining somatic time in relation to eunuchs. I will argue that this idea of naturalized time can also be seen in rabbinic discussions of eunuchs, which the rabbis use to establish the way gendered bodies should move and develop through time generally. In the next section, I will begin to explore these questions.

"OLD MEN ARE LIKE EUNUCHS": EUNUCH BODIES AS ANALOGIES

Our sugya appears to be held together loosely by traditions connected to eunuchs. While the opening of the sugya treats the topic of eunuchs and levirate marriage, several other types of cases are introduced that cover a range of different ritual and legal areas. Between the sheer array of laws and the fact that the sugya is organized counterintuitively (moving from old age to birth, and then to puberty), it would be easy to dismiss this discussion as a lightly edited stream of consciousness. Instead, I argue that the composition of the sugya is deliberately shaped to curate a broader meditation on the imbrication of eunuchs and time. In this section, eunuch bodies carry the weight of failing to conform to gendered expectations of age and devel-

---

16. Freeman, *Time Binds*, 3. Clearly Freeman's notion of "productive" bodies in the context of late capitalism is formed out of a different historical moment than the rabbinic conceptualization of "productive" (and reproductive) bodies. At the same time, Freeman's chrononormativity provides a theoretical model to describe the regulatory relationship among time, gender, and embodiment; feminist scholarship on the Mishnah demonstrates that all three of these categories are entangled in tannaitic thought.

17. Others in the field of rabbinics have established that representations of the body naturalize asymmetrical power relations. See Fonrobert, "Regulating the Human Body," 271.

opment. In the process, eunuchs both delineate and undo the boundaries of normative somatic time.

The sugya begins with a discussion of the laws of levirate marriage. I will briefly remind readers of the laws of levirate marriage again here, although I discussed them at length in previous chapters. Levirate marriage is first described in the Hebrew Bible. When a married man dies without children, his widow is obligated to marry his brother. Any children that result from the union carry on the lineage of the dead husband. Alternatively, the widow and the brother-in-law may perform a ritual to dissolve the obligation to marry and to free the widow to marry another person. Either levirate marriage or the ritual must be performed.

Normally, marriage between a widow and her brother-in-law would be prohibited. It is *only* in the case where the husband dies without children that the laws of levirate marriage transform what would otherwise be a proscribed relationship into a mandated one. Since levirate marriage authorizes an otherwise forbidden relationship for the explicit purpose of procreation, the rabbis question what happens when one of the parties is a eunuch.

Our discussion begins with a technical debate of Rabbi Akiva's position in the Mishnah (which I discussed at length in the last chapter).[18] In this mishnah, Rabbi Akiva asserts that the acquired saris should perform the ritual to dissolve the obligation to enter into levirate marriage, whereas the born saris should not. There is a problem, however. Another tradition attributed to Rabbi Akiva seems to contradict this statement. The second statement would seem to imply that the acquired saris transgresses biblical law if they participate in levirate marriage.[19]

---

18. There is a debate in the Mishnah about which kind of eunuch is obligated to perform the ritual to dissolve the obligation to levirate marriage. Rabbi Akiva argues that the man who becomes a eunuch later in life performs the ritual to dissolve levirate marriage because he had a time (in the past) when he had the capacity to procreate. Rabbi Eliezer, on the other hand, argues that the born saris should perform it because he has the potential to be cured (and therefore has a potential to procreate in the future). See m. Yevamot 8:4 and my discussion of this mishnah in the previous chapter.

19. The conflict, which is complex, is as follows: Rabbi Akiva argues that an acquired saris performs the ritual of ḥalizah in the Mishnah. Elsewhere, Rabbi Akiva states that those who have transgressed negative commandments do not participate in levirate marriage or ḥalizah (see, for example, m. Yevamot 4:13). One statement seems to imply that the acquired saris participates in the ritual in order to dissolve levirate marriage, while the other seems to say that he would be ineligible, since doing so transgresses a negative commandment.

The latter statement suggests that the eunuch's marriage transgresses a negative commandment. This refers to Deuteronomy 23:2 which prohibits the genitally damaged men from "entering into the congregation of the LORD." The rabbis interpret the phrase "entering into the congregation of the LORD" as the ability to marry certain kinds of Israelite women. In other words, the conflict becomes: why would Rabbi Akiva allow the acquired saris to perform the ritual of ḥalizah if the eunuch is also prohibited from "entering into the congregation of the LORD" by Deuteronomy?

This argumentative move is quite common in the Babylonian Talmud; later layers of text often point out a contradiction between two statements attributed to the same earlier sage. However, the effect of this line of argumentation is not pro forma. Here the biblical prohibition that the acquired saris is transgressing refers to Deuteronomy 23:2. Technically, the verse in Deuteronomy prohibits "genitally damaged" men (the *p'zua daka'* and *krut shafkhah*) from marrying Israelite women.[20] By applying the verse to the acquired saris, however, the editors of the sugya naturalize the idea that the acquired saris and the genitally damaged man are one and the same.[21] In other words, the sugya begins with a technical discussion of a potential conflict in Rabbi Akiva's thought. It would be easy to miss, however, that eunuchs and "genital damage," two frameworks that are entirely separate biblically, become collapsed in this move. This was not necessarily a fait accompli; the rabbis retained distinct terms for genital damage and eunuchs, and by doing so left open the possibility of separating out these two frameworks.

Read expansively, this collapse between genital damage and castration raises profound questions about the nature of both. Is castration the same as "damage"? Are all eunuchs then considered "damaged?" Are we to judge those people born as a saris damaged as well? What are the theological implications for considering the born saris damaged? A very simple attempt to draw an equivalency between genitally "damaged" men and the saris raises complex questions.

When a later layer of rabbinic literature points out a contradiction in an earlier sage's thinking, the rabbis sometimes solve the contradiction by narrowing the circumstances to which the ruling applies. By narrowing the case, the two traditions attributed to the same sage will no longer be in conflict. In the next line of our sugya, Rabbi Ami, a later Amoraic sage, does precisely that. Rabbi Ami attempts to solve the contradiction in Rabbi Akiva's earlier teachings by suggesting that the ruling about the acquired saris is only applicable in a certain case. He argues that Rabbi Akiva permits the acquired saris to participate in levirate marriage only when the widow is a convert.[22]

---

20. I will use the term "damaged" when I think that rabbinic texts are situating various bodies as damaged. My intent is not to reiterate the ableist language of the rabbis. See the introduction to my last chapter for a more thorough discussion of the question of sexed variance as "damage."

21. There are earlier traditions that connect Deuteronomy 23:2 to the eunuchs; see t. Yevamot 11:2, a variant of the baraita that will be cited in our sugya and p. Yevamot 8:3 (9c-d). By arguing that both the creators of the sugya and Rabbi Ami are connecting the verse to the saris, I do not mean to suggest that the Babylonian Talmud is the first place where that happens. Rather, the editors of this sugya cement and naturalize a particular interpretation that the verse applies to the acquired saris.

22. Again, this is somewhat technical, so I will describe the argument in the notes. If the prohibition in Deuteronomy also applies to the acquired saris, then Rabbi Akiva must be discussing a case where the widow of the eunuch's brother is a convert to Judaism. Since she is a convert, and was not born an Israelite woman, the eunuch would not be transgressing the laws that prohibit "entering into the congregation" and is thereby obligated to perform the ritual with his brother's widow. Note that

Rabbi Ami's solution to the dilemma of Rabbi Akiva plays with the language of the biblical prohibition itself. Deuteronomy 23:2 states: "No one whose testes are crushed or member is cut off shall be admitted into the congregation of the LORD." The rabbis interpret that phrase, "entering into the congregation of the LORD," as a prohibition against marriage to an Israelite woman—a woman who was born Jewish and free. Rabbi Ami states his logic as follows: "Rabbi Akiva reasons like Rabbi Yose, who said: a congregation of converts is not called a congregation [of the LORD]."²³ In other words, in order to be considered a part of the "congregation," one must have been born Jewish. If the widow is a convert, then the acquired saris has not "entered the congregation."

Circumcision is the genital cut associated with becoming part of the Israelite community for men. And yet, as we saw in the last chapter, too much cutting renders the genitally damaged man unable to access the "congregation" through marriage. Rabbi Ami rhetorically strengthens that point by citing a tradition that plays with the term "congregation" itself. Congregations of converts are not called "congregations of the LORD." In one and the same gesture, then, Rabbi Ami associates castration with genital damage to consolidate an impermeable definition of the "congregation of the LORD." As such, sex, sexuality, ethnicity, and gender are all constitutive of the boundaries of the "congregation." Again, this is a technical solution to an apparent conflict in Rabbi Akiva's thought, but it raises much broader considerations about the boundaries of identity and community.

Having solved the apparent conflict between the two statements by Rabbi Akiva, the sugya entertains an additional challenge from an early (tannaitic) source. This tradition is cited because it seems to contradict the idea that the acquired saris performs the ritual to dissolve the obligation to enter into levirate marriage.²⁴ The tradition states: "Genitally damaged men, the acquired saris, and the elderly man either perform the ritual to dissolve the obligation to enter into levirate marriage or [they enter into a] levirate marriage."²⁵ In this source, genitally

---

none of this is explicit in the earlier layers in the Mishnah—the whole conflict in Rabbi Akiva's thought arises only when the verse in Deuteronomy is applied to the eunuch. The more straightforward solution to the "conflict" in Rabbi Akiva's thought would be to argue that he did not believe that the verse applied to the acquired saris.

23. Munich 95 is missing the word "not" (*lo'*), but Munich 141 and other manuscripts have it. The fuller debate between Rabbi Yehudah and Rabbi Yose on the question of what constitutes community is found in b. Kiddushin 72b–73a.

24. I am skipping over a fascinating discussion in our sugya that questions whether Rabbi Akiva also permits the acquired saris to participate in levirate marriage, or just *ḥaliẓah*. Because the material in the sugya is dense enough that a full explication would be difficult for general readers to follow, I am emphasizing the portions of the sugya that are most relevant to the theme of temporality.

25. Rabbah is citing the tradition. See t. Yevamot 11:2. This baraita is apparently attributed to Rabbi Akiva, although nowhere does the sugya explicitly state that. However, since this baraita suggests that the acquired eunuch performs *ḥaliẓah* or levirate marriage, and it omits the born saris, we can see why

damaged men, acquired eunuchs, and old men are all grouped together. All three groups of men seem to be able to participate in levirate marriage.

While the tradition does not offer its reasoning for adding the elderly man to the list of men being discussed, we can speculate as to the logic. Presumably, there are doubts about the procreative abilities of all four categories of men, including the elderly man.[26] This assumes that men's bodies have natural reproductive seasons, and that old age precludes reproduction. Since the purpose of levirate marriage is to ensure reproduction, there are reasons why old men might appear alongside other types of infertile men on the list.

And yet, even if the acquired saris and the old man are similarly infertile, the end of the text makes sense only in reference to eunuchs. If the genitally damaged man, the acquired saris, or the old man participate in levirate marriage, despite the fact that they were not supposed to, there are consequences:

> [then] whatever action they took has legal force, and [if] they had sex with the widow, they acquired her [as their wife.] [However], it is forbidden to maintain [the marriage], because of the verse [in Deuteronomy]: "Genitally damaged men should not enter into the congregation of the LORD."[27]

If any of these men engage in any aspect of levirate marriage, then their actions have legal force. But, the tradition continues, those actions will need to be undone; if these men enter into a levirate marriage, the marriage must be dissolved with a writ of divorce. The tradition also provides a reasoning for its ruling: the levirate

---

this would accord with Rabbi Akiva's position in the Mishnah. Lieberman's version in the Tosefta differs slightly from the variant cited in our sugya, but the differences are not substantive, except for the fact that the Tosefta adds that "if they had sex with the widows, then they acquired them and exempted their co-wives." The last clause appears in all the manuscripts that Lieberman cites that have the source.

26. Rabbi Akiva describes the acquired saris as a man who had had a time when he was capable of procreation (before castration.) By that definition, the acquired saris and the old man are parallel cases—both may have been able to procreate at an earlier stage of life.

This is not the only time we see a question of aging considered alongside other "conditions"—see the debate about animals on b. Bekhorot 41a, which provides the logic for why the Mishnah groups together the sick, elderly, and smelly animals. One strand of argument found there is that you need to exclude all three because otherwise you might assume aging is a natural process unlike becoming sick. Alternatively, the Gemara suggests that sick animals can become healthy again, while old animals do not become young once more. These traditions similarly seem to debate whether bodily processes like aging or illness are natural, and the normative trajectory of bodily change.

27. The beginning of the tradition specifies the actions that the men took. In the Tosefta it discusses both cases—the old men/genitally damaged men/acquired saris as levir, and as the dead husband. The former is as follows: "If [the genitally damaged men, acquired saris or old man] made a betrothal agreement with the widow, or if they gave [the widow] a bill of divorce, or performed [the ritual of] ḥalizah [to dissolve the obligation to levirate marriage] . . ." Those actions have legal effect ex post facto, and therefore must be undone, suggesting that they are not permitted ab initio.

union must be ended because of the biblical prohibition against "entering into the congregation of the LORD."

As mentioned, the verse in Deuteronomy originally specifies only genitally damaged men. We have already seen the suggestion that the prohibition for "genitally damaged men" should also be applied to the acquired saris. With the citation of this tradition, old men are now prohibited from "entering into the congregation of the LORD." Now, old men (and not just infertile eunuchs) are analogous to men with "genital damage." Read literally, this means that aging becomes a type of genital damage.

This *baraita* (an early tradition that was not incorporated into the Mishnah) and its inclusion of the old man highlight the tension between the frameworks of "damage" and infertility.[28] The category of the old man suggests that there are those whose time of procreative capability has ended. The acquired saris acts as a bridge between genital damage and infertility, because both the acquired saris and the old man had a period during which they had the ability to procreate. And yet, the inclusion of the elderly man in this ruling is less obvious than it first appears.[29] We must either consider the old man as genitally damaged, or we must see this tradition as intervening in the idea of "damage" as irregular. Perhaps, then, "damage," even genital damage, is simply a part of the seasons of life. When the old man is understood as damaged, then damage becomes a part of the normative life cycle.

Moreover, this conclusion throws the entire enterprise of levirate marriage into an uneasy light: sometimes men's bodies are not procreative, even in the absence of any injury or illness. This fundamental truth is, in fact, the very reason why levirate marriage is said to be necessary; any married man may die without children. If we start excluding eunuchs, then it seems that other classes of men should be excluded as well. The entire system of levirate marriage, itself necessitated by a failure in procreation, seems to point to the illogic of this exclusion.

---

28. For an analysis of the figure of the old man, see Wyn Schofer, *Confronting Vulnerability*, 21–53.

29. I am not the only one who finds the inclusion of the old man strange, although Lieberman, in his notes on the variant found in the Tosefta, (t. Yevamot 11:2) argues that there is no doubt about the language. See Lieberman's notes on Tosefta Yevamot (*Tosefta K'fshuta: Yevamot–Nezirot*, 106–7). There are also texts that associate elderly women with the aylonit (see m. Soṭah 4:3). The commentators are quite bothered by this baraita, which seems unique in its conclusions; I have found no other instance in the corpus where Deuteronomy 23:2 is applied to the elderly man. None of the medieval commentators can accept the conclusion that the elderly man is prohibited from levirate marriage because of the prohibition against the *p'zua daka'/krut shafkhah*. Rashi (Rabbi Shlomo Yiẓḥaki, the medieval French commentator) attempts to solve the issue by stating that the end of the baraita does not apply to the elderly man. I see no evidence to support his reading, and the parallel structure between this text and the first half of the baraita that is cited in the Tosefta makes his claim even more difficult to support. Moshe Isserles, (the sixteenth-century Talmudist) suggests that the problem is that the elderly man is simply not fit for intercourse because he is too weak. These solutions merely highlight the fact that the ruling itself is quite difficult.

The discussion continues with an objection to the idea that the acquired saris can participate in levirate marriage:[30]

> Read here [the verse Deuteronomy 25:6, which introduces the biblical rationale for levirate marriage]: "to establish a name for his brother" [through procreation]. And the acquired saris is not capable of this [because he cannot procreate]. (b. Yevamot 79b)

There is a fundamental problem with any eunuchs participating in levirate marriage. Regardless of whether the acquired saris could have children in the past, or the born saris may be "cured" at some point in the future (as is discussed in the Mishnah), neither of them has the ability to reproduce at the present moment. If the point of levirate marriage is to carry on the name of the dead brother, then why should eunuchs be included in levirate marriage at all? There is an easy solution: exclude all eunuchs. This basic question has hovered in the background of our discussion from the start; it is startling that it is explicitly posed only at this point.

An answer to this fundamental challenge comes in the form of another analogy between eunuchs and infirmity. Rava, a new figure in the discussion, argues:

> If [the man's ability to procreate is the problem], then there is no woman that is fit [Heb. kosher] for levirate marriage, since her husband is made a born saris an hour before his death. (b. Yevamot 79b)

The eunuch was analogous to an old man before; Rava now creates a new analogy between the born saris and a man in the moment before his death. The function of the analogy is similar: sterility does not occur only in eunuchs, and non-eunuch men also have periods of sterility. As Rava points out, all men become incapable of procreation in the moment before their deaths.[31] Moreover, the moment of death is not predictable, so we are not able to anticipate that period of sterility. Therefore, if we accept the logic that the born saris cannot participate in levirate marriage, then no woman should ever participate in levirate marriage, because no husband can procreate in his final hour. Rava's answer invokes the inevitable slide of bodies toward death, where fertility is one of the expected losses.

Rava's statement is a masterful response to the challenge of the sterility of eunuchs. At the same time, however, there are several contradictions embedded in his point. First, there is a disjunction between the question, as stated by the crea-

---

30. I am skipping an argument in the sugya that adjudicates the question of whether the positive commandment to perform levirate marriage takes precedence over the negative commandment not to engage in improper sexual relations. While fascinating, it is a technical discussion not germane to my analysis on time.

31. Mira Balberg and Haim Weiss have argued that in rabbinic literature, the old man is a liminal figure associated with the juncture between life and death: Balberg and Weiss, "'That Old Man Shames Us,'" 17–41.

tors of the sugya, and the answer, in the form of the tradition attributed to Rava. The question, as asked, is why the acquired saris participates in levirate marriage if he cannot procreate? In this question, the eunuch is the *brother* of the dead husband. The answer to the question, in the form of a tradition cited by Rava, on the other hand, makes an analogy between the (dying) husband and eunuchs. In other words, the question refers to the brother of the dead man, while the answer refers to the eunuch as dying husband.

This slippage between the two types of cases (the eunuch as *levir* and the eunuch as the one who dies) is accompanied by a second slippage: Rabbi Akiva permits the *acquired* saris to participate, while Rava makes an analogy between a dying husband and a *born* saris. This analogy to the born saris is awkward: If the term "born saris" is generally used to designate those who have been eunuchs from birth, then someone who becomes a eunuch in the moment before death is not a born saris. Instead, the moment before death seems most analogous to an acquired saris. That is precisely why the previous analogy was between an elderly man and an acquired saris; both had the ability to procreate in the past. By analogizing the man before his death to a born saris, Rava's comment emphasizes an innate (perhaps even natural) movement between procreative to nonprocreative states.

This is perhaps the furthest we have seen the sugya stray from the trope of eunuch as damaged man. The frame of "damage" imagines a whole, unblemished, and undamaged body as the norm; damage marks the body as nonnormative. But in these two analogies, both the weakness that accompanies death and the inevitability of becoming a eunuch before death are preordained and universal (male) phenomena. In other words, all men have a time when they become eunuchs. Now there have been two analogies in a row that make a connection between the eunuch and a time when men are conceived of as naturally unable to procreate.

Rava's statement is also striking for its androcentrism. It is women who are not "kosher," or fit, to marry their levir, even though it is their husbands who become eunuchs before they die. In the last chapter, we saw the question of kosher "fitness" describing genitally damaged men. In this context, fitness is still linked to marriage, but now the infertility of the male body makes women unfit for levirate marriage. The focal point is still the bodily status of a man, evaluated through his relationship to a woman. Fitness is connected to access to women in both cases.

What is particularly tricky about Rava's point, however, is timing. If old age is a period of sterility for all men, then all men will predictably arrive at their eunuch-stage of life, although perhaps at different points in the aging process. The moment right before death, however, is singularly unpredictable. Deathbed sterility may strike at any time. It is also retroactive: if a dying man recovers, he may also recover his ability to procreative. It is death that renders his sterility retroactively permanent. Timing in Rava's example functions by working backward to designate the eunuch after his death.[32]

This emphasis on incurable sterility is an opening for the sugya to respond to Rava:

> [In the case of a man in the hour before his death,] it is weakness overtaking him, [not sterility as in the case of the born saris]. (b. Yevamot 79b)[33]

Faced with Rava's sweepingly universalizing statement that all men become eunuchs, the creators of the sugya respond that weakness is not the same as sterility. This move reinscribes a minoritized understanding of the eunuch: eunuchs are constitutionally different from temporarily weak or infertile men. All three of these positions (the baraita, Rava, and the creators of the sugya) collude to implicitly link reproduction with health, youth, strength, and vitality. The question is whether the eunuch should be singled out in the face of the universal possibility of masculine procreative failure. There are two contrasting positions: one that understands infertility as a potentially universal experience of (masculine) embodiment, and another that establishes kosher levirate marriage through disqualifying eunuchs.[34]

Contemporary scholars of disability studies have responded to the idea that disability is a natural stage of life, and that all bodies will become disabled as they age. Rosemarie Garland-Thomson posits that the able-bodied do not wish to admit that we all become disabled if we live long enough. In her view, the propensity to become disabled is what makes the category of disability more threatening to normates.[35] Allison Kafer, on the other hand, critiques the ableism of the idea that disability comes (in the future) to all, pointing out that this assumes an able-bodied present. Jasbir Puar has drawn attention to the fact that not all people are allowed to live long enough to acquire the disabilities of old age. Puar argues there

---

32. This retroactive designation of the eunuch after death resonates with Alice Domurat Dreger's history of intersexuality. Dreger points out that when mixed gonads became the definition of the "true" hermaphrodite in the 19th century, the diagnosis could only be confirmed through dissection after death. As such, not only was the definition of hermaphrodite narrowed, excluding many who would have previously fallen into the category, but the only "true" hermaphrodite was a dead one. It is fascinating that Rava's invocation of the retroactive eunuch is precisely what *widens* the definition of eunuch. See Dreger, *Hermaphrodites and the Medical Invention of Sex*, 139–67.

33. The creators of the sugya ask whether Rava's answer stands as a refutation of Rabbi Eliezer's position in the Mishnah, which is that the born saris participates in *ḥaliẓah*.

34. In playing with the language of "universalized" and "minoritized" eunuchs, I am referring to Eve Sedgwick's work. Minoritizing homosexuality means positing that a relatively stable and small community of homosexuals exists. Sedgwick, *Epistemology of the Closet*, 1–66.

35. On the concept of normates (those whose bodies are not subject to stigma) and Garland-Thomson's assessment of the concept's importance in disability studies, see the preface to the twentieth anniversary edition of *Extraordinary Bodies*, vii–xviii.

is a racialized logic governing the inevitability of impairment; only some bodies are supposed to be (and remain) able-bodied.

These tensions over the "universality" of disability in our futures (and its base assumption of able-bodiedness in the present), are also at play in the rabbis' descriptions of eunuchs and levirate marriage.[36] The laws of levirate marriage may be the staging ground, but these debates over the bodies of eunuchs embroil reproduction and masculinity. Eunuchs serve as a site where the rabbis consider the ways in which masculine bodies change through time; eunuchs are a place from which to imagine how sex changes.

DIAGNOSING THE EUNUCH: THE SOMATIC SIGNS OF MALE AND FEMALE EUNUCHS

In the last section we saw how the tension between universalizing and minoritizing conceptualizations of the eunuch played out through analogies to aging and death. In this section of the sugya, we move backward from old age to infancy. In the process, the eunuch's body becomes the site of scrutiny and judgment; the pathologized eunuch is the conceptual opposite of the universalized eunuch. Reproduction continues to be the backdrop against which the rabbis stage broader conceptual debates about eunuchs and masculinity.

After distinguishing between the weakness of men before death and the born saris, the topic abruptly switches. The sugya notes that the discussion has not, in fact, defined a born saris:

> What born saris [is being discussed]? Rav Yiẓḥak bar Yosef said in the name of Rabbi Yoḥanan: anyone who has not seen even one moment of fitness. (b. Yevamot 79b-80a)

This is a simple variant of the definition of a born saris from the Mishnah (as we saw in the last chapter). In the Mishnah, a born saris was defined as someone who has never seen a period of "fitness"—in other words, a born saris has never been able to procreate.[37] This definition uses the language of being "kosher," which I render as "fitness" in my translation. The born saris and the acquired saris define each other: the acquired saris has had a procreative time that the born saris lacked.

One of the methods of transing that I employ throughout this book is to embrace a "bad" or literal reading strategy. I have demonstrated that reading strategy in several chapters already. Here, too, I want to read "badly" and literally, to illustrate the rhetorical effects of Rabbi Yoḥanan's statement. If we take the definition of the born

---

36. Kafer, *Feminist, Queer, Crip*, 25–26, and Puar, *The Right to Maim*, 84–88.

37. The quotation is essentially parallel to Rabbi Akiva's definition of the acquired saris in the Mishnah. Rabbi Akiva stated that the born saris lacked a procreative time and Rabbi Yoḥanan said that a born saris has not seen even a moment of fitness; Rabbi Yoḥanan's statement is an intensification.

saris—which says that the born saris has never experienced *a single moment* of reproductivity—literally, then we have to consider to consider the procreative capacity of a person's entire life span. We have just seen the image of the doubtfully procreative elderly man (or man on his deathbed). This definition of a born saris invokes a pathologized nonprocreative infant. What does it mean for an infant not to be fit for procreation?

The citation of Rabbi Yoḥanan's statement introduces the striking oddity of what it means to be kosher for procreation. The text seems to be describing something more than the simple ability to reproduce. How does one test the procreative capabilities of an infant? How do we ascertain whether, in the course of the changes that bodies undergo, the infant's infertility will be a constant? Rabbi Yoḥanan's eunuch infant exposes the oddities of defining normative masculinity through constant procreation. Given the link between sex, sexuality, and reproduction, the nonprocreative infant may sound particularly strange to our ears; we tend to exclude sexuality from contemporary conceptualizations of childhood.[38]

Evidence of fertility is most obviously established through reproduction itself, but how is a lack of fertility recognized? The creators of the sugya ask this question:

> How do we know [that a person is a born saris]? Abaye says: Anyone who urinates without the urine forming an arc. Where does [this condition] come from? [From] his mother baking at midday [i.e., a hot time of day] and drinking diluted[39] beer while pregnant.[40] Rav Yosef said: I heard from Ami that "[the born saris is] anyone who is damaged [Heb. *lakuy*] [already in his] mother's womb," and I did not know to what case he was referring.[41]

---

38. Kathryn Bond Stockton argues that the absence of sexuality defines childhood. Thus, for example a queer child can only ever be established retrospectively. Stockton's book, however, explicitly contrasts trans emergence in childhood with the exclusion of queerness from childhood. See Stockton, *The Queer Child*, 7–8. One wonders how her discussion of delay might be enhanced had she engaged with the fight over access to puberty blockers, for example. For a genealogy of the trans child, see Gill-Peterson, *Histories of the Transgender Child*.

39. I translate the word *marka'* as "diluted" in accordance with Sokoloff, who suggests that it comes from an Akkadian root. See Sokoloff, *A Dictionary of Jewish Babylonian Aramaic*, 711. The traditional commentator Rashi (Rabbi Shlomo Yiẓḥaki), on the other hand, reads this as particularly strong beer instead of diluted beer. There are other texts that describe the etiology for "birth defects": see b. Ketubbot 60b–61a.

40. I have not found evidence of parallel traditions in other contemporaneous literatures about baking during pregnancy as the etiology of eunuchs. However, temperature plays a significant role in medical discourse, physiognomy, and theories of conception in Greco-Roman medicine. See Lieber, "The Hippocratic 'Airs, Waters, Places,'" 351–69. Lieber discusses a group of Scythians who had a disease that caused them to become eunuchs in Hippocrates. Moreover, for both Hippocrates and Galen, the temperature of the part of the uterus within which the seed implanted affects the gender of the child.

41. The phrase *"v'lo yada'na' may nihu"* (roughly: and I did not know what he was referring to) could be stated in relation to either of two things, as Rashi points out: it could mean that Rav Yosef is

Abaye's diagnostic criteria provide a methodology for recognizing that a male infant is a born saris: if the child cannot pee in an arc, then he is a potential eunuch. Peeing in an arc, as a sign of infertility, broadens the question of a time of being fit or kosher for reproduction into a discussion of the function of the penis generally.

There is also an etiology for the condition of a born saris: a eunuch is created through the actions of their pregnant mother while the fetus is in utero.[42] This tradition situates the condition of the born saris as preventable damage, and it functions as a kind of public health warning about the effects of heat on a fetus in utero. The proximity to Rav Yosef's use of the word *lakuy* (damaged, afflicted) strengthens this association. In contrast to Rava's universalist and naturalizing framing that every man becomes a born saris in the hour before his death, Rav Yosef's born saris has been damaged in utero by his mother's actions.[43] The clock rewinds even further—now it is not only the eunuch infant who cannot pee in an arc but the fetus in utero that is already damaged before birth. We have moved from a question of diagnosis to cause and, by implication, prevention. Diagnosis and cure are linked in an implied gendered eugenics.[44]

Both the suggested etiology and Rav Yosef's emphasis on the mother's womb center women in the discussion of the cause of the born saris's condition. "Damaged" men are produced through their mother's incautious behaviors. Far from a natural occurrence, then, this occurs because women push the development of their fetuses off course. Up until this point in the discussion, the only women who appear in our sugya have been there instrumentally, to measure the fitness of damaged men for levirate marriage. Even the aylonit is completely absent from the discussion.[45]

Infertile fetuses (and incautious mothers) are marshaled to diagnose the eunuch at birth. Abaye ascertains the somatic signs that an infant is a eunuch, so that he may be recognized. But the proposed definition for a born saris is sweeping: it is not just that the infant must be born a eunuch but also that the person remains infertile throughout his life span. How do we know that the infant's sterility is not

---

not sure what the etiology of the born saris is; such uncertainty makes sense in the immediate context of folk beliefs concerning the causes of birth defects. And yet, it is also equally plausible that Rav Yosef is not sure exactly what Ami's statement pertains to.

42. On the connections of heat and gender in rabbinic embryology, see Kessler, *Conceiving Israel*, 89–127. Sarra Lev also explores these questions in relation to temperature and the signs of the eunuch body in "Genital Trouble," 189–91.

43. Sarit Kattan Gribetz explores the association of time and women's bodies in "Women's Bodies as Metaphors for Time," 173–204.

44. Disability theorists argue that diagnosis and a desire to cure disability (and prevent the reproduction of disability) are all linked to eugenics. See Clare, *Brilliant Imperfection*, 103–25. See also Jake Pyne's discussion of the Ashley X case in "Arresting Ashley X," 95–123.

45. The temporality of pregnancy is not the focus; instead, the rabbis are focused on "a moment" of reproduction. But that does not entirely explain why the aylonit is sidelined in this discussion.

a temporary condition? If the requirement is that the born saris must never have a moment of fitness, then to identify an adult eunuch we must also be able to say that from the time of infancy, the eunuch never heals:

> Should we suspect that he might have been healed [in the interim] between [birth and adulthood]? Since his beginning and ending were damaged, we are not concerned [with the possibility that he might have healed for a period in between].
> (b. Yevamot 80a)

To qualify as a born saris, he must remain a eunuch. If he begins life as a eunuch and enters adulthood as a eunuch, the rabbis argue that there is no reason to suspect that he might have healed in the interim. The infant's body does not slip in and out of the category of eunuch; the condition of being a eunuch is stable.

It is the Mishnah that raises the prospect of a born saris healing (when the possibility of a cure for the born saris is mentioned). So there are formal reasons why we may be discussing the potential of healing at this point. But the specter of a eunuch that heals and then becomes damaged again reflects broader questions about the nature of eunuchs. Is the born saris afflicted permanently by a "defect" caused in utero through his mother's behavior? Or is the born saris temporarily ill, and therefore curable? Again, these are ontological questions about the nature of born eunuchs, similar to the questions raised about the nature of the acquired saris. But it is simultaneously a meditation on the plasticity of bodies and their capacity to be molded and to change through time.[46]

The sugya explores this question of the constancy of the eunuch body further:[47]

---

46. On the racialization of plasticity as it relates to trans children, see Gill-Peterson, *Histories of the Transgender Child*, 35–59. I will discuss Gill-Peterson more fully in the conclusion of the book.

47. The beginning of this discussion is technical and I am skipping it in the main text because it would be difficult for general readers: Rav Mari challenges the idea that if the born saris begins and ends as damaged, then we can assume that they did not heal in the interim. He cites the case of a cataract in a sacrificial animal's eye, in which Rabbi Ḥanina ben Antigonus rules that we must check three times in the course of eighty days to ensure that it is a fixed blemish as opposed to a temporary blemish. This implies that one needs to check in the middle, not *just* the end and the beginning. Rabbi Ḥanina ben Antigonus' statement also appears in m. Bekhorot 6:3.

Fixed and temporary blemishes are legal categories that appear within the context of the bodies of priests, sacrificial animals, and marriage contracts. In the latter cases, the husband has the right to divorce his wife without paying out her marriage contract if she has a blemish that was not disclosed before the marriage. Like the transphobic trope of the transsexual who "hides" their trans status, bodies whose "damage" is not immediately apparent are presented as deceitful. This requires us to understand specific bodies as available for surveillance. On blemishes, see Rosen-Zvi, "*Haguf V'ha'mikdash*," 49–87 and Belser, "Brides and Blemishes," 401–29. For a discussion of the transphobic trope of trans bodies as deceitful or "counterfeit," see Halberstam, *In a Queer Time and Place*, 47–76.

If it is one limb, we are concerned lest [it heal in the interim], but if it [is a defect that involves] the whole body, we do not worry [that it might have healed]. (b. Yevamot 80a)

The rabbis dismiss the possibility of a born saris healing in between infancy and adulthood by arguing that eunuchs are different from others with "birth defects." The born saris is categorically different from someone with a cataract, for example. Whereas a cataract affects only one part of the body, a born saris is affected in his entire body.

In this analogy, being a eunuch is not confined to the genitals or gonads. The inability to procreate, then, is no merely local issue; the entire body of the eunuch is marked. This teaching establishes both the stability of the eunuch's body and its systematic differences from the non-eunuch body. Earlier the born saris was a universal stage of the masculine life cycle: all men become a born saris before death. In this passage the born saris is rather systemically different from men.

The text that follows is found also in early rabbinic (tannaitic) literature, and as such has been discussed by those scholars who have investigated portrayals of eunuchs in tannaitic literature. These scholars primarily conclude that the early rabbis depict both the born saris and the aylonit as nonprocreative but as fundamentally fully men and women.[48] In all the early texts, there is only one exception to the portrayal of eunuchs as stable men and women, and this exceptional source is also cited here in the Babylonian Talmud. Abaye establishes the signs of eunuchs as infants, so the discussion now turns to determining the signs of the eunuch in the adult body:[49]

> The rabbis taught: Who is a born saris? Everyone who is twenty years old and has not grown two [pubic] hairs,[50] and even if he grew two [pubic hairs] subsequently, he is considered a eunuch in all respects. And these are the signs [that he is a eunuch]:

---

48. For both Fonrobert and Lev, the treatment of eunuchs as men and women is markedly distinct from the Greco-Roman discourses about eunuchs, which are invariably negative and occasionally vitriolic in tone. See Fonrobert's assertion: "The halakhic literature nowhere suggests that the saris or the aylonit are in fact not 'really' man or woman" (Fonrobert, "Semiotics," 92). Fonrobert therefore states that the word saris would be better translated as a "sterile man" than a eunuch. See also Lev's conclusions in, "Genital Trouble."

49. I am skipping a technical discussion of the infant born in the eighth month; the discussion would be difficult to translate for a general reader. The eighth-month infant is included because of its analogy with the born saris in that there are certain signs that must be deciphered in order to identify them. The exploration of the eighth-month infant is one of the ways in which the sugya explores the connection between bodies and time.

50. David Kraemer concludes that for the rabbis, childhood and adolescence are separate periods. He demonstrates that while the advent of puberty triggered some legal responsibilities, there is a second major transitional age, at twenty years, that is considered the beginning of full adulthood. Kraemer, "Images of Childhood and Adolescence," 65–80.

anyone who does not have a beard, and his hair is smooth, and his skin is soft.⁵¹ Rabban Shimon ben Gamliel says in the name of Rabbi Yehudah ben Yair: Anyone whose urine does not foam. And there are those who say: anyone who urinates and the [urine] does not form an arc. And there are those who say: anyone whose semen is watery.⁵² And there are those who say: anyone whose urine does not ferment. Others say: anyone who bathes in the rainy season and his skin does not steam. Rabbi Shimon ben Elazar says: anyone whose voice is damaged and [the listener] cannot recognize whether it is a man or woman [speaking].

The first part of this source gives us the criterion to identify a born saris. Any man who reaches the age of twenty and has not grown two pubic hairs is a born saris. This definition implies that the eunuch's body does not experience puberty in the ways the rabbis expect a body to experience puberty. Pubic hairs, as a bodily sign, must appear during the right stage of life; even if he grows two pubic hairs after the age of twenty, these hairs no longer have the power to signify puberty. The first part of this source gives both an age marker (twenty years old) and a somatic marker (two pubic hairs) for indicating the successful onset of puberty.⁵³

The latter half of the source adds many other signs. It is not entirely clear how this preponderance of signs should be weighed alongside the age of twenty/two pubic hairs system. Are these signs meant to be additional diagnostic criterion? What happens if a person has two pubic hairs, but his urine does not foam? These additional measures are related to the function of the genitalia (e.g., watery semen), but they are also gendered markers. Temperature, for example, is connected to gendered medicine in many different Greco-Roman sources, so the ability of a

51. These are classic physiological signs attributed to eunuchs in different Greco-Roman medical texts. You can find similar discussion in Galen, Aretaeus of Cappadocia, and the Hippocratic corpus, which all associated hairlessness and smooth skin with eunuchs. For a discussion of the way these ideas migrate into early Christian literature, see Horstmanshoff, "Who is the True Eunuch?" 101–18.

52. This line is difficult to translate. The verb literally means to repel. Charlotte Fonrobert translates the phrase as: "Anyone whose seminal ejaculation is delayed" ("Semiotics," 88) but does not comment specifically on what that refers to. Sarra Lev translates the phrase literally as "repel" and also does not comment directly on it ("Genital Trouble," 330.) Elsewhere (b. Gittin 57a), the phrase "semen repels" is used in the context of a story where the sages were trying to determine whether a spill was semen or egg white. They test the spill, relying on a key difference between the two substances: semen is either repelled or absorbed into the sheet by flame while egg white is not. There, however, it is precisely "normal" semen that is repelled or absorbed. The commentator Shimon Kayyara's Halakhot Gedolot (*Hilchot Niddah*) discusses gonorrheal flux. In addition to other signs, the flux repels (is spread out) while semen is connected. Possibly our text is referring to semen that looks more like flux –watery might be another way to describe spread out. The phrase, however, is difficult to interpret.

53. This dual system of pubic hair and age is also found in Roman legal discourse, and Tirzah Meacham finds that the presence of pubic hair is an older system in both tannaitic and Roman legal discourse. See Meacham, "Halakhic Limitations on the Use of Slaves," 33–48. See m. Niddah 6:11 which comments directly on the relationship of pubic hairs and the ability to contract levirate marriage.

body to steam in the rainy season is a gendered sign.[54] The signs of being a eunuch are written over the entire body.

The source continues by listing the signs of being an aylonit. The aylonit, who is the counterpart of the born saris; is also born infertile.[55]:

> And who is an aylonit? Anyone who is twenty years old and has not grown two [pubic] hairs, even if she grew [two pubic hairs] subsequently, she is considered an aylonit in all respects. And these are the signs [that she is an aylonit]: Anyone who does not have breasts, and [for whom] intercourse is painful. Rabban Shimon ben Gamliel says: anyone who does not have a mons veneris like women do.[56] Rabbi Shimon ben Elazar says: Anyone whose voice is thick and [the listener] cannot recognize whether it is a man or woman [speaking.][57] (b. Yevamot 80b)

This passage suggests a number of ways in which the body of the aylonit does not experience puberty as expected. The system for identifying the aylonit is parallel to the system for identifying the born saris: she must have reached twenty years of age and produced two pubic hairs. At the same time, however, the source also lists a number of other signs of her bodily difference. These are specifically gendered, as the lack of breasts and the deep voice suggest. In many respects, the aylonit is treated as a parallel case to the born saris in this tradition.

I want to pause for a moment to discuss the background of the figure of the aylonit, because, while we have already discussed the born saris extensively, I have only briefly treated the aylonit in the last chapter. The defining characteristic of the aylonit, like that of the born saris, is her infertility. The rabbis have a well-established tradition of discussing fertility in the Hebrew Bible to draw on. The injunction to "be fruitful and multiply" (Genesis 1:28) may be the most well-known verse on the subject, but the Hebrew Bible is rife with discussions of (in)fertility,[58] primarily directed

---

54. For a full discussion of all the relevant Greco-Roman medical literature on this source in particular, see Lev, "Genital Trouble," 184–248 and 318–38. In the first section she contextualizes these signs within physiognomic readings of gender found in the second sophistic movement (hairlessness, body temperature, etc.), in addition to the medical literature.

55. Sarra Lev has argued that the symptoms of the born saris and aylonit are parallel, suggesting that they were conceptualized together: "*How the 'Aylonit* Got Her Sex," 297–316.

56. I have translated the phrase as mons veneris, along with Sarra Lev, although Fonrobert translates it as lower abdomen. See Lev, "Genital Trouble," 322 and Fonrobert, "Semiotics."

57. Sarra Lev cites a selection of manuscript variations for the last line, in order to demonstrate the ambiguity of whether it is the voice or the person whose gender cannot be discerned. The Vienna manuscript muddies the waters. The Erfurt manuscript is clearer, and the grammar in this version can refer only to the aylonit herself, not her voice. Lev "Genital Trouble," 321–23. See also the discussion of age of majority in m. Niddah 5:9. A variant of this tradition is also found in t. Yevamot 10:6–7.

58. For example, Deuteronomy promises: "You shall be blessed above all other peoples; there shall be no sterile male ('*akar*) or female ('*akarah*) among you or among your livestock." (7:14) Joel Baden argues that conception requires God's opening of the womb, and the default state of the womb is closed. See Baden, "The Nature of Barrenness in the Hebrew Bible," 13–27.

at women.⁵⁹ Barrenness plays a large role in central narrative portions of the Bible.⁶⁰ Some Second Temple sources interpret these verses to propose a blanket ban on castration and deliberate sterilization, although this ban does not exist in the Hebrew Bible explicitly.⁶¹ The rabbis expand on this biblical interest in fertility and the forces that thwart it. In this context, they develop the category of the barren woman ('akarah).⁶² Given the deep biblical engagement with the figure of the barren woman, why would the rabbis invent the category of the infertile aylonit?⁶³

In response to this quandary, some scholars argue that the two categories are essentially the same, and so they translate the saris and aylonit as a sterile man and woman, rather than as eunuchs.⁶⁴ This makes a certain amount of sense; the rabbis discuss the category of male and female eunuchs mainly in relation to procreation.⁶⁵ And yet, this tendency in the scholarship to collapse the category of the eunuch with infertility makes the least sense in relation to the aylonit, precisely because the rabbis invent the latter category; they surely did not need to invent the aylonit when they already had the category of the barren woman.

One explanation for the aylonit would be that the rabbis are drawing on contemporaneous Greco-Roman categories. There is no obvious counterpart among those categories for the aylonit, but, given the description of her bodily signs, we

---

59. Susan Ackerman argues that women in ancient Israel were accorded a certain power because they wielded reproductive magic. See Ackerman, "'I Have Hired You with my Son's Mandrakes,'" 15–30. In earlier sources, scholars have argued that women's infertility functioned as a disability. See, for example, Walls, "The Origins of the Disabled Body," 13–30.

60. There are five narratives of barren women in the Bible (Hannah, Sarah, Rebekah, Rachel, and the unnamed mother of Samson). Candida Moss and Joel Baden speculate that the focus on fertility in the Hebrew Bible may be connected to Israel's emergence during the population collapse in the Iron Age. See Moss and Baden, *Reconceiving Infertility*, 27–30. On questions of gender and male infertility, see Budin, "Fertility and Gender in the Ancient Near East," 30–50.

61. In rabbinic literature, there are sources that describe people deliberately imbibing a sterilizing potion. Barry Wimpfheimer discusses these texts. See Wimpfheimer, "Footnotes to *Carnal Israel*," 161–201.

62. Philo condemns marriage to a barren woman, thereby taking a position that is more stringent than that of the rabbis (see Philo, *On the Special Laws* III.VI.34–36.)

63. Of course, the category of the 'akar/barren man overlaps with male infertility in the Bible. In that sense, the born saris could also be understood as redundant. The aylonit is unique, however, in that there is no precise biblical equivalent. The rabbis briefly discuss an etymology for the aylonit that compares her to a ram who does not bear children. This seems also to associate her infertility with a gendered deviance. See b. Ketubbot 11a. There is also a tradition that the matriarch Sarah was an aylonit. This passage makes a clear distinction between the 'akarah/barren woman and the aylonit, and stresses that Sarah did not have "a place" for a child; in other words, Sarah had no womb. See b. Yevamot 64b.

64. See, for example, Fonrobert, "Gender Identity in Halakhic Discourses."

65. In English, the term eunuch is almost universally applied to men. When the rabbis make the aylonit parallel to the born saris, however, they are essentially connecting the two. I am therefore using "eunuch" as an umbrella term for the saris and the aylonit.

can draw some parallels. Depictions of so-called "mannish women" abound.[66] So, for example, the physical exercise required to train as a dancer was thought to sterilize women, an idea that perhaps drew on Hippocrates's theories that exercise causes the womb to shift location.[67] Some sources, therefore, depict dancers as both infertile and mannish.[68]

Other sources in Greco-Roman literature also seem to suggest a connection between mannish women and infertility. Judith Hallett surveys the literary depiction of the *tribas* (a word that comes from the Greek to "rub"), a category that can be broadly understood to indicate a woman who has sex with other women.[69] In Roman literature the tribas is associated primarily with women who penetrate other women. Diana Swancutt, building on Hallet's work, argues that the tribas was a category invented by the Romans, and that it constituted a distinct gender, a phallic woman, whose body had been transformed by gender-deviant sex.[70] For Swancutt, the "foreign" Greek quality of the category of the tribas in Roman literature was an indication of the way that she threatened Roman male imperial domination. While the aylonit is not portrayed as a classic phallic woman in rabbinic literature, these various Greco-Roman discourses that connect gender-deviance and infertility in women may be the conceptual backdrop for early rabbinic sources.

---

66. For a discussion of Philo's usage of the term, see Szesnat, "Philo and Female Homoeroticism," 140–47. For the category of women-men in Greco-Roman Egypt, see DePauw, "Notes on Transgressing Gender Boundaries in Ancient Egypt," 49–59. There are also descriptions of circumcision for women, although the evidence for the practice in Egypt is equivocal—Strabo and other literary sources attest to the practice, and there is some papyrological evidence. Of course, female circumcision does not render someone infertile. However, it leaves open the question of why clitoridectomy was being practiced. See Bernadette Brooten's analysis of Soranos's advocacy for clitoridectomy (Brooten, *Love Between Women*, 162–71).

67. For Hippocrates's etiology of the mannish woman, consider this quotation: "But if the man's secretions be female and the woman's male, and the female gains the mastery, growth takes place after the same fashion, but the girls prove more daring than the preceding, and are named 'mannish' [*andreiai*]." Hippocrates, *Regimen* XXIX.5–11. See Hippocrates, vol. 4, *Nature of Man*, trans. W. H. S. Jones, Loeb Classical Library 150 (Cambridge, MA: Harvard University Press, 1931): 270–71.

68. Montserrat, *Sex and Society in Graeco-Roman Egypt*, 62.

69. Judith Hallett, "Female Homoeroticism and the Denial of Roman Reality," 209–27. Hallett describes a range of Latin categories, including categories that are adopted from the Greek. In rabbinic literature, the most obvious counterpart for the *tribas* is the "rubbing" or "sporting" woman. See, for example, b. Shabbat 65a and also the well-known text that describes women marrying women: Sifra, 'Aḥarei Mot, 13:10 to Leviticus 18:3 Admiel Kosman and Anat Sharbat address these sources and the categories in Kosman and Sharbat, "'Two Women Were Sporting with Each Other,'" 37–73.

70. Diana Swancutt notes that, unlike Roman discussions of male-male sexuality, which make sharp distinctions between the active penetrating role and the "passive" penetrated figure (who was more stigmatized), the discussions of female-female sex do not seem to place as much emphasis on active and passive roles. See Swancutt, "*Still Before Sexuality*," 11–61.

There is one major difference, however, between the barren woman (*akarah*) and the aylonit. One of the problems presented by the barren woman is that her infertility is invisible and there is no way to ascertain, in advance of marriage, whether she is infertile.[71] By contrast, at least in this text, the aylonit's infertility is written across her body. The rabbis are conceptualizing a woman's body that does not progress in accordance with their ideas of normative temporal, gendered, and reproductive development. Thus the infertile woman and the aylonit are not coextensive in all rabbinic sources.

Although this tradition does not employ the kinds of gendered vitriol found in some contemporaneous literary sources, the rhetoric of diagnosis positions the aylonit and the saris so that their bodies must be "read" to offer up their truths. An otherwise potentially invisible quality (the ability to procreate) is written on the body in such a way that those with sufficient knowledge may interpret it.

These early traditions suggest that there are two systems to identify the born saris and the aylonit: the first system uses the age marker and pubic hairs, and the second is a catalog of symptoms. Given the different methods for determining the status of the saris and aylonit, we are left with two simultaneous impressions. First, if all the signs are supposed to function concurrently, then the bodies of the born saris and aylonit must be so changed as to be obviously different. Second, on the contrary: if we require so many diagnostic methods and signs, then the bodies of the aylonit and the born saris must have the potential to deceive the viewer. Therefore, much like the Greco-Roman sciences of physiognomy, the truth must be discovered arduously.[72] The age marker/pubic hair system for determining the age of majority is applied not only to eunuchs. And yet, this surveillance of bodily signs, meant to ferret out nonbinary sex/gender, lends a disturbing undertone to this scrutiny of eunuch bodies.

An inscrutable voice and the lack of breasts or a beard are gendered signifiers, but they also signal age. Certain bodily attributes are considered pathological only to the degree that they are present (or absent) at the wrong stage of life. The lack of breast development and pubic hair[73] both point to a difficulty manifesting the somatic signs

---

71. Sarra Lev provides us with a compelling theory on why the rabbis introduce the aylonit when the category seems redundant. She notes that the criterion for determining barrenness occurs after marriage, when a woman does not get pregnant after a sufficient number of years has passed. The aylonit, however, is presumably known to be infertile before marriage. Introducing the aylonit allows the rabbis to explore the permissibility of marrying someone who is infertile from the start. See Lev, "How the 'Aylonit,'" 297–316. I discuss the aylonit and sexuality in the previous chapter.

72. The question of whether all the signs are required to identify a eunuch is taken up by Daniel Malakh ("B'Din Hagdarat Saris Chammah v'Aylonit," 329–42). The idea that bodies can "lie" has been the foundation for much antitrans violence in contemporary times.

73. Charlotte Fonrobert, in her discussion of the somatic signs, points out that pubic hair is not in itself gendered, since it is used as the standard for both male and female bodies. And yet the inclusion of both an "upper" (breast development) and "lower" (pubic hair) sign betrays an extra investment in regulating female embodiment. See Fonrobert, *Menstrual Purity*, 128–60.

of puberty but these are also the legal signs of becoming an adult woman.[74] The inability to develop pubic hair is an issue only when the male or female eunuch is twenty years old, precisely because it can be considered normal until that age.

We have now seen the eunuch analogized to old age and the eunuch as infant. With this tradition, which describes the problem of crossing into adult gender, we move into the realm of puberty, situating the eunuch in a liminal space between the axes of age and of gender. Puberty is a time when the body is expected to undergo sexed changes. And yet, eunuch bodies stubbornly refuse to conform with those expectations. Puberty is a normative sex change that the body of the eunuch does not undergo.

In the next section, I continue to investigate a discussion of the boundaries between childhood and adulthood in rabbinic literature. I will also begin to draw some conclusions about the connections between time and the bodies of the aylonit and the born saris.

RETROACTIVE CHILDHOOD: THE DEVELOPMENT OF THE BORN SARIS

The list of somatic characteristics that identify eunuchs begins with a text that gives both an age marker (twenty years of age) and a somatic sign (two pubic hairs). In her work on the laws of menstrual impurity, Charlotte Fonrobert describes the rabbinic system of checking for the signs of puberty and *indagatio corporis*, its counterpart in Roman law. She notes that almost every time the rabbis raise the question of puberty, they do so in the context of levirate marriage.[75] While this makes a certain formal sense, it also has the effect of collapsing the signs of puberty and the signs of reproductive capability. Moreover, the choice of pubic hair (as opposed to underarm hair, for example) lends weight to the theory that a central component of rabbinic ideas about puberty is procreativity and, by extension, sexuality.

The confluence of reaching the age marker without achieving the somatic signs is what diagnoses the aylonit and the born saris as both adults and eunuchs. The two methods of measuring the age of majority (age and pubic hair) work in concert, since it is the tension between the two that makes it possible for the eunuch to be identified as such. It is perhaps most true for the aylonit and the born saris that a dual system of markers functions together.

---

74. The category of the minor is found ubiquitously in the legal corpus, often accompanied by women when they are exempted from participating in a legal obligation. For a recent approach to the minor, see Hezser, "Passover and Social Equality," 91–107. Jonathan Wyn Schofer treats Mishnah Avot 5:21, which outlines rabbinic stages of life. See Schofer, "The Different Life Stages," 327–43.

75. See Fonrobert, *Menstrual Purity*, 272nn30–31.

The system of an age marker and pubic hairs is meant to address the way that the advent of puberty is not predictable; some people experience puberty later than others. The flexible timing of puberty is a fundamental conceptual problem for eunuchs: how can we determine the difference between a case of delayed puberty and the case of a born saris or aylonit, whose bodies may never exhibit the signs of puberty?[76] For some people, there can be a gray period when it is difficult to determine whether they will eventually develop, or whether they will be designated as an aylonit or a born saris. This gray period presumes that in certain moments of life, eunuchs are not easily distinguishable from "normal" teenagers; after all, "normal" development occurs at very different rates.

There is a growing body of work in rabbinics on temporality. Sacha Stern analyzes rabbinic concepts of time in his monograph, *Time and Process in Ancient Judaism*. Rather than taking for granted the notion that rabbinic ideas about time mirror our own, Stern investigates the ways that time is measured in rabbinic texts. Stern notes the various factors that mark adulthood and the stages on the way to achieving full adult status. The age marker and somatic milestones constitute the end result in a process that is supposed to unfurl.[77] Thus the rabbis have a notion of the progressive development of bodies in time.

Lynn Kaye, in her analysis of temporality in the Babylonian Talmud, calls this kind of progressive bodily time "natural" time: "Bavli texts view certain temporal processes as present in the material world (natural time) and beyond the control of rabbinic conceptualization. This kind of temporality is treated as a stable foundation upon which to build imaginative temporalities."[78] Kaye's work skillfully dissects two competing registers of temporality in the Babylonian Talmud: a kind of "natural" time (in our case, somatic time) that progresses, and a legal/imaginative time. We see these two temporal registers combining for the eunuch: there is an expectation about somatic time and puberty that is linked to the concept of reaching the age of legal majority. The eunuch, however, separates these two versions of time, since puberty cannot function as the eunuch's marker of adulthood.

Trans studies has similarly engaged concepts of somatic time as process. Eva Hayward has argued that the teleological account of transition as a journey from

---

76. I am skipping a fascinating section of the sugya that explores an apparent contradiction in Rabbi Eliezer's statements, in a parallel to the opening of the sugya. That section works to establish gendered expectations around aging, but the material is quite technical for a general reader.

The Palestinian Talmud contains a shorter version of this entire sugya. In the Bavli, after attempting a solution that does not exist in the Palestinian Talmud, Rabbi Elazar states that the mishnah in Niddah relates to penalties. While this tradition exists, none of the various baraitot that follow are cited by the Palestinian Talmud, and its placement in introducing a conversation about various age and development markers does not occur in the corresponding sugya. See p. Yevamot 8:4–5 (9d).

77. Stern, *Time and Process*.

78. Kaye, *Time in the Babylonian Talmud*, 110.

an unlivable body to a livable whole may resonate for some, but in her conception, to be comfortable in her body is not synonymous with being complete. Instead, "it is to be able to embody the body's multiplicities, its vicissitudes, its (our) ongoing process of materialization."[79] As an alternative to the naturalization of the somatic development of the body, Hayward's understanding of transition invites us to think about inhabiting a body as an ongoing engagement with materialization, rather than a fixed destination. In that sense, both Hayward and Stern are emphasizing an idea of time as process, albeit to different effects.

The eunuchs in our sugya outline the expectations of how bodies are supposed to move through time. In some sources, eunuchs thwart an orderly process of development. In others, eunuchs demonstrate the fact that all bodies are expected to transition through time. The problem that eunuchs pose, however, arises because of the rabbinic anticipation of normative (teleological) processes of development. These expectations are expressed instrumentally through eunuchs.

The sugya brings a series of examples of different legal dilemmas regarding eunuchs. These dilemmas focus on cases for which it would matter whether the person who has transgressed has reached the age of majority. In each example, there is a discussion of when the born saris should count as an adult under the law. As there are several cases in a row, I have chosen a representative example to illustrate the debate over retroactive adulthood. Rather than focusing on the complicated and technical specifics of the law, I wish to focus our attention on how temporality functions here.

Our sugya cites a case concerning retroactive adulthood:

> It was stated: [In the case of one who ate biblically] prohibited fats[80] [between] the ages of twelve plus one day until the age of eighteen and exhibited signs of being a born saris and later grew two pubic hairs, Rav said: He becomes a eunuch retroactively [and therefore is judged to be an adult retroactively,[81] that is, during the period when he transgressed the prohibition against eating the fats]. And Shmuel says: he was a minor at that time. (b. Yevamot 80a)

The disagreement between Rav and Shmuel centers around the time period between the ages of twelve and eighteen. Implicitly, the debate assumes that this is when most people would experience puberty. During this time period, someone who has not exhibited the signs of puberty could be either a child or a eunuch.

---

79. Hayward, "More Lessons from a Starfish," 73.
80. Leviticus 7:23 prohibits the consumption of certain kinds of fats, called *ḥelev*. These laws require the removal of the fats of certain animals before the meat can be consumed.
81. There is a problem with the text here, since twelve and eighteen are the age markers of the aylonit (unless they are following the opinion of Shammai), not the born saris, and yet the text uses the word saris. Some commentators solve this by arguing that the text is discussing the aylonit.

Their transgressions may be judged as the transgressions either of a minor or of someone who is an adult but cannot manifest the signs of puberty. If a person who is subsequently designated a eunuch transgresses a prohibition during this liminal period, are they subject to the same penalties as adults would be?[82]

The two rabbis cited disagree: Rav designates the born saris as an adult retroactively. Once the eunuch has reached the age marker (for Rav, eighteen years of age) without the bodily signs of adulthood, then they are retroactively an adult during this liminal period. Shmuel disagrees, and argues that in this case, the born saris was a minor during that liminal period.

Retroactive thinking is not rare in rabbinic literature. Retroactivity is found in cases that treat a diverse array of topics, from the legitimacy of ritual immersions performed in an invalid ritual bath to the question of whether a witness who commits perjury taints the trustworthiness of their earlier testimony.[83] The mere fact that we are discussing whether the eunuch's adulthood is established retroactively is not in itself necessarily significant. And yet, it is *only* in hindsight that we can distinguish between the vagaries of bodily timing and the normal development of a eunuch. Eunuch adults are created by looking backward. The effect of this definition of adulthood is deferral for the born saris and aylonit. What must it feel like to live in that extended liminal moment?

We have moved through conceptualizations of the eunuch as old man, the eunuch as a man who is about to die, the eunuch as a fetus or an infant, and the eunuch in puberty. At each stage of this deconstructed life cycle, the born saris and the aylonit are instrumental in a broader meditation on the unruliness of bodies. How perverse is the body that steadfastly refuses to produce two pubic hairs, only to grow hair after the cut-off date of twenty years old! How very unpredictable is

---

82. The case is slightly more complicated than that, however, since the person in question does eventually grow two pubic hairs, but only after the cut-off date. Do somatic signs produced after the age of eighteen indicate adulthood that had been delayed, and therefore mean that the diagnosis as a eunuch was a mistake? Or do pubic hairs that manifest only after the age of eighteen no longer signify normative adulthood/gender? In other words, Rav and Shmuel's debate touches obliquely on the question of a cure for the born saris. This is not the only case where the rabbis discuss pubic hairs not grown in the correct time frame. They also query what happens when pubic hair is grown too early, and whether it still signifies physical maturity. See, for example, t. Niddah 6:2 and Tirzah Meacham's commentary on it (Meacham, "Halakhic Limitations on the Use of Slaves," 40–41).

83. There are over a hundred instances of the word *l'mifra'*, although some of them mean "abnormal" or "out of order" as opposed to "retroactive." For example, the term is used in the discussion of the recitation of the Shema in m. Berakhot 2:3. Leib Moscovitz considers the development of both terms. See Moscovitz, *Talmudic Reasoning*. Lynn Kaye argues that retrospective legal decisions comprise an example of imaginative time existing alongside natural time in the Babylonian Talmud. See Kaye, *Time in the Babylonian Talmud*, especially chapter 4. Whether these two phrases function interchangeably is a matter of debate; Kaye cites Nissim Luk on the question. See "Bererah and the Status of Time," 199–258.

the body's infertility, when death can strike at any time. And how difficult are bodies to decipher, when somatic time is so highly variable. Eunuchs do not have difficult bodies; bodies themselves are problems to be solved in this rabbinic discussion.

It is that fundamental problem that haunts the ontological debates over the eunuch and the discussions of the degree to which the eunuch's infertility is analogous to normal procreative failures, or whether the eunuch is uniquely embodied. My point is not to adjudicate between one position as more "subversive" than the other; a universalized eunuch, whose body is fundamentally similar to all bodies, may be eviscerated of meaning. On the other hand, a eunuch whose embodiment is singled out for surveillance and regulation (the flip side of "visibility") is not intuitively liberating. Rather than privileging one reading of the eunuch over another, I am noting a tension over the unruliness of bodies, played out through temporality, sex, and gender.

In her contemporary memoir, Thea Hillman relays her first memory of being told she was intersex. Her parents offer her an explanation of her "condition":

> My mother tells me about the diagnosis. She tells me I have an imbalance. And that I have to wear a medic alert bracelet. I love jewelry and find this news very exciting. She tells me I'll have to have a lot of blood tests and that I'll have to take medication, maybe for the rest of my life. I think this makes me very grown up, because adults take pills, especially my grandparents, who line them up beside their glass of orange juice each morning. She tells me about periods, and that I might get mine early. I can't wait. She tells me that I won't have more pubic hair than anyone else, just that I got mine earlier. I love the idea that I have something other kids don't. I decide this makes me special.[84]

Hillman's description of coming to awareness of her bodily differences takes place in two time periods simultaneously. There is the narrative time, as the reader, who already knows that Hillman is intersex, relives Hillman's discovery through her child-comprehension. There is Hillman's own backward glance as she remembers her mother's explanations of her condition through the lens of her own adult understanding. The adult and child versions of Hillman are both present in this scene, as her bracelets toggle between a symbol of her "condition" and jewelry.

Hillman interprets her body through the ways she experiences time: from the pills that seem to signal her precocious old age, to the pubic hair that sets her apart from her peers. Intersex time is not pathology, at least not for Hillman as a child: it signifies a precocious adulthood. Hillman does not mourn the loss of her childhood in this scene of her coming to consciousness as an intersex person, nor does she evince nostalgia for a pre-intersex past.

---

84. Thea Hillman, *Intersex (for lack of a better word)*, 18.

Intersex time also lurks in the silences within her recollection, as Hillman retrospectively interjects what her mother did not say:

> What she doesn't tell me is that CAH [Congenital Adrenal Hyperplasia] is a condition that can result in hermaphrodism in girls ....She doesn't tell me that CAH speeds up brain maturity, or that she worries about me being socially advanced beyond my peers and the hardships that might cause. She doesn't tell me many of the girls with CAH end up being bisexual or lesbian .... It's not that I think she should have told me these things. It's just that they were there, between us and around me, hovering behind every word and gesture.[85]

The revelation of her "condition" is wrapped through with her mother's desire to protect her childhood, shaped by an understanding that sexuality is the death of childhood. We see in Hillman's words the normative gendered expectations of bodily time, which exist in the future threat of masculinization, in the queerly lurking danger of lesbianism or bisexuality, and in the specter of her infertility.

There are parallels between our sugya and Hillman's story: in both, the connection between bodily time and the naturalized expectations of aging is disrupted by a body that does not conform to the expectations of sex and gender. Hillman's premature experience of medication displaces her in time and connects her to her grandparents. Similarly, if we reverse Rava's analogy, the born saris is like an old man. And the development of pubic hair for Hillman (early, as opposed to late, as in our sugya) is problematic only because it happens out of synch with expectations. Two bodies are juxtaposed in this passage by Hillman: the intersex body that is conceptualized as damaged and pathologized, and the intersex body that is shaped by the expectations of normative bodily time. Without adjudicating between these two tropes of intersex bodies, I want to emphasize that neither representation is a fait accompli.

In weaving Hillman into the rabbinic discussion of eunuchs, I am not arguing for a kind of trans-historical intersex time, along the lines of "women's temporality" in apologist defenses of positive time-bound commandments. I do not think Hillman's intent is to demonstrate the ways in which intersex bodies naturally interfere with time. There are obvious differences between the sugya and the memoir: Hillman describes early puberty, while the eunuchs are framed in terms of delayed puberty, for example. In fact, many of the temporal shifts in Hillman's account are not solely about her body: taking pills renders her old before her time because, in her view as a small child, pills are the prerogative of adults.

---

85. Hillman, *Intersex*, 18. The representation of a disjunction between age and body/mind development is often used to justify medical intervention or institutionalization in the case of disability. See Alison Kafer's discussion of Ashley X, where a family intervened in a woman's physical development so that her body would match her "cognitive age." See Kafer, *Feminist, Queer, Crip*, 47–69. On the rhetoric of intersex bodies, see Karkazis, *Fixing Sex*, 1–30.

While there are many differences between the saris and CAH temporalities however, both accounts demonstrate the expectations of the ways bodies are supposed to move in time, and what happens to those who thwart those expectations. In our sugya, eunuchs elaborate a kind of intersex/trans/crip temporality. A case of infertility reveals the arbitrary nature of the division between childhood and adulthood, and the way adulthood is deeply entwined with gendered notions of reproductivity. When eunuchs inhabit a doubtful age, they expose the difficulties of legislating unruly embodiment, and the fiction of orderly development and progression. We can begin to see the traces of rabbinic chrononormativity in its breach: the rabbinic expectation of the particular somatic stages of aging, leading to reproductive adulthood. Even the structure of the *sugya* is strangely ordered: it begins with old age and the moment before death, moves backwards in time to the born saris as an infant, and then proceeds through the fuzzy line between puberty and adulthood. Time moves differently in rabbinic literature when eunuchs are involved.

Conclusion

Rereading the Rabbis (Again)

Until quite recently, eunuchs and androgynes have largely been treated as a footnote to discussions of gender and sexuality in rabbinic literature. I have argued throughout this book that centering androgynes and eunuchs transforms our narratives about sex/gender in rabbinic literature. Transing rabbinic literature has allowed me to attend to the heightened levels of scrutiny directed at eunuchs and androgynes. Transing has pointed to the ways in which the rabbis do not invest in a stable system of binary sex; nor, on the whole, do they attempt to "correct" sex or disambiguate bodies. I will use these conclusions to describe the ways that contemporary transphobic appeals to a Judeo-Christian gender binary are not simply inadequate, but, in some cases, deliberately efface Jewish texts and their long history of engaging nonbinary bodies. Finally, I will argue that rabbinic interest in the changeability of sex establishes the rabbis' expertise in interpreting the body.[1]

. . .

In rabbinic literature, the drama of regulating unruly embodiment plays out over and against the bodies of androgynes and eunuchs. Eunuchs and androgynes experience the vicissitudes of reproductive failures, uneven and idiosyncratic bodily development through time, the vulnerable penetrability of the body, and the

---

The title of this chapter is a reference to Judith Hauptman's foundational feminist work *Rereading the Rabbis*.

1. This line of reasoning is indebted to thinkers in trans studies like Jules Gill-Peterson, as will become apparent in the body of the chapter. But it is also deeply indebted to Charlotte Fonrobert's arguments in *Menstrual Purity*.

uncertainties of sex changes. In response to these "failures," the rabbis subject eunuchs and androgynes to heightened levels of bodily surveillance, including genital scrutiny. This fascination with the bodies of eunuchs and androgynes elides the ways that it is not just eunuchs and androgynes that are subject to penetrability, reproductive failures, and stubborn idiosyncratic development. I have argued, therefore, that in the sources I have analyzed in this book, the rabbis displace the fragility and changeability of all bodies onto androgynes and eunuchs. And yet, the very attempts to define what makes androgynes and eunuchs unique point to the changeability of bodies and to the way all bodies may refuse to develop in accordance with normative gendered expectations.

Transing rabbinic literature has not, for me, located a gender-subversive core at the heart of rabbinic discourse. The rabbinic sources that I analyze in this book are often invested in shaping the entanglement of sex, sexuality, and embodiment, and are embedded within a (perhaps imaginary, but no less violent) disciplinary system. And yet, sometimes these stories also seem to offer an implicit critique of the feasibility or even desirability of the regulation of gender. Take, for example, the story of the androgyne with which I began this book and which I discussed at length in chapter 3:

> Rabbi [Yehudah HaNasi] relayed [the following story]: "When I went to learn rabbinic teachings with Rabbi Elazar ben Shamua, his students banded together against me like the [famously aggressive] roosters of Beit Bukiya.[2] They allowed me to learn only one teaching [and it was this]: "Rabbi Eliezer says that [in the case of the] androgyne: [the man who penetrates the androgyne anally] is liable for [the penalty of] stoning [for transgressing the prohibition against sex with a man, just] as [he would be if he had anal sex with a non-androgyne] male." (b. Yevamot 84a)

This is the story of Rabbi Yehudah HaNasi, who goes to learn from a teacher. Students block Rabbi Yehudah HaNasi's access to their teacher. Because of the interference of the students, Rabbi Yehudah HaNasi manages to learn only one teaching. This teaching is that a man who has anal sex with an androgyne transgresses the biblical prohibition against "lying with a man."

There are certainly ways to read this story as a critique of heteronormative gender. The penetrable body of the androgyne subverts the hypermasculine territorial boundary erected by the students. In that reading, the permeability of the androgyne is a metaphor for the potential for cross-fertilization when boundaries are transgressed. In other words, it is possible to interpret this story as a criticism, not just of aggressive masculinity but also of the value of maintaining strict dichotomies and boundaries. The story's critique focuses on scholarly boundaries; but

---

2. Beit Bukiya is a place name. I explore this text further (and have a longer note on it) in chapter 3 of this book.

through the inclusion of the body of the androgyne, that critique can be extended to other dichotomies, including the gender binary. In the debate over which kinds of penetrative sex with an androgyne constitute "lying with a man," the very sex of the androgyne seems to shift and morph.

The discussion of sex with an androgyne not only draws our attention to the instability of sexed embodiment; it also clearly demonstrates an awareness of sexed variation outside of a binary.[3] In other texts, such as the source I analyze in chapter 2, which asks the questions, "how is the androgyne like men, women, both, and neither?" the androgyne is called a "unique creation" (rather than male or female). This suggests that not all beings will (or should) fit into a binary. The framework of "unique creation" clearly gestures at the unsustainability of binary thinking around sex and gender, even though (as I argue in chapter 2) this move also excludes the androgyne from rabbinic legal obligation. At the very least, then, this book functions as further evidence of the ways in which we must understand binary gender as a historically and culturally situated phenomenon. As Leah DeVun, a medieval historian who writes about nonbinary embodiment has argued:

> An expansive chronology of sexual difference can be a powerful corrective to assertions that sex and gender binaries have simply always been with us. The complex notions of sex and gender that preceded our era by many centuries, and the heated debates that surrounded them, whether or not we know about those debates, continue to affect our world.[4]

Similarly, my work serves to contextualize the naturalization of binary gender as a modern innovation. When contemporary antitrans arguments reach toward a "Judeo-Christian" argument in support of binary gender, they must ignore the history of classical Jewish sources, which describe a more complex and uneven picture.

At the same time, the basic concept that sex is mutable is not necessarily subversive or resistant. Jules Gill-Peterson, in the book *Histories of the Transgender Child*, painstakingly traces the rise of the idea of sexed plasticity in US medicine. Gill-Peterson has argued that while the concept of the plasticity of sex plays a role in the development of trans medicine, it is also linked to racialized sciences and eugenics. Moreover, techniques for sex change were developed through medical experimentation on intersex infants. For example, experiments carried out at the clinic at Johns Hopkins were often practiced on white children who were understood to have the potential to be normalized. Doctors deemed white children's lives uniquely worth preserving and assumed that Black sexed "deviance" was a product of Blackness itself. Thus, sex change is also predicated on the fungibility of Black bodies, and we can directly link plasticity to the persistent dehumanizing

---

3. See Kessler, "Rabbinic Gender," 353–70.
4. DeVun, *The Shape of Sex*, 205.

anti-Blackness practiced at the Johns Hopkins clinic, and its ongoing effects on the residents of the surrounding Black neighborhoods in Baltimore. In other words, sexed plasticity has, at times, been deadly.[5] Moreover, as Gill-Peterson argues, researchers establish their own authority as interpreters of sex and gender through these experiments that were carried out on intersex bodies. There is significant harm when the mutability of sex can be used to create a class of expertise designed to hoard the authority to interpret sex.

Similarly, when the rabbis explore the instability of sex and gender, they set themselves up as interpreters of sexed materiality.[6] The endless rabbinic debates shaping and reshaping the connection among genitals, sex, gender, and sexuality scrutinize and define eunuch and androgyne bodies. In turn, the rabbinic definitional and regulatory interests in sexed embodiment bring eunuchs and androgynes into the realm of halakhah and therefore into rabbinic jurisdiction.[7] It is the very fact that the rabbis do not invest in either stable sex, or in a clear binary, that enables them to become interpreters of sex.

When the rabbis absorb eunuchs and androgynes into halakhah, then, they position themselves as experts on sex, with the ability to interpret bodies and assign roles, rituals, and obligations on the basis of that interpretation. When, for example, the rabbis rename the anus of the androgyne as the "masculine orifice," they are mapping the body. Renaming can often function as a powerful tool of trans resignification. I was not born with the name "Max," for example. Trans people rename body parts to match our embodied self-knowledge as well. And yet, in this case, renaming is a type of mapping that colonizes the territory it describes.

At the same time, while the mutability of sex enables rabbinic halakhic expertise, it also has paradoxical effects. Even as the rabbis position themselves as interpreters of sex through their close scrutiny of the ways in which sex can change (either through time or owing to transformations of the body), this very mutability also

---

5. Gill-Peterson, *Histories of the Transgender Child*. See, particularly, chapters 1 and 2, which describe the prehistory of transsexuality and the early racialized constitution of the plasticity of sex.

6. See Fonrobert, "Regulating the Human Body," 270–94. There is a broader field that speaks to medicine and rabbinic authority. See, for example, Balberg, "Rabbinic Authority, Medical Rhetoric, and Body Hermeneutics," 323–46; Lehmhaus, "*Listenwissenschaft,*" 59–100; Neis, "Fetus, Flesh, Food," 181–210; Kessler, *Conceiving Israel*.

7. Feminists have questioned whether the genre of halakhah can be transformed: "halakhah is part of the system that women did not have a hand in creating. How can we presume that if women add our voices to tradition, law will be our medium of expression and repair?" (Plaskow, *Standing Again at Sinai*, 9). Similarly, in trans studies, scholars have critiqued law as a site of trans liberation. As Dean Spade writes, "[A critical trans politics means] . . . acknowledging that legal equality demands are a feature of systemic injustice, not a remedy. It is confronting the harms that come to trans people at the hands of violent systems structured through law itself—not by demanding recognition and inclusion in those systems, but by working to dismantle them while simultaneously supporting those most exposed to their harms" (Spade, *Normal Life*, 41).

makes eunuchs and androgynes difficult to regulate. When the rabbis discuss in lengthy and intimate detail the ways in which sex changes for androgynes and eunuchs, the changeability of bodies is precisely what makes it so difficult to definitively "know" a person's sex. For example, as we saw in chapter 3, if the disambiguating surgery practiced on the tumtum does not wholly demonstrate their capacity for reproduction, then there are limits to our ability to determine masculine reproductivity from the scrutiny of sexed bodies. In chapter 4 we explored the way in which changes to genitalia, and the consequent halakhic judgment of some genitals as kosher, are connected to a social system of access to women. Because sexed embodiment can change at any time, this kind of genital surveillance, which is linked to social consequences, speaks to the ultimate impossibility of definitively determining which men are fit for which kind of marriages. The very same emphasis on mutability, then, simultaneously undermines the possibilities for stable knowledge about sex/gender. In many of the sources I have analyzed in this book, there are visible cracks in the rabbis' ability to definitively identify and assign sex/gender.

I have not located sources that suggest that androgynes and eunuchs pushed back against rabbinic expertise in this book. The texts themselves provide only the faintest potential traces of gender-marginalized historical figures, such as the partly nameless figure of the Tumtum of Biri. And yet, I find another kind of historical trace in the echoes of stubbornly resistant embodiment. Take, for example, the source that describes the signs of the bodies of the born saris and aylonit. This early rabbinic source lists a number of bodily signs that can help identify the body of eunuchs, as well as a system of age markers. In response to the lack of clarity about the point when eunuchs reach the age of adulthood if they do not experience puberty, the rabbis give them until the age of twenty to grow two pubic hairs. That way, those people who come to puberty late can be distinguished from the born saris and aylonit. And yet, this source discusses the problem of a person who grows two pubic hairs after reaching the cutoff age of twenty. In other words, even after the rabbis grant an extended timeline for puberty in order to ascertain the borderlines between eunuchs and non-eunuchs, they describe a body that perversely refuses to cooperate. One can explain these instances in the way I have—as the rabbis investing in establishing themselves as interpreters of sex. And yet, while this bodily resistance does not point to transcestors in any recoverable sense, it does hint at bodies that may have pushed back against taxonomical impulses.[8]

---

8. There are various attempts (artistic and otherwise) to think through the concept of transcestors. I am reminded of the recent publication in *Trans Studies Quarterly* of Julian Carter's zine, which describes attempts to connect (sexually, affectively) across generations. See "Sex Time Machine," 691–706. See also Leah DeVun's discussion of the importance of Leslie Feinberg's work in *The Shape of Sex*, 1–16.

188 CONCLUSION

The bodies of eunuchs and androgynes seem, on occasion, to thwart rabbinic attempts at mapping, and to actively refuse to cooperate with rabbinic timelines.

I have nevertheless been cautious throughout this book about trumpeting the subversive potential of eunuchs and androgynes. This is, in part, because it is almost impossible for me to know the cost of that subversion to the people who inhabited those categories at the time. The mutability of sex and gender has, at different historical times and in diverse places, led to classifying certain bodies as incoherent. As we know from more recent history, the repercussions of gendered incoherency can sometimes be deadly. Violence (whether rhetorical or material) underlies many of the rabbinic sources. Subversion, then, may be bought at too high a price when we lack an ability to account adequately for harm. In this respect, I remain stubbornly attached to the "bad" literal reading of the materiality of sex, of bodies that existed in the world, and what it might have meant to them to navigate contested and changing terrain.

My research on eunuchs and androgynes poses a series of larger questions that are ultimately beyond the scope of this book: Since bodies change through time, and bodily functions are not entirely within our control, are there limits to the rabbis' ability to regulate the body? How do the rabbis address this seemingly endless variability of bodies within the structure of halakhah without sacrificing the idea that halakhah is flexible enough to address every situation? There is an inherent tension in the way that bodies exceed the strictures of halakhah, in parallel to the way that bodies exceed their own boundaries: the rabbis extensively contemplate bodies that leak or bleed, become "damaged," lose bodily integrity, or challenge orderly taxonomies. Texts that address gender, sexuality, ethnicity, and disability tend to foreground these questions. Perhaps the rabbis invoke these categories to grapple with the regulation of the body and the limits of the halakhic enterprise itself.

NAMING THE PAST: HERMAPHRODITUS, HERMAPHRODITE, INTERSEX

When Jeffrey Eugenides published *Middlesex* in 2002, the novel garnered glowing critical reviews and, eventually, a Pulitzer Prize. *Middlesex* rode the wave of public interest in intersex issues, following hard on the heels of several articles written by activists for the popular press in the 1990s.[9] The novel features an intersex protagonist named Cal, a reference to Calliope, the Greek muse (whom Ovid

---

9. Fausto-Sterling, "The Five Sexes," 20–24; Fausto-Sterling, "How Many Sexes are There?" In response to Fausto-Sterling, Cheryl Chase/Bo Laurent published a groundbreaking letter in 1993 that announced the founding of the Intersex Society of North America (ISNA). See Chase, "Letters from Readers," 3.

describes). Even though the story is set mostly in the modern period, this reference to Cal is one of several that *Middlesex* makes to Greco-Roman literature. For example, in one scene, Cal performs the story of Hermaphroditus, the figure who is created when a nymph and an attractive male youth are conjoined by the gods. The name Hermaphroditus comes from a fusion of the names Hermes and Aphrodite. Greco-Roman mythology and literary traditions are incorporated into the plot of the novel. Thus, *Middlesex* draws connections between contemporary intersex lives and late antique literary traditions.

Several intersex activists publicly criticized *Middlesex*. Thea Hillman describes her reaction to the novel in her memoir *Intersex (for lack of a better word)*. Hillman penned a critical op-ed in response to Eugenides's novel; this op-ed was ultimately rejected by the *New York Times*. After receiving the rejection, she attended a reading of the novel, where Eugenides used the word "hermaphrodite" all through the talk "as if it were appropriate."[10]

Hillman is disturbed by both the frequent references to Greco-Roman mythology and the way the term "hermaphrodite" features so prominently in the novel. Intersex activists reject the use of this term. As Hillman puts it, "While the myth of Hermaphroditus has captured the imagination for ages, it traps real human beings in the painfully small confines of story. Someone else's story."[11] In this passage, Hillman refuses the connection between the story of Hermaphroditus and contemporary intersex lives. Hillman, in the process of producing her own narrative memoir, invites us to think about the way intersex narratives can be both prescripted and confining. In an odd way, the late antique term "hermaphrodite," with all its mythological connotations, has eclipsed the contemporary term "intersex." It is as if the story of Hermaphroditus, popularized by Ovid in the first century, becomes a more culturally relevant frame for discussing contemporary intersex experiences than Hillman's own embodied knowledge.

I have been clear throughout this book that the terms "trans" and "intersex" have their own histories and genealogies and should not be conflated with the androginos, tumtum, saris, or aylonit. I have been particularly concerned with the anachronistic insertion of specific contemporary regimes of sex and gender into the past. So, for example, in this book I have argued that the antitrans theological reach toward Genesis as the creation story of binary gender imposes a woefully anachronistic reading of sex and gender onto Jewish pasts.[12]

10. Hillman, *Intersex (for lack of a better word)*, 25.
11. Hillman, *Intersex (for lack of a better word)*, 29.
12. David Halperin's groundbreaking monograph *How to Do the History of Homosexuality* lays out his methodology for studying premodern sexuality. Halperin describes (with more sympathy than in his previous work) the desire of some contemporary gay men to connect to Greco-Roman sexual mores in order to negotiate contemporary culture wars. At the same time, as a part of this theoretical reframing, Halperin assumes that the modern subject has the "epistemic and social privilege" to interpret

And yet, in Hillman's case, the problem is not the imposition of the framework of intersex onto the (defenseless) Hermaphroditus; it is, in fact, quite the opposite. The hermaphrodite is reanimated over and against contemporary intersex identification. Hillman's attempts to exorcise Hermaphroditus are only partly successful; it is as if the imperative to address hermaphrodites is inescapable. This reach toward the classical world is simultaneously a racialized imagining, used to construct a narrative of Western continuity and an unbroken cultural legacy by mythologizing nonbinary sex.[13]

The implication of Hillman's story is also, of course, that the mainstream literary marketplace is challenged by contemporary intersex narratives, but not by fictional portrayals of intersex bodies, nor by intersexuality marked in some way as "past." Hillman suggests that we have a collective investment in rendering gender and sexed variation as historical and mythical. This, in turn, can naturalize (or theologize) a straightened definition of sex and gender in the here and now. Or it can authorize a neoliberal narrative that relies on the proliferation and commodification of gender as a sign of progress.

I am not invoking Hillman to argue against projects of intersex or trans history. I am, however, pointing to the unique and specific ontological stakes of trans and intersex historical projects. Jules Gill-Peterson has argued that the way trans children have been figured as a "new" social problem not only ignores trans children in the history of the United States but also deprives trans children of a history that might work to empower them. The erasure of trans history, in this case, is not neutral; it is a deliberate forgetting in the service of subjecting trans children to medical authority. Leah DeVun argues that trans historical projects make visible the transgression of gender in the past, and also give us insights into the formation of systems of classification themselves.[14]

Similarly, as Iain Morland points out in his afterword "Genitals are History," the intent of intersex treatments is to efface the history of the intersex body. Morland argues that we need to rethink surgical practice, which has often been portrayed as cementing male or female sex. Instead, surgeons create an accepted version of the appearance of sexed congruity, and work to erase the presurgical body. In that

---

(and identify) these historical continuities and discontinuities. As we can see from the example of Hillman's memoir, however, not all epistemic and social privilege is created equally. See Halperin, *How to do the History of Homosexuality*, 20. For a critique of Halperin's earlier work, see Sedgwick, *Epistemology of the Closet*, 44–48. For a discussion of these questions more broadly, and an engagement with Bernadette Brooten's important contribution to this conversation, see Marchal, *Appalling Bodies*, 16–29.

13. For an analysis of *Middlesex* through the lens of critical race studies, and a discussion of the way that orientalism structures the relationship between Cal and Julie in the novel, see Hsu, "Ethnicity and the Biopolitics of Intersex," 87–110; and Kojima, "Trans-Pacific Imaginaries and Queer Intimacies," 57–61. The latter article is part of a roundtable discussing *Middlesex*.

14. Gill-Peterson, *Histories*, 195–209; DeVun, *The Shape of Sex*, 1–16.

sense, surgery memorializes the contact of a body with someone who sought to erase it.[15] One might argue, then, that the "rediscovery" of intersex issues by the mainstream media every few years is predicated on the consistent forgetting of intersexuality. In that sense, the colonizing "rediscovery" is an extension of the aims of surgery. Like surgery, this manufactured "forgetting" is designed to suppress the possibility of intersex history. In the face of such historical suppressions, trans and intersex histories become all the more crucial.

In chapter 2, I analyzed the theology of the Mississippi "bathroom bill," which purports to protect religious beliefs in straight marriage and binary gender. In that chapter, I read the language of the law closely and argued that the antiqueer theology embedded within it assumes that queer marriage should not exist. The belief that queer marriage should not exist (and that marriage *should* be straight) tacitly acknowledges that queerness does, in fact, already exist. In the same bill, however, antitrans theologies are written differently. The "bathroom bill" protects a belief that trans people *do* not exist—in other words, that trans people are an impossibility.[16] I argued that antiqueer and antitrans theologies do not work in parallel ways within the logics of religious freedom laws.[17] The distinction between "should not exist" and "does not exist" has subjected trans people to disproportionate levels of violence. Trans historical projects, then, function within an ontology in which trans people are told that they do not exist.

The contemporary negation of trans and intersex existence means that trans and intersex historical projects are always caught up in contemporary ontological dilemmas. If, as Morland writes, genital surgeries both indicate the attempted erasure of intersex history, and also function as the marker of that history, then contemporary contests over intersex and trans embodiment are already embroiled in both history and ontology. A history of sexuality approach, which has in the past been primarily organized around the dangers and possibilities of constructing a gay (and sometimes lesbian) past, will be insufficient to address these very specific concerns. While trans and intersex historical projects are not totally distinct from the field of history of sexuality, they are also not entirely contiguous with it either. Trans history cannot fight the ontological battles of the present by itself, but the project of trans history is not divorced from this contemporary struggle. In this book, I have tried to address and attend to some of those specificities, both by rooting my analysis within the context of the study of eunuchs and androgynes in

15. Morland, "Afterword: Genitals are History," 209-15.
16. In chapter 2 I also engage Eva Hayward's work on trans ontology. See Hayward, "Don't Exist," 191-94.
17. The Mississippi law is completely silent about intersex people. The bill assumes that genetics and morphology align at birth, thus erasing the possibility of certain kinds of intersex variations. In that sense, the law presumes intersex nonexistence, thereby completing the erasures of nonconsensual surgeries.

late antiquity, and by making explicit the connection to the contemporary ontologies of sex and gender that govern trans and intersex existence.

In the next section I will turn to the ways contemporary trans and intersex activists, artists, and rabbis are reaching to late antiquity to (re)animate the past. Before I turned to these activist attempts, however, I invoked Hillman's memoir to remind us of the struggle to name (or claim) the past. Contemporary trans and intersex Jews who reach toward androgynes and eunuchs in rabbinic literature are naming their past. They do so within a contested landscape.

IMAGINING A "JUDEO-CHRISTIAN" BINARY GENDER

The claim that "Judeo-Christian" values support binary sex and gender is found throughout contemporary antitrans conservative thinking. Take, for example, the position statement of Focus on the Family, a Christian evangelical organization founded in 1977 by James Dobson. Their position statement on "transgenderism" was last updated in 2018. In addition to interpreting Genesis as establishing binary gender as central to God's plan, the authors state: "We disagree with revisionist gay and transgender theologies as contradictory to foundational Christian doctrine and the Judeo-Christian sexual ethic."[18] Thus, gay and transgender theologies are positioned as neither Christian nor compatible with Judeo-Christian sexual values. The phrase "Judeo-Christian," which, in this case, is invoked by Christian evangelicals, purports to create a kind of hybrid Jewish-Christian sexual ethics while actually choosing a particular strain of Christian interpretation and ascribing it to Judaism. Thus, the authors imagine a shared "sexual ethics" that excludes the possibility of gay and trans theology.

While Christian evangelicals have imagined a Jewish antitrans sexual ethics, Jewish communities have similarly struggled with halakhah and transition. Questions about gender variance and sexed change within Jewish law are not abstract; these concepts continue to be debated. A recent court case in England, for example, involved a custody dispute in an ultra-Orthodox Jewish family with five children. One of the parents came out as a trans woman and the couple obtained a divorce. The nontrans mother, who remained within the ultra-Orthodox community, argued that if the children continued to have contact with their transgender parent, the entire family would be socially shunned. The question was decided in the secular courts.

---

18. See "Transgenderism—Our Position," Focus on the Family, February 1, 2018, https://www.focusonthefamily.com/get-help/transgenderism-our-position/. As recently as 2017, former Vice President Mike Pence attended an anniversary event for Focus on the Family, to lay out the values shared between the Trump administration and Christian evangelicals. Questions of religious freedom continue to shape the political and legal debate over trans embodiment in the United States.

During the legal battle, both sides brought expert witnesses who testified to the status of trans people within Jewish law. The former head of the religious courts for the Federation of Synagogues, Dayan Yisroel Yaakov Lichtenstein, was quoted as saying, "I can state categorically that Jewish law does not recognise any change in sex of male to female or female to male under any circumstances."[19] The judge "regretfully" accepted the argument that the children would be harmed by contact with their transgender parent. To protect the children from stigma, he refused the transgender parent direct contact with her children. She is permitted to send letters four times a year to each child.[20] The secular court, therefore, was called on to adjudicate between competing opinions about the relationship between Judaism and sex change. In contemporary debates over the position of sex change within Jewish law, the widespread (and often unsubstantiated) claims that "Judeo-Christian" values preclude sex change seek to resolve these issues in advance.

Custody cases are one area where we can see contestation over Judaism and transgender embodiment, but it is not the only one. It is possible to find other statements by Orthodox authorities that mimic Lichtenstein's assertion that Judaism does not permit transsexuality. Joy Ladin, a tenured professor at the Orthodox institution Yeshiva University, famously wrote about having to fight for her job after coming out as trans.[21] Ladin describes the press coverage in the secular news media, which quoted colleagues (some of whom were not specialists in Jewish law per se) giving similar statements about the incompatibility of transition with Jewish law.

On the other hand, Orthodox authorities who have written directly about the status of transgender people in halakhah often leave subtle room for maneuvering. The most famous work on the status of trans people is Rabbi Idan Ben-Efrayim's book *Dor Tahapuchot*. In it, Ben-Efrayim asserts all the reasons that transsexuality is impermissible, citing the prohibition in Deuteronomy on cross-dressing, for example. At the same time, scholars who have studied Ben-Efrayim's work note that the net effect of his writing is often to soften the prohibitions against transition.[22] So, for example, he rules that the ban on castration only applies to the surgeon who

---

19. The expert witness also cites Rabbi Eliezer Waldenberg, a famous decisor who is particularly known for his work on medicine and Jewish law. There was another witness who argued that Orthodox Judaism recognizes nonbinary and transgender identities. See Rabbi Ariel Abel's testimony. J v. B and the Children, [2017] EWFC4, AG, IM (Fam.), accessed October 24, 2021, https://www.familylaw.co.uk/news_and_comment/j-v-b-and-the-children-ultra-orthodox-judaism-transgender-2017-ewfc-4.

20. This case is one example of the larger phenomenon of *haredi* custody cases. A recent panel at the Association for Jewish Studies conference spoke to the gendered politics of these types of cases. See Joffe et al., "Leave the Faith, Lose Your Kids."

21. Ladin, *Through the Door of Life*.

22. See Ben-Efrayim, *Dor Tahapuchot*; Irshai, "The Contemporary Discourse on Sex-Reassignment Surgery"; Gray, "The Transitioning of Jewish Biomedical Law," 81–107. Ronit Irshai, in addition to writing on Ben-Efrayim, has published articles on responsa (legal decisions) in a range of Jewish movements. See, for example, Irshai, "*Livror Amdat HaRav Waldenberg b'inyan Nituchim l'shinui Min*," 123–51.

performs it, not the person who undergoes it, leaving room for non-Jewish surgeons to provide gender-affirming surgeries. While seemingly small, these interventions have carved space for transition within contemporary Orthodox Judaism.

Jewish authors often draw on the examples of eunuchs and androgynes to offer rulings on a variety of halakhic questions that pertain to intersex and trans Jews. Rabbinic sources about androgynes and eunuchs have been cited in legal opinions (*responsa*) on issues as diverse as the adjudication of the medical ethics of intersex surgeries and the legal efficacy of sex change.[23] One of the sources that I analyze in this book, the debate over which kinds of sex with an androgyne count as "penetrating a man," has even been used as a prooftext to argue against the ordination of lesbian and gay rabbis.[24] (I disagree with that scholar's interpretation of the source in chapter 3 of this book.)

The idea of "Jewish law" as a unified entity is a fiction, and rulings often draw on centuries of different layers of debate, codes, and responsa, alongside medical and scientific knowledge, among other sources. Still, even as "Jewish law" is not synonymous with rabbinic literature, it is my hope that the analysis in this book undermines simple and straightforward narratives about halakhah and sex change. While the rabbinic sources are not radical from a contemporary trans and queer perspective, they incorporate eunuchs and androgynes into halakhic discussion, and they do so at length. In most cases, this extensive engagement with eunuchs and androgynes cannot be explained by any formal relationship with the Hebrew Bible. The rabbis chose to situate nonbinary people at the heart of rabbinic discussions of sex and gender. At the same time, when they discuss eunuchs and androgynes, the rabbis embed the mutability of sex within those conversations. Sexed mutability is inscribed from the very earliest layers of the sources. These rabbinic sources should complicate any easy appeal to a (singular) position of halakhah on sex changes.

At the very least, rabbinic sources make laughable any appeal to a "Judeo-Christian" consensus on transsexuality. The Christian evangelical citation of Genesis as a prooftext for binary gender disregards the rest of the Hebrew Bible and the

---

23. For an example of a paper that addresses intersex surgeries and medical ethics, see Cohen, "Tumtum and Androgynous," 62–85. On the Conservative movement's recent responsa on several legal questions concerning trans people, including transition, see Sharzer, "Transgender Jews and Halakhah."

24. For the use of the androgyne in the question of gay ordination in the Conservative movement, and the permissibility of gay male sex generally, see the minority opinion by Joel Roth, "Homosexuality Revisited." In it, Roth reads the sugya on the androgyne and the Levitical prohibition of sex between men to define all sex between men as prohibited, not just anal sex. I disagree with his reading of a key word in the sugya—namely, *zakhrut*. Roth thinks the phrase refers to the penis, while I believe that in this case it refers to the anus. While he is correct that the word means penis in other places, in this case, the sugya is remarkable precisely because the meaning of the word shifts in relation to the body of the androgyne, as I argue in chapter 3.

various categories of sex and gender that circulate biblically. But it also completely ignores any development in Judaism after the advent of Christianity. Given the rich and complex late antique discussions of eunuchs and androgynes in rabbinic literature that are roughly contemporaneous with the Christian Bible, ignoring all postbiblical Jewish texts is nonsensical. Of course, Focus on the Family and its ilk are not trying to construct careful scholarly and philological genealogies of sexed changes within Judaism (or Christianity, for that matter). Still, this book arises out of a context in which Jewish ideas about sex and gender are both imagined and enlisted in the service of Christian evangelical aims. These deeply theological statements purport to represent Jewish opposition to trans theology as self-evident. In turn, this betrays a deeply supercessionist understanding of Judaism while simultaneously staking a claim for Christianity's ability to speak authoritatively for Jewish ethics and values. On occasion, contemporary Jewish thinkers similarly assume a Jewish antagonism to trans theology in the absence of any specific arguments or interpretations of texts. These ungrounded statements can be understood as colluding with a Christian evangelical agenda.

Similarly, within Jewish communities there is a persistent message that trans and intersex bodies are a question to be adjudicated, even when some halakhic decisions rule in favor of trans or intersex "inclusion." It should not surprise us, then, that trans and intersex Jewish activists have increasingly turned to biblical and rabbinic sources to interpret the tradition directly. As such, Jewish activists, rabbis, and artists have responded in turn, drawing on androgynes and eunuchs to provide proof of existence. In the face of the current drive to argue that trans and intersex people generally, and trans and intersex Jews specifically, should not exist, activists turn to the past to write themselves into history.

I began this book by relaying my first encounter with androgynes and eunuchs in the Talmud in a queer and trans Jewish setting. I want to end the book by turning to these contemporary trans, intersex, and queer engagements with androgynes and eunuchs. Each year sees the publication of new zines, rituals, poetry, and sermons. A comprehensive summation and analysis of all the contemporary receptions of androgynes and eunuchs (and all the current innovations of trans and intersex Judaism) is beyond the scope of what I can accomplish here. Instead, I want to offer a series of sketches that outline trans and intersex engagements with androgynes and eunuchs. Many of these activists and artists reading through a trans and intersex lens imagine Jewish transcestors.

DESIRING TRANSCESTORS

Micah Bazant produced their groundbreaking zine, *Timtum*, in the late 1990s. *Timtum* is the Yiddish word that evolves out of the rabbinic category of the tumtum, the figure in rabbinic literature who is often portrayed as not-yet-sexed but having a sex that may be revealed.[25] Bazant begins the zine with a formal definition of *timtum* borrowed from *The Joys of Yiddish* and retyped carefully.[26] In the postrabbinic period, the word *timtum* has accrued some negative connotations, and it is now connected to words with meanings like "simple" or "stupid." Bazant reclaims the term by adding their own definition, handwritten with a sharpie: "A sexy, smart, creative, productive, Jewish genderqueer."[27] Bazant's redefinition is also a deliberate translation equating timtum with genderqueer in order to create a language for genderqueer Judaism. The very first page of the zine, therefore, establishes Bazant's connection with the figure of the timtum and identifies their shared characteristics as sexy, smart, and creative genderqueers. It also plays with the way Bazant borrows from Jewish pasts and at the same time redefines them.

In addition to naming the zine *Timtum,* Bazant works to produce a narrative of Jewish trans history throughout its pages. The zine invokes historical Jewish nonbinary figures, most notably Claude Cahun, a French Jewish photographer and resistance fighter in World War II. Bazant weaves together history with dream sequences, a family history of the Holocaust, and personal narratives of their attempts to find a synagogue in Portland, Oregon. The juxtaposition of historical figures with Bazant's experiences of exclusion in different synagogue settings suggests that it is not only external antisemitism, but also transphobia within the Jewish community that suppresses a Jewish trans past. In response to that transphobia, Bazant works to grant Jewish trans people their proper inheritance by writing trans Jews back into Jewish history and, in the process, creating the conditions for a trans Judaism to emerge.

Bazant is not the only artist to connect with the figure of the tumtum.[28] Gil Yefman, a mixed media artist who has worked at the intersection of trans/Judaism,

25. I did not invent the term "trancestors." Activists, authors, and scholars have been using the term; there is a hashtag on Twitter and on Instagram; and it was the title of a museum exhibition about gender in the Jewish tradition in Montreal. In other words, the term is in wide circulation, although I have not identified a specific origin of it.

26. Rosten, *The Joys of Yiddish*.

27. Bazant, *Timtum: A Trans Jewish Zine*. Bazant believes that the zine was released in 1999, although they are not precisely sure. The zine refers, in two separate sections, to Bazant as being both twenty-six and twenty-seven years old. In the zine, Bazant counters the characterization of the timtum as stupid with their own adjective of "smart." Bazant would be more critical of the ableist formulations of gender deviance today.

28. I am focusing on Micah Bazant and Gil Yefman as two artists who have addressed androgynes and eunuchs specifically, but there are numerous important trans and intersex Jewish artists working today: Tobaron Waxman, and Nicki Green have worked on creating trans Jewish art and ritual objects, while the band Schmeckel used the phrase "100% trans Jewcore" to describe their music. Some more recent artists have taken inspiration from earlier artwork. So, for example, Rena Yehuda Newman's zine *House of Jacob/People Israel: A Trans Jewish Zine* explicitly lists Micah Bazant as an influence.

FIGURE 4. *Timtum*, cover art of the zine *Timtum*, Micah Bazant, 1999.

created a sculpture titled *Tumtum*. The sculpture resembles a suspended, colorful, large, knitted ball, with a surface comprised of three-dimensional body parts and orifices. These orifices ooze and drip large knit droplets of bodily fluids. In the center of the suspended sculpture is a place where the artist can stand, mostly concealed by this external knitted skin, with only feet and lower legs visible. In his description of the sculpture, Yefman quotes the medieval rabbi Rambam's discussion of the tumtum and androgyne in relation to the laws of impurity and skin ailments. Yefman notes that the Rambam plays with the meaning of tumtum, since the word *tumtum* sounds like *tum'ah*—the Hebrew word for impurity. By quoting Rambam's (invented) etymology, Yefman plays with the kinds of social exclusions that are tied to skin ailments in the Hebrew Bible, and the stigma that attaches to contemporary gender variant bodies. In Jewish law, impurity is often conveyed by the leaking body. Yefman's knitted leaking body alludes to the ways law has attempted (unsuccessfully) to domesticate the sex/gender indeterminate body, which continues to exceed orderly boundaries. At the same time, the artist is recreating their external skin by knitting from within the sculpture. For Yefman, the very attempt at violent social exclusion is what creates the potential of the tumtum to effect social transformation.[29] The figure of the tumtum is literally knitted around Jewish trans and intersex bodies, but also offers a way to describe the propensity for stigma to become a source of resistance.

Intersex and trans rabbis have also engaged eunuchs and androgynes. Seven years after Micah Bazant released the zine *Timtum*, Elliot Kukla wrote his thesis "A Created Being of Its Own" in fulfillment of the requirements for his ordination as a Reform rabbi. The title of the thesis is a reference to the androgyne lists found in early rabbinic literature, which pose the question of how the androgyne is like a man, woman, both and neither. The final attributed line of the list states that the androgyne is a unique creation, and that the sages could not decide about them whether he is a man or she is a woman. "A Created Being of Its Own" is therefore both a citation from early rabbinic literature and an allusion to the unique status of the androgyne, who does not fit neatly into a binary.

Kukla was the first openly trans person to be ordained by the Reform movement; his thesis was therefore groundbreaking in several ways.[30] Kukla begins his thesis by describing his encounter with the figure of the tumtum in a yeshiva (a traditional site of Jewish learning.) When he reads about the tumtum in the sources, he asks the teacher to define the tumtum, and the teacher responds that it

---

29. Gil Yefman, "Tumtum."

30. Elliot Kukla is certainly not the only trans rabbi. While Reuben Zellman became the first openly trans and intersex person to be accepted into the Reform seminary, Elliot Kukla came out as trans in rabbinical school and was the first to graduate. Rabbi Emily Aviva Kapor-Mater was privately ordained earlier than either Zellman or Kukla. Abby Stein received ordination from an Orthodox yeshiva in 2011 and, since coming out as trans, has worked to create support groups for trans Orthodox Jews. See Stein, *Becoming Eve*. Numerous rabbis speak publicly about being intersex; these include not only Reuben Zellman but also Rabbi Bobbie Rosenberg, for example. Recently there have been increasing numbers of trans and intersex rabbinic ordinations. As a result, there are now trans and intersex rabbis representing a variety of different denominations of Judaism, including nondenominational movements. There are also several rabbinical students moving through the ordination pipeline currently. This is a US-focused list, and it is therefore very incomplete. There are more trans rabbis (and trans rabbinical students) each year, along with more trans Jewish zines, blessings, poems, and art.

FIGURE 5. Timtum-Yefman, Gil Yefman, TUMTUM, 2012, knitting, Faraday cage, sound, additional performance, 200 × 200 × 200 cm. Installation view at Petah Tikva Museum of Art. Photo: Elad Sarig.

is a mythical beast "kind of like a unicorn."[31] For Kukla, who identifies with the tumtum, this explanation is unsatisfactory. He writes:

> The tumtum and the androgynos are a resource not just for *destabilizing* modern dichotomous sexes, but also for *stabilizing* wholly new and surprising constructions of sexual identity. I believe that gender multiplicity in the texts of Jewish antiquity do

31. Kukla, "A Created Being of Its Own," 1.

not just offer the reader *more* options for finding a home within a gender. These texts indicate an opening towards *infinite* locations for belonging that are still authentically connected to our histories and communities.³²

Here Kukla argues that the tumtum and androginos can serve to undermine both our contemporary naturalized gender binary and also our drive to disambiguate bodies into a sexed binary (through cosmetic surgery, among other tactics). What this offers Kukla is not just a way of identifying with the tumtum, but also a language out of which to construct new identities. Kukla's writing suggests that this reappropriation is deliberate, creative, and engenders a sense of the distance between the tumtum and modern trans and intersex identities, even as it attempts to collapse that distance. For Kukla, the tumtum constitutes a kind of textual home within Judaism.

Trans and intersex Jews are innovating not just by drawing on rabbinic sources; they are redefining ritual and producing art that challenges the role of gender in Judaism. S. J. Crasnow, in their article on contemporary trans Jewish ritual innovation, describes a series of trans interventions in immersion (*mikvah*) rituals.³³ The space of the ritual bath is usually segregated by sex, and it therefore seems unpromising, on the face of it, as a site for trans ritual innovation. And yet, in Crasnow's review of the rituals and blessings written by rabbi Emily Aviva Kapor-Mater, there is an investment in transforming the space of the mikvah. Kapor-Mater describes trans people as partners in (re)creation with God in her blessings surrounding immersion, and she places ritual immersion at the heart of ritualizing

---

32. Elliot Kukla, "A Created Being of Its Own," 58. It is possible to challenge the language of "authentic" connections, but for my purposes here it is not required. Kukla's thesis is older, and he would not be invested in the notion of an "authentic" tradition today. The language is an implicit response to the ways in which the tumtum is mythologized or dematerialized and the desire to substantiate a trans Judaism within canonical sources.

33. Crasnow, "On Transition: Normative Judaism and Trans Innovation," 403–15. In addition to trans and intersex rabbis and artists, there are also numerous activists within the trans Jewish community who have been making inroads into Jewish institutions and rituals: Levi Ethan Alter is both a rabbi and the president of FTM International, and he is also known for his work on intersex issues. Joy Ladin's written work addresses the trans/Jewish intersection in both poetry and theology. See Ladin, *The Soul of the Stranger*. Noach Dzurma edited an award-winning anthology about trans Judaism, and S. Bear Bergman and J. Wallace Skelton have both written on the trans Jewish experience. See Dzurma, ed., *Balancing on the Mechitza*; Bergman, *Blood, Marriage, Wine, and Glitter*. Svara, a radical yeshiva dedicated to queer and trans learning, has also trained trans Jews to read traditional texts, and has trans-identified teachers (including Laynie Solomon). Congregation Beit Simchat Torah convened a group of trans Jews in 2019 in a conference led by Seth Marnin, Jillian Weiss, and Rafi Daugherty. In other words, we are in the midst of a flourishing of trans Judaism. This list is focused on the Jewish community in North America, as that is the community with which I am most familiar, but there are numerous international trans Jewish movements. Ido Katri, who works at the intersection of trans law in Israel/Palestine, and Surat Shaan Knan, an activist who works on international human rights and also writes about trans Judaism in England, are some examples of international figures in this movement.

transition in Judaism. Artist Nicki Green has also played with creating trans ritual objects around immersion, and artist Tobaron Waxman has a series of photos in which he immerses himself. These types of innovations, which draw on both rituals and objects that are traditionally restricted by gender, can be understood as a simultaneous critique of the ways in which Jewish spaces have been constituted as transphobic spaces, and the possibilities for their transformation.[34]

I have written this book out of the conviction that reading the rabbis with trans and intersex theory can open up new vistas on the sources. At the same time as I write within a world that debates trans existence, I also write within and toward a world where trans and intersex Judaism is currently flourishing. The work of trans and intersex rabbis, activists, and artists grounds me. I want these activists to have their *yerushah*—their inheritance. And when their inheritance falls short, I write with hope for the transformation that these poets, artists, and activists will bring.

---

34. Waxman, "Levush Project," 400–402; Green and Crasnow, "Artifacts from the Future," 403–8.

BIBLIOGRAPHY

Abel, Elizabeth. "Bathroom Doors and Drinking Fountains: Jim Crow's Racial Symbolic." *Critical Inquiry* 25, no. 3 (Spring 1999): 435–81.

Abusch, Ra'anan. "Eunuchs and Gender Transformation: Philo's Exegesis of the Joseph Narrative." In *Eunuchs in Antiquity and Beyond,* edited by Shaun Tougher, 103–22. Swansea: Classical Press of Wales, 2002.

Ackerman, Susan. "The Blind, the Lame, and the Barren Shall Not Come into the House." In *Disability Studies and Biblical Literature*, edited by Candida Moss and Jeremy Schipper, 29–47. New York: Palgrave Macmillan, 2011.

———. "'I Have Hired You with my Son's Mandrakes': Women's Reproductive Magic in Ancient Israel." In *Sex in Antiquity: Exploring Gender and Sexuality in the Ancient World*, edited by Mark Masterson, Nancy Sorkin Rabinowitz, and James Robson, 15–30. New York: Routledge, 2014.

Adler, Rachel. *Engendering Judaism: An Inclusive Theology and Ethics.* New York: Jewish Publication Society, 1998.

Ahbabi, Mahin. "A Comparative Study of *Zahhak's* Dual Character in Mythology, History, and Archeological Findings in Iran and Tajikistan." *Anthropology and Archeology of Eurasia* 55, nos. 3–4 (2016): 301–15.

Ahmed, Sara. *Queer Phenomenology: Orientations, Objects, Others.* Durham, NC: Duke University Press, 2006.

Aitken, James. "Why is the Giraffe Kosher? Exoticism in Dietary Laws of the Second Temple Period." *Biblische Notizen* 164, no. 1 (2015): 21–34.

Aizura, Aren Z. *Mobile Subjects: Transnational Imaginaries of Gender Reassignment.* Durham, NC: Duke University Press, 2018.

Ajootian Aileen. "The Only Happy Couple: Hermaphrodites and Gender." In *Naked Truths: Women, Sexuality, and Gender in Classical Art and Archaeology,* edited by Ann Olga Koloski-Ostrow, 220–42. New York: Routledge, 1997.

Albeck, Hanoch. Mechqarim b'baraita v'Tosefta v'Yachasan l'Talmud. Jerusalem: HaRav Kook Press, 1969.

Alliance Defending Freedom. "Alliance Defending Freedom Statement of Faith." Accessed September 9, 2021. https://www.adflegal.org/about-us/careers/statement-of-faith.

Alon, Gedaliah. *The Jews in Their Land in the Talmudic Age, 70- 640 CE*. Edited and translated by Gershon Levi. Cambridge, MA: Harvard University Press, 1989.

American Civil Liberties Union. "Past Anti-LGBT Religious Exemption Legislation Across the Country." Accessed September 9, 2021. https://www.aclu.org/other/past-anti-lgbt-religious-exemption-legislation-across-country?redirect=anti-lgbt-religious-refusals-legislation-across-country.

Amin, Kadji. "Temporality." *Trans Studies Quarterly* 1, nos. 1–2 (2014): 219–22.

Anderson, William S. *Ovid's Metamorphoses: Books 1–5*. Norman: University of Oklahoma Press, 1997.

Asad, Talal. *Formations of the Secular: Christianity, Islam, Modernity*. Stanford, CA: Stanford University Press, 2003.

Åshede, Linnea. "*Neutrumque et Utrumque Videntur*: Reappraising the Gender Role(s) of Hermaphroditus in Ancient Art." In *Exploring Gender Diversity in the Ancient World*, edited by Allison Surtees and Jennifer Dyer, 81–95. Edinburgh: Edinburgh University Press, 2020.

Asher-Greve, Julia M. "The Essential Body: Mesopotamian Conceptions of the Gendered Body." *Gender and History* 9, no. 3 (1997): 432–61.

Asikainen, Susanna. "'Eunuchs for the Kingdom of Heaven': Matthew and Subordinated Masculinities." In *Biblical Masculinities Foregrounded*, edited by Ovidiu Creangă and Peter-Ben Smit, 156–88. Sheffield: Sheffield Phoenix Press, 2014.

Assante, Julia. "Men Looking at Men: The Homoerotics of Power in the State Arts of Assyria." In *Being a Man: Negotiating Ancient Constructs*, edited by Ilona Zsolnay, 42–83. New York: Routledge, 2017.

Avalos, Hector. *Illness and Health Care in the Ancient Near East: The Role of the Temple in Greece, Mesopotamia, and Israel*. Atlanta: Scholars Press, 1995.

Baden, Joel S. "The Nature of Barrenness in the Hebrew Bible." In *Disability Studies and Biblical Literature*, edited by Candida Moss and Jeremy Schipper, 13–27. New York: Palgrave Macmillan, 2011.

Baker, Cynthia M. *Rebuilding the House of Israel: Architectures of Gender in Jewish Antiquity*. Stanford, CA: Stanford University Press, 2002.

Balberg, Mira. *Purity, Body, and Self in Early Rabbinic Literature*. Berkeley: University of California Press, 2014.

———. "Rabbinic Authority, Medical Rhetoric, and Body Hermeneutics in Mishnah Nega'im." *AJS Review* 35, no. 2 (2011): 323–46.

Balberg, Mira, and Haim Weiss. "'That Old Man Shames Us': Aging, Liminality, and Antimony in Rabbinic Literature." *Jewish Studies Quarterly* 25 (2018): 17–41.

Barber v. Bryant. 193 F. Supp. 3d 677 (S.D. Miss. 2016), reversed, 860 F.3d 345 (5th Cir. 2017).

Bardel, Ruth. "Eununchizing Agamemnon: Clytemnestra, Agamemnon and *Maschalismos*." In *Eunuchs in Antiquity and Beyond*, edited by Shaun Tougher, 51–71. Swansea: Classical Press of Wales, 2002.

Baril, Alexandre. "'Doctor, Am I an Anglophone Trapped in a Francophone Body?': An Intersectional Analysis on 'Trans-crip-t Time' in Ableist, Cisnormative, Anglonormative Societies." *Journal of Literary and Cultural Disability Studies* 10, no. 2 (2016): 155–72.

Bar-Ilan, Meir. "The Attitude Toward *Mamzerim* in Jewish Society in Late Antiquity." *Jewish History* 14, no. 2 (2000): 125–70.

Barker, Joanne. Introduction to *Critically Sovereign: Indigenous Gender, Sexuality, and Feminist Studies*, 1–44. Edited by Joanne Barker. Durham, NC: Duke University Press, 2017.

Baskin, Judith R. *Midrashic Women: Formations of the Feminine in Rabbinic Literature*. Hanover, NH: Brandeis University Press, 2002.

Bazant, Micah. *Timtum: A Trans Jewish Zine*. Portland, OR: Self-published, 1999.

Beardsley, Christina, and Michelle O'Brien, eds. *This is My Body: Hearing the Theology of Transgender Christians*. London: Darton, Longman, and Todd, 2016.

Beauchamp, Toby. *Going Stealth: Transgender Politics and U.S. Surveillance Practices*. Durham, NC: Duke University Press, 2019.

Beier, Claudia. "Fighting Animals: An Analysis of the Intersections between Human Self and Animal Otherness on Attic Vases." In *Interactions Between Animals and Humans in Graeco-Roman Antiquity*, edited by Thorsten Fögen and Edmund Thomas, 275–305. Berlin: De Gruyter, 2017.

Belkin, Samuel. "Levirate and Agnate Marriage in Rabbinic and Cognate Literature." *JQR* 60, no. 4 (1970): 275–329.

Bellwether, Mira. *Fucking Trans Women: A Zine about the Sex Lives of Trans Women*. No. 0. Self-published, 2010.

Belser, Julia Watts. "Brides and Blemishes: Queering Women's Disability in Rabbinic Marriage Law." *Journal of the American Academy of Religion* 84, no. 2 (June 2016): 401–29

———. "Disability, Animality, and Enslavement in Rabbinic Narratives of Bodily Restoration and Resurrection." *Journal of Late Antiquity* 8, no. 2 (Fall 2015): 288–305.

———. "Queering the Dissident Body: Race, Sex, and Disability in Rabbinic Blessings on Bodily Difference." In *Unsettling Science and Religion: Contributions and Questions from Queer Studies*, edited by Lisa Stenmark and Whitney Bauman, 161–81. Lanham, MD: Lexington Books, 2018.

———. *Rabbinic Tales of Destruction: Gender, Sex, and Disability in the Ruins of Jerusalem*. Oxford: Oxford University Press, 2017.

Benaim, Rachel. "Harvard Conference Examines Jewish Law and Trans Identity." Tablet. April 4, 2017. https://www.tabletmag.com/scroll/228890/harvard-conference-examines-jewish-law-and-trans-identity.

Ben-Efrayim, Idan. *Dor Tahapuchot*. Jerusalem: self-published, 2004.

Bennett, Jane. *Vibrant Matter: A Political Ecology of Things*. Durham, NC: Duke University Press, 2010.

Bergman, S. Bear. *Blood, Marriage, Wine, and Glitter*. Vancouver: Arsenal Pulp Press, 2013.

Berkowitz, Beth A. *Animals and Animality in the Babylonian Talmud*. Cambridge: Cambridge University Press, 2018.

———. *Execution and Invention: Death Penalty Discourse in Early Rabbinic and Christian Cultures*. Oxford: Oxford University Press, 2006.

———. "What is the Place of Philology and Source Criticism in Talmudic Studies? Yesterday, Today, and Tomorrow." Panel presentation (response) at the Association for Jewish Studies Annual Conference, Boston, MA, December 17, 2018.

Bernabé, Carmen. "Of Eunuchs and Predators: Matthew 19:12 in a Cultural Context." *Biblical Theology Bulletin* 33, no. 4 (2003): 128–34.

Berthold, Dana. "Tidy Whiteness: A Genealogy of Race, Purity, and Hygiene." *Ethics and the Environment* 15, no. 1 (2010): 1–26.

Bettcher, Talia Mae. "Evil Deceivers and Make-Believers: On Transphobic Violence and the Politics of Illusion." *Hypatia* 22, no. 3 (2007): 43–65.

———. "'When Tables Speak': On the Existence of Trans Philosophy." *Daily Nous*. May 30, 2018. http://dailynous.com/2018/05/30/tables-speak-existence-trans-philosophy-guest-talia-mae-bettcher/.

Bey, Marquis. "The Trans*ness of Blackness, the Blackness of Trans*ness." *Transgender Studies Quarterly* 4, no. 2 (2017): 275–95.

Biale, Rachel. *Women and Jewish Law: The Essential Texts, Their History, and Their Relevance for Today*. New York: Schocken, 1984.

Bickart, Noah Benjamin. "'Overturning the Table': The Hidden Meaning of a Talmudic Metaphor for Coitus." *Journal of the History of Sexuality* 25, no. 3 (2016): 489–507.

Boellstorff, Tom. "Dubbing Culture: Indonesian Gay and Lesbi Subjectivities and Ethnography in an Already Globalized World." *American Ethnologist* 30, no. 2 (2003): 225–42.

———. *The Gay Archipelago: Sexuality and Nation in Indonesia*. Princeton, NJ: Princeton University Press, 2006.

Bolle, Helena M., and Stephen R. Llewelyn. "Intersectionality, Gender Liminality, and Ben Sira's Attitude to the Eunuch." *Vetus Testamentum* 67, no. 4 (2017): 546–69.

Boswell, John. *Christianity, Social Tolerance, and Homosexuality: Gay People in Western Europe from the Beginning of the Christian Era to the Fourteenth Century*. Chicago: University of Chicago Press, 1980.

Boustan, Ra'anan. "Negotiating Difference: Genital Mutilation in Roman Slave Law and the History of the Bar Kokhba Revolt." In *The Bar Kokhba War Reconsidered*, edited by Peter Schäefer, 77–78. Tübingen: Mohr Siebeck, 2003.

Boyarin, Daniel. "Against Rabbinic Sexuality: Textual Reasoning and the Jewish Theology of Sex." In *Queer Theology: Rethinking the Western Body*, edited by Gerard Loughlin, 131–47. Malden, MA: Blackwell Publishing, 2007.

———. "Are There Any Jews in 'The History of Sexuality.'" *Journal of the History of Sexuality* 5, no. 3 (Jan. 1995): 333–55.

———. *Borderlines: The Partition of Judaeo-Christianity*. Philadelphia: University of Pennsylvania Press, 2011.

———. *Carnal Israel: Reading Sex in Talmudic Culture*. Berkeley: University of California Press, 1993.

———. "Gender." In *Critical Terms for Religious Studies*, edited by Mark Taylor, 117–36. Chicago: University of Chicago Press, 1998.

———. "The Great Fat Massacre: Sex, Death, and the Grotesque Body in the Talmud." In *People of the Body: Jews and Judaism from an Embodied Perspective*, edited by Howard Eilberg-Schwartz, 69–99. Albany: State University of New York Press, 1992.

———. *A Radical Jew: Paul and the Politics of Identity.* Berkeley: University of California Press, 1994.

———. *Socrates and the Fat Rabbis.* Chicago: University of Chicago Press, 2009.

———. *Unheroic Conduct: The Rise of Heterosexuality and the Invention of the Jewish Man.* Berkeley: University of California Press, 1997.

Boylan, Jennifer Finney. *She's Not There: A Life in Two Genders.* New York: Broadway Books, 2003.

Bradford, Micky. "The Trans Tipping Point or Loretta Lynch is Like Our Auntie." *SONG* (blog). May 11, 2016. http://southernersonnewground.org/2016/05/the-trans-tripping-point-or-loretta-lynch-is-like-our-auntie.

Brintnall, Kent. "North Carolina's HB2 and the Shifting Battle over LGBT Rights." *Religion and Politics.* May 9, 2016. https://religionandpolitics.org/2016/05/09/north-carolina-hb2-religion-shift-battle-lgbt-rights.

Brisson, Luc. *Sexual Ambivalence: Androgyny and Hermaphroditism in Graeco-Roman Antiquity.* Translated by Janet Lloyd. Berkeley: University of California Press, 2002.

Brodsky, David. "Sex in the Talmud: How to Understand Leviticus 18 and 20: *Parashat Kedoshim* (Leviticus 19:1–20:27)." In *Torah Queeries: Weekly Commentaries on the Hebrew Bible*, edited by Gregg Drinkwater, Joshua Lesser, and David Shneer, 157–70. New York: New York University Press, 2009.

Brody, Robert. "Irano-Talmudica: The New Parallelomania?" *Jewish Quarterly Review* 106, no. 2 (2016): 209–32.

Brooks, Ernest W. "Arabic Lists of the Byzantine Themes." *Journal of Hellenistic Studies* 21 (1901): 67–77.

Brooten, Bernadette J. "Jewish Women's History in the Roman Period: A Task for Christian Theology." *Harvard Theological Review* 79, nos. 1–3 (1986): 22–30.

———. *Love Between Women: Early Christian Responses to Female Homoeroticism.* Chicago: University of Chicago Press, 1996.

———. *Women Leaders in the Ancient Synagogue: Inscriptional Evidence and Background Issues.* Providence: Brown Judaic Studies, 1982.

Brower, Gary Robert. "Ambivalent Bodies: Making Christian Eunuchs." PhD diss., Duke University, 1996. ProQuest (AAT 9625625).

Budin, Stephanie Lynn. "Fertility and Gender in the Ancient Near East." In *Sex in Antiquity: Exploring Gender and Sexuality in the Ancient World*, edited by Mark Masterson, Nancy Sorkin Rabinowitz, and James Robson, 30–50. New York: Routledge, 2014.

Bullough, Vern L. "Eunuchs in History and Society." In *Eunuchs in Antiquity and Beyond*, edited by Shaun Tougher, 1–17. London: Classical Press of Wales, 2002.

Burke, Sean D. "Queering Early Christian Discourse: The Ethiopian Eunuch." In *Bible Trouble: Queer Readings at the Boundaries of Biblical Scholarship*, edited by Teresa Hornsby and Ken Stone, 175–91. Atlanta: Society of Biblical Literature, 2011.

Butler, Judith. "Afterword." In *Bodily Citations: Religion and Judith Butler*, edited by Ellen Armour and Susan St.Ville, 276–93. New York: Columbia University Press, 2006.

———. *Bodies that Matter: On the Discursive Limits of "Sex."* New York: Routledge, 1993.

———. "Doing Justice to Someone: Sex Reassignment and Allegories of Transsexuality." *GLQ: A Journal of Lesbian and Gay Studies* 7, no. 4 (2001): 621–36.

———. *Gender Trouble: Feminism and the Subversion of Identity*. New York: Routledge, 1990.

Butler, Shane. "Notes on a Membrum Disiectum." In *Women and Slaves in Greco-Roman Culture: Differential Equations*, edited by Sandra Joshel and Sheila Murnaghan, 236–55. London: Routledge, 1998.

Bychowski, M. W., Howard Chiang, Jack Halberstam, Jacob Lau, Kathleen P. Long, Marcia Ochoa, C. Riley Snorton, Leah DeVun, and Zeb Tortorici. "Trans*Historicities: A Roundtable Discussion." *Transgender Studies Quarterly* 5, no. 4 (2018): 658–85.

Cadden, Joan. *The Meaning of Sex Difference in the Middle Ages: Medicine, Science, and Culture*. Cambridge: Cambridge University Press, 1993.

Cahana, Jonathan. "Gnostically Queer: Gender Trouble in Gnosticism." *Biblical Theology Bulletin* 41, no. 1 (2011): 24–35.

Callisen, Sterling A. "The Iconography of the Cock on the Column." *Art Bulletin* 21, no. 2 (1939): 160–78.

Campanile, Domitilla, Filippo Carlà-Uhink, and Margherita Facella, eds. *TransAntiquity: Cross- Dressing and Transgender Dynamics in the Ancient World*. New York: Routledge, 2017.

Caner, Daniel. "The Practice and Prohibition of Self-Castration in Early Christianity." *Vigiliae Christianae* 51, no. 4 (November 1997): 396–415.

Cárdenas, Micha. "Pregnancy: Reproductive Futures in Trans of Color Feminism." *Transgender Studies Quarterly* 3, nos. 1–2 (2016): 48–57.

Carmichael, Calum M. "Forbidden Mixtures in Deuteronomy 22:9–11 and Leviticus 19." *Vetus Testamentum* 45, no. 4 (1995): 433–48.

Carter, Julian B. "Sex Time Machine for Touching the Transcestors." *Transgender Studies Quarterly* 5, no. 4 (2018): 691–706.

Cavanagh, Sheila L. "Gender, Sexuality, and Race in the Lacanian Mirror: Urinary Segregation and the Bodily Ego." In *Psychoanalytic Geographies*, edited by Paul Kingsbury and Steve Pile, 323–39. New York: Routledge, 2014.

Chase, Cheryl. "Hermaphrodites With Attitude: Mapping the Emergence of Intersex Political Activism." In *The Transgender Studies Reader*, edited by Susan Stryker and Stephen Whittle, 316–30. New York: Routledge, 2013.

———. "Letters from Readers." *Sciences* (July/August 1993): 3.

Chase, Cheryl/Bo Laurent. "Hermaphrodites with Attitude: Mapping the Emergence of Intersex Political Activism." *GLQ: A Journal of Lesbian and Gay Studies* 4, no. 2 (1998): 189–211.

Chen, Mel Y. *Animacies: Biopolitics, Racial Mattering, and Queer Affect*. Durham, NC: Duke University Press, 2012.

Chew, Kathryn. "Virgins and Eunuchs: Pulcheria, Politics, and the Death of Emperor Theodosius II." *Historia* 55, no. 2 (2006): 207–27.

Chiang, Howard. *After Eunuchs: Science, Medicine, and the Transformation of Sex in Modern China*. New York: Columbia University Press, 2018.

Chosky, Jamsheed K. "Zoroastrianism." In *Encyclopedia of Religion*, edited by Lindsay Jones, 9988–10005. Detroit: Macmillan Reference, 2005.

Cioffi, Robert L. "A Trugeranos for Seleukos? An Animal Name and the Power of the Exotic in Philemon, Neaira, Fr. 49 K-A." *Rheinisches Museum für Philologie* 158, no. 2 (2015): 209–13.

Clare, Eli. *Brilliant Imperfection: Grappling with Cure*. Durham, NC: Duke University Press, 2017.
Cohen, Alfred. "Tumtum and Androgynous." *Journal of Halacha and Contemporary Society* 38 (Fall 1999): 62–85.
Cohen, Shaye. "The Place of the Rabbi in Jewish Society of the Second Century." In *The Galilee in Late Antiquity*, edited by Lee Levine, 157–73. New York: Jewish Theological Seminary, 1992.
———. "Sabbath Law and Mishnah Shabbat in Origen De Principiis." *Jewish Studies Quarterly* 17 (2010): 160–89.
———. *Why Aren't Jewish Women Circumcised? Gender and Covenant in Judaism*. Berkeley: University of California Press, 2005.
Cohn, Naftali S. *The Memory of the Temple and the Making of the Rabbis*. Philadelphia: University of Pennsylvania Press, 2012.
Cohn, Naftali S, Pratima Gopalakrishnan, Andrew W. Higginbotham, Max Strassfeld, and John Robert Mandsager. "The Boundaries of Text, Gender, and Space in Mishnah Bikurim." Panel presentation at the Association for Jewish Studies Annual Conference, Boston, MA, December 13, 2015.
Coloru, Omar. "Ancient Persia and Silent Disability." In *Disability in Antiquity*, edited by Christian Laes, 61–74. New York: Routledge, 2016.
Cook, Johann. "On the Role of External Traditions in the Septuagint." In *Septuagint and Reception: Essays Prepared for the Association for the Study of the Septuagint in South Africa*, edited by Johann Cook, 17–37. Boston: Brill, 2009.
Coogan, Michael David, ed. *The New Oxford Annotated Bible: New Revised Standard Version*. 3rd ed. Oxford: Oxford University Press, 2001.
Cooper, Kate. "Gender and the Fall of Rome." In *A Companion to Late Antiquity*, edited by Phillip Rousseau and Jutta Raithel, 187–200. Oxford: Wiley Blackwell, 2007.
Cornelius, Sakkie. "'Eunuchs'? The Ancient Background of *Eunouchos* in the Septuagint." In *Septuagint and Reception: Essays Prepared for the Association for the Study of the Septuagint in South Africa*, edited by Johann Cook, 321–35. Leiden: Brill, 2009.
Cornwall, Susannah. *Sex and Uncertainty in the Body of Christ: Intersex Conditions and Christian Theology*. New York: Routledge, 2014.
Couey, J. Blake. "Isaiah, Jeremiah, Ezekiel, Daniel, and the Twelve." In *The Bible and Disability: A Commentary*, edited by Sarah Melcher, Mikeal Parsons, and Amos Yong, 215–73. Waco, TX: Baylor University Press, 2017.
Couzin, Robert. "Uncircumcision in Early Christian Art." *Journal of Early Christian Studies* 26, no. 4 (2018): 601–29.
Crasnow, S. J. "On Transition: Normative Judaism and Trans Innovation." *Journal of Contemporary Religion* 32, no. 3 (2017): 403–15.
Csapo, Eric. "The Cultural Poetics of the Greek Cockfight." *Australian Archaeological Institute at Athens* 4 (2006): 20–37.
———. "Deep Ambivalence: Notes on a Greek Cockfight (Part I)." *Phoenix* 47, no. 1 (1993): 1–28.
Currah, Paisley, Richard M. Juang, and Shannon Price Minter, eds. *Transgender Rights*. Minneapolis: University of Minnesota Press, 2006.

Dalley, Stephanie. "Evolution of Gender in Mesopotamian Mythology and Iconography with a Possible Explanation of Ša Rēšēn, 'the Man with Two Heads.'" In *Sex and Gender in the Ancient Near East: Proceedings of the 47th Recontre Assyriologique Internationale Helsinki July 2–6, 2001 part I*, edited by Simo Parpola and R. M. Whiting, 117–22. Helsinki: University of Helsinki, 2002.

Dasen, Véronique. "Multiple Births in Graeco-Roman Antiquity." *Oxford Journal of Archaeology* 16, no. 1 (1997): 49–63.

David, Lennard J. *Enforcing Normalcy: Disability, Deafness, and the Body*. London: Verso Books, 1995.

Davis, Stephen J. "Crossed Texts, Crossed Sex: Intertextuality and Gender in Early Christian Legends of Holy Women Disguised as Men." *Journal of Early Christian Studies* 10, no. 1 (2002): 1–36.

DeFranza, Megan K. *Sex Difference in Christian Theology: Male, Female, and Intersex in the Image of God*. Grand Rapids, MI: Eerdmans, 2015.

De Hoop, Raymond. "The Interpretation of Isaiah 56:1–9: Comfort or Criticism?" *Journal of Biblical Literature* 127, no. 4 (2008): 671–95.

Delacourt, Marie. *Hermaphrodite: Myths and Rites of the Bisexual Figure in Classical Antiquity*. Translated by Jennifer Nicholson. London: Studio Books, 1961.

Deller, Karlheinz. "The Assyrian Eunuchs and their Predecessors." In *Priests and Officials in the Ancient Near East: Papers of the Second Colloquium on the Ancient Near East*, edited by Kazuko Watanabe, 303–11. Heidelberg: Universitätsverlag C. Winter, 1999.

DeVun, Leah. "The Jesus Hermaphrodite: Science and Sex Difference in Premodern Europe." *Journal of the History of Ideas* 69, no. 2 (April 2008): 193–218.

———. *The Shape of Sex: Nonbinary Gender from Genesis to the Renaissance*. New York: Columbia University Press, 2021.

DeVun, Leah, and Zeb Tortorici, eds. "Trans*historicities." *Transgender Studies Quarterly* 5, no. 4 (2018): 515–719.

DePauw, Mark. "Notes on Transgressing Gender Boundaries in Ancient Egypt." *Zeitschrift für Ägyptische Sprache* 130, no. 1 (2003): 49–59.

Diamond, Eliezer. *Holy Men and Hunger Artists: Fasting and Asceticism in Rabbinic Culture*. Oxford: Oxford University Press, 2004.

Diamond, Milton. "Sexual Identity, Monozygotic Twins Reared in Discordant Sex Roles and a BBC Follow-up." *Archives of Sexual Behavior* 11, no 2. (1982): 181–85.

Dietrich, Ernst Ludwig. "Der Urmesnsch als Androgyn." *Zeitschrift für Kirchengeschichte* 58 (1939): 297–345.

Dinshaw, Carolyn. *Getting Medieval: Sexualities and Communities, Pre- and Postmodern*. Durham, NC: Duke University Press, 1999.

Dinshaw, Carolyn, Lee Edelman, Roderick A. Ferguson, Carla Freccero, Elizabeth Freeman, J. Halberstam, Annamarie Jagose, Christopher S. Nealon, and Tan Hoang Nguyen. "Theorizing Queer Temporalities: A Roundtable Discussion." *GLQ: A Journal of Lesbian and Gay Studies* 13, nos. 2–3 (2007): 177–95

Dohrmann, Natalie B. "Reading as Rhetoric in Halakhic Texts." In *Of Scribes and Sages*, vol. 2, *Early Jewish Interpretation and Transmission of Scripture*, edited by Craig Evans, 90–115. London: T & T Clark, 2004.

Dolgopolski, Sergey. *The Open Past: Subjectivity and Remembering in the Talmud*. New York: Fordham University Press, 2013.
Doniger, Wendy. "Bisexuality in the Mythology of Ancient India." *Diogenes* 52, no. 4 (2005): 50–60.
———. *Women, Androgynes, and Other Mythical Beasts*. Chicago: University of Chicago Press, 1980.
Dor, Menachem. "Ma'aley-Hageyrah b'Mikra uv'Mishnah: T'o, R'aym (Dishon), Shor haBar, M'ri, Coy." *Beit Mikra: Journal for the Study of the Bible and Its World* 37, no. 2 (1992): 122–30.
Dorman, Johanna Helena Wilhelmina. "The Blemished Body: Deformity and Disability in the Qumran Scrolls." PhD diss., University of Groningen, 2007.
Douglas, Mary. *Purity and Danger: An Analysis of Concepts of Pollution and Taboo*. New York: Routledge, 2002. First published 1966 by Routledge and Kegan Paul (London).
Dover, Kenneth James. *Greek Homosexuality*. Cambridge, MA: Harvard University Press, 1989.
Downing, Lisa, Iain Morland, and Nikki Sullivan, eds. *Fuckology: Critical Essays on John Money's Diagnostic Concepts*. Chicago: University of Chicago Press, 2015.
Dreger, Alice Domurat. *Hermaphrodites and the Medical Invention of Sex*. Cambridge, MA: Harvard University Press, 1998.
Dundes, Alan. "Projective Inversion in the Ancient Egyptian "Tale of Two Brothers." *Journal of American Folklore* 115, no. 457/458 (2002): 378–94.
Dzurma, Noach. *Balancing on the Mechitza: Transgender in Jewish Community*. Berkeley, CA: North Atlantic Books, 2010.
Elman, Yaakov. "'He in His Cloak and She in Her Cloak': Conflicting Images of Sexuality in Sasanian Mesopotamia." In *Discussing Cultural Influences: Text, Context, and Non-Text in Rabbinic Judaism*, edited by Rivka Ulmer, 129–65. Lanham, MD: University Press of America, 2007.
———. "Order, Sequence, and Selection: The Mishnah's Anthological Choices." In *The Anthology in Jewish Literature*, edited by David Stern, 53–81. Oxford: Oxford University Press, 2004.
Epstein, Louis M. *Marriage Laws in the Bible and the Talmud*. Cambridge, MA: Harvard University Press, 1942.
Epstein, Yakov N. *Mavo L'Nusach HaMishnah-Chelek Shayni*. Jersualem, Magnes: 1964.
———. *M'vo'ot l'Sifrut haTanaim: Mishnah, Tosefta, u'midrashei halachah*. Jerusalem: Magnes, 1957.
Eugenides, Jeffrey. *Middlesex*. London: Picador Books, 2002.
Everhart, Janet S. "The Hidden Eunuchs of the Hebrew Bible: Uncovering an Alternate Gender." PhD diss., University of Denver Colorado Seminary, 2003 (AAT 3095069).
Faderman, Lillian. "A Usable Past." In *The Lesbian Premodern*, edited by Noreen Giffney, Michelle Sauer, and Diane Watt, 171–78. New York: Palgrave Macmillan, 2011.
Fausto-Sterling, Anne. "The Five Sexes: When Male and Female Are Not Enough." *Sciences* (March/April 1993): 20–24.
———. "How Many Sexes Are There?" *New York Times*, March 12, 1993, A29.
———. *Sexing the Body: Gender Politics and the Construction of Sexuality*. New York: Basic Books, 2000.

Fear, A. T. "Cybele and Christ." In *Cybelle, Attis, and Related Cults: Essays in memory of M. J. Vermaseren*, edited by Eugene N. Lang, 37–51. Leiden: Brill, 1996.

Feder, Ellen K. "Imperatives of Normality: From Intersex to DSD." *GLQ: A Journal of Lesbian and Gay Studies* 15, no. 2 (2009): 225–47.

Feldblum, Chai R. "Rectifying the Tilt: Equality Lessons from Religion, Disability, Sexual Orientation, and Transgender." *Maine Law Review* 54 (2002): 159–95.

Fishbane, Simcha. *Deviancy in Early Rabbinic Literature: A Collection of Socio-Anthropological Essays*. Leiden: Brill, 2007.

———. "The Ritual of Kapparot." *Jewish Journal of Sociology* 50, nos. 1 and 2 (2008): 67–75.

Flemming, Rebecca. *Medicine and the Making of Roman Women: Gender, Nature, and Authority from Celsus to Galen*. Oxford: Oxford University Press, 2000.

Focus on the Family Issue Analysts. "Transgenderism—Our Position." Focus on the Family. February 1, 2018. http://www.focusonthefamily.com/socialissues/sexuality/transgenderism/transgenderism-our-position.

Fonrobert, Charlotte Elisheva. "Gender Duality and Its Subversions in Rabbinic Law." In *Gender in Judaism and Islam: Common Lives, Uncommon Heritage*, edited by Firoozeh Kashani-Sabet and Beth Wenger, 106–25. New York: New York University Press, 2014.

———. "Gender Identity in Halakhic Discourses." *Jewish Women: A Comprehensive Historical Encyclopedia*. December 31, 1999. https://jwa.org/encyclopedia/article/gender-identity-in-halakhic-discourse.

———. "The Handmaid, The Trickster, and the Birth of the Messiah: A Critical Appraisal of the Feminist Valorization of Midrash Aggadah." In *Current Trends in the Study of Midrash*, edited by Carol Bakhos, 245–77. Leiden: Brill, 2006.

———. "'Humanity was Created as an Individual': Synechdochal Individuality in the Mishnah as a Jewish Response to Romanization." In *The Individual in the Religions of the Ancient Mediterranean*, edited by Jörg Rüpke, 489–523. Oxford: Oxford University Press, 2013..

———. *Menstrual Purity: Rabbinic and Christian Reconstructions of Biblical Gender*. Stanford, CA: Stanford University Press, 2000.

———. "On Carnal Israel and its Consequences: Talmudic Studies since Foucault." *Jewish Quarterly Review* 95, no. 3 (2005): 462–69.

———. "Regulating the Human Body: Rabbinic legal discourse and the making of Jewish gender." In *The Cambridge Companion to the Talmud and Rabbinic Literature*, edited by Charlotte Elisheva Fonrobert and Martin Jaffee, 270–94. Cambridge: Cambridge University Press, 2007.

———. "The Semiotics of the Sexed Body in Early Halakhic Discourse." In *Closed and Open: Readings of Rabbinic Texts*, edited by M. A. Kraus, 69–96. Piscataway, NJ: Gorgias Press, 2006.

Forsyth, Ilene H. "The Theme of Cockfighting in Burgundian Romanesque Sculpture." *Speculum* 53, no. 2 (1978): 252–82.

Foucault, Michel. *Herculine Barbin (Being the Recently Discovered Memoirs of a Nineteenth Century French Hermaphrodite)*. Translated by Richard McDougall. New York: Vintage Books, 1980.

———.The *History of Sexuality*. Vol. 1, *An Introduction*. Translated by Robert Hurley. New York: Vantage Books, 1990. First published 1978 by Pantheon (New York).

Fox, Nili Sacher. *In the Service of the King: Officialdom in Ancient Israel and Judah.* Cincinnati: Hebrew Union College Press, 2000.
Foxhall, Lin, and John Salmon, eds. *When Men were Men: Masculinity, Power, and Identity in Classical Antiquity.* New York: Routledge, 1998.
Fraade, Steven D. "Introduction to the Symposium: What is (the) Mishnah?" *AJS Review* 32, no. 2 (Nov. 2008): 221–23.
Frankel, Zechariah. *Darchei HaMishnah: Chelek Rishon.* Leipzig: Sumptibus Henrici Hunger, 1859.
Fredriksen, Paula. "*Secundum Carnem*: History and Israel in the Theology of St. Augustine." In *The Limits of Ancient Christianity: Essays on Late Antique Thought and Culture in Honor of R. A. Markus*, edited by William Klingshirn and Mark Vessey, 26–41. Ann Arbor: University of Michigan Press, 1999.
Freeman, Elizabeth. *Time Binds: Queer Temporalities, Queer Histories.* Durham, NC: Duke University Press, 2010.
Friedman, Shamma. "Pereq ha'Ishah Rabah b'Bavli, b'Tzeyruf Mavo Clali al Derekh Cheqer haSugya." In *Mechqarim u'M'qorot: Ma'asaf l'Madei haYahadut*, vol. 1, edited by H. Z. Dimitrovsky, 275–441. New York: Jewish Theological Seminary Press, 1977.
Gabbay, Uri. "The Akkadian Word for 'Third Gender': The *kalû* (gala) Once Again." *Studies in Ancient Oriental Civilization* 62 (2008): 49–56.
Gafni, Isaiah. "Rabbinic Historiography and Representations of the Past." In *The Cambridge Companion to the Talmud and Rabbinic Literature*, edited by Charlotte Elisheva Fonrobert and Martin Jaffee, 295–313. Cambridge: Cambridge University Press, 2007.
Gardner, Jane F. "Sexing a Roman: Imperfect Men in Roman Law." In *When Men Were Men: Masculinity, Power, and Identity in Classical Antiquity*, edited by Lin Foxhall and John Salmon, 136–52. New York: Routledge, 1998.
Garland-Thomson, Rosemarie. *Extraordinary Bodies: Figuring Physical Disability in American Culture and Literature.* New York: Columbia University Press, 1996.
Geertz, Clifford. "Common Sense as a Cultural System." *Antioch Review* 33, no. 1 (1975): 5–26.
———. "Deep Play: Notes on the Balinese Cockfight." *Daedalus* 101, no. 1 (1972): 1–37.
Geiger, Yosef. "Hag'zeirah al hamilah u'mered Bar Kochba." *Zion* 41, no. 2 (1976): 139–47.
Geller, Markham J. "Akkadian Healing Therapies in the Babylonian Talmud, Preprint 259." Berlin: Max Planck Institute for the History of Science, 2004.
Ghorayshi, Azeen. "A Landmark Lawsuit About an Intersex Baby's Genital Surgery Just Settled for $440,000." BuzzFeed. July 27, 2017. https://www.buzzfeednews.com/article/azeenghorayshi/intersex-surgery-lawsuit-settles.
Gibbon, Edward. *The History of the Decline and Fall of the Roman Empire.* 8 vols. Philadelphia: William Birch and Abraham Small, 1804.
Gill-Peterson, Jules. *Histories of the Transgender Child.* Minneapolis: University of Minnesota Press, 2017.
Ginzburg, Carlo. *Wooden Eyes: Nine Reflections on Distance.* Translated by Martin Ryle and Kate Soper. New York: Columbia University Press, 2001.
Gleason, Maud W. *Making Men: Sophists and Self-Presentation in Ancient Rome.* Princeton, NJ: Princeton University Press, 1995.
Goldberg, Sylvie-Anne. "Is Time a Gendered Affair? Category and Concept: 'Women' and 'Mitzvah.'" In *Tov 'Elem: Memory, Community, and Gender in Medieval and Early*

Modern Jewish Societies—Essays in Honor of Robert Bonfil, edited by Elisheva Baumgarten Ammon Raz-Krakotzkin and Roni Weinstein, 15–29. Jerusalem: Bialik Institute/Hebrew University, 2011.

Goodman, Martin. "The Function of *Minim* in Early Rabbinic Judaism." In *Judaism in the Roman World: Collected Essays*, 163–73. Ancient Judaism and Early Christianity 66. Leiden: Brill, 2007.

Gordon, Demoya, and Ryan Rasdall. "Stalled Progress: Combatting Bathroom Bullies' Attacks on Transgender People." Presentation at the Philadelphia Trans Health Conference, Philadelphia, PA, June 9, 2016.

Gossett, Che, and Juliana Huxtable. "Existing in the World: Blackness at the Edge of Trans Visibility." In *Trap Door: Trans Cultural Production and the Politics of Visibility*, edited by Reina Gossett, Eric Stanley, and Johanna Burton, 39–55. Cambridge, MA: MIT Press, 2017.

Gossett, Reina, Eric A. Stanley, and Johanna Burton. *Trap Door: Trans Cultural Production and the Politics of* Visibility. Cambridge, MA: MIT Press, 2017.

Graumann, Lutz Alexander. "Monstrous Births and Retrospective Diagnosis: The Case of Hermaphrodites in Antiqutiy." In *Disabilities in Roman Antiquity*, edited by Chrisian Laes, Chris Goodey, and M. Lynn Rose, 181–211. Leiden: Brill, 2013.

Greatrex, Geoffrey, and Jonathan Bardill. "Antiochus the "Praepositus": A Persian Eunuch at the Court of Theodosius II." *Dunbarton Oaks Papers* 50 (1996): 171–97.

Green, Erica, Katie Benner, and Robert Pear. "'Transgender' Could Be Defined Out of Existence Under Trump Administration." *New York Times*, October 21, 2018. https://nyti.ms/2R9W1jB.

Green, Jamison. *Becoming a Visible Man*. Nashville: Vanderbilt University Press, 2004.

Green, Nicki, and S. J. Crasnow. "Artifacts from the Future: The Queer Power of Trans Ritual Objects." *Trans Studies Quarterly* 6, no. 3 (2019): 403–8.

Greenberg, Julie A. *Why Sex Matters: Intersexuality and the Law*. New York: New York University Press, 2012.

Gray, Hillel. "Not Judging by Appearances: The Role of Genotype in Jewish Law on Intersex Conditions." *Shofar* 30, no. 4 (Summer 2012): 126–48.

———. "The Transitioning of Jewish Biomedical Law: Rhetorical and Practical Shifts in Halakhic Discourse on Sex-Change Surgery." *Nashim* 29 (Fall 2015): 81–107.

Gribetz, Sarit Kattan, David M. Grossberg, Martha Himmelfarb, and Peter Schäefer, eds. *Genesis Rabbah in Text and Context*. Tübingen: Mohr Siebeck, 2016.

Groves, Robert. "From Statue to Story: Ovid's Metamorphosis of Hermaphroditus." *Classical World* 109, no. 3 (2016): 321–56.

Guyot, Peter. *Eunuchen als Sklaven und Freigelassene in der griechisch-römischen Antike*. Stuttgart: Ernst Klett, 1980.

Hacohen, Aviad. "'Kol Ish Asher Bo Mum lo Yikarev?' Ma'amadam shel anashim im mugbalut b'olamah she torat yisrael." In *V'chai Achechah Imchah*, edited by Moshe Rachimi, 51–77. Rehovot: Orot College Press, 2011.

Halberstam, J. *In a Queer Time and Place: Transgender Bodies, Subcultural Lives*. New York: New York University Press, 2005.

———. *The Queer Art of Failure*. Durham: Duke University Press, 2011.

———. *Trans*: A quick and Quirky Account of Gender Variability*. Berkeley: University of California Press, 2018.

———. "Transgender Butch: Butch/FTM Border Wars and the Masculine Continuum." *GLQ: A Journal of Lesbian and Gay Studies* 4, no. 2 (1998): 287–310.

Halberstam, J., and C. Jacob Hale. "Butch/FTM Border Wars: A Note on Collaboration." *GLQ: A Journal of Lesbian and Gay Studies* 4, no. 2 (1998): 283–85.

Halbertal, Moshe. *The Birth of Doubt: Confronting Uncertainty in Early Rabbinic Literature*. Providence: Brown Judaic Studies, 2020.

Hales, Shelley. "Looking for Eunuchs: The *Galli* and Attis in Roman Art." In *Eunuchs in Antiquity and Beyond*, edited by Shaun Tougher, 87–103. London: Classical Press of Wales and Duckworth, 2002.

Hall, Radclyffe. *The Well of Loneliness*. New York: Random House, 2016. First published 1928 by Jonathan Cape (London).

Hallett, Judith. "Female Homoeroticism and the Denial of Roman Reality in Latin Literature." *Yale Journal of Criticism* 3, no. 1 (1989): 209–27.

Hallett, Judith, and Marilyn Skinner, eds. *Roman Sexualities*. Princeton, NJ: Princeton University Press, 1997.

Halperin, David M. *How to Do the History of Homosexuality*. Chicago: University of Chicago Press, 2002.

Halsall, Guy. "Gender and the End of Empire." *Journal of Medieval and Early Modern Studies* 34, no. 1 (2004): 17–39.

Handelman, Susan A. *The Slayers of Moses: The Emergence of Rabbinic Interpretation in Modern Literary Theory*. Albany: State University of New York Press, 1983.

Hannabach, Cathy. "Imagine Otherwise." Ideas on Fire. Podcast. Accessed September 13, 2021. https://ideasonfire.net/imagine-otherwise-podcast/.

Hanson, Richard P. C. "A Note on Origen's Self-Mutilation." *Vigiliae Christianae* 20 (1966) 81–82.

Hartke, Austen. *Transforming: The Bible and the Lives of Transgender Christians*. Louisville: Westminster John Knox Press, 2018.

Hasan-Rokem, Galit. "Erotic Eden: A Rabbinic Nostalgia for Paradise." In *Paradise in Antiquity: Jewish and Christian Views*, edited by Guy Stroumsa and Markus Brockmuehl, 156–66. Cambridge: Cambridge University Press, 2010.

———. *Tales of the Neighborhood: Jewish Narrative Dialogues in Late Antiquity*. Berkeley: University of California Press, 2003.

Hasan-Rokem, Galit, and Israel Jacob Yuval. "Myth, History, and Eschatology in a Rabbinic Treatise on Birth." In *Talmudic Transgressions: Engaging the Work of Daniel Boyarin*, edited by Charlotte Elisheva Elisheva Fonrobert, Ishay Rosen-Zvi, Aharon Shemesh, Moulie Vidas, and James Adam Redfield, 243–73. Leiden: Brill, 2017.

Haselhoff, Günther. "Salin's Style I." *Medieval Archaeology* 18 (1974): 3.

Hauptman, Judith. "Feminist Perspectives on Rabbinic Texts." In *Feminist Perspectives on Jewish Studies*, edited by Lynn Davidman and Shelly Tenenbaum, 40–61. New Haven, CT: Yale University Press, 1996.

———. *Rereading the Mishnah*. Tübingen: Mohr Siebeck, 2005.

———. *Reading the Rabbis: A Woman's Voice*. Boulder, CO: Westview Press, 1998.

Hawkins, John D. "Eunuchs Among the Hittites." In *Sex and Gender in the Ancient Near East: Proceedings of the 47th Recontre Assyriologique Internationale Helsinki, July 2–6, 2001*, vol. 1, edited by Simo Parpola and R. M. Whiting, 217–33. Helsinki: University of Helsinki, 2002.

Hayes, Christine E. *Gentile Impurities and Jewish Identities: Intermarriage and Conversion from the Bible to the Talmud*. Oxford: Oxford University Press, 2002.

———. "Intermarriage and Impurity in Ancient Jewish Sources." *Harvard Theological Review* 92, no. 1 (1999): 3–36.

———. "Law in Classical Rabbinic Judaism." In *The Cambridge Companion to Judaism and Law*, edited by Christine Hayes, 76–128. Cambridge: Cambridge University Press, 2017.

Hayward, Eva. "Don't Exist." *Transgender Studies Quarterly* 4, no. 2 (2017): 191–94.

———. "More Lessons from a Starfish: Prefixial Flesh and Transspeciated Selves." *Women's Studies Quarterly* 36, no.3/4 (2008): 64–85.

———. "Transxenoestrogenesis." *Transgender Studies Quarterly* 1, nos. 1–2 (2014): 255–58.

Hayward, Eva, and Jami Weinstein. "Introduction: Tranimalities in the Age of Trans* Life." *Transgender Studies Quarterly* 2, no. 2 (2015): 195–208.

Hester, J. David. "Eunuchs and the Postgender Jesus: Matthew 19.12 and Transgressive Sexualities." *Journal for the Study of the New Testament* 28, no. 1 (2005): 13–40.

———. "Queers on Account of the Kingdom of Heaven: Rhetorical Constructions of the Eunuch Body." *Scriptura: International Journal of Bible, Religion, and Theology in Southern Africa* 90 (2005): 809–23.

Hezser, Catherine. "Passover and Social Equality: Women, Slaves, and Minors in *Bavli Pesachim*." In *A Feminist Commentary on the Babylonian Talmud*, edited by Tal Ilan, 91–107. Tübingen: Mohr Siebeck, 2007.

———. "Roman Law and Rabbinic Legal Composition." In *The Cambridge Companion to the Talmud and Rabbinic Literature*, edited by Charlotte Elisheva Fonrobert and Martin Jaffee, 144–63. Cambridge: Cambridge University Press, 2007.

Hidary, Richard. *Rabbis and Classical Rhetoric: Sophistic Education and Oratory in the Talmud and Midrash*. Cambridge: Cambridge University Press, 2018.

Hillman, Thea. *Intersex (for lack of a better word)*. San Francisco: Manic D Press, 2008.

Hippocrates. *Regimen I*. In *Hippocrates*, vol. 4, translated by W. H. S. Jones, 223–96. Loeb Classical Library 150. Cambridge, MA: Harvard University Press, 1931.

Hoffman, Lawrence A. *Covenant of Blood: Circumcision and Gender in Rabbinic Judaism*. Chicago: University of Chicago Press, 1996.

Hollenback, George M. "Who is Doing What to Whom Revisited: Another Look at Leviticus 18:22 and 20:13." *Journal of Biblical Literature* 136, no. 3 (2017): 529–37.

Holmes, Morgan. *Intersex: A Perilous Difference*. Selinsgrove, PA: Susquehanna University Press, 2008.

———. "Re-membering a Queer Body." *Undercurrents* 6 (May 1994): 11–13.

Hopkins, Keith. "Eunuchs in Politics in the Later Roman Empire." *Cambridge Classical Journal* 9 (1963): 62–80.

———. "The Political Power of Eunuchs." In *Conquerors and Slaves: Sociological Studies in Roman History*, vol. 1, 172–97. London: Cambridge University Press, 1978.

Horstmanshoff, Manfred. "Who is the True Eunuch? Medical and Religious Ideas About Eunuchs and Castration in the Works of Clement of Alexandria." In *From Athens to Jerusalem: Medicine in Hellenized Jewish Lore and in Early Christian Literature; Papers of the Symposium in Jerusalem, 9–11 September 1996*, edited by Samuel Kottek and Manfred Horstmanshoff, 101–18. Rotterdam: Erasmus Publishing, 2000.

Hsu, Stephanie. "Ethnicity and the Biopolitics of Intersex in Jeffrey Eugenides's *Middlesex*." *Melus* 36, no. 3 (2011): 87–110.

Hunt, Ailsa. "Elegiac Grafting in Pomona's Orchard: Ovid, Metamorphosis 14. 623–771." *Materiali e discussioni per l'analisi dei testi classici* 65 (2010): 43–58.

Hunter, Lourdes Ashley. "Every Breath a Black Trans Woman Takes is an Act of Revolution." *HuffPost*. February 6, 2015. https://www.huffpost.com/entry/every-breath-a-black-tran_b_6631124.

Ilan, Tal. *Jewish Women in Greco-Roman Palestine: An Inquiry into Image and Status*. Tübingen: Mohr Siebeck, 1995.

Ilan, Tal, Tamara Or, and Dorothea M. Salzer, Christiane Steuer, and Irina Wandrey, eds. *A Feminist Commentary on the Babylonian Talmud: Introduction and Studies*. Tübingen: Mohr Siebeck, 2007.

Intersex Society of North America. "Why is ISNA Using DSD?" Accessed September 13, 2021. http://www.isna.org/node/1066.

Irshai, Ronit. "The Contemporary Discourse on Sex-Reassignment Surgery in Orthodox Jewish Religious Law, as Reflected in *Dor Tahapuchot* (*A Generation of Perversions*)." Paper presented at the Symposium on Transgender/Religion, Harvard Law School, Cambridge, MA, May 29–30, 2017.

———. "Livror Amdat HaRav Valdenberg b'inyan Nituchim l'shinui Min: Iyun b'fsika ha'orthodoksit v'ha'konservativit b'ikvut Tshuvatav." *Shnaton HaMishpat HaIvri* 29 (2011–13): 123–51.

Israeli, Anat. "Jewish Women and Positive Time-Bound Commandments: Reconsidering Rabbinic Texts." *Women in Judaism* 12, no. 1 (2015): 1–27.

Jackson, Bernard S. "Liability for Animals in Roman Law: An Historical Sketch." *Cambridge Law Journal* 37, no. 1 (1978): 122–44.

Jaffee, Martin S. *Torah in the Mouth: Writing and Oral Tradition in Palestinian Judaism 200 BCE–400 CE*. New York: Oxford University Press, 2001.

Jastrow, Marcus. *A Dictionary of the Targumim, the Talmud Bavli and Yerushalmi, and the Midrashic Literature*. London: G. P. Putnam's Sons, 1903.

Jennison, George. *Animals for Show and Pleasure in Ancient Rome*. Philadelphia: University of Pennsylvania Press, 2005.

Jewish Publication Society. *Hebrew-English Tanakh: The Traditional Hebrew Text and the New JPS Translation*. 2nd ed. Philadelphia: Jewish Publication Society, 1999.

Joffe, Lisa Fishbayn, Jessica Lang, Miriam Moster, and Chavie Weisberger. "Leave the Faith, Lose Your Kids: A Multidisciplinary Exploration of Custody Disputes Among Formerly Orthodox Parents." Panel presentation at the at the Association for Jewish Studies Annual Conference, San Diego, CA, December 15–17, 2019.

Johns, Catherine. *Sex or Symbol? Erotic Images of Greece and Rome*. New York: Routledge, 1982.

Johnston, Patricia A., Attilio Mastrocinque, and Sophia Papaioannou, eds. *Animals in Greek and Roman Religion and Myth*. Cambridge: Cambridge Scholars Publishing, 2016.
Josephus. *Jewish Antiquities*. Vol. 2. Translated by H. St. J. Thackeray and Ralph Marcus. Loeb Classical Library 490. Cambridge, MA: Harvard University Press, 1930.
Junior, Nyasha, and Jeremy Schipper. "Mosaic Disability and Identity in Exodus 4:10, 6:12, 30." *Biblical Interpretation* 16, no. 5 (2008): 428–41.
J v. B and the Children (Ultra-Orthodox Judaism: Transgender). January 30, 2017. https://www.judiciary.uk/judgments/j-v-b-and-the-children-ultra-orthodox-judaism-transgender/.
Kadish, Gerald E. "Eunuchs in Ancient Egypt." In *Studies in Honor of John A. Wilson*, edited by E. B. Hauser, 55–67. Chicago: University of Chicago Press, 1969.
Kafer, Alison. *Feminist, Queer, Crip*. Bloomington: Indiana University Press, 2013.
Kağnici, Gökhan. "Insights from Sumerian Mythology: The Myth of Enki and Ninmaḫ and the History of Disability." *Tarih Incelemeleri Dergisi* 33, no. 2 (2018): 429–50.
Kalidos, Raju. "Ardhanari in Early South Indian Cult and Art." *Proceedings of the Indian History Congress* 52 (1991): 1037–43.
Kalla, Gábor. "Date Palms, Deer/Gazelle, and Birds in Ancient Mesopotamian and Early Byzantine Syria: A Christian Iconographic Scheme and Its Sources in the Ancient Orient." In *Across the Mediterranean—Along the Nile*, vol. 2, edited by Tamás A. Bács, Ádám Bollók, and Tivadar Vida, 863–901. Budapest: Archaeolingua, 2018.
Karkazis, Katrina. *Fixing Sex: Intersex, Medical Authority, and Lived Experience*. Durham, NC: Duke University Press, 2008.
Kattan Gribetz, Sarit. *Time and Difference in Rabbinic Judaism*. Princeton, NJ: Princeton University Press, 2020.
———. "Time, Gender, and Ritual in Rabbinic Sources." In *Religious Studies and Rabbinics: A Conversation*, edited by Elizabeth Shanks Alexander and Beth Berkowitz, 139–57. New York: Routledge, 2018.
———. "Women's Bodies as Metaphors for Time in Biblical, Second Temple, and Rabbinic Literature." In *The Construction of Time in Antiquity: Ritual, Art, and Identity*, edited by Jonathan Ben-Dov and Lutz Doering, 173–204. Cambridge: Cambridge University Press, 2017.
Kattan Gribetz, Sarit, and Lynn Kaye. "The Temporal Turn in Ancient Judaism and Jewish Studies." *Currents in Biblical Research* 17, no. 3 (2019): 332–95.
Kaye, Lynn. *Time in the Babylonian Talmud: Natural and Imagined Times in Jewish Law and Narrative*. Cambridge: Cambridge University Press, 2018.
Keegan, Cáel M. "In Praise of the Bad Transgender Object: *Rocky Horror*." Flow: A Critical Forum on Media and Culture. November 28, 2019.. https://www.flowjournal.org/2019/11/in-praise-of-the-bad/. https://www.colorado.edu/gendersarchive1998-2013/2013/06/01/moving-bodies-sympathetic-migrations-transgender-narrativity.
———. "Moving Bodies: Sympathetic Migrations in Transgender Narrativity." *Genders* 57, June 1, 2013.
Kelley, Nicole. "Deformity and Disability in Greece and Rome." In *This Abled Body: Rethinking Disabilities in Biblical Studies*, edited by Hector Avalos, Sarah Melcher, and Jeremy Schipper, 31–47. Atlanta: Society of Biblical Literature, 2007.

Kelly, Peter. "Intersex and Intertext: Ovid's Hermaphroditus and the Early Universe." In *Exploring Gender Diversity in the Ancient World*, edited by Allison Surtees and Jennifer Dyer, 95–106. Edinburgh: Edinburgh University Press, 2020.

Kessler, Gwynn. "Bodies in Motion: Preliminary Notes on Queer Theory in Rabbinic Literature." In *Mapping Gender in Ancient Religious Discourses*, edited by Caroline Vander Stichele and Todd Penner, 389–430. Leiden: Brill, 2007.

———. *Conceiving Israel: The Fetus in Rabbinic Narratives*. Philadelphia: University of Pennsylvania Press, 2009.

———. "Rabbinic Gender: Beyond Male and Female." In *A Companion to Late Ancient Jews and Judaism: Third Century BCE to Seventh Century CE*, edited by Naomi Koltun-Fromm and Gwynn Kessler, 353–70. Hoboken, NJ: Wiley & Sons, 2020.

Kessler, Suzanne J. *Lessons from the Intersexed*. New Brunswick, NJ: Rutgers University Press, 1998.

Kiel, Yishai. "Negotiating 'White Rooster' Magic and Binitarian Christianity: Mapping the Contours of Jewish Babylonian Culture in Late Antiquity." *Journal of Ancient Judaism* 9 (2018): 259–79.

———. *Sexuality in the Babylonian Talmud: Christian and Sasanian Contexts in Late Antiquity*. Cambridge: Cambridge University Press, 2016.

King, Helen. *The One-Sex Body on Trial: The Classical and Early-Modern Evidence*. London: Routledge, 2016.

Klein, Samuel. *Neue Beiträge zur Geschichte und Geographie Galiläas*. Vienna: Menorah, 1923.

Kogan, Terry S. "Sex-Separation in Public Restrooms: Law, Architecture, and Gender." *Michigan Journal of Gender and Law* 14, no. 1 (2007–8): 1–58.

Kojima, Dai. "Trans-Pacific Imaginaries and Queer Intimacies in the Ruins of Middlesex." *Goose* 17, no. 1 (2018): 57–61.

Kolesnikov, A. "Eunuchs: ii. The Sasanian Period." In *Encyclopaedia Iranica*, edited by Ehsan Yarshater, 9:64–69. Leiden: Brill, 1998. https://iranicaonline.org/articles/eunuchs#ii.

Kosman, Admiel, and Anat Sharbat. ""Two Women Were Sporting with Each Other": A Reexamination of the Halakhic Approaches to Lesbianism as a Touchstone for Homosexuality in General." *Hebrew Union College Annual* 75 (2004): 37–73.

Koyama, Emi. "From 'Intersex' to 'DSD': Toward a Queer Disability Politics of Gender." Intersex Initiative. Accessed September 14, 2021. http://intersexinitiative.org/articles/intersextodsd.html.

———. "Intersex Critiques: Notes on Intersex, Disability, and Biomedical Ethics." Zine. Portland: Self-published, 2003.

Kraemer, David. "Images of Childhood and Adolescence in Talmudic Literature." In *The Jewish Family: Metaphor and Memory*, edited by David Kraemer, 65–80. Oxford: Oxford University Press, 1989.

———. *Reading the Rabbis: The Talmud as Literature*. Oxford: Oxford University Press, 1996.

Kraemer, Ross S. *Unreliable Witnesses: Religion, Gender, and History in the Greco-Roman Mediterranean*. Oxford: Oxford University Press, 2010.

Kuefler, Matthew. *The Manly Eunuch: Masculinity, Gender Ambiguity, and Christian Ideology in Late Antiquity*. Chicago: University of Chicago Press, 2001.

Kukla, Elliot R. "A Created Being of Its Own." Master's thesis, Hebrew Union College, 2006.

Kunzel, Regina G. *Criminal Intimacy: Prison and the Uneven History of Modern American Sexuality*. Chicago: University of Chicago Press, 2010.

Labovitz, Gail S. "The Language of the Bible and the Language of the Rabbis: A Linguistic Look at *Kiddushin*." *Conservative Judaism* 63, no. 1 (Fall 2011): 25–42.

———. "A Man Spinning on His Thigh: Gender, Positive Time-Bound Commandments, and Ritual Fringes in Mishnah *Mo'ed Katan* 3:4." *Nashim* 28 (2015): 75–87.

———. *Marriage and Metaphor: Constructions of Gender in Rabbinic Literature*. Lanham, MD: Lexington Books, 2009.

Ladin, Joy. *The Soul of the Stranger: Reading God and Torah from a Transgender Perspective*. HBI Series on Jewish Women. Waltham, MA: Brandeis University Press, 2019.

———. *Through the Door of Life: A Jewish Journey Between Genders*. Madison: University of Wisconsin Press, 2013.

LaFleur, Greta. *The Natural History of Sexuality in Early America*. Baltimore: Johns Hopkins University Press, 2018.

Lane, Jamie M. "Reproducing Intersex Trouble: An Analysis of the M. C. Case in the Media." Master's thesis, University of South Florida, 2018. ProQuest (AAT 10752074).

Langmuir, Gavin I. *Toward a Definition of Antisemitism*. Berkeley: University of California Press, 1990.

Laqueur, Thomas. *Making Sex: Body and Gender from the Greeks to Freud*. Cambridge, MA: Harvard University Press, 1990.

Lateiner, Donald. Review of *Eunuchs in Antiquity and Beyond*, edited by Shaun Tougher. *Bryn Mawr Classical Review*, October 12, 2003. https://bmcr.brynmawr.edu/2003/2003.10.12/.

Latham, Jacob. "'Fabulous Clap-Trap': Roman Masculinity, the Cult of Magna Mater, and Literary Constructions of the *Galli* at Rome from the Late Republic to Late Antiquity." *Journal of Religion* 92, no. 1 (2012): 84–122.

Lederberg, Nathaniel. "'HaIshah Niqnayt b'Shalosh D'rakhim': She'elat Arichatan v'Etzuvan shel haMishnayot b'Perek haRishon shel Masekhet Kidushin." *Netuim* 15 (2008): 25–41.

Lee, Peter A., Christopher P. Houk, S. Faisal Ahmed, and Ieuan A. Hughes. "Consensus Statement on the Management of Intersex Disorders." *Pediatrics* 118, no. 2 (August 2006): 488–500.

Lehman, Marjorie. "The Gendered Rhetoric of Sukkah Observance." *Jewish Quarterly Review* 96, no. 3 (2006): 309–35.

———. "Imagining the Priesthood in Tractate Yoma: Mishnah Yoma 2:1–2 and BT Yoma 23a." *Nashim* 28 (Spring 2015): 88–105.

Lehmhaus, Lennart. "Listenwissenschaft and the Encyclopedic Hermeneutics of Knowledge in Talmud and Midrash." In *In the Wake of the Compendia: Infrastructural Contexts and the Licensing of Empiricism in Ancient and Medieval Mesopotamia*, edited by J. Cale Johnson, 59–103. Berlin: De Gruyter, 2015.

Lehmhaus, Lennart, and Matteo Martelli. *Collecting Recipes: Byzantine and Jewish Pharmacology in Dialogue*. Berlin: De Gruyter, 2017.

Lemos, Tracy M. "'Like the Eunuch Who Does Not Beget': Gender, Mutilation, and Negotiated Status in the Ancient World." In *Disability Studies and Biblical Literature*, edited by Candida Moss and Jeremy Schipper, 47–67. New York: Palgrave Macmillan, 2011.

———. *Violence and Personhood in Ancient Israel and Comparative Contexts*. Oxford: Oxford University Press, 2017.
Lerner, Judith A., and Prods Oktor Skjaervø. "A Seal of a Eunuch in the Sasanian Court." *Journal of Inner Asian Art and Archaeology* 1 (2006): 113–19.
Lev, Sarra. "Defying the Binary? The Androgynous in Tosefta *Bikkurim*." Paper presented at the Association for Jewish Studies Annual Conference, Washington, DC, December 18–20, 2011.
———. "Genital Trouble: On the Innovations of Tannaitic Thought Regarding Damaged Genitals and Eunuchs." PhD diss., New York University, 2004 (AAT 3127457).
———. "How the *Aylonit* Got Her Sex." *AJS Review* 31, no. 2 (2007): 297–316.
———. "They Treat him as a Man and See him as a Woman: The Tannaitic Understanding of the Congenital Eunuch." *Jewish Studies Quarterly* 17, no. 3 (2010): 213–43.
Leven, K. H. "At Times These Ancient Facts Seem to Lie Before me Like a Patient on a Hospital Bed: Retrospective Diagnosis and Ancient Medical History." In *Magic and Rationality in Ancient Near-Eastern and Graeco-Roman Medicine*, edited by H. F. J. Horstmanshoff and M. Stol, 369–86. Leiden: Brill, 2004.
Levine, Baruch A. "'Seed' versus 'Womb': Expressions of Male Dominance in Biblical Israel." In *Sex and Gender in the Ancient Near East*, vol. 2, edited by Simo Parpola and Robert Whiting, 337–43. Helsinki: Neo-Assyrian Text Corpus Project, 2002.
Levinson, Joshua. "Cultural Androgyny in Rabbinic Literature." In *From Athens to Jerusalem: Medicine in Hellenized Jewish Lore and Early Christian Literature—Papers of the Symposium in Jerusalem 9–11 September 1996*, edited by Samuel Kottek and Manfred Horstmanshoff, 119–40. Rotterdam: Erasmus Publishing, 2000.
Lévi-Strauss, Claude. *The Elementary Structures of Kinship*. Translated by James Harle Bell, John Richard von Sturmer, and Rodney Needham. Boston: Beacon Press, 1971.
Lewis, Charlton T., and Charles Short. *A Latin Dictionary*. Rev. ed. Oxford: Clarendon Press, 1879.
Lewis, Sian, and Lloyd Llewellyn-Jones. *The Culture of Animals in Antiquity: A Sourcebook with Commentaries*. New York: Routledge, 2018.
Lidell, Henry G., and Robert Scott. *A Greek-English Lexicon*. 9th ed. Oxford: Oxford University Press, 1995.
Lieber, Elinor. "The Hippocratic 'Airs, Waters, Places' on Cross-Dressing Eunuchs: 'Natural' yet also 'Divine.'" In *Sex and Difference in Ancient Greece and Rome*, edited by Mark Golden and Peter Toohey, 351–70. Edinburgh: Edinburgh University Press, 2003.
Lieberman, Saul. *Greek in Jewish Palestine/Hellenism in Jewish Palestine*. New York: Jewish Theological Seminary Press, 2012. First published 1994 by Jewish Theological Seminary Press (New York).
———. *Tosefta Kifshuta*. New York: Jewish Theological Seminary Press, 2007.
Lieu, Samuel N. C., ed. *The Emperor Julian*. Liverpool: Liverpool University Press, 1986.
Light, Little. "The Seam of Skin and Scales." *Taking Steps* (blog). January 15, 2004. http://takingsteps.blogspot.com/2007/01/.
Lightfoot, Jane L. "Sacred Eunuchism in the Cult of the Syrian Goddess." In *Eunuchs in Antiquity and Beyond*, edited by Shaun Tougher, 71–87. Swansea: Classical Press of Wales, 2002.

Llewellyn-Jones, Lloyd. "Eunuchs and the Royal Harem in Achaemenid Persia (539–331 BC)." In *Eunuchs in Antiquity and Beyond*, edited by Shaun Tougher, 19–51. Swansea: Classical Press of Wales, 2002.

Lloyd, Erin. "From the Hospital to the Courtroom: A Statutory Proposal for Recognizing and Protecting the Legal Rights of Intersex Children." *Cardozo Journal of Law and Gender* 12 (2005–6): 155–97.

Lombardo, Paul A. *Three Generations, No Imbeciles: Eugenics, the Supreme Court, and Buck v. Bell*. Baltimore: Johns Hopkins University Press, 2010.

Love, Heather. *Feeling Backward: Loss and the Politics of Queer History*. Cambridge, MA: Harvard University Press, 2009.

Luk, Nissim. "Breyrah u'Mimad haZeman: Iyun b'Shitat Rashi." *Gullot* 4 (1995): 199–258.

MacDonald, Dennis Ronald. "Corinthian Veils and Gnostic Androgynes." In *Images of the Feminine in Gnosticism*, edited by Karen L. King, 276–92. Minneapolis: Fortress Press, 1988.

MacKenzie, D. Neal. "Bundahišn." In *Encyclopaedia Iranica*, edited by Ehsan Yarshater, 4:547–51. Leiden: Brill, 1989. http://www.iranicaonline.org/articles/bundahisn-primal-creation.

Macuch, Maria. "The Case Against Mār Abā, the Catholicos, in the Light of Sasanian Law." *Aram* 26, no. 1 (2014): 47–58.

Magubane, Zine. "Spectacles and Scholarship: Caster Semenya, Intersex Studies, and the Problem of Race in Feminist Theory." *Signs* 39, no. 3 (Spring 2014): 761–85.

Mahmood, Saba. "Agency, Performativity, and the Feminist Subject." In *Pieties and Gender: International Studies in Religion and Society*, vol. 9, edited by Lori Beamon and Peter Beyer, 11–45. Leiden: Brill Publishing, 2009.

Malakh, Daniel. "B'Din Hagdarat Saris Chammah v'Aylonit." In *Sefer Refa'el: Ma'amarim u-Mekhkarim bTorah Uve-Mada'e haYahadut Lezikhro Shel Dr. Yitzhak Refa'el, Zal*, edited by Yosef Eliyahu Moshovitz, 329–42. Jerusalem: Moshav Harav Kuk, 2000.

Malatino, Hilary. *Queer Embodiment: Monstrosity, Medical Violence, and Intersex Experience*. Lincoln: Nebraska University Press, 2019.

Mandelbaum, Irving. *A History of the Mishnaic Law of Agriculture: Kilayim—Translation and Exegesis*. Chico, CA: Scholars Press, 1982.

Mandsager, John Robert. "To Stake a Claim: The Making of Rabbinic Agricultural Spaces in the Roman Countryside." PhD diss., Stanford University, 2014. ProQuest (AAT 28121181).

Marchal, Joseph A. *Appalling Bodies: Queer Figures before and after Paul's Letters*. Oxford: Oxford University Press, 2019.

———. "Bodies Bound for Circumcision and Baptism: An Intersex Critique and the Interpretation of Galatians." *Theology and Sexuality* 16, no. 2 (2010): 163–82.

———. "The Corinthian Women Prophets and Trans Activism: Rethinking Canonical Gender Claims." In *Bible Trouble: Queer Readings at the Boundaries of Biblical Scholarship*, edited by Teresa Hornsby and Ken Stone, 223–47. Atlanta: Society of Biblical Literature, 2011.

———. "Who Are You Calling a Eunuch?! Staging Conversations and Connections between Feminist and Queer Biblical Studies and Intersex Advocacy." In *Intersex, Theology, and the Bible: Troubling Bodies in Church, Text, and Society*, edited by Susannah Cornwall, 29–54. London: Palgrave Macmillan, 2015.

Marcone, Arnaldo. "A Long Late Antiquity? Considerations on a Controversial Periodization." *Journal of Late Antiquity* 1, no. 1 (2008): 4–19.
Margalit, David. "Tumtum v'Androginos." *Korot* 6, nos. 11–12 (1975): 777–80.
Margalit, Natan. "Not By Her Mouth Do We Live: A Literary/Anthropological Reading of Gender in Mishnah Ketubbot, Chapter 1." *Prooftexts* 20, no. 1 (2000): 61–86.
Marx, Tzvi C. *Disability in Jewish Law*. London: Routledge, 2002.
Mason, H. J. "Favorinus' Disorder: Reifenstein's Syndrome in Antiquity?" *Janus* 66 (1979): 1–13.
Massumi, Brian. *What Animals Teach Us about Politics*. Durham, NC: Duke University Press, 2014.
Matić, Uroš. "Gender in Ancient Egypt: Norms, Ambiguities, and Sensualities." *Near Eastern Archaeology* 79, no. 3 (2016): 174–83.
McCaffrey, Kathleen. "Reconsidering Gender Ambiguity in Mesopotamia: Is a Beard Just A Beard." In *Sex and Gender in the Ancient Near East: Proceedings of the 47th Recontre Assyriologique Internationale Helsinki July 2–6, 2001*, vol. 2, edited by Simo Parpola and R. M. Whiting, 379–91. Helsinki: University of Helsinki, 2002.
McCoskey, Denise Eileen. *Race: Antiquity and its Legacy*. Oxford: Oxford University Press, 2012.
McDonough, Scott J. "A Question of Faith? Persecution and Political Centralization in the Sasanian Empire of Yazdgard II (438–457 CE)." In *Violence in Late Antiquity: Perceptions and Practice*, edited by H. A. Drake, 69–85. Aldershot: Ashgate Press, 2006.
McRuer, Robert. "Crip Eye for the Normate Guy: Queer Theory and the Disciplining of Disability Studies." *PMLA* 120, no. 2 (2005): 586–92.
———. *Crip Theory: Cultural Signs of Queerness and Disability*. New York: New York University Press, 2006.
Meacham, Tirzah. "Halakhic Limitations on the Use of Slaves in Physical Examinations." In *From Athens to Jerusalem: Medicine in Hellenized Jewish Lore and in Early Christian Literature—Papers of the Symposium in Jerusalem, 9–11 September 1996*, edited by Samuel Kottek and Manfred Horstmanshoff, 33–48. Rotterdam: Erasmus Publishing, 2000.
Meeks, Wayne A. "The Image of the Androgyne: Some Uses of a Symbol in Earliest Christianity." *History of Religions* 13, no. 3 (1974): 165–208.
Melcher, Sarah J., Mikeal C. Parsons, and Amos Yong, editors. *The Bible and Disability: A Commentary*. Waco, TX: Baylor University Press, 2017.
Meyerowitz, Joanne. *How Sex Changed: A History of Transsexuality in the United States*. Cambridge, MA: Harvard University Press, 2002.
———. "A New History of Gender." Paper presented at Trans/forming Knowledge, Center for Gender Studies, University of Chicago, Chicago, IL, February 16–17, 2006.
Michaels, Samantha. "We Tracked Down the Lawyers Behind the Recent Wave of Anti-Trans Bathroom Bills." *Mother Jones*, April 25, 2016. https://www.motherjones.com/politics/2016/04/alliance-defending-freedom-lobbies-anti-lgbt-bathroom-bills/.
Milgrom, Jacob. *Leviticus 17–22*. Anchor Bible Series. New York: Random House, 2000.
———. *Leviticus: A Book of Ritual and Ethics*. Minneapolis: Fortress Press, 2004.
Miller, Patricia Cox. "Is There a Harlot in This Text? Hagiography and the Grotesque." *Journal of Medieval and Early Modern Studies*, 33 no. 3 (2003): 419–35.

———. "Shifting Selves in Late Antiquity." In *Religion and the Self in Antiquity*, edited by David Brakke, Michael Satlow, and Steven Weitzman, 15–40. Bloomington: Indiana University Press, 2005.

Mitchell, David T. "Body Solitaire: The Singular Subject of Disability Autobiography." *American Quarterly* 52, no. 2 (June 2000): 311–15.

Mitchell, David T., and Sharon L. Snyder. *Narrative Prosthesis: Disability and the Dependencies of Discourse*. Ann Arbor: University of Michigan Press, 2000.

Mock, Janet. *Surpassing Certainty: What my Twenties Taught Me*. New York: Simon & Schuster, 2017.

Mokhtarian, Jason S. *Rabbis, Sorcerors, Kings, and Priests: The Culture of the Talmud in Ancient Iran*. Berkeley: University of California Press, 2015.

Montserrat, Dominic. *Sex and Society in Graeco-Roman Egypt*. London: Kegan Paul International, 1996.

Morgan, Kathryn A. "Plato's Goat-Stags and the Uses of Comparison." In *Plato and the Power of Images*, edited by Radcliffe Edmonds III and Pierre Destreé, 179–98. Leiden: Brill, 2017.

Morland, Iain. "Afterword: Genitals are History." *Postmedieval* 9, no. 2 (2018): 209–15.

———, ed. "Intersex and After." *GLQ: A Journal of Lesbian and Gay Studies* 15, no. 2 (2009): 191–313.

———. "Introduction: Lessons from the Octopus." *GLQ: A Journal of Lesbian and Gay Studies* 15, no. 2 (2009): 191–92.

———. "Postmodern Intersex." In *Ethics and Intersex*, edited by Sharon E. Sytsma, 319–32. Dordrecht: Springer, 2006.

———. "What Can Queer Theory Do For Intersex?" *GLQ: A Journal of Lesbian and Gay Studies* 15, no.2 (2009): 285–312.

Morrigan, Clementine. "Trauma Time: The Queer Temporalities of the Traumatized Mind." *Somatechnics* 7, no. 1: 50–58.

Moscovitz, Leib. *Talmudic Reasoning: From Casuistics to Conceptualization*. Tübingen: Mohr Siebeck, 2002.

Moslener, Sara. *Virgin Nation: Sexual Purity and American Adolescence*. Oxford: Oxford University Press, 2015.

Moss, Candida R. "Mark and Matthew." In *The Bible and Disability: A Commentary*, edited by Sarah Melcher, Mikeal Parsons, and Amos Yong, 275–301. Waco, TX: Baylor University Press, 2017.

Moss, Candida R., and Joel S. Baden. *Reconceiving Infertility: Biblical Perspectives on Procreation and Childlessness*. Princeton, NJ: Princeton University Press, 2015.

Moss, Candida R., and Jeremy Schipper, eds. *Disability Studies and Biblical Literature*. New York: Palgrave Macmillan, 2006.

Muñoz, José Esteban. *Cruising Utopia: The Then and There of Queer Futurity*. New York: New York University Press, 2009.

Murison, Charles Leslie. "Cassius Deo on Nervan Legislation (68.2.4): Nieces and Eunuchs." *Historia: Zeitschrift für Alte Geschichte* 53, no. 3 (2004): 343–55.

Najmabadi, Afsaneh. *Professing Selves: Transsexuality and Same-Sex Desire in Contemporary Iran*. Durham, NC: Duke University Press, 2013.

Namaste, Viviane. *Invisible Lives: The Erasure of Transsexual and Transgendered People*. Chicago: University of Chicago Press, 2000.

Neis, R. "Fetus, Flesh, Food: Generating Bodies of Knowledge in Rabbinic Science." *Journal of Ancient Judaism* 10, no. 2 (2019): 181–210.

———. "The Reproduction of Species: Humans, Animals, and Species Nonconformity in Early Rabbinic Science." *Jewish Studies Quarterly* 24, no. 4 (2017): 289–317.

———. "The Seduction of Law: Rethinking Legal Studies in Jewish Studies." *Jewish Quarterly Review* 109, no. 1 (2019): 119–38.

———. *The Sense of Sight in Rabbinic Culture: Jewish Ways of Seeing in Late Antiquity*. Cambridge: Cambridge University Press, 2013.

Newman, Rena Yehuda. "House of Jacob/People Israel: A Trans Jewish Zine." Self-published, 2017.

Neusner, Jacob. *How the Rabbis Liberated Women*. Tampa, FL: University of South Florida, 1999.

———. *The Idea of History in Rabbinic Judaism*. Leiden: Brill, 2003.

———. *Nashim: A History of the Mishnaic Law of Women; The Mishnaic System of Women*. Vol. 5. Leiden: Brill, 1980.

———. *Three Questions of Formative Judaism: History, Literature, and Religion*. Boston: Brill Academic Publishers, 2002.

Nguyen, Tan Hoang. *A View from the Bottom: Asian American Masculinity and Sexual Representation*. Durham, NC: Duke University Press, 2014.

Nissan, Ephraim, and Zohar Amar. "What They Served at the Banquet for the Wedding of Shim'on Nathan's Daughter: Considerations on the Sense of *tsvi* in Sources from East and West." *Australian Journal of Jewish Studies* 26 (2012): 95–129.

Nissinen, Martti. "Relative Masculinities in the Hebrew Bible/Old Testament." In *Being a Man: Negotiating Ancient Constructs of Masculinity*, edited by Ilona Zsolnay, 221–47. New York: Routledge, 2017.

N'Shea, Omar. "Royal Eunuchs and Elite Masculinity in the Neo-Assyrian Empire." *Near Eastern Archaeology* 79, no. 3 (2016): 214–21.

Nugent, George. "This Sex Which Is Not One: De-Constructing Ovid's Hermaphrodite." *differences* 2, no. 1 (1990): 160–85.

Nussbaum, Martha C. "Platonic Love and Colorado Law: The Relevance of Ancient Greek Norms to Modern Sexual Controversies." *Virginia Law Review* 80, no. 7 (1994): 1515–1651.

Olyan, Saul M. "'And with a Male you Shall not Lie the Lying Down of a Woman': On the Meaning and Significance of Leviticus 18:22 and 20:13." *Journal of the History of Sexuality* 5, no. 2 (October 1994): 179–206.

———. "Defects, Holiness, and Pollution in Biblical Cultic Texts." In *Sybils, Scriptures, and Scrolls: John Collins at Seventy*, vol. 2., edited by Joel Baden, Hindy Najman, and Eibert Tigchelaar, 1018–28. Leiden: Brill, 2017.

———. *Disability in the Hebrew Bible: Interpreting Mental and Physical Differences*. Cambridge: Cambridge University Press, 2008.

———. *Rites and Rank: Hierarchy in Biblical Representations of Cult*. Princeton, NJ: Princeton University Press, 2000.

Oppenheimer, Aharon. "Rabbi Judah Ha-Nasi and Babylonia: Ties and Tensions." In *"Follow the Wise": Studies in Jewish History and Culture in Honor of Lee I. Levine*, edited by Zeev Weiss and Lee Levine, 297–318. Winona Lake, IN: Eisenbraus, 2010.

Organisation Intersex International. "The Terminology of Intersex." OII Intersex Network. November 14, 2010. http://oiiinternational.com/2602/terminology-intersex/.

Ovid. *Ovid in Six Volumes: The Metamorphoses*. Translated by Frank Justus Miller. 2nd ed. Cambridge, MA: Harvard University Press, 1984.

Paige, Chris. *OtherWise Christian: A Guidebook for Transgender Liberation*. Madison, NJ: OtherWise Engaged Publishing, 2019.

Pamela and John Mark Crawford v. Medical University of South Carolina, South Carolina Department of Social Services and Greenville Hospital Systems. 2013CP4002877 (July 27, 2017). https://www.documentcloud.org/documents/3901419-Final-Settlement.html.

Pardes, Ilana. *Countertraditions in the Bible: A Feminist Approach*. Cambridge, MA: Harvard University Press, 1993.

Patel, Nigel. "Violent Cisterns: Trans Experience of Bathroom Space." *Agenda: Empowering Women for Gender Equity* 31, no. 1 (2017): 51–63.

Payne, Richard E. "Sex, Death, and Aristocratic Empire: Iranian Jurisprudence in Late Antiquity." *Comparative Studies in Society and History* 58, no. 2 (2016): 519–49.

Peled, Ilan. *Masculinities and Third Gender: The Origins and Nature of an Institutionalized Gender Otherness in the Ancient Near East*. Münster: Ugarit-Verlag, 2016.

Pellegrini, Ann, and Janet R. Jakobsen. *Love the Sin: Sexual Regulation and the Limits of Religious Tolerance*. Boston: Beacon Press, 2004.

Perry-Gal, Lee, Adi Erlich, Ayelet Gilboa, and Guy Bar-Oz. "Earliest Economic Exploitation of Chicken Outside East Asia: Evidence from the Hellenistic Southern Levant." *Proceedings of the National Academy of Sciences of the U.S.* 112, no. 32 (2015): 9849–54.

Pettipiece, Timothy. "Many Faced Gods: Triadic (Proto-) Structure and Divine Androgyny in Early Manichean Cosmogony." *Open Theology* 1, no. 1 (2015). https://doi.org/10.1515/opth-2015-0010.

Peskowitz, Miriam B. *Spinning Fantasies: Rabbis, Gender, and History*. Berkeley: University of California Press, 1997.

Philo. *On Abraham*. In *Philo*, vol. 6, translated by F. H. Colson, 1–137. Loeb Classical Library 289. Cambridge, MA: Harvard University Press, 1935.

———. *On Dreams*. In *Philo*, vol. 5, translated by F. H. Colson and G. H. Whitaker, 285–580. Loeb Classical Library 275. Cambridge, MA: Harvard University Press, 1934.

———. *The Works of Philo: Complete and Unabridged*. Translated by C. D. Yonge. Carol Stream, IL: Tyndale House Publishers, 1993. First published 1855 by Henrickson (Peabody, MA).

Plantzos, Dimitris. "Hellenistic Cameos: Problems of Classification and Chronology." *Bulletin of the Institute for Classical Studies* 41, no. 1 (1996): 115–32.

Plaskow, Judith. *Standing Again at Sinai: Judaism From a Feminist Perspective*. New York: Harper Collins, 1991.

———. "Taking a Break: Toilets, Gender, and Disgust." *South Atlantic Quarterly* 115, no. 4 (2016): 748–54.

Plato. *The Statesman*. Translated by Harold Fowler. London: William Heinemann, 1925.

———. *Symposium*. In *Plato*, vol. 3, translated by W. R. M. Lamb. Loeb Classical Library 166. Cambridge, MA: Harvard University Press, 1925.

Plemons, Eric. *The Look of a Woman: Facial Feminization Surgery and the Aims of Trans-Medicine*. Durham, NC: Duke University Press, 2017.

Pliny the Elder. *Natural History*. Translated by H. Rackham. Cambridge, MA: Harvard University Press, 1947.

Pollitt, Jerome Jordan. *Art in the Hellenistic Age*. Cambridge: Cambridge University Press, 2006.

Poppers, H. L. "The Déclassé in The Babylonian Jewish Community." *Jewish Social Studies* 20, no. 3 (July 1958): 153–79.

Porton, Gary G. *The Stranger Within Your Gates: Converts and Conversion in Rabbinic Literature*. Chicago: University of Chicago Press, 1994.

Pratt, Minnie Bruce. *S/he*. Ann Arbor, MI: Firebrand Books, 1995.

Preuss, Julius. *Biblical and Talmudic Medicine*. Translated and edited by Fred Rosner. New York: Sanhedrin Press, 1993. First published 1978 by Sanhedrin Press (New York).

———. *Biblisch-talmudische Medizin: Beiträge zur Geschichte der Heilkunde und der Kulturüberhaupt*. Berlin: S. Karger, 1911.

Prosser, Jay. *Second Skins: The Body Narratives of Transsexuality*. New York: Columbia University Press, 1998.

Puar, Jasbir K. *The Right to Maim: Debility, Capacity, Disability*. Durham, NC: Duke University Press, 2017.

Pyne, Jake. "Arresting Ashley X: Trans Youth, Puberty Blockers, and the Question of Whether Time is on Your Side." *Somatechnics* 7, no. 1 (2017): 95–123.

Ramsay, William M. *The Historical Geography of Asia Minor*. Vol. 4. London: John Murray, 1890.

Raphael, Rebecca. *Biblical Corpora: Representations of Disability in Hebrew Biblical Literature*. New York: T & T Clark, 2008.

Reeg, Gottfried. *Die Ortsnamen Israels Nach der Rabbinischen Literatur*. Wiesbaden: Dr. Ludwig Reichert Verlag, 1989.

Reign, Cypress Amber. "The Justice Fleet: Fostering Healing Through Art, Dialogue, and Play." The Justice Fleet. Accessed September 13, 2021. https://www.thejusticefleet.com/.

Reis, Elizabeth. *Bodies in Doubt: An American History of Intersex*. Baltimore: Johns Hopkins University Press, 2009.

Retief, Francoise P., J. F. G. Cilliers, and S. P. J. K. Riekert. "Eunuchs in the Bible." *Acta Theologica* 26, no. 2 (2006): 247–58.

Richlin, Amy, ed. *Arguments with Silence: Writing the History of Roman Women*. Ann Arbor: University of Michigan Press, 2014.

———. *The Garden of Priapus: Sexuality and Aggression in Roman Humor*. Oxford: Oxford University Press, 1992. First published 1983 by Yale University Press (New Haven, CT).

———. "Making Up a Woman: The Face of Roman Gender." In *Off with Her Head! The Denial of Women's Identity in Myth, Religion, and Culture*, edited by Howard Eilberg-Schwartz and Wendy Doniger, 185–213. Berkeley: University of California Press, 1995.

———. "Not before Homosexuality: The Materiality of the Cinaedus and the Roman Law against Love Between Men." *Journal of the History of Sexuality* 3, no. 4 (1993): 523–73.

———. "Reading Ovid's Rapes." In *Pornography and Representation in Greece and Rome*, edited by Amy Richlin, 158–80. Oxford: Oxford University Press, 1992.

Rizki, Cole. "Latin/x American Trans Studies: Towards a *Travesti*-Trans Analytic." *Trans Studies Quarterly* 6, no. 2 (2019): 145–55.

Robinson, Matthew. "Salmacis and Hermaphroditus: When Two Become One* (Ovid, Met. 4.285- 388)." *Classical Quarterly* 49, no. 1 (1999): 212–23.

Romano, Allen J. "The Invention of Marriage: Hermaphroditus and Salmacis at Halicarnassus and in Ovid." *Classical Quarterly* 59, no. 2 (2009): 543–61.

Ronis, Sara A. "Different Approaches to Rabbinics Research: Between the United States and Israel." Panel presentation at the Association for Jewish Studies Annual Conference, Boston, MA, December 16–18, 2018.

Rose, Martha L. *The Staff of Oedipus: Transforming Disability in Ancient Greece*. Ann Arbor: University of Michigan Press, 2006.

Rosen-Zvi, Ishay. "*Haguf v'ha'mikdash: R'shimat Mumay Hacohanim b'Mishnah u'm'komo shel Hamikdash b'vayt Hamidrash Hatana'i*." *Mada'ei Hayahadut* 43 (2005): 49–87.

———. *HaTekes she-lo haya: Mikdash, Midrash, u-Migdar b'Masechet Sotah*. Jerusalem: Magnes Press, 2008.

———. "Usual Suspects: On Trust, Doubt, and Ethnicity in the *Mishnah*." In *The Role of Trust in Conflict Resolution: The Israeli- Palestinian Case and Beyond*, edited by Ilai Alon and Daniel Bar-Tel, 117–27. Cham: Springer International Publishing, 2016.

Rosenberg, Jordy. *Confessions of the Fox*. New York: One World, 2018.

Rosten, Leo. *The Joys of Yiddish*. New York: McGraw Hill, 1968.

Roth, Joel. "Homosexuality Revisited." Rabbinical Assembly. December 6, 2006. https://www.rabbinicalassembly.org/sites/default/files/assets/public/halakhah/teshuvot/20052010/roth_revisited.pdf.

Rozenfeld, Ben Tsiyon. *Torah Centers and Rabbinic Activity in Palestine, 70–400 CE: History and Geographic Distribution*. Translated by Chava Cassel. Leiden: Brill, 2010.

Ruane, Nicole J. "'Male Without Blemish': Sacrifice and Gender Ideologies in Priestly Ritual Law." PhD diss., Union Theological Seminary, 2005. ProQuest (AAT 3172920).

Rubin, Gayle S. "The Traffic in Women: Notes on the Political Economy of Sex." In *Toward an Anthropology of Women*, edited by Rayna Reiter, 157–210. New York: Monthly Review Press, 1975.

Rubinstein, Jeffrey L. *The Culture of the Babylonian Talmud*. Baltimore: Johns Hopkins University Press, 2004.

———. "On Some Abstract Concepts in Rabbinic Literature." *Jewish Studies Quarterly* 4 (March 1997): 33–73.

Runions, Erin. *How Hysterical: Identification and Resistance in the Bible and Film*. London: Palgrave Macmillan, 2003.

Salamon, Gayle. *The Life and Death of Latisha King: A Critical Phenomenology of Transphobia*. New York: New York University Press, 2018.

Salah, Trish. "'Time isn't after Us': Some Tiresian Durations." *Somatechnics* 7, no. 1 (2017): 16–33.

Saldarini, Anthony J. "'Form Criticism' of Rabbinic Literature." *Journal of Biblical Literature* 96, no. 2 (June 1977): 257–74.

Sanders, Joel, and Susan Stryker. "Stalled: Gender-Neutral Public Bathrooms." *South Atlantic Quarterly* 115, no. 4 (2016): 779–88.
Satlow, Michael L. "Beyond Influence: Towards a New Historiographic Paradigm." In *Jewish Literatures and Cultures: Context and Intertext*, edited by Anita Norich and Yaron Eliav, 37–53. Atlanta: Society of Biblical Literature, 2008.
———. *Jewish Marriage in Antiquity*. Princeton, NJ: Princeton University Press, 2001.
———. *Tasting the Dish: Rabbinic Rhetorics of Sexuality*. Atlanta: Society of Biblical Literature, 2014. First published 1995 by Brown Judaic Studies (Providence).
———. "'They Abused Him Like a Woman': Homoeroticism, Gender Blurring, and the Rabbis in Late Antiquity." *Journal of the History of Sexuality* 5, no. 1 (Jul. 1994): 1–25.
Schalk, Sami. *Bodyminds Reimagined: (Dis)ability, Race, and Gender in Black Women's Speculative Fiction*. Durham, NC: Duke University Press, 2018.
Scherer, Bee. "Variant Dharma: Buddhist Queers, Queering Buddhism." In *Queering Paradigms VI: Interventions, Ethics, and Glocalities*, edited by Bee Scherer, 253–73. Bern: Peter Lang, 2016.
Schiffman, Lawrence H. "The Eschatological Community of the *Serekh Ha-'Edah*." *Proceedings for the American Academy of Jewish Research* 51 (1984): 105–29.
———. "Exclusion from the Sanctuary and the City of the Sanctuary in the Temple Scroll." *Hebrew Annual Review* 9 (1986): 301–20.
Schilt, Kristen, and Laurel Westbrook. "Bathroom Battlegrounds and Penis Panics." *Contexts* 14, no. 3 (Summer 2015): 26–31.
Schipper, Jeremy. "Deuteronomy 24:5 and King Asa's Foot Disease in 1 Kings 15:23b." *Journal of Biblical Literature* 128, no. 4 (2009): 643–48.
———. *Disability Studies and the Hebrew Bible: Figuring Mephibosheth in the David Story*. New York: T & T Clark, 2006.
Schipper, Jeremy, and Jeffrey Stackert. "Blemishes, Camouflage, and Sanctuary Service: The Priestly Deity and His Attendants." *Hebrew Bible and Ancient Israel* 2, no. 4 (2013): 458–78.
Schofer, Jonathan Wyn. *Confronting Vulnerability: The Body and the Divine in Rabbinic Ethics*. Chicago: University of Chicago Press, 2010.
———. "The Different Life Stages: From Childhood to Old Age." In *The Oxford Handbook of Jewish Daily Life in Roman Palestine*, edited by Catherine Hezser, 327–43. (Oxford: Oxford University Press, 2010).
Scholz, Piotr O. *Eunuchs and Castrati: A Cultural History*. Princeton, NJ: Markus Wiener, 2001.
Schremer, Adiel. *Zachar u'Nekayvah B'ra'am: HaNisuim b'Shilhay Yimey haBayit haSheyni u'vT'kufat haMishnah v'haTalmud*. Jerusalem: Merkaz Zalman Shazar Le'Toldot Yisrael, 2003.
———. "Thinking About Belonging in Early Rabbinic Literature: Proselytes, Apostates, and 'Children of Israel,' or: Does it Make Sense to Speak of Early Rabbinic Orthodoxy?" *Journal for the Study of Judaism* 43 (2012): 249–75.
Schwartz, Rafi. "Tennessee Inmates Are Being Offered a Horrifying Choice: Jail Time or Sterilization." Splinter. July 20, 2017. https://splinternews.com/tennessee-inmates-are-being-offered-a-horrifying-choice-1797100263.
Schwartz, Seth. *Imperialism and Jewish Society 200 BCE—640 CE*. Princeton, NJ: Princeton University Press, 2001.

Scott, Joan Wallach. "Sexularism." Ursula Hirschmann Annual Lecture on Gender and Europe, Robert Schuman Centre for Advanced Studies, April 23, 2009, Florence, Italy. https://cadmus.eui.eu/bitstream/handle/1814/11553/RSCAS_DL_2009_01.pdf?sequence=1&isAllowed=y.

Scurlock, JoAnn, and Burton Anderson. *Diagnoses in Assyrian and Babylonian Medicine: Ancient Sources, Translations, and Modern Medical Analysis*. Urbana: University of Illinois Press, 2005.

Sears, Clare. *Arresting Dress: Cross-Dressing, Law, and Fascination in Nineteenth-Century San Francisco*. Durham, NC: Duke University Press, 2014.

Secunda, Shai. "The Construction, Composition, and Idealization of the Female Body in Rabbinic Literature and Parallel Iranian Texts: Three Excurses." *Nashim* 23 (Spring–Fall 2012): 60–86.

———. *The Iranian Talmud: Reading the Bavli in its Sasanian Context*. Philadelphia: University of Pennsylvania Press, 2016.

Sedgwick, Eve Kosofsky. *Espistemology of the Closet*. Berkeley: University of California Press, 2008. First published 1990 by University of California Press (Berkeley).

Seidman, Naomi. *Faithful Renderings: Jewish-Christian Difference and the Politics of Translation*. Chicago: University of Chicago Press, 2006.

Sellew, Melissa Harl. "Reading the *Gospel of Thomas* from Here: A Trans-Centred Hermeneutic." *Journal for Interdisciplinary Biblical Studies* 1, no. 2 (2020): 61–96.-

Sexton, Jared. "The Social Life of Social Death: On Afro-pessimism and Black Optimism." In *Time, Temporality, and Violence in International Relations*, edited by Anna Agathangelou and Kyle Killian, 61–75. Abingdon: Routledge, 2016.

Shackleton Bailey, D. R., trans. *Memorable Doings and Sayings*. Cambridge, MA: Harvard University Press, 2000.

Shanks Alexander, Elizabeth. *Gender and Timebound Commandments in Judaism*. Cambridge: Cambridge University Press, 2013.

———. *Transmitting Mishnah: The Shaping Influence of Oral Tradition*. Cambridge: Cambridge University Press, 2006.

Sharpe, A. N. *Transgender Jurisprudence: Dysphoric Bodies of Law*. London: Cavendish Publishing, 2002.

Sharzer, Leonard A. "Transgender Jews and Halakhah." Rabbinical Assembly. June 7, 2017. https://www.rabbinicalassembly.org/sites/default/files/public/halakhah/teshuvot/2011-2020/transgender-halakhah.pdf.

Shasha, Roy. "The Forms and Functions of Lists in the Mishnah." PhD diss., University of Manchester, 2006. ProQuest (AAT 11009832).

Shemesh, Aharon. "'The Holy Angels are in their Council:' The Exclusion of Deformed Persons from Holy Places in Qumranic and Rabbinic Literature." *Dead Sea Discoveries* 4, no. 2 (1997): 179–206.

Sherry, A. P. *Osef Kitve haYad shel haTalmud Bavli b'Sifriyat haVatican b'Roma*. Jerusalem: Makor, 1972–74.

Simon-Shoshan, Moshe. "Halakhic Mimesis: Rhetorical and Redactional Strategies in Tannaitic Narrative." *Dine Israel* 24 (2007): 101–23.

Sizgorich, Thomas. "Reasoned Violence and Shifty Frontiers: Shared Victory in the Late Roman East." In *Violence in Late Antiquity: Perceptions and Practice*, edited by H. A. Drake, 167–79. Aldershot: Ashgate Press, 2006.

Skjaervø, Prods Oktor. "A Postscript on the Seal of a Eunuch in the Sasanian Court." *Journal of Inner Asian Art and Archaeology* 2 (2007): 39.

Snorton, C. Riley. *Black on Both Sides: A Racial History of Trans Identity*. Minneapolis: University of Minnesota Press, 2017.

Snorton, C. Riley, and Jin Haritaworn. "Trans Necropolitics: A Transnational Reflection on Violence, Death, and the Trans of Color Afterlife." In *The Transgender Studies Reader 2*, edited by Susan Stryker and Aren Aizura, 66–76. New York: Routledge, 2013.

Somerville, Siobhan. *Queering the Color Line: Race and the Invention of Homosexuality in American Culture*. Durham, NC: Duke University Press, 2000.

Sokoloff, Michael. *A Dictionary of Jewish Babylonian Aramaic of the Talmudic and Geonic Periods*. Baltimore: Johns Hopkins University Press, 2003.

Sørenson, Lone Wriest. "Here There Be Monsters: Hybrids Painted on Cypriot Iron Age Pottery." In *Tradition: Transmission of Culture in the Ancient World*, edited by Jane Fejfer, Mette Moltesen, and Annette Rathje, 427–50. Copenhagen: Museum Tusculanum Press, 2015.

Spade, Dean. *Normal Life: Administrative Violence, Critical Trans Politics, and the Limits of Law*. Durham, NC: Duke University Press, 2015.

Speiser, Ephraim A. *The Anchor Bible: Genesis*. New York: Doubleday, 1964.

Spillers, Hortense J. "Mama's Baby, Papa's Maybe: An American Grammar Book." *Diacritics* 17, no. 2 (1987): 65–81.

Stein, Abby. *Becoming Eve: My Journey from Ultra-Orthodox Rabbi to Transgender Woman*. New York: Seal Press, 2019.

Steinberg, Avraham. *The Encyclopedia of Jewish Medical Ethics*. Translated by Fred Rosner. Jerusalem: Feldheim Publishers, 1998.

Steinmetz, Devora. *Punishment and Freedom: The Rabbinic Construction of Criminal Law*. Philadelphia: University of Pennsylvania Press, 2008.

Stern, Sacha. *Jewish Identity in Early Rabbinic Writings*. Leiden: Brill, 1994.

———. *Time and Process in Ancient Judaism*. Oxford: Littman Library of Jewish Civilization, 2003.

Stevenson, Walter. "Eunuchs and Early Christianity." In *Eunuchs in Antiquity and Beyond*, edited by Shaun Tougher, 123–42. Swansea: Classical Press of Wales, 2002.

Stewart, David Tabb. "Leviticus-Deuteronomy." In *The Bible and Disability: A Commentary*, edited by Sarah Melcher, Mikeal Parsons, and Amos Yong, 57–91. Waco, TX: Baylor University Press, 2017.

———. "Sexual Disabilities in the Hebrew Bible." In *Disability Studies in Biblical Literature*, edited by Candida Moss and Jeremy Schipper, 67–89. New York: Palgrave Macmillan, 2011.

Stockton, Kathryn Bond. *The Queer Child, or Growing Sideways in the Twentieth Century*. Durham, NC: Duke University Press, 2009.

Stone, Sandy. "The *Empire* Strikes Back: A Posttranssexual Manifesto." *Camera Obscura* 10, no. 2 (1992): 150–76.

Strack, Hermann L., and Günter Stemberger. *Introduction to the Talmud and Midrash.* Translated by Markus Bockmuehl. Minneapolis: Fortress Press, 1996.

Strassfeld, Max. "Translating the Human: The *Androginos* in Tosefta Bikkurim." *Transgender Studies Quarterly* 3, nos. 3–4 (2016): 587–604.

———. "'You and I Have Bodies that Make People Pray': Queer Bodies and Religion." *Scholar and Feminist On-line* 14, no. 2 (2017). https://sfonline.barnard.edu/queer-religion/you-and-i-have-bodies-that-make-people-pray-queer-bodies-and-religion/.

Stryker, Susan. "(De)Subjugated Knowledges: An Introduction to Transgender Studies." In *The Transgender Studies Reader*, edited by Susan Stryker and Stephen Whittle, 1–17. New York: Routledge, 2013.

———. "My Words to Victor Frankenstein Above the Village of Chamounix: Performing Transgender Rage." *GLQ: A Journal of Lesbian and Gay Studies* 1, no. 3 (1994): 237–54.

———. "The Transgender Issue: An Introduction." *GLQ: A Journal of Lesbian and Gay Studies* 4, no. 2 (1998): 145–58.

———. "Transgender Studies: Queer Theory's Evil Twin." *GLQ: A Journal of Lesbian and Gay Studies* 10, no. 2 (2004): 212–15.

Stryker, Susan, Paisley Currah, and Lisa Jean Moore. "Introduction." *Women's Studies Quarterly* 36 nos. 3–4 (Fall/Winter 2008): 11–22.

Sullivan, Winnifred Fallers, Elizabeth Shakman Hurd, Saba Mahmood, and Peter G. Danchin, eds. *The Politics of Religious Freedom.* Chicago: University of Chicago Press, 2015.

Sundén, Jenny. "Temporalities of Transition: Trans-Temporal Femininity in a Human Musical Automaton." *Somatechnics* 5, no. 2 (2015): 197–216.

Surtees, Allison, and Jennifer Dyer, eds. *Exploring Gender Diversity in the Ancient World.* Edinburgh: Edinburgh University Press, 2020.

Sussman, Ya'acov. *Talmud Yerushalmi: According to Ms. Or. 4720 (Scal 3) of the Leiden University Library with Restorations and Corrections.* Jerusalem: Academy for the Hebrew Language, 2001.

Swancutt, Diana. "*Still* Before Sexuality: 'Greek' Androgyny, the Roman Imperial Politics of Masculinity and the Roman Invention of the *Tribas*." In *Mapping Gender in Ancient Religious Discourses*, edited by Caroline Vander Stichele and Todd Penner, 11–63. Leiden: Brill, 2007.

Swidler, Leonard. "Jesus Was a Feminist." *Catholic World* 212 (1971): 177–83.

Szesnat, Holger. "Philo and Female Homoeroticism: Philo's use of γύνανδρος and Recent Work on 'tribades.'" *Journal for the Study of Judaism in the Persian, Hellenistic, and Roman Period* 30, no. 2 (1999): 140–47.

Tadmor, Hayim. "The Role of the Chief Eunuch and the Place of Eunuchs in the Assyrian Empire." In *Sex and Gender in the Ancient Near East: Proceedings of the 47th Recontre Assyriologique Internationale Helsinki July 2–6, 2001*, vol. 2, edited by Simo Parpola and R. M. Whiting, 603–11. Helsinki: University of Helsinki, 2002.

———. "Was the Biblical *Saris* a Eunuch?" In *Solving Riddles and Untying Knots: Biblical, Epigraphic and Semitic Studies in Honor of Jonas C. Greenfield*, edited by Ziony Zevit, Seymour Gitin, and Michael Sokoloff, 317–27. Winona Lake, IN: Eisenbrauns, 1995.

Tafażżoli, Ahmad. "An Unrecognized Sasanian Title." *Bulletin of the Asia Institute* 4 (1990): 301–5.

Talbott, Rick. "Imagining the Matthean Eunuch Community: Kyriarchy on the Chopping Block." *Journal of Feminist Studies in Religion* 22, no. 1 (Spring 2006): 21–43.
Tavakoli-Targhi, Mohamad. "Contested Memories: Narrative Structures and Allegorical Meanings of Iran's pre-Islamic History." *Iranian Studies* 29, nos. 1–2 (1996): 149–75.
Tottoli, Roberto. "At Cock-Crow: Some Muslim Traditions About the Rooster." *Zeitschrift für Geschichte und Kultur des Islamischen Orients* 76 (1999): 139–47.
Tougher, Shaun. "Eunuchs in the East, Men in the West? Dis/Unity, Gender, and Orientalism in the Fourth Century." In *East and West in the Roman Empire of the Fourth Century*, edited by Roald Dijkstra, Sanne van Poppel, and Daniëlle Slootjes, 147–63. Leiden: Brill, 2015.
———. "In or Out? Origins of Court Eunuchs." In *Eunuchs in Antiquity and Beyond*, edited by Shaun Tougher, 143–61. Swansea: Classical Press of Wales, 2002.
———. *The Roman Castrati: Eunuchs in the Roman Empire*. London: Bloomsbury Academic, 2020.
Towner, Wayne S. *The Rabbinic Enumeration of Scriptural Examples: A Study of a Rabbinic Pattern of Discourse With Special Reference to Mekhilta D'R Ishmael*. Leiden: Brill, 1973.
Transgender Europe. "Trans Rights Europe Map 2017." TGEU. Accessed September 14, 2021. https://tgeu.org/wp-content/uploads/2017/05/Map2017-PRINT.pdf.
Tuell, Steven S. "The Evidence of the 'Foreigner': Evidence of Competing Polities in Ezekiel 44:1–4 and Isaiah 56: 1–8." In *Constituting the Community: Studies on the Polity of Ancient Israel in Honor of S. Dean McBride Jr.*, edited by John T. Strong and Steven S. Tuell, 183–205. Winona Lake, IN: Eisenbrauns, 2005.
Valentine, David. *Imagining Transgender: An Ethnography of a Category*. Durham, NC: Duke University Press, 2007.
Van der Gracht, Stefanie Lauren. "Hermaphroditism in Greek and Roman Antiquity." Master's thesis, University of Calgary, 2009. ProQuest (AAT MR54415).
Van der Horst, Pieter W. "Two Notes on Hellenistic Lore in Early Rabbinic Literature." *Jewish Studies Quarterly*, 1, no. 3 (1993/1994): 252–62.
Van Tine, R. Jarrett. "Castration for the Kingdom and Avoiding the αἰτία of Adultery." *Journal of Biblical Literature* 137, no. 2 (2018): 399–418.
Velde, H. Te. *Seth God of Confusion: A Study of his Role in Egyptian Mythology and Religion*. Leiden: Brill, 1977.
Vidas, Moulie. *Tradition and the Formation of the Talmud*. Princeton, NJ: Princeton University Press, 2014.
Vikman, Elisabeth. "Ancient Origins: Sexual violence in warfare, part I." *Anthropology and Medicine* 12, no. 1 (2005): 21–31.
Villalobos, Manuel. "Bodies *Del Otro Lado* Finding Life and Hope on the Borderland: Gloria Anzaldúa, the Ethiopian Eunuch of Acts 8:26–40, y Yo." In *Bible Trouble: Queer Readings at the Boundaries of Biblical Scholarship*, edited by Teresa Hornsby and Ken Stone, 191–223. Atlanta: Society of Biblical Literature, 2011.
Viloria, Hida. *Born Both: An Intersex Life*. New York: Hachette Books, 2017.
von Bothmer, Dietrich. "The Tawny Hippalektryon." *Metropolitan Museum of Art Bulletin* 11, no. 5 (1953): 132–36.
von Stackelberg, Katherine T. "Garden Hybrids: Hermaphrodite Images in the Roman House." *Classical Antiquity* 33, no. 2 (2014): 395–426.

Walls, Neal H. "The Origins of the Disabled Body: Disability in Ancient Mesopotamia." In *This Abled Body: Rethinking Disabilities in Biblical Studies*, edited by Hector Avalos, Sarah Melcher, and Jeremy Schipper, 13–30. Atlanta: Society of Biblical Literature, 2007.

Walsh, Jerome T. "Leviticus 18:22 and 20:13: Who is Doing What to Whom?" *Journal of Biblical Literature* 120, no. 2 (2001): 201–9.

Warmington, E. H., trans. *Remains of Old Latin: Lucilius; The Twelve Tables*. Vol. 3. Loeb Classical Library 329. Cambridge. MA: Harvard University Press, 1938.

Wasserman, Mira B. *Jews, Gentiles, and Other Animals: The Talmud after the Humanities*. Philadelphia: University of Pennsylvania Press, 2017

Waxman, Tobaron. "Levush Project." *Trans Studies Quarterly* 6, no. 3 (2019): 400–402.

Wegner, Judith Romney. *Chattel or Person? The Status of Women in the Mishnah*. Oxford: Oxford University Press, 1988.

———. "Tragelaphos Revisited: The Anomaly of Women in the Mishnah." *Judaism* 37, no. 2 (1988): 160–72.

Weheliye, Alexander G. *Habeas Viscus: Racializing Assemblages, Biopolitics, and Black Feminist Theories of the Human*. Durham, NC: Duke University Press, 2014: 75–76.

Weisberg, Devora E. "The Babylonian Talmud's Treatment of Levirate Marriage." *Review of Rabbinic Judaism* 3, no. 1 (2000): 35–66.

———. *Levirate Marriage and the Family in Ancient Judaism*. Waltham, MA: Brandeis University Press, 2009.

———. "The Widow of our Discontent: Levirate Marriage in the Bible and Ancient Israel." *Journal for the Study of the Old Testament* 28, no. 4 (2004): 403–29.

Weismantel, Mary. "Towards a Transgender Archaeology: A Queer Rampage through Prehistory." In *The Transgender Studies Reader 2*, edited by Susan Stryker and Aren Aizura, 319–35. New York: Routledge, 2013.

Weiss Halivni, David. *Mekorot U'Mesorot: Biurim b'Talmud l'seder Nashim*. Tel Aviv: D'vir, 1968.

———. *Midrash, Mishnah and Gemara: The Jewish Predilection for Justified Law*. Cambridge, MA: Harvard University Press, 1986.

West, Isaac. *Transforming Citizenships: Transgender Articulations of Law*. New York: New York University Press, 2013.

Whatmore, Sarah, and Lorraine Thorne. "Wild(er)ness: Reconfiguring the Geographies of Wildlife." *Transactions of the Institute of British Geographers*, n.s. 23, no 4 (1998): 435–54.

White, Heather R. *Reforming Sodom: Protestants and the Rise of Gay Rights*. Chapel Hill: University of North Carolina Press, 2015.

Williams, Craig A. "The Meanings of Softness: Some Remarks on the Semantics of *mollitia*." *Eugesta* 3 (2013): 240–63.

———. *Roman Homosexuality: Ideologies of Masculinity in Classical Antiquity*. Oxford: Oxford University Press, 1999.

Wilson, Brittany E. "'Neither Male nor Female': The Ethiopian Eunuch in Acts 8:26–40." *New Testament Studies* 60 (2014): 403–22

Wimpfheimer, Barry Scott. "Footnotes to *Carnal Israel*: Infertilty and the Legal Subject." In *Talmudic Transgressions: Engaging the Work of Daniel Boyarin*, edited by Charlotte Elisheva Fonrobert, Ishay Rosen-Zvi, Aharon Shemesh, Moulie Vidas, and James Redfield, 161–201. Leiden: Brill, 2017.

———. *Narrating the Law: A Poetics of Talmudic Legal Stories.* Philadelphia: University of Pennsylvania Press, 2011.

Wittig, Monique. *Les Guérillères.* Translated by David Le Vay. Boston: Beacon Press, 1971.

Wright, Jacob L., and Michael J. Chan. "King and Eunuch: Isaiah 56:1–8 in Light of Honorific Royal Burial Practices." *Journal of Biblical Literature* 131, no. 1 (2012): 99–119.

Yalçin, Serdar. "Men, Women, Eunuchs, etc.: Visualities of Gendered Identities in Kassite Babylonian Seals (ca. 1470–1155 B.C.)." *Bulletin of the American School of Oriental Research* 376 (November 2016): 121–50.

Yeivin, Israel. *Osef Kit'ei Ha-Genizah shel ha-Mishnah be-nikud Bavli: Be-livyat te'ur Kitvei ha-yad.* Jerusalem: Makor, 1974.

Yefman, Gil. "Tumtum." Accessed September 14, 2021. https://www.gilyefman.com/tumtum.

Yerushalmi, Yosef Hayim. *Zakhor: Jewish History and Jewish Memory.* Seattle: University of Washington Press, 1982.

Zajko, Vanda. "'Listening With' Ovid: Intersexuality, Queer Theory, and the Myth of Hermaphroditus and Salmacis." *Helios* 36, no. 2 (Fall 2009): 175–202.

Zellman, Reuben, Jhos Singer, Max Strassfeld, Elliot Kukla, Joy Ladin, Ari Lev Fornari, and Micah Bazant. "Resources." TransTorah. Accessed September 13, 2021. http://transtorah.org/resources.html.

Ziffer, Irit. "The First Adam, Androgyny, and the 'Ain Ghazal Two-headed Busts in Context?" *Israel Exploration Journal* 57, no. 2 (2007): 129–52.

Zuckerberg, Donna. *Not All Dead White Men: Classics and Misogyny in the Digital Age.* Cambridge, MA: Harvard University Press, 2018.

Zuckermandel, Moses Samuel. *MS Tosefta Based on the Erfurt and Vienna Codices.* Jerusalem: Wahrman Books, 1970.

GLOSSARY

Abbreviations used:

adj. adjective

n. noun

pl. plural

v.t. verb, transitive

Words that are entries in this glossary, including plural forms of entry words, are indicated in small capitals.

Entry words listed in italics are not commonly used in English; their language is indicated in parentheses following the part of speech. They appear in italics in the running text when they are first used; afterward, they are set in roman. Many of the words in this glossary are both English and Aramaic or Hebrew, but they may be found in English dictionaries and other English-language publications. For an example of this distinction, compare the entry for "HALAKHAH" to the entries for "KOY" and "TRAGELAPHOS."

Only entry words that are not commonly used in English, including in discussions of the relevant topic, are given here in italics.

Acquired *saris* — *noun phrase* In rabbinic literature, a person assigned male at birth whose body subsequently changes in a way that precludes reproduction. Literally, the Hebrew phrase, *s'ris 'adam*, means a "SARIS of human," usually glossed as one made a SARIS by a human act or misadventure.

Aggadah — *n.* (1) (*proper noun*) The body of non-legal rabbinic literature, consisting of stories, teachings, sayings, illustrations of ethical and legal principles, and biblical commentary. (2) (*common noun*; AGGADOT, *pl.*) A nonlegal rabbinic text presenting a story, a teaching, a saying, an illustration of an ethical or HALAKHIC principle, a biblical commentary, or some combination of these. While AGGADAH and AGGADOT are often contrasted to legal materials in rabbinic literature (such as in this definition), contemporary scholarship has problematized the boundaries between these two genres.

Aggadic   *adj.* Consisting of or pertaining to AGGADAH.

Amora   *n.* (AMORAIM, *pl.*) One of the rabbis from the second rabbinic period, usually dated between the third century CE and 500, whose teachings and discussions form a significant portion of the Talmud.

Amoraic   *adj.* Being or pertaining to the AMORAIM.

Androginos   *n.* In Judaism, a person whose body includes both genitalia traditionally regarded as female and genitalia traditionally regarded as male. This Hebrew word derives from the Greek term, which combines the Greek words for "man" and "woman."

Aylonit   *n.* In Judaism, one who is assigned female at birth but who has physiological characteristics that make her infertile. She is sometimes described through her bodily differences from non-AYLONIT women, such as a lack of breasts or a low voice.

Babylonian Talmud   *n.* The recension of the TALMUD consisting of discussions of the MISHNAH among both Palestinian and Babylonian AMORAIM, REDACTED by rabbinic sages usually dated approximately to the sixth century CE, and including HALAKHIC arguments, stories about the sages, creative interpretations of the Hebrew Bible, and parables. The Babylonian Talmud is generally the more famous of the two RECENSIONS of the Talmud.

Baraita   *n.* An early rabbinic (TANNAITIC) text that was not included in the MISHNAH, such as any of those cited in the TALMUD or anthologized in the TOSEFTA.

Born *saris*   *noun phrase.* In rabbinic literature, a person understood to be male but born with a body that will preclude reproduction. (Literally, the Hebrew phrase *s'ris ḥamah* translates as "sun SARIS," and it is sometimes glossed as someone who is a SARIS before their first encounter with the sun's rays.)

Eunuch   *n.* (1) One understood to be male who lacks testicles, a penis, or both, whether congenitally or due to removal. See also SARIS. (2) In this book, one who is either a SARIS or an AYLONIT.

Halakhah   *n.* (1) (*proper noun*) Jewish law. (2) (*proper noun*) The body of rabbinic legal texts. (3) (*common noun;* halakhot, *pl.*) A Jewish law, legal ruling, or legal text. While the Hebrew term. "HALAKHAH," is often translated as "law" in English, the traditional texts comprising this material contain all kinds of medical, ritual, and narrative elements that we do not always associate with the term "law" in English. *Alternate spellings:* halacha, halachah, halakha.

Halakhic	*adj.* Being, containing, of pertaining to HALAKHAH.
Kil'ayim	*n. dual* Mixtures (as of fabric) or hybrids (as of plants or animals) that are forbidden for use or cultivation by the Hebrew Bible.
Koy	*n.* In rabbinic literature, a hybrid between a wild and a domesticated animal. Many rabbis understood the *Koy* as any such hybrid animal, while others understood it as a specific form of hybrid, although they did not all agree on the form. For example, one opinion understood the *Koy* as a hybrid between a goat and a doe. See also TRAGELAPHOS.
Levirate marriage	*noun phrase* In Judaism, the institution of marriage between a childless widow and the brother of her deceased husband for the purpose of ensuring a line of descent for, and a continuity of the name of, the deceased.
Midrash	*n.* (MIDRASHIM, *pl.*) (1) In Judaism, an interpretive commentary on the Hebrew Bible. (2) (*proper noun*) A collection of such commentaries, especially one compiled between antiquity to the early middle ages.
Midrashic	*adj.* (1) Being or pertaining to a MIDRASH or body of MIDRASHIM. (2) Being or pertaining to a method of interpretation used in MIDRASHIM.
Mishnah	(1) (*proper noun*) The written collection of oral rabbinic traditions developed over centuries and compiled in Roman Palestine in the third century CE in a REDACTION traditionally attributed to Rabbi Yehudah HaNasi. The MISHNAH consists of six thematic ORDERS, which are, in turn, subdivided into individual books, or TRACTATES. (2) (*common noun*) An individual passage, teaching, or legal ruling within the larger collection of the MISHNAH. When referencing an individual passage, the word is not capitalized. *Alternate spelling:* Mishna.
Mishnaic	*adj.* Being or pertaining to the MISHNAH.
Order	*n.* A division of the MISHNAH, and therefore also of the TALMUD, structured on the basis of broad subject matter. There are six orders, which are further subdivided into TRACTATES.
Palestinian Talmud	*n.* The version of the TALMUD REDACTED by rabbinic sages in the fourth or early fifth century in Roman Palestine and containing discussions of the MISHNAH, primarily among Palestinian AMORAIM. As in the BABYLONIAN TALMUD, the discussions include creative interpretations of the Hebrew Bible, HALAKHIC arguments, stories about the sages, and parables.

Rabbanan	*n. pl.* The rabbis.
Rabbis, the	*n. pl.* The Jewish sages of Judea and Babylonia, including the TANNAIM and the AMORAIM, who led the movement that is traditionally credited with shifting the center of Judaism from the Temple to the study hall and who developed the traditions that form the core of HALAKHAH. The historic period of THE RABBIS began before the Common Era and continued into the sixth century CE.
Rabbinic	*adj.* Being of or pertaining to THE RABBIS.
Recension	*n.* (1) The process of creating a critical REDACTION of a text, particularly a religious text. (2) The version of a text created by such a process.
Redact	*v.t.* To compile a body of work orally or in writing.
Redaction	*n.* (1) The process of compiling or editing of body of work, especially in written form, as for publication. (2) A version or edition of a written work.
Saris	*n.* In rabbinic literature, a person understood to be male but with a body that precludes reproduction. Often translated as "eunuch."
Stammaim	*n. pl.* According to some scholars, the rabbis of the generation that redacted the BABYLONIAN TALMUD, following the AMORAIC period and preceding the Gaonic period of the early Middle Ages. The name "stamma" comes from the work of scholar David Weiss Halivni and a theory that interprets the unattributed materials in a SUGYA as a later editorial layer. Medieval authors use the term "Savoraim" to describe the latest layers of the Babylonian Talmud. I sometimes use the term "creators of the SUGYA" to refer to the people who were responsible for shaping the latest layers of discussion (based on the scholarship of Moulie Vidas), and I sometimes use the word STAMMAIM for them. The question of the redaction of the Talmud and the process by which the latest layers were formed remains open in the field.
Stammaitic	*adj.* Being or pertaining to the STAMMAIM.
Sugya	*n.* In the TALMUD, a literary unit compiled from disparate sources into a coherent discussion, often organized around a single passage from the Mishnah. A SUGYA typically includes a series of questions, back-and-forth responses, and sometimes narrative.
Talmud	*n.* (1) a. A primary, postbiblical text of Judaism, consisting of the Mishnah and rabbinic discussions organized around the Mishnah, and existing in two versions, the BABYLONIAN TALMUD and the PALESTINIAN TALMUD. b. Either of these two versions. (2) The portion of the TALMUD (*definition 1 above*) consisting of rabbinic discussions about the MISHNAH and including HALAKHIC

	arguments, stories about the sages, creative interpretations of the Hebrew Bible, and parables.
Tanna	*n.* (*TANNAIM, pl.*) One of the Jewish sages from the earliest rabbinic period, often dated approximately between the first and the third centuries CE, whose teachings comprise the MISHNAH, TOSEFTA, and additional *BARAITOT*.
Tannaitic	*adj.* Being or pertaining to the *TANNAIM* or the time period during which they were active.
Tosefta	*n.* The collection of oral rabbinic TRADITIONS compiled during roughly the same period as the MISHNAH. (The exact dating is contested, as with most rabbinic compositions). The TOSEFTA is similar to the MISHNAH in both language and organization, and often seems to be in dialogue with it.
Tractate	*n.* A subdivision of the MISHNAH, and therefore also of the TALMUD, within the larger division of an ORDER, and akin to a book or volume within a larger written work. Like ORDERS, TRACTATES are organized on the basis of subject matter.
Tradition	*n.* In rabbinics, a rabbinic precept or set of precepts, such as those presented in the TALMUD.
Tragelaphos	*n.* (Greek) A hybrid between a goat and a stag. See also *Koy*.
Tumtum	*n.* (*TUMTUMIM, pl.*) In rabbinic literature, one not assigned a binary sex, whether owing to insufficient genital indications or to a flap of skin covering the genitalia.

INDEX

Abaye, 166, 167, 169
able-bodiedness. *See* abled
abled, 117n6, 132, 136, 140, 143, 165
ableism, 5, 23n46, 83n92, 94n17, 111–13, 118, 128, 149, 158n20, 164, 196n27
Abraham (biblical), as tumtum, 91–92
Achaemenid period, 46, 130
adulthood, 168, 169, 175–79, 181, 187
aging, 20, 160n26, 161, 163, 165, 176n76, 180, 181
Akiva, Rabbi, 137, 140, 142, 142n88, 143, 145n96, 157–59, 160n25–26, 163
Alliance Defending Freedom, 55n3, 81, 84n97
Ami, Rabbi, 95, 158, 159, 166
Ammonites, 44n39, 121n22, 128, 130, 132, 133n65
anachronism, 3, 4, 6, 7, 18, 19n36, 26, 29, 31, 53, 56, 189
androcentrism, 3, 23, 31, 66, 72n60, 73, 134, 146, 150, 163
androginos, 5, 8, 9, 56, 57, 65, 68, 79n82, 94n18, 97–106, 110, 113, 114
androgyne: human rights of, 75, 76; inclusion of, 74, 76, 185; injury of, 74–76; as legal subject, 73–75; two-headed, 58, 59; types of, 7, 49, 58; as unique creation, 79, 80, 86, 185, 198
androgyne bodies, 6, 57, 58, 59, 65, 79, 184, 186, 188, 189, 200
animacy, 78
animality, 25, 68–72, 75, 78, 80
anti-Blackness, 5, 19, 76, 83n92, 84n96, 85, 186

anti-Judaism, 22n42, 23
antiqueer theology, 191
anti-trans law, 6, 53, 56, 85
anti-trans theology, 81, 84, 85, 191
antiquity, 6, 16, 20, 30, 56, 58, 70, 81, 199; late, 9, 12, 17, 26, 34–54, 60, 61, 63, 77, 86, 109, 118, 128n49, 192
Aristophanes, 58, 69, 108
Association for Jewish Studies, 24, 193n20
Aylonit, 5, 8, 27, 144–50, 151, 153, 167, 169, 171–78, 187, 189

Babylonian Talmud. *See* Talmud, Babylonian
bad readings, 7, 16–19, 26, 40, 153, 165, 188
baraita, 161, 164
Bardel, Ruth, 44, 131
Bar Hamduri, 102, 103
Barrenness, 118, 120n21, 121n25, 147–48, 172, 174n71
Baskin, Judith, 58, 77
"bathroom" bills, 6, 26, 82, 83n94
Bazant, Micah, 195–98
Beit Bukiya, 1, 2, 105, 107, 109, 111, 184
Belser, Julia Watts, vii, viii, 25n53, 86n103, 141, 144n93, 168n47
Ben-Efrayim, Idan, Rabbi, 193
Berkowitz, Beth, 24, 25n53, 70, 71, 100n35
Bettcher, Talia Mae, 78
Bikkurim, 26, 55–87

binary, in gender, 3, 4, 13, 15, 17, 74–80, 84, 85, 101, 174, 183, 185, 186, 189, 191, 192, 194, 198, 200
BIPOC, ix, 89, 112
Black feminist thought/theory, 19n37, 75, 76, 84, 112
Blackness, 4, 19, 28n58, 90, 112, 113, 184–85
Black trans women, 83
Bostock v. Clayton County, 55, 56
Boswell, John, 87
Boyarin, Daniel, viii, 23n45, 29n61, 34n6, 57, 58n9, 98n30, 101n39, 106, 110n68, 125n42, 129n50
Brooten, Bernadette, 20n39, 22, 173n66, 190n12
Buck v. Bell, 112

Cahun, Claude, 196
capitalism, racialized, 113
castration, 3n7, 6, 36–49, 51n72, 118, 128, 131, 132, 138, 158, 159; ban on, 52, 129n49, 172, 193
Christian feminists, 22
Christianity, 11, 35, 37, 49, 195
Christians, 12, 23, 34, 47, 82, 192
1 Chronicles, 38, 39
Chrononormativity, 155, 156, 181
Cicero, 50
circumcision, 8n22, 19, 45n45, 121, 123, 128, 129, 159
Clare, Eli, 94n17, 112n77, 141, 167n44
cockfights, 2, 105–10
cocks. *See* roosters
colonialism, 19, 34n4
complementarian theology, 84
Constantine, 12, 35
Couey, J. Blake, 118
Cox, Laverne, 85
Crasnow, S.J., 200
created beings, 59, 81, 189
creation stories: androgynes in, 57, 59, 60, 81; anti-trans readings of, 81, 189; Babylonian, 59 Genesis and rabbinic, 57; in Plato, 59; Zoroastrian, 58
crip activists, ix
cripping/crip theory, 116, 151n5, 154, 181. *See also* disability theory
critical race theory, 25, 28, 117, 190n13
crossbreeding, 67
cross-dressing, 49, 193
cure, politics of, 94, 141, 142, 167, 168
custody cases, 193
Cybele (Magna Mater), 34, 44, 131; castrated priests of (*galli*), 37, 43, 44, 45, 52n75, 131

Dalley, Stephanie, 59
denaturalizing, 16
Deuteronomy, 41, 42, 67, 119, 120, 126, 134, 158, 159, 160, 161, 162, 193
deviance, 20n40, 35, 39n29, 149
DeVun, Leah, 4n12, 17n29, 36n12, 50n67, 59n18, 82n89, 185, 190
disability, 27, 42, 115, 116, 125, 128, 141, 142, 147, 150, 154, 164, 165, 188
disability theory, 25, 27, 28, 117, 125, 141, 150, 164, 164n45, 172n63, 173, 185, 196
divorce, 79n82, 142n86, 160, 192
Domestication, 71, 72, 80, 81
DSD. *See* intersex
du parẓuf, 8n22, 57, 59n18

Elazar ben Shamua, Rabbi, 1, 2, 100n34, 102, 105, 106, 109, 184
elderly men, 159–61, 163, 166
Eliezer, Rabbi, 1, 99, 100, 101, 102n41, 103n44, 105, 140–42, 142n88, 157n18, 164n33, 176n76, 184
emasculation, 35, 36, 60n23
embodiment, 155, 184, 187; disabled, 137; for eunuchs, 153, 174, 179; female, 150, 174n73; gendered/sexed,156, 185, 186, 187; masculine, 164; unruly, 94, 143, 181, 183, 187, 188. *See also* intersex embodiment; trans embodiment
Enuma Elish, 59
erasure, 53, 78, 85, 86, 190, 191
ethnicity, 23, 27, 159, 188
eugenics, 112, 167, 185
Eugenides, Jeffrey, 188, 189
eunuchphobia, 36
eunuch embodiment, 6, 47, 48, 153, 174, 175, 179, 184, 186, 188
eunuchs, taxonomies of, 5, 7, 139, 188
expertise, rabbinic, 27, 80n85, 183, 186, 187
exposure, 50, 52

Favorinus, 43, 44, 139, 115n1
Federation of Synagogues, 193
female embodiment, 65, 150, 174
feminist activists, ix
feminist rabbinics, 23, 154, 155
feminist scholarship/ theory, 16, 17, 21, 22, 24, 25, 71, 75, 76, 77n72, 85, 117
Fonrobert, Charlotte, vii, 22n44, 25, 66n40, 73, 75n67, 80n85, 169n48, 170n52, 171n56, 174n73, 175, 183n1
Fraade, Steven, 27

Freeman, Elizabeth, 155–56
Fungibility, 185

gala and galli. See Cybele
Gardner, Jane, 51, 52, 143n90
Garland-Thomson, Rosemarie, 164
gatekeeping, 23
gender: ableist, 113; biblical, 81; as binary, 3, 74, 76, 80, 84, 185, 189, 192, 194; as category, 3, 7, 40, 51, 56, 67n46, 73, 80, 195; as dichotomy, 17, 76; grammatical, 31, 52, 103; identity, 55, 84, 100, 153n9; racialized, 4, 5, 19, 36, 113, 190
gendered embodiment, 90
gendered law, 3, 53, 64, 72, 74
gendered markers, 170
gendered politics, 22–24, 56, 77, 193n20
gendered space, 15
gender studies/theory, 23, 25
Genesis, 41–43, 57–59, 67n46, 80–82, 86, 87, 91, 92, 171, 189, 192
genitalia, 9, 27, 51, 99n31, 100, 101, 107, 128, 169, 170, 186; "damaged," 5, 38, 41, 115, 120–27; dual, 8, 9, 51, 63, 97, 100, 149; of Hermaphroditus, 61; hidden, 94, 95; as immutable, 149 kosher, 121–25 128, 133, 143, 148, 150, 167, 187; as mutable, 15, 16, 18, 41, 187; privileged, 73; subject to surgery, 89; of tumtum, 91, 93, 91n7, 93–95; uncut, 133
Gibbon, Edward, 35, 36, 53, 54
Gill-Peterson, Jules, 5, 185, 186, 190
Gleason, Maud, 43, 139, 139n80
Grafting, 61, 65
Greco-Roman antiquity, 26
Greco-Roman sources, 9, 43, 44n38, 45–47, 58, 65, 69, 86n103, 108, 130, 131, 133n66, 136, 139, 169n48, 170, 173, 189
Greco-Roman world, 34, 36, 97, 125, 166n40, 172, 174
Green, Nicki, 201

Halakhah, 13, 22n44, 17, 80, 81, 86, 87, 155, 186, 188, 192–94
Halberstam, Jack, 17, 18
Hales, Shelley, 45
Hallett, Judith, 173
harlots, 148
Hauptman, Judith, 24, 77n72, 149n102
Hayward, Eva, 14, 85, 86, 176, 177, 191n16
Heave offerings, 67n48, 119n16, 121n25, 123–28, 143, 148
HB 1523. *See* Mississippi HB 1523

Hecabe, 44, 131
hermaphrodite, 30, 51, 60n21, 85n101, 113, 143n90, 152n7, 164n32, 189, 190
Hermaphroditus, 49, 60, 60n20, 60n22, 60n23, 61–63, 65, 66, 188–90
Hillman, Thea, 1, 151, 179, 180, 189, 190, 192
hermeneutics, 19
homophobia, 22
hybridity, 26, 59, 61, 66–72, 75, 76, 78–81, 86, 98, 192
hypermasculinity, 2, 39, 106, 110, 184

identity, 17, 39, 44, 55, 61, 84, 153n9, 155n14, 159, 199. *See also* gender, identity
immutability, 55, 81–86, 149
indagatio corporis, 175
infertility, 91, 140n82, 141, 161, 163, 166, 167, 171–74, 179–81
infidelity, 96
interact, 89, 112
intersex activists, 6, 27, 30, 84, 86, 87, 89, 90, 111, 113, 126, 152n6, 152n7, 188, 189, 192, 195, 201
intersex bodies, 5, 16, 30, 94, 180, 186, 190, 195
intersex children, 89, 90, 110, 112, 113, 179–80, 185
intersex category, 94
intersex Christians, 23
intersex embodiment, 5, 23, 94, 152, 153, 191, 198
intersex identity, 5, 84, 152–53n9
intersex history, 3, 4, 15, 16, 27, 40n60, 53, 90, 112, 152n6, 164n32, 187–91, 195
intersex Jews, vii, 6, 86, 111, 192, 194–96, 198, 200
Intersex Justice Project, 89, 90n4
intersex politics, 7, 21, 63, 190n13
intersex studies/theory, 3, 5, 15, 21, 25, 26, 82n89, 117, 153, 201
intersex surgery. *See* surgery, intersex
intersexuality, 8, 30, 112n74, 152, 164n32, 190, 191
intersex youth, vii, 89
Isaiah, 44n39, 107n55, 118, 133n68, 144n92
Islam, 12, 34

Jesus, 22, 109n64
Jewish activists, 22, 27, 80, 86, 87, 195, 201
Johns Hopkins, 185, 186
Josephus, 10, 43, 44, 47, 121n24
"Judeo-Christian" arguments, 183, 185, 192, 194
Justinian's Digest, 45, 29n52, 131, 143n90

Kafer, Allison, 116, 151n5, 164, 165n36, 180n85
Kapor-Mater, Emily Aviva, 198n30, 200–201
Kaye, Lynn, 154n12, 176, 178n83

Kessler, Gwynn, 3n6, 25n53, 56n4, 76n70, 80n83, 91n9, 144n93, 167n42, 184n3, 185n6
Ketubbot, 66
Kiddushin, 155n14; Mishnah, 130n52, 154; Talmud, 109n66, 125n38; Tosefta, 132n64
Kiel, Yishai, 106, 107n54, 109, 126n43
kil'ayim, 66n44, 67, 71n58, 86n102, 98, 238
kosher masculinity, 27, 115, 116, 122, 125, 133, 137, 140, 141, 143, 162–67
kosher women, 163
koy, 64, 65, 67–72, 73n63, 76, 78, 79n80, 81
Kuefler, Matthew, 47n57, 51, 52, 138n75,
Kukla, Elliot, 8, 72n60, 198–200

LaFleur, Greta, 4
Labovitz, Gail, 66, 71n59, 128n48, 155n15
Ladin, Joy, 192, 199n33
Lappe, Benay, Rabbi, 1
Laqueur, Thomas, 15, 16, 18
Lev, Sarra, vii, 21, 73, 121n24, 122n30, 125n37, 144n94, 147n99, 167n42, 170n52, 171n54–47, 174n71
levirate marriage, 5, 91–96, 97n25, 106, 118n10, 133–37, 139–48, 156–65, 167, 175
Leviticus, 41, 43, 97–100, 102–4, 119, 120, 128, 134,
LGBTQ people, 83, 111
Lichtenstein, Dayan Yisroel Yaakov, 193
Lieberman, Saul, 31, 63, 64, 92n27, 100n34, 161n29
Lightfoot, J. L., 44–45
lineage, 39, 91, 106, 107n54, 135, 148, 149n102, 157
lists, 63n33, 64, 65, 67, 72n61, 79, 81, 119, 129n51, 130n52, 132n64, 198
literal reading, 16–19, 40, 153, 161, 165, 188
Lourdes, Ashley Hunter, 4
Lurie Children's Hospital, 89
lying with a man, 2, 26, 90, 97–100, 102, 103, 184, 185

Magna Mater. *See* Cybele
Malatino, Hillary, 94
Marchal, Joseph, vii, viii, 4n8, 6, 19n35
marginalized bodies, 90, 187
markers: of age, 176n76, 177n81, 187; of gender, 170, 175
masculine bodies, 21, 27, 65, 101, 105, 129, 143, 164, 165
masculine orifice, 101, 102, 186
masculinity, 2, 42, 73n63, 151; abled, 140; aggressive, 184; Assyrian, 39; rabbinic, 96, 100, 104, 107, 110, 116, 125, 128, 132, 133, 136, 143, 144, 165, 166; Roman, 35, 40, 44n38; toxic, 24; transgressive, 27
Matthew (New Testament), 47–49, 137–39
M. C., 89, 90, 10–13
medical ethics, 194
medical experimentation, 112, 185, 186
medicine, Talmudic, 13, 38, 115,
Mesopotamia, 11, 37, 38n25, 59n17, 92n10
Mishnah, 1n2, 6, 12, 13, 27, 31, 63, 64, 65n36, 66, 67n44, 68, 69n52, 70n56, 71, 72n61, 79n80, 93, 95, 97n27, 99n31, 116, 117, 121–30, 132, 133, 135, 137, 139–42, 144–49, 154, 156, 157, 159n22, 161, 162, 165, 168
Misogyny, 18, 19, 22–25, 77, 82n91
Mississippi HB 1523, 82, 83, 85
Moabites, 44n39, 121n22, 130n52, 132, 133n65
Mock, Janet, 151
modernity, 22, 23
monogamy, 84
monstrous birth, 50–52
Morland, Iain, 152–53, 190–91
mutability of sex, 3, 4, 27, 90, 128, 186, 188, 194

Near East, 26, 37, 49
necropolitics, 78n77
Nerva, 45, 131
Neusner, Jacob, 77, 78
New Testament. *See* Matthew
nonbinary activists, 80
nonbinary bodies, 80, 90, 183, 194
nonbinary embodiment, 72n60, 86, 90, 183, 185
nonbinary frameworks, 17
nonbinary gender, 2
nonbinary identity, 193
nonbinary pronouns, 31
nonbinary sex, 49, 80, 190
nonbinary space, 3
noneunuchs, 162, 169, 187
nontrans people, 151, 192
normates, 164
normativity, 17n31, 18. *See also* chrononormativity

ontology, 77–79, 85, 86, 88, 94, 191
orientalizing, 36
Ovid, 60, 61n31, 65, 188–89

Pagan religion and ritual, 34, 37, 43, 48, 70
Pagonis, Pidgeon, 89, 90
Palestinian Talmud. *See* Talmud, Palestinian
Parthian dynasty, 111

INDEX   247

penetration: of the androgyne, 99, 100, 101, 102, 103, 104; of men, 73, 98n30, 100
penetrability: of the androgyne, 103, 104, 183; masculine, 26, 98, 101, 105
Persian Empire, 11, 12, 34, 44, 46, 131
Philo, 41, 42, 47, 58n9, 60n44, 108, 121n24, 139, 172n62
Plasticity, 5, 168, 185, 186
Pliny the Elder, 50n67, 51, 108
Plutarch, 69
polemics, Christian, 19, 22
polemics, interreligious, 34
postcolonial theory, 25
Preuss, Julius, 38
priestly bodies, 41, 119, 125
priests, 10, 41, 43–46, 119, 120, 123, 124, 125n39, 126, 127, 129, 131, 143, 146n98, 147, 148, 168n47
procreation, 43, 92, 135, 136, 140, 143n90, 145n96, 157, 160n26, 161, 162, 166
pronouns, 31, 72n60
property, 66, 70, 71, 124n35
Prosser, Jay, 18
proto-trans remains, 37n18
Puar, Jasbir, 164
Puberty, 20, 27, 151, 153, 158, 166n38, 169n50, 170, 171, 175–78, 180, 181, 187

queer liberation, 15
queer scholarship, 24, 25,
queer studies/theory, 16, 17, 21, 22, 25, 28
Qumran, 41n32, 42n35, 149n102

Rabban Shimon ben Gamliel, 170, 171
rabbinics, 7, 21–30, 38, 57, 63, 116, 154, 176
racialization, 4, 19, 104n48, 116, 141, 168n46
rape, 66
Rashi, 95n22, 151n29, 166n39
Rav, 99, 100, 177, 178
Rava, 102, 127n45, 162–64, 167, 180
reproductive capability, 138, 175
reproductive failure, 20, 27, 96, 98, 135, 140, 142, 150, 183, 184
reproduction, 8, 27, 43, 66, 91–97, 105, 106, 107n54, 110, 113, 119, 133, 140, 141, 143, 147–49, 160, 164–67, 187. *See also* procreation
responsa, 194
resurrection, 141
retroactivity, 175, 177, 178
Roman Empire, 6, 10–12, 33–36, 45, 46, 50, 52, 53, 131, 132

Roman legal sources, 9, 45, 46, 49–52, 69, 130, 131, 132, 133, 143n90, 175
Roman Palestine, 9, 12
Ronis, Sara, 24
roosters (cocks), 1, 2, 105, 107–11, 113, 184
Rubenstein, Jeffrey, 101n40, 106, 107,

Sarah (biblical), as tumtum, 91
saris, 5, 7, 8, 27, 38, 39, 41, 42, 47–49, 94, 97n25, 118, 121n24, 133, 135, 137, 138, 139–47, 150, 153, 157–81, 189
Sasanian dynasty/Empire, 11, 12, 46
Sasanian culture, 9, 13, 26, 34, 53, 107n54, 109
Sasanian period, 11, 46, 130
Secunda, Shai, 58
Seleucid rule, 11
Semenya, Caster, 112
seminal emissions, 8, 73
sexed embodiment, 5, 16, 18, 84, 137, 150, 152, 153, 185–87. *See also* embodiment
sexed variance, 7, 50, 112n74, 150, 158n20, 192
sexism, 21, 24, 25, 76
sex signs, 50, 91, 97, 175, 187
sexuality, 2, 3, 9, 15, 20, 21, 23, 25, 27, 40, 56, 66, 84, 90, 91, 96, 100, 102, 116, 144, 148, 149, 150, 154, 159, 166, 175, 180, 183, 184, 186, 188, 191
Shmuel (Amoraic rabbi), 177–78
Snorton, C. Riley, 4n14, 5, 19, 82n91
somatic signs, 165–78
Southern Poverty Law Center, 112
Sophocles, 44, 131
Spade, Dean, 83, 186n7
Stackleberg, Katharine von, 66
stammaitic argumentation, 29
sterility, 52, 142, 162–64, 167
sterilization, 172, 173; forced, 90, 112, 141
Stern, Sacha, 176
surgery: on the androgyne, 90; gender-affirming, 117, 149; on intersex people, 30, 48n60, 89, 90, 111, 112, 191, 200; on tumtumim, 93, 94, 96, 187
surveillance, bodily/genital, 18, 168, 174, 179, 184, 187
Swancutt, Diana, 173
Svara, 1, 200n33

Tadmor, Hayim, 39
Tal, Ilan, 22, 23
Talmud, Babylonian, 12, 13, 26–29, 70, 106–9, 153, 158, 169, 176

Talmud, Palestinian, 1n2, 30n64, 31, 32, 91n6, 107, 109, 147n100, 176n76
tannaitic literature/sources, 3n6, 8n22, 11, 26–30, 53, 63, 69n53, 70n56, 72, 79n82, 86, 87, 97n6, 93n14, 94n15, 101n40, 115n2, 121n25, 122n27, 124n35, 129n51, 132n63, 142n86, 148, 156n16, 159, 169, 170n53. *See also* Mishnah,
taxonomy, 9, 71, 81, 97n26, 139
teleological development, 176–77
Temple, the, 9, 10, 65, 119, 120n21, 124n30; offerings in, 65, 67; Second, 12, 41, 126n44
temporality, 27, 142, 151–81
theology: anti-trans, 81, 85, 19; complementarian, 84; gendered, 85; trans, 82, 192, 195
time, 5; concepts of, 29, 177; as gendered, 154–56, 179, 180, 183; rabbinic, 29; in relation to medical treatments, 152–53; retroactive, 178; somatic, 141–43, 151, 153, 156, 157, 161, 163, 165–68, 169n49, 175–79, 171, 186
timtum, 195–99
Tosefta, 1n2, 31, 63, 64, 65n36, 93n14, 97n25, 99n31, 122n28, 123n31, 127n46, 160n25, 160n27, 161n29
tragelaphos, 67n45, 68n49, 69, 70n56
trans activists, vii, ix, 27, 72n60, 80, 85–87, 192, 195, 201
transcestors, vii, 187, 195, 196
trans children, 166n38, 168n46, 190
trans Christians, 23
trans embodiment, 5, 6, 16, 17, 18, 21, 26, 56, 81, 83–86, 191, 192, 193, 195, 198
trans femininity, 152n5
trans history, 3, 15, 16, 19–21, 33, 49, 54, 56, 115, 154n11, 180, 185, 186–91, 195–96, 200
trans identity, 5, 17, 19, 84, 193n19
transing, 13–15, 19–21, 25–26, 33, 36, 40, 53–54, 56, 117, 168
transition, 13, 14, 94n17, 151, 152n5, 176–77, 192–94, 200n33
trans Jews, vii, 6, 87, 111, 192, 194–98, 200
trans liberation, ix, 14–16, 186n7
transmasculinity, 18, 19n36, 24, 151
transmisogyny, 18, 19, 24n48, 82n91
trans parents, 192, 193
transphobia, 6, 22, 36, 53, 81–88, 117, 149, 168n47, 183, 196
trans politics, 7, 19, 21, 22, 23, 63, 186n7
transsexuality, 17, 18, 18n32, 18n34, 82, 85, 186n5, 193, 194
trans studies/theory, vii, viii, 3, 5, 14, 15, 17, 19n35, 19n37, 21, 22, 25, 26, 36n14, 85, 176, 183n1, 186n7

Trans Studies Initiative, viii
trans theology, 82, 192, 195
Transtorah, vii
trans women, 14, 18, 19, 78, 79, 83, 85, 86
trans women of color, 14, 18n33, 83, 85, 86
tribas, 173
tumtumim, 5, 9, 56n4, 79n82, 90, 91–99, 104n47, 113, 187, 189, 194n23, 196–200
tumtum of Biri, 91, 95–97, 187

Ulpian, 47, 51, 52, 138, 143n90
Uncircumcision, 133
universalizing, 164–65
Ur Nanshe, 37
US Department of Health and Human Services, 55, 82, 84n97

Varro, 65, 65n38, 66, 108n64
Vidas, Moulie, 28, 28n59

WAITRRS, vii
Waxman, Tobaron, 196n28, 201
Wegner, Judith Romney, 25, 77, 77n73
Weheliye, Alexander, 75, 75n68
Williams, Craig, 39n29
Wissenschaft des Judentums, 22, 23, 63n33, 186n6

Yehoshua, Rabbi, 136, 137, 140
Yehudah ben Yair, Rabbi, 170
Yehuda haNasi, Rabbi, 1–2, 6, 12, 15, 20, 105, 106, 109, 110, 113, 184
Yehudah, Rabbi, 93, 95, 96, 147, 148
Yefman, Gil, 196–99, 198n29
Yerushalmi, Yosef Hayim, 29, 29n62
Yeshiva University, 193
Yevamot 32, 91n6, 97n25, 132n64; b. 1, 26, 27, 90, 93, 94n17, 95, 98n27, 99, 100, 101n39, 102, 103, 105, 106n53, 123n32, 127n45, 153, 162, 164, 165, 168, 169, 171, 172, 177, 184; Mishnah, 27, 43n35, 79n82, 93, 93n13, 94n17, 116, 121, 122, 124, 126, 129, 136; p. 101n38, 142n86, 145, 147, 157n18, 158n21, 176; t. 102, 123n31, 140n83, 158n21, 159n25, 161n29
Yiẓḥak bar Yosef, Rav, 165
Yoḥanan, Rabbi, 105, 165, 166
Yosef, Rav, 165–67
Yose, Rabbi, 79–81, 86, 159

Zoroastrianism, 11, 13, 46, 58, 97, 109, 131n55, 134n70. *See also* creation stories, Zoroastrian

Founded in 1893,
UNIVERSITY OF CALIFORNIA PRESS
publishes bold, progressive books and journals
on topics in the arts, humanities, social sciences,
and natural sciences—with a focus on social
justice issues—that inspire thought and action
among readers worldwide.

The UC PRESS FOUNDATION
raises funds to uphold the press's vital role
as an independent, nonprofit publisher, and
receives philanthropic support from a wide
range of individuals and institutions—and from
committed readers like you. To learn more, visit
ucpress.edu/supportus.

www.ingramcontent.com/pod-product-compliance
Lightning Source LLC
Chambersburg PA
CBHW021402230426
43666CB00006B/616